A FEW ACRES OF ICE

A FEW ACRES OF ICE

Environment, Sovereignty, and *Grandeur* in the French Antarctic

Janet Martin-Nielsen

CORNELL UNIVERSITY PRESS   ITHACA AND LONDON

Thanks to generous funding from KTH-Sweden, the ebook editions of this book are available as open access volumes through the Cornell Open initiative.

Copyright © 2023 by Cornell University

The text of this book is licensed under a Creative Commons Attribution-NonCommercial-NoDerivatives 4.0 International License: https://creativecommons.org/licenses/by-nc-nd/4.0/. To use this book, or parts of this book, in any way not covered by the license, please contact Cornell University Press, Sage House, 512 East State Street, Ithaca, New York 14850. Visit our website at cornellpress.cornell.edu.

First published 2023 by Cornell University Press

Library of Congress Cataloging-in-Publication Data

Names: Martin-Nielsen, Janet, 1982– author.
Title: A few acres of ice : environment, sovereignty, and grandeur in the French Antarctic / Janet Martin-Nielsen.
Description: Ithaca [New York] : Cornell University Press, 2023. | Includes bibliographical references and index.
Identifiers: LCCN 2022059451 (print) | LCCN 2022059452 (ebook) | ISBN 9781501772092 (hardcover) | ISBN 9781501772108 (paperback) | ISBN 9781501772115 (epub) | ISBN 9781501772122 (pdf)
Subjects: LCSH: Geopolitics—Antarctica—Adélie Coast. | Adélie Coast (Antarctica)—Discovery and exploration—French. | Adélie Coast (Antarctica)—Environmental conditions. | Adélie Coast (Antarctica)—History.
Classification: LCC G890.A4 M34 2023 (print) | LCC G890.A4 (ebook) | DDC 320.1/2—dc23/eng/20230606
LC record available at https://lccn.loc.gov/2022059451
LC ebook record available at https://lccn.loc.gov/2022059452

Cover art: Bernard Buffet, *Piste de la Terre Adélie*, timbre T.A.A.F. poste aérienne no. 124, non dentelé, 1992.

For Richard, who never once doubted I would write a second book

Contents

List of Illustrations	ix
Acknowledgments	xi
Introduction: The French Antarctic	1
1. "All That Is Required Is to Discover It"	9
2. An Unexpected Territory	26
3. Apathy and Neglect	44
4. Formalizing Sovereignty	62
5. Science and Presence	77
6. Growing Maturity	101
7. Crisis and Choices	131
8. Environmental Authority	148
9. An Uncertain Future	175
Epilogue: An Antarctic Power *Malgré Soi*	187
Notes	197
References	219
Index	257

Illustrations

Figure 1. Oronce Fine, *Mappemonde en forme de cœur* (World map in the form of a heart), 1536   11

Figure 2. Philippe Buache, *Carte des Terres Australes* (Map of the southern lands), 1739   18

Figure 3. Path of the Dumont d'Urville expedition between Hobart and the Antarctic, 1840   34

Figure 4. Léon Jean Baptiste Sabatier, *Prise de possession de la Terre Adélie le 21 janvier 1840* (Taking possession of Terre Adélie on 21 January 1840), 1846   35

Figure 5. Clément Adrien Vincendon-Dumoulin, *Carte de la Terre Adélie et régions circum-polaires* (Map of Terre Adélie and circumpolar regions), 1840   36

Figure 6. France's Antarctic and sub-Antarctic possessions   47

Figure 7. Claimed territories in the Antarctic, 1933   68

Figure 8. Path of the *Commandant Charcot* (first voyage 1948–1949, second voyage 1949–1951)   86

Figure 9. At the Port-Martin site in Terre Adélie, 1950   90

Figure 10. Procession of Emperor penguins and chicks, Pointe Géologie archipelago, 1957   92

Figure 11. Raoul Desprez and Michel Barré with a sugar model of Port-Martin, 1951   94

Figure 12. The Port-Martin base burns, 23 January 1952   95

Figure 13. The first two buildings of the Dumont-d'Urville base, built for the International Geophysical Year, 1956   111

Figure 14. Station Charcot buried in the snow, 1957   113

Figure 15. A French International Geophysical Year stamp highlighting Terre Adélie   115

Figure 16. A Dragon rocket rises in a plume of combustion gases, 1967   128

Figure 17. A surgical operation in the improvised operating room in Terre Adélie, 1951   150

Figure 18. The Terre Adélie airstrip plan, 1983   152

Figure 19. Greenpeace activists at the airstrip construction site, 1990   157

Figure 20. High-altitude aerial view showing the airstrip under construction, 1990   172

Acknowledgments

With many thanks to Peder Roberts, who brought me on board the GRETPOL (Greening the Poles: Science, the Environment, and the Creation of the Modern Arctic and Antarctic) project and made this book possible—and for years of friendship spanning so many countries.

This book was written in Vilnius during the first two years of the COVID-19 pandemic. It was a mental lifesaver in a very uncertain time. Given the travel restrictions, it could not have been accomplished without the immense help of research assistants, librarians, and archivists, as well as the impressive digitization efforts of the Bibliothèque nationale de France. My thanks to Anna Svensson, Maël Goumri, Christian Kehrt, Michelle Andringa, Vincent Reniel, Marion Barlet, and Aude Sonneville, as well as to Alexandre Simon for providing me with an advance copy of his dissertation. At Cornell University Press, Bethany Wasik answered my many questions with patience and kindness. The book is stronger for the detailed comments of three anonymous reviewers. Richard Martin-Nielsen, Ole Nielsen, Peder Roberts, and Jasmine Elson read through the manuscript at a later stage and provided both helpful comments and encouragement.

The GRETPOL project, centered at KTH Stockholm and the University of Stavanger, received funding from the European Research Council (ERC) under the European Union's Horizon 2020 research and innovation program (grant agreement no. 716211). The images and maps have been reproduced with the kind permission of the Bibliothèque nationale de France, Archipôles, and the National Library of Australia. The book was spoken with Apple voice recognition software.

I would never have had the pleasure of researching and writing this book if my parents, Ole and Kathy Nielsen, had not put me into French language education from the get-go.

Finally, all my thanks to Richard, who made my maps and dealt with all the technical difficulties of the manuscript and references, and who was confident and enthusiastic throughout the entire project—and to my two boys, Lars Ole and Ian Niels, who never let me forget that writing a book is pretty much the coolest thing ever.

Introduction

THE FRENCH ANTARCTIC

Nearly half of Earth's circumference separates Paris from its Antarctic territory, Terre Adélie, a sliver of the white continent as far removed from France's capital as geography, environment, and climate allow. Since its discovery by a French navigator in 1840, Terre Adélie has given France a strategic foothold in the Antarctic, and today France is one of the seven states laying claim to part of the white continent.

France's entry into the Antarctic sphere was unexpected, a product of rivalries, last-minute changes of plan, and royal decree. For King Louis-Philippe, who sent the explorer and navigator Jules Sébastien César Dumont d'Urville south in 1837, the appeal of Antarctica (at that point, not yet proved to be a continent) was based in imperial rivalry: a desire to best both Britain, France's old enemy, and the United States, the emerging commercial rival. When Dumont d'Urville discovered and claimed Terre Adélie for France in 1840, his country was by no means ready to act on that claim. Indeed, no Frenchman would again set foot in the territory for over a century. For much of that long period, it was all but forgotten and the French claim lay dormant. While France's empire was second only to Britain's in terms of size and wealth by the end of the nineteenth century, little geopolitical or strategic significance was ascribed to Terre Adélie. It was not until Britain and its Dominions began to carve up the continent in the 1920s that France enacted decrees in support of Terre Adélie. But the decrees were legal instruments, utilitarian and practical, prompted by the threat of annexation rather than by genuine interest. They were not accompanied by expeditions and the Antarctic was all but absent from the French political and cultural imaginations.

Even after World War II, as the geostrategic importance of the Antarctic grew, it was neither a government initiative nor priority. France's return to Terre Adélie was championed by a private individual, Paul-Emile Victor, who had the connections necessary to finally make the territory matter. By using science to perform sovereignty, Victor launched French presence in Terre Adélie. And as France's second colonial empire collapsed and Charles de Gaulle returned to power at the end of the 1950s, Terre Adélie took on new meaning as a secure overseas region: remote, often overlooked, and yet increasingly relevant to de Gaulle's desire for France to remain a *puissance mondiale moyenne* (midsized world power).

But Terre Adélie has also drawn harsh criticism at home, to the extent that the 1970s and 1980s saw open debate over whether France should give up its Antarctic territory. With no permanent population, no electors, and no clear economic potential, Terre Adélie does not fit into normal political structures. As the political class openly questioned the value of retaining the territory, France's commitment to the Antarctic fell into crisis. New life was injected at the very end of the 1980s when questions of environment and sovereignty came together to make Terre Adélie matter at the highest political levels. As President François Mitterrand and Prime Minister Michel Rocard took personal interest in the white continent, France engineered the success of the Madrid Protocol in support of Antarctica's environment. Since then, France's relationship with Terre Adélie has been guided by environmental principles, not always consistently and not always successfully, but with a force that persists to the present day. Today, there is a conviction that the Antarctic offers France a privileged and strategic space. Still, the money necessary to support Terre Adélie is sorely lacking. The territory also retains a low profile in the public sphere: the French have never felt an intimate connection to the Antarctic, in contrast to what Rohan Howitt describes for Australians and Francis Spufford for Britons.[1]

By analyzing Terre Adélie's place in evolving political contexts, from imperial expansion to postwar reconstruction and from the Cold War to the environmental turn, this book shows how France became and has remained an Antarctic power *malgré soi*, that is, despite only intermittent political and cultural interest at home. With no sense of urgency surrounding Terre Adélie and few clear, immediate advantages to be gained from the territory, successive French governments had nothing to lose by ignoring it, often for long periods. Each stage in France's journey to its present position as a claimant state and Antarctic Treaty System (ATS) power was propelled less by internal desire or motivation than by a deep need to respond to an adversary, whether it be another state or a more nebulous threat. The idea of losing Terre Adélie to a rival has always been anathema, and France has long used the territory to try to show itself superior to other states, from Britain in the far past to the United States during the Cold War to China and Russia today. More broadly, since World War II, Terre Adélie has become central to *grandeur*, faraway and yet essential to the redefinition of France as a global political entity following decolonization, resonating as strongly for geopolitical purposes as for environmental ones. The story of France in the Antarctic is rooted in national pride and honor rather than strictly in territory. This pattern of French involvement with Terre Adélie is also representative of the territory's outlier status in broader French conceptions of colonialism and empire.

Terre Adélie is the strangest of possessions: France's claim to the territory is only recognized by a handful of other nations, and this claim is at present "frozen" by the Antarctic Treaty. In this geopolitical environment, to perform sovereignty is to at once build a moral (and potentially future legal) claim to territory, to shore up support at home for an expensive yet faraway endeavor, and to continue building a historical legacy in what could well one day again be an openly disputed region—all part of the construction of Antarctica's legal geography.[2] Toward these ends, performances of sovereignty—the practices and narratives, both physical and intellectual, that countries employ to build identity and authority over a place—take center stage. How, Klaus Dodds asks, do "the representatives of claimant states 'speak' and the discourses and practices they deploy . . . construct their identities as claimants with sovereign rights"?[3] From postage stamps to airstrips, from flag raising to childbirth, sovereignty performances have long been (and continue to be) used to demonstrate commitment and respond to challenges to legitimacy in the Antarctic—despite the Antarctic Treaty's freeze on territorial claims. Science plays a preeminent role here: it is one of the leading ways in which countries, and particularly claimant states, have justified their presence and built power bases on the white continent.[4] While science was at the heart of the establishment of French presence in Terre Adélie in the 1950s, today French Antarctic science is underfunded, a black mark for the claim. Science, environment, and sovereignty go hand in hand not only in the Antarctic but also in other remote and uninhabited regions of the world where territorial claims push at the edge of international law. In these contexts, the creation of new knowledge about a space is a means of asserting and justifying authority over that space in the absence of more traditional symbols of sovereignty; knowledge, quite literally, is power. To this end, this book also looks to France's sub-Antarctic possessions, scattered islands and archipelagos whose history is entwined with Terre Adélie.

The history of sovereignty claims in the Antarctic can be separated neither from the history of the Antarctic environment, as Adrian Howkins emphasizes, nor from the physical materiality underpinning presence in the region.[5]

Sovereignty—control, authority, and legitimacy over territory—is integral to environmental history, especially as it affects geopolitical interaction with natural environments. In this context, Terre Adélie's environment has been shaped by the political desire for authority and prestige and constructed to fit ideas of a global France set out in Paris. The geopolitics of Antarctic space affected the relationship of French politicians, diplomats, and scientists with the white continent—even though many, indeed most, of these actors never set foot there. As such, this story takes place as much in Paris, the seat of the French political scene, as it does in the Antarctic (and, to a lesser extent, other parts of France and other countries). It is a story as much of the navigators, explorers, and scientists who discovered, explored, and investigated Terre Adélie as of the promoters, public servants, elected officials, and environmental activists who have so shaped the territory. It is also a story of how Terre Adélie fit into imperial, political, economic, and diplomatic ideas and plans set out in and controlled by Paris—and into France's more recent environmental diplomacy. By looking at these relationships, this book responds to Stéphane Frioux and Vincent Lemire's call to elucidate the absorption of environmental questions into the fabric of political and public action in France.[6]

France's relationship with Terre Adélie is deeply connected to physical environmental realities: in a place where human interaction with the natural environment is severely constrained by the harshness of that environment, and where even access to the territory in question is impeded by geography and natural phenomena—distance, pack ice, wind, and polar extremes—Antarctic activity requires a high level of human-environment engagement. By mischance of discovery, France's Antarctic territory constitutes one of the least accessible portions of the continent, something that has long been a source of woe. From the construction of the first French base in Terre Adélie in 1950 to the present day, France has never had fully secure, year-round, independent access to the territory. Over the decades, it has depended on maritime access, most often by leasing foreign ships, but ships can only reach Terre Adélie for a very few months each year. At its worst, pack ice can entirely block maritime access to the coast even in the austral summers. The need for assistance from other countries, regular and emergency, air and sea, is far from rare. In the 1980s, these challenges led the French to build an airstrip as a way of beating the hostile sea environs near the territory. While the airstrip's construction harmed Terre Adélie's living environment, this was considered by the project's drivers as more than acceptable in light of the control over territory it offered. But the airstrip project ultimately failed, destroyed by a ferocious storm before it was ever put to use. By the time of the storm, Antarctica's evolving political dynamics had changed the debate in France and a high-level political decision was made to strike an environmental course. Since the end of the 1980s, France has deliberately and explicitly invoked the environment as central to the maintenance of political power in the Antarctic. France's identity as a claimant state and a leader in the Antarctic Treaty System, too, has been constructed, shaped, and altered by the physicality of the Antarctic environment and the materiality of Antarctic space. The weight of authority invested in the materiality of French bases and installations (and even the unused airstrip) forms a key link in the backbone of France's moral and legal argument for its claim to Terre Adélie.

While in the postwar decades Antarctica's environment was seen as an enemy, a hostile force to be conquered, the gradual emergence of the polar regions as part of a growing environmental consciousness has changed the human relationship with the continent.[7] As conceptions of Antarctic space and landscape (real and imagined) evolved, so too did the activities conducted there.[8] In the case of France, the production of scientific knowledge about Terre Adélie's natural environment (first through mapping and meteorology, then through glaciology, biology, and other sciences) was appended by the explicit protection of that environment through physical and legal acts. For France, environmental protection also went hand in hand with efforts to reinforce its own claims to legitimacy and authority in the Antarctic. In this sense, the environment acts as a lens through which French attitudes toward Antarctica have evolved, ultimately emerging as a politicized responsibility, to build on Alice Ingold's conceptualization.[9] Indeed, changing French perceptions of the interrelationship between Antarctica's environment and the preservation of political power shed light on how environmental authority has been brought to bear on sovereignty issues, especially since the late 1980s.[10] This environmental turn has been motivated as much by political calculations, domestic and international, as by concern for the natural world.

The disregard of environmental degradation, and especially anthropogenic pollution, for political borders, combined with the trend toward global environmental thinking, is challenging the ways in which states conceive of sovereignty—something that emerging environmental practices and policies are increasingly being forced to recognize. How, Karen Litfin asks, do attempts to deal with environmental problems contribute to the reconfiguration of political space and to new norms for sovereignty?[11] Since the end of the 1980s, France has used environmental authority as a tool for solving the thorny political problems facing Antarctica in its own favor, to support its claim to Terre Adélie and to justify political control on the white continent. Just as Thom Kuehls argues in the case of the Brazilian rain forest, the environmental importance of Antarctica extends far beyond the territorial borders of individual claims, and the environmental politics of any individual Antarctic claim cannot be restricted to that specific place.¹² By explicitly recognizing this in the Madrid Protocol proposal, France (together with Australia) held that the sum of the Antarctic is greater than its parts—an argument that increased the moral authority of the Antarctic Treaty System. By mollifying the developing country group and the environmental non-governmental organizations (ENGOs) that had been challenging Antarctica's management, the Madrid Protocol relegitimized the ATS's voice through environmental policy.¹³ This illustrates a way in which a privileged group of countries can use the environment—indeed manipulate it—to maintain power. But today we are beginning to see the limits of this greening, and once again France is being forced to step up to support its interests.

Despite an increasing focus on Antarctica in the literature, there is still a disconnect between Antarctic history and imperial history.¹⁴ In the French case, the historical connection between Terre Adélie and empire is particularly interesting: while Terre Adélie always stood apart from the French imperial project, it was still intimately connected to identity and prestige during and after the collapse of the second colonial empire. This is a story neither of domination nor of traditional colonialism, but one of imperial motivation and global ambition nonetheless. As the French empire collapsed after World War II, remote and uninhabited possessions such as Terre Adélie took on more significance as part of France's overseas identity. The first postwar expeditions to Terre Adélie were both a means of securing the claim and a way of raising a devastated nation's morale, part of what Gabrielle Hecht calls the broader "metaphysical and physical (re) building of the French nation."¹⁵ By the end of the 1950s, it was clear that the vision of the French state as a territorial entity that reached around the world—something intrinsic to the Fifth Republic's 1958 constitution—would now be dependent on smaller and more remote possessions. In this rapidly changing order, Terre Adélie took on a new role, providing a means to maintain French presence in all the world's major oceans, rebuild prestige and international weight, and underline France's independence from the United States, all central to the Gaullist worldview. While the Antarctic did not have the same resonance as de Gaulle's other major projects—building an independent French nuclear deterrent and pulling out of the North Atlantic Treaty Organization—still, in its own way, it lent weight to *grandeur*, a geopolitical statement in one of Earth's most remote areas. Moreover, Terre Adélie offered a territory immune from the anger and stain of decolonization, unscarred by its shameful history. By virtue of being devoid of Indigenous inhabitants, too, and never dispossessed, Terre Adélie and France's sub-Antarctic islands floated above the thorny problem of how to reconcile the Algerian War with the myth, so integral to French identity, of the *mission civilisatrice* (civilizing mission). Terre Adélie has now become symbolic of French environmental diplomacy, part of a larger strategic foreign policy. In this sense, Terre Adélie offers a lens into the struggle to reimagine Frenchness and French identity, and to redefine the French nation as an international political entity, in the postwar world.[16] Still today, Terre Adélie offers to France both a means and a rationale for maintaining the status of a midsize world power.

Today, France is engaged in new power plays in the Antarctic. As the changing balance of great powers calls into question the political status quo on the white continent, high-level political interest has emerged and France is increasingly vocal about Chinese and Russian interference in the Antarctic, as well as the dangers posed by tourism. These threats have fed a French drive to push the "science and peace" agenda of the Antarctic Treaty System, a system in which France is highly invested. President Emmanuel Macron is urging his country to develop an overarching Antarctic policy, one that is future oriented and less piecemeal than in the past—something other claimant states are also pursuing.[17] Still, while Macron officially projects confidence with respect to Terre Adélie's status and future, internally there is fierce debate over how the cost of maintaining Antarctic presence will be met. When Jérôme Chappellaz, the director of France's polar institute, addressed the National Assembly in mid-2019, he sounded the alarm: France's Antarctic budget is too low, France trails behind other countries in terms of science and logistics, and the French Antarctic base is decrepit, he said.[18] "A central question today is, 'Do we still want to play a role in the Antarctic?'" Chappellaz asked. If more investment is not forthcoming, he continued, "not only will we lose our rank as a nation currently located at the forefront of scientific production in Antarctica, but France's weight in the Antarctic diplomatic context as well as its initial claim of sovereignty in Terre Adélie could be called into question." These questions were almost verbatim those asked through the crises of the 1970s and 1980s, and capture the peak and trough, on-and-off-again nature of France's relationship with Terre Adélie.

The importance of the Antarctic to our world, to Earth's future, cannot be underestimated. As the planet warms, fragile Antarctic ecosystems are being disrupted. Penguin colonies are shrinking or disappearing, floating ice shelves are melting, and average summer temperatures are rising alarmingly. These changes have global consequences, from sea levels to the absorption of excess heat and carbon dioxide to the frequency of extreme weather events.[19] In this context, understanding the position (historical and present) of all states with significant Antarctic interests is essential. While Antarctica's history has received appreciable attention, France has all but been left out of this work. Based on a thorough study of French government, military, institutional, non-governmental, and private archives, this book brings France into the literature. In doing so, it explains critical aspects of Antarctic history in new and illuminating ways, broadening our understanding of the white continent's geopolitical position. In particular, the analysis of the environmental turn presented here provides a much-needed counterpoint to work on the Antarctic interests of other states.[20] By bringing in newspaper and film archives, diaries, and photography collections, too, this book further links the cultural, personal, and social to the political.

Today, Terre Adélie is seen to give France a privileged space, one that contributes to maintaining its status as a political entity reaching around the globe. But while the environmental approach that emerged in the late 1980s has provided a clear narrative for France's course in the Antarctic, Terre Adélie is by no means securely supported today: it suffers from chronically low funding for scientific research, weak logistics, crumbling infrastructure, and burned-out personnel. While there have been signs of greater positive engagement at high political levels, especially in response to Chinese and Russian actions, real commitment in the form of euros is lacking. The undeniable effects of climate change in the Antarctic offer both an immense challenge and a critical opportunity for France to step up to the plate and lead. With an evolving geopolitical situation that once again threatens to reconfigure political space and destabilize governance on the continent, the need to strengthen environmental governance and better integrate Antarctic space into French political discourse is pressing.

1
"ALL THAT IS REQUIRED IS TO DISCOVER IT"

The idea of a great southern continent permeated geographical dreams and theorizing from antiquity.[1] The ancient Greeks postulated that the Southern Hemisphere was home to a vast unknown continent, part of a larger speculative cosmology that wove together scientific thinking and an intellectual and aesthetic desire for symmetry, or ideal harmony. For the terrestrial masses to be in equilibrium, a southern continent was needed to counterbalance the known northern lands of Europe, Asia, and North Africa. Ancient philosophers, mappers, and cosmographers alike were attracted by the idea of a vast austral continent, with its connotations of otherness, extremity, and geographic symmetry. The word we use today to name that continent, Antarctica, stems from the Greek word *antarktikos*, "opposite the Arctic"—*arktos* being the Greek term for bear, representing the eponymous constellation that graces the northern sky. While the ancient Greeks defined this land in terms of their knowledge of the European world, early ideas of such lands were not restricted to Europe: Polynesian narratives describe the seventh-century voyage of Hui Te Rangiora to the white land of the frozen southern ocean and Māori legends, too, recount that such lands existed.[2]

In European medieval geography, the Antipodes (to use the term generally attributed to the Spanish scholar and cleric Isidore of Seville) lay at the heart of debate over Earth's configuration and the extent of its habitation.[3] For non-Christian classical scholars such as Servius and Macrobius, land beyond that which was known—if it existed—was conceivably populated. For Christians, however, this idea was unacceptable. Augustine and other Christian writers rejected the idea of inhabited southern lands because of the threat they posed to the integrity of scripture and to Christian thought itself—namely, the spread of salvation to all people. If people lived on the other side of the globe, and if this place was unreachable from the Northern Hemisphere due to the impassability of the torrid regions, as it was thought, how could Christ's instruction to evangelize all people be fulfilled?

In the Renaissance, the rediscovery of ancient texts (in particular, Ptolemy's *Geographica*, translated into Latin in 1409) brought about renewed interest in the idea of a vast continent occupying the southern portion of the globe, an idea that was widely cultivated in the intellectual milieux of this era. Cartographers and geographers began to conceive of southern lands in visual and spatial terms, and they became a regular feature on sixteenth-century maps. Despite being the product of imagination and speculation, albeit rooted in classical and medieval ideas, maps of the time evolved to show a fair degree of consistency in their depictions of a great southern land. Its coastline, topography, and toponyms were recognizable and even well-known (if invented) geographic features. Christopher Columbus's voyage of 1492 to the New World—the western Antipodes—also gave cartographers of the imagined southern continent a real and yet just-discovered place to mirror. More broadly, as Alfred Hiatt writes, by showing that antipodal spaces were indeed reachable from the known world, Columbus's voyages turned the question of the evangelization of antipodal peoples into a real, practical problem with political as well as religious consequences.[4]

One of the earliest of these maps, French mathematician, cartographer, and artist Oronce Fine's influential 1536 cordiform map of the world, shows a massive austral continent covering the South Pole region and reaching far up the coasts of South America and Africa, separate from other lands (figure 1). Alongside mountain ranges jutting skyward near a coastline speckled with intricate inlets and bays, Fine inscribed the words "nvper inventa, sed nondvm plene examinata" (lately discovered but not yet fully examined)—a reference to Ferdinand Magellan's great voyage of 1522. Indeed, it was Magellan's sighting of land to the south of the furthest known extent of South America—the land he named Tierra del Fuego—that gave new cogency to the idea of a southern continent. It is thought that Fine was the first to baptize this continent "Terra Australis," which, alongside "Terra Australis Incognita," soon became widely used. Fine's cartography combines cosmographic and geographic theorizing; ideas passed down from classical and medieval traditions; and the new discoveries and travel narratives, varied in their authenticity, from traders, navigators, and evangelists, which flooded Europe through the sixteenth century. That maps of the era showed nearly equal ratios of land to sea in both hemispheres is a reminder that, far from being simply speculative, Terra Australis was equally the result of cal-

FIGURE 1. Oronce Fine, *Mappemonde en forme de cœur* (World map in the form of a heart), 1536, 52×59.5 cm, 2 assembled sheets (Bibliothèque nationale de France).

culation, mathematical and precise, driven by the ancient ideals of symmetry and balance.

While in the sixteenth century Terra Australis Incognita was often represented as stretching high up toward (or even joined to) Africa, Oceania, and South America, this imagined land gradually lessened in size as navigators and explorers brought back observations from their epic voyages.[5] Speaking to broader visions of man's place in the world, in seventeenth-century Europe Terra Australis manifested itself in political views of colonial expansion and romantic ideals in literature. While today the Antarctic evokes images of endless ice, a white and barren environment, empty and unable to support human life, until well into the eighteenth century Terra Australis was conceived of entirely differently, with ample, fertile lands, blessed with a temperate or even hot climate, thought to be inhabited by people, possibly highly civilized—elements from the known world brought to bear on the unknown, used to give meaning and shape to the unseen. On maps, animals, people, and plants—many fantastical but with groundings in the known (and especially the newly discovered)—filled the continent's blank spaces, which were being explored by thought and imagination even before they were explored in reality.

At the opening of the eighteenth century, Terra Australis Incognita was still a mystery, unseen, a place of lore and fable, despite its appearance on maps for centuries. At this time, the New World was increasingly well-known, and the Pacific and Indian Oceans had been extensively explored. While Terra Australis had never been sighted, its existence was presumed. It called to navigators and explorers, to scientists and writers, to cartographers and philosophers enchanted by its possibilities and by speculation of the riches and glory that might be found there. The continent was often still drawn as a huge landmass filled with people and the splendors of nature. At a time when exotic countries and faraway lands were à la mode in European intellectual circles, Terra Australis drove discussions of known versus unknown, distance and the reach of human knowledge, and otherness. This space was informed as much by classical and medieval ideas disseminated over the centuries as by the age of exploration as by imagination, fancy, and desire. As observations from Pacific explorations were disseminated, especially from Dutch navigators, the boundaries of the unknown continent slowly receded. So too did the dream of tropical or even warm climates, of habitation, and eventually of riches. As geographic experience pushed out the older conceptions, the land slowly took the shape of the Antarctic Continent we know and recognize today. The hinge point in this transformation was the famed British explorer and cartographer James Cook's great southern circumnavigation of 1772–1775, which brought back evidence of impenetrable pack ice south of vast ice-free seas, finally and conclusively disproving the idea of a temperate and abundantly populated southern continent as had been dreamed about from antiquity on.

Early Ideas of the Antarctic in France

Sixteenth- and seventeenth-century maps and illustrations of Terra Australis Incognita caught the imagination of French cartographers, traders, and writers. Fantastical imagery and lavish descriptions served only to feed this imagination, which soon led to plans for exploration, colonization, and expansion. Inspired by compatriot Oronce Fine as well as by Flemish cosmographer and cartographer Gerardus Mercator, Norman mapmakers paid particular attention to Terra Australis, which dominated the southern portion of their resplendent mid-sixteenth-century maps. Known as the Dieppe maps, these were drawn for royal and wealthy patrons, and showed Terra Australis as a vast landmass stretching from the tip of South America across to present-day Australia. In the Dieppe school's Pierre Desceliers's rendering from 1550, a sumptuous color map two and a half meters long, the continent is elaborately detailed with exotic beasts and plants and a scallop-edge coastline. And Guillaume Le Testu, a French privateer and one of the preeminent cartographers of the Dieppe school, drew Terra Australis replete with human figures with ears as long as their bodies, described as "idolatres ignorans Dieu" (idolaters ignorant of God) inhabiting a land rich in nutmeg, cloves, and fruits.[6] That this Terra Australis was imagined rather than known was something the Dieppe mapmakers emphasized: "The so-called Terra Australis [is] unknown to us because all that is passed off on this subject is nothing but the work of imagination and unfounded opinion," wrote Le Testu.[7]

Putting images and ideas into action, in the late sixteenth century André and Francisque d'Albaigne, Italian merchants from Lucca, proposed to Charles IX a voyage to explore and colonize what they called "la tierce partie du monde" (the third part of the world).[8] The brothers reminded the king about France's mistake in dismissing Columbus and spoke of the benefits that would accrue from discovering a new part of the world with "lands and realms abundant and rich in gold, silver, precious stones, drugs and spices." While not much is known about the brothers and their project, the late nineteenth-century erudite scholar Ernest-Théodore Hamy's careful argument that they were referring to Terra Australis is widely but not unanimously accepted.[9] Gaspard de Coligny, the admiral of France and a Huguenot, looked favorably on the proposal, offering as it did prospects similar to his earlier venture to secure a haven for persecuted French Protestants.[10] But when Coligny was killed along with tens of thousands of Huguenots in the Saint Bartholomew's Day Massacre of 1572, the d'Albaigne project died too.

The "third part" of the world, as distinct from the Old World of Europe and the New World of the Americas, beckoned with the opportunity to extend European exploration and colonization of faraway lands and with the hope to correct some of the excesses and abuses associated with European incursions into the New World. In France, these dual possibilities were taken up by the Huguenot historian and writer Henri Lancelot Voisin de La Popelinière (1541–1608). His book *Les Trois Mondes*, published in 1582, combined geography, religious history, and political advice to offer a vision of French colonial expansion to the new promised land of Terra Australis—that immense land of "all kinds of good and things of excellence," discovered by Magellan and "belonging to nobody."[11] This was offered as much as an antidote to the Portuguese and Spanish hold over the New World as a refuge for French Protestants. With the New World divided up between the Iberian powers—a result of the Papal Bull of 1493 and the subsequent Treaty of Tordesillas—France was excluded from that region of the globe. That France had empowered Spain's political and military position by failing to colonize the Indies was strongly felt even as France was subsumed by the Wars of Religion. For La Popelinière, Terra Australis offered a way for his country to redeem itself, a new hope, at once a means of strengthening the French state and of atoning for the violent behavior inflicted in other newly discovered territories. From these swirling ideas, La Popelinière is thought to have departed from La Rochelle in May 1589 with three ships in search of Terra Australis. "All that is required," he had written seven years prior, "is to discover it."[12] It is hard to reconstruct his voyage. It seems that he turned around upon reaching Cap Blanc in western Africa, for reasons that are opaque, and returned home with one of the ships. The other two ships continued on to South America.

While La Popelinière elicited interest in the idea of Terra Australis as a place for French renewal, for sixty years after his aborted voyage no further French expeditions set out for the unknown southern continent. Engrossed by the Wars of Religion, which stretched from 1562 until the end of the century and took perhaps three million lives, the country was divided and exhausted. This only changed in the first half of the seventeenth century as the Counter-Reformation elicited tremendous interest in missionary work and evangelization. With this push to renew the French Catholic Church, asserting Christianity beyond France's European borders and searching for new peoples to convert took center stage. In this context, the "third world" offered a speculative space for France to realize these aims without encroaching on rival powers and a place in which the church could absolve itself after the devastation of the Wars of Religion. Eager for France to build an empire to rival Spanish holdings in the Americas, Abbé Jean Paulmier de Courtonne, the canon of Saint-Pierre Cathedral in Lisieux (Normandy), argued that France was obligated to discover and evangelize this unknown third part of the world. He proposed to the pope a mission to "Terre Australes" in a series of drafts and publications in the 1650s and 1660s.[13] This was not the Antarctic as we conceive of it today, but a southern land whose borders, location, and climate were not yet known.

In his writings, de Courtonne told of a French navigator, Binot Paulmier de Gonneville, who had discovered "Terre Australes" in 1504.[14] According to de Courtonne, Gonneville left the Norman port of Honfleur aboard *L'Espoir* in 1503, heading for the Spice Islands—but after reaching the Cape of Good Hope, his ship was blown by a storm to "the great austral land," where he spent six months. De Courtonne describes this land as rich and well populated, with friendly natives, plentiful food, and an ideal climate for settlement. He adds that Gonneville took possession of the land in the name of Pope Alexander VI, King Louis XII, and the Amiral de Graville. But scarce evidence remains of this voyage: while Gonneville returned to Rouen in 1505, de Courtonne wrote, his logbook was lost during an attack by an English corsair. "Terre de Gonneville" has subsequently been identified as being in places ranging from southern Brazil to Patagonia to New Zealand to Madagascar.[15] De Courtonne himself claimed (rather doubtfully) to be a descendant of a native of Gonneville's land, Essomeric, the son of a chieftain.

But who was Gonneville and why had he never been heard of before de Courtonne's account? After all, his purported discovery took place in 1504, while de Courtonne wrote of him a century and a half later. And why does there seem to be no original documentation about him or his voyage? These problems have led to controversy, with some suggesting that Gonneville's voyage, and perhaps even the man himself, are entirely fictional, invented by de Courtonne—conclusions supported by the evidence.[16] But regardless of the account's veracity, and regardless of where the land was thought to be, its impact was significant: for more than a century, the allure of imagined southern lands, and Gonneville's purported discovery in particular, beckoned to French explorers who were eager to rediscover this lost paradise and colonize it for their country. De Courtonne himself was the first to propose an expedition to refind the lost land. Despite uncertainties surrounding its location, the king and the pope were both drawn to the proposal. Owing to internal church bickering over the granting of bishoprics, however, de Courtonne's plan was soon shelved. Still, his ideas took hold, motivating extensive French exploration of the southern oceans over the next century.

With de Courtonne's accounts, Gonneville, theretofore unheard of, was widely believed in mid-to-late seventeenth- and eighteenth-century France to have discovered a new land, and numerous French and foreign expeditions set out in search of it. His writings were well-timed, offering a balm in an era when the English and the Dutch were far outpacing the French in the South Pacific. They also fit well with Cardinal Richelieu's view of the colonial enterprise as a means of developing commerce, opening routes for emigration, and heightening national glory, as well as a political tool to combat Spanish hegemony. Richelieu's government built a strong navy, giving a firm foundation to dreams of exploration, something that only increased with Jean-Baptiste Colbert's arrival in power. Further, by crediting Gonneville with the discovery of a land far to the south, de Courtonne gave to France a moral legitimacy toward Terra Australis parallel to that of Amerigo Vespucci in the New World. His description of a fertile, temperate climate sparked the imagination of French explorers and writers, and the search for the unknown land wove a thread through subsequent French exploration in the Southern Hemisphere. To refind "Terre de Gonneville" and, with it, a great southern continent, had an unparalled allure. It was only with Cook's penetrating explorations of the southern seas in the 1770s that this French quest for the fabled southern continent, warm and full of lush life, abated. With Cook's voyage, the massive extent of the southern pack ice was finally exposed—but still there was no knowledge of what lay beyond the forbidding ice, whether it be open sea, land, or more ice.

Through the eighteenth century, French interest in Terra Australis—whether it be a vast southern continent or specific territories in and near present-day Australia—grew in line with public fascination with faraway lands and the scientific, commercial, and colonial questions they raised. When the philosopher and mathematician Pierre Louis Moreau de Maupertuis wrote to Prince Frédéric de Prusse that southern lands offered important possibilities for science and commerce, his letter gained much attention in France's flourishing literary salons.[17] By the middle of the century, these ideas preoccupied scientific, intellectual, and social circles. The attraction also spoke to geopolitics, power, and rivalry: if France could find and exploit these lands, the country could "catch up" in the race for exploration and colonization, and it would also help restore France's naval position at a time when British naval power was in ascendence. Navigators, especially from the French East India Company, were fascinated with the idea of establishing an "Austral France" in a land that, they thought, contained riches to outstrip even those of El Dorado.

Expeditions, however, were at the mercy of changing political winds. In the opening years of the eighteenth century, until 1715, the accession of Philip V to the Spanish throne and the subsequent transformations on the European political scene facilitated French maritime activity. During the War of Spanish Succession (1701–1714), several French voyages set out for the southern seas, including that of Pierre Perrée du Coudray de la Villestreux, who became one of the first to navigate the Strait of Magellan. But this burst of activity ended in 1715 with the Treaty of Utrecht, which stripped France of many of its overseas possessions, especially in what is now maritime Canada and the West Indies. For the following fifty years, Britain ruled the waves while French mariners slumped into a period of lethargy, with no coherent policies to guide them. Still, this period did see one explicit effort to search for Terra Australis: that of the French East India Company's Jean-Baptiste Charles Bouvet de Lozier (1705–1786).

Like many at the time, Bouvet was as inspired by de Courtonne's writings as he was frustrated by his inability to find original accounts of Gonneville's voyage. Between 1734 and 1738, the experienced navigator petitioned the East India Company three times before receiving approval for his voyage to rediscover "Terre de Gonneville." There, Bouvet hoped to evangelize the natives, develop commerce opportunities, and establish a depot to serve navigators sailing between France and the Far East. Bouvet left France with two ships, *L'Aigle* and *Le Marie*, in mid-1738. On the first day of the new year, he caught sight of snow-covered land south of the Cape of Good Hope, but all attempts to disembark were blocked by thick fog and unnavigable ice. Forced to turn around, Bouvet returned to France with descriptions of towering icebergs, freezing seas teeming with whales, and odd black and white birds, unable to fly but gracefully agile in the water. Thinking that he had seen the advanced part of a great austral continent, Bouvet named his land "Cap de la Circoncision" in reference to the religious day on which he sighted it, the Feast of the Circumcision of Christ. A map made based on Bouvet's expedition by the pioneering geographer Philippe Buache in 1739 shows a large bipartite southern continent encircling but not covering the South Pole, with Cap de la Circoncision highlighted in red at the tip of the smaller continental section (figure 2). While the French East India Company had initially thought that Terre Australe might offer strategic advantages—including a rest and resupply station for ships, a site for a new colony, and even a base for war—it did not find Bouvet's description of a snowy and fog-frozen land enticing and declined to pursue the idea further. While Bouvet thought he had discovered a southern continent, his land was later shown to be insular.[18] Still, the idea of a great southern land ripe for colonization and domination, analogous to other waiting parts of the globe, persisted.

Soon after Bouvet's return, the French naturalist Georges Louis Leclerc de Buffon proposed a route through the Pacific Ocean toward Terre Australe, the unknown continent, which he thought to be as big as Europe, Asia, and Africa put together. Buffon had an open mind as to the climate of this land, writing that conflicting reports made it impossible to know whether Terre Australe was colder than the Arctic or possessed a temperate or even warm climate.[19] His close friend, the writer and Bourguignon magistrat Charles de Brosses (1709–1777), took up the idea. De Brosses's five-volume history of the search for Terre Australe, written in the 1750s, drew from navigators' logbooks and journals of the previous two centuries to evidence a huge land situated in the austral region but with the climate, opulence, and allure of the tropics. His interest in French colonial expansion and commercial gain was both political and personal; he thought that the successful colonization of Terre Australe could counter Britain's profligate imperial expansion and, as a shareholder in the French East India Company, he saw the control of new lands on the route to India as a means of lifting the company's fortunes—and thus his own.[20] De Brosses called on the king to pursue this idea: "For a king, it would be an enterprise much more glorious than a war, than a conquest. The most celebrated of the modern monarchs will be he who gives his name to the austral world. . . . It is France above all who must attempt this, France which, until now, has let herself be bested by other nations in the domain of austral discoveries."[21] But de Brosses had the misfortune of advancing his proposals at the opening of the Seven Years' War (1756–1763). With that war, France lost its best remaining colonies as well as access to the lucrative spice trade in India. Conquered on the sea, too, where Britain now

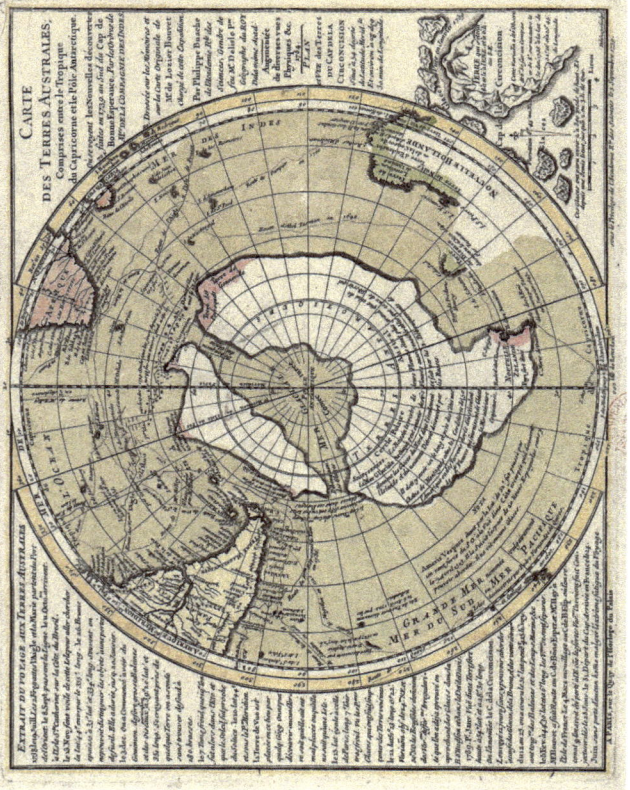

FIGURE 2. Philippe Buache, *Carte des Terres Australes, comprises entre le Tropique du Capricorn et le Pole Antarctique, où se voyent les Nouvelles découvertes faites en 1739 au Sud du Cap de Bonne Esperance par les Ordres de Mrs de la Companie des Indes, dressée sur les Memoires et sur la Carte originale de Mr de Lozier Bouvet chargé de l'expédition* (Map of the southern lands, between the Tropic of Capricorn and the Antarctic Pole, where the new discoveries made in 1739 to the south of the Cape of Good Hope on the Orders of Messieurs of the Company of India are seen, drawn up according to the notes and the original map by Mr. de Lozier Bouvet, in charge of the expedition), 1739, 25×32 cm (Bibliothêque nationale de France).

reigned supreme, France was a country humiliated—all the more so since less than a decade earlier, France had arguably been the most powerful nation in Europe.

In a push to rebuild France's empire, Louis XV, fascinated by geography and encouraged by Bouvet's voyage, ordered expeditions anew. Together with his principal counselor, the Duc de Choiseul, the king sought to restore his navy's prestige with grand expeditions to the Pacific. This push continued with the accession of Louis XVI in 1774. With the new king's interest in maritime affairs, the French Navy entered a period of prosperity. From 1766 to 1840, France surpassed all other countries in grand exploratory voyages in search of unknown lands, especially in the Pacific. The men who led these expeditions served the monarch, chosen for their proficiency as sailors and their courage proven in earlier battles; their names are still today well-known in France. While some of these navigators set out explicitly to discover Terre Australe, and several thought they did so, none of them made it as far as the Antarctic Continent. They did play an important role in the discovery of the sub-Antarctic possessions France retains today.

This era of Pacific exploration falls into two parts, separated by the French Revolution. Between the 1760s and the Revolution, French navigators set out on a series of well-equipped, state-funded, scientifically oriented voyages to the southern Pacific and Indian Oceans. Beginning with Louis-Antoine de Bougainville, these voyages—including those of Jean-François Marie de Surville, Yves Joseph de Kerguelen de Trémarec, Marc Joseph Marion Dufresne, Jean François de Galaup, comte de La Pérouse, and, during the Revolution itself, Antoine Reymond Joseph Bruny d'Entrecasteaux and Nicolas Baudin—exemplify the archetype of grand, exploratory, ethnocentric voyages in the French cultural imagination. They mark the beginning of a *grand dessein* for the Pacific for which enthusiasm was profound and long-lasting.[22] Nourished by the philosophy and intellectual pursuits of the Enlightenment, these voyages also offered new hope to a defeated country, a means of rebuilding French prestige through faraway exploits. The discovery of strange societies, too, perceived in France as the incarnation of the philosophical ideal of nature, underwrote the French belief in the dual progress of the nation and the human spirit.

Of these many voyages, it is those of Kerguelen and Marion Dufresne that are important for the sub-Antarctic islands France possesses today. Having joined the navy at the age of sixteen, Kerguelen (1734–1797) rose steadily through its ranks, serving in the Antilles during the Seven Years' War and subsequently in the North Atlantic. Inspired by Bouvet and by the idea of Terre Australe, all the rage in scientific and literary circles, Kerguelen dreamed of launching a grand exploratory campaign to find the unknown southern land. In September 1770, he presented his ideas to the Duke of Praslin, the influential minister of the marine. Soon, he received orders to find and explore the large continent thought to occupy the southern part of the globe, an immense and unpenetrated space. Kerguelen was instructed to disembark, examine any existing production and manufacturing facilities, evaluate commerce possibilities, and begin building a trade relationship with the natives.

With two ships (the second commanded by Louis François Marie Aleno de Saint-Aloüarn) and more than three hundred sailors, Kerguelen headed south.[23] In mid-February 1772, sailing through strong winds and snow in the southern Indian Ocean, the French captain caught sight of land and, thinking it the famous continent, baptized it *France Australe*. An ensign, Charles de Boisguehenneu, managed to disembark and claim the uninhabited land for France, a simple *prise de possession* unimpeded by the complexities of territorial claim in populated regions.[24] In the ensuing violent storm, the two ships were separated. Kerguelen and his men made their way back to France, arriving in Brest in mid-1772. The navigator went straight to Versailles to recount his voyage to the king and court, telling of a land that was likely to contain wood, minerals, diamonds, rubies, precious stones, and marble. With his lavish descriptions of the elusive Terra Australis, Kerguelen was, in the words of the naval officer and explorer La Pérouse, received in France "like a new Christopher Columbus."[25]

Given the appeal of his report, it is no surprise that Kerguelen convinced the king to authorize a second, more ambitious voyage. Kerguelen left France again in March 1773 and soon refound his promised land—but the sailors and future colonists aboard the ships quickly realized that their captain's idyllic descriptions bore no resemblance to reality. The inhospitable coasts and ferocious weather—nothing but relentless cold, fog, and icy winds—allowed for only a short debarkation. Early in the new year of 1774, the men renewed the French claim from two years prior: to the accompaniment of musketry fire, they wired a bottle containing a piece of parchment with the king's name and the date to a rock in Baie de l'Oiseau (named for one of the expedition's ships). But the dream was shattered. Fearing mutiny, Kerguelen returned to France despondent, penning a letter to the court en route admitting his failure.[26] In the meantime, Louis XV had died and Kerguelen's support at the Ministry of the Marine had evaporated. With his extravagant claims about the supposed austral continent shown to be false, he was stripped of his rank, struck from the list of officers, and imprisoned.[27]

Despite Kerguelen's personal misfortunes, his voyages laid claim to the islands for France. When James Cook arrived at the seal-dotted archipelago on Christmas Day 1776, he found and respected the French *prise de possession*. He did add his own declaration of debarkation to the French parchment—and, of more immediate value, his surgeon, William Anderson, found the abundant Kerguelen cabbage to be a potent antiscorbutic.[28] While he was tempted to name the archipelago "Desolation Islands," Cook ultimately chose to name it for the demoted French navigator, "but that I would not rob Monsieur de Kerguelen of the honour of it bearing his name."[29] Port Christmas (or Christmas Harbor), of course, was named for the day of Cook's arrival. That these names were given by Cook is a reminder that, despite the French claim to the islands, France had neither presence in nor control over them at the time.[30] While the islands were frequented by British and US sealers in the years following Cook's visit, they only became of political interest much later.

In the same year as Kerguelen set out on his first voyage, so too did another French navigator with similar intentions: Marc Joseph Marion Dufresne (1724–1772). Born into a rich Saint-Malo family with significant interests in the French East India Company, Marion Dufresne had the sea in his blood.[31] As a privateer during the War of the Austrian Succession, he captured several English ships and aided in the rescue of "Bonnie" Prince Charles Stuart from Scotland in 1746 before being taken prisoner. After being exchanged and returned to France, Marion Dufresne joined the East India Company, venturing as far as China. With the dissolution of the company in 1769, the navigator settled on Isle de France. Soon, he embarked on a dual mission: to return Aotourou, a Tahitian presented at the court of Versailles by Bougainville, to his home country, as well as to explore the southern seas with a view to finding Gonneville's long-lost land—and, he hoped, to make his fortune through trading. More than a century after de Courtonne's writing, Gonneville's land still beckoned to explorers.

Marion Dufresne, who was financing the voyage largely from his own funds, left Isle de France in October 1771. After Aotourou died of smallpox at Port Dauphin, Madagascar, Marion Dufresne continued south to the Cape of Good Hope, where he took on fresh supplies and then set out eastward. In early 1772, he sighted a number of islands shrouded by fog. His second-in-command, Julien Marie Crozet, took possession of some of these islands for France—the *prise de possession* which today backs French sovereignty over the Crozet archipelago.[32] Marion Dufresne did not, however, refind Gonneville's land or Bouvet's Cap de la Circoncision—and his voyage ended badly. With his ships damaged from a collision in heavy fog, he set sail in search of a place to make repairs and treat his scurvy-ridden crew. In March 1772 they reached Van Diemen's Land (now Tasmania), previously sighted by Europeans 130 years earlier on Dutch seafarer Abel Tasman's voyage. But a lack of materials forced the Frenchmen to depart quickly, heading north toward New Zealand. In mid-June, Māoris killed Marion Dufresne and nearly two dozen of his men, most likely after they fished in taboo waters.

While these voyages did secure sub-Antarctic possessions for France, they provided little in the way of new information about Terra Australis. It was Cook's momentous expedition that showed that if there was a southern continent, it was necessarily much further to the south than had previously been thought. Cook's circumnavigation of the globe in the high southern latitudes indicated that any such continent would be a permanently cold and icy land, devoid of the exotic riches long thought to exist there and not suitable for colonization. When he reached the Antarctic polar circle at 71°10 south in early 1774—the furthest south that anyone had penetrated to date—his efforts to push farther were blocked by ice. "The risque one runs in exploring a coast in these unknown and icy seas," Cook wrote, "is so very great that no man will ever venture farther than I have done, and that the lands which may lie to the South will never be explored."[33] With Cook's findings, the Antarctic question took on its modern aspect. For their part, the French were greatly discouraged by Cook's successes. Cook had done so much, La Pérouse complained, that little was left for others to explore.[34]

In the narrow window between Cook's second voyage and the outbreak of the French Revolution, and despite his grumbling about the British captain's accomplishments, La Pérouse set out on a grand exploratory voyage to the Pacific. He had been personally chosen by Louis XVI to lead an expedition to try to link up Cook's and Bougainville's earlier voyages. The choice of La Pérouse reflected his long experience: already forty-four years old, he had distinguished himself in the Americas and the West Indies during the Seven Years' War and the Anglo-French War. He was much admired for capturing two British forts on the coast of Hudson Bay in the summer of 1782, and particularly for his treatment of the governor of the Prince of Wales Fort. Charged with refinding Bouvet's land and examining the far southern archipelagos discovered by Cook—instructions that hinted at the global scale of French-British rivalry—La Pérouse's expedition also included sixteen scientists who undertook meticulously planned work in physics, astronomy, mineralogy, zoology, geography, botany, and meteorology.

La Pérouse left Brest in mid-1785, a huge crowd cheering on his ships.[35] Their departure marked the beginning of a remarkable three-year voyage that took them from Africa to South America to Alaska before crossing the Pacific and arriving in Macao in early 1787. The ships then sailed the China and Japan Seas, making La Pérouse the first European navigator to penetrate these waters, passing through the strait that now bears his name, dividing the Russian island of Sakhalin from the northern part of Japan's Hokkaidō Island. When he reached Petropavlosk in September 1787, La Pérouse dispatched Barthélémy de Lesseps (uncle to Ferdinand de Lesseps, the developer of the Suez Canal) to return to France via Siberia, taking with him reports to be presented in Versailles—a decision that would prove prescient. La Pérouse's ships then proceeded south to

Australia. It is from Botany Bay that the navigator wrote his last known messages to Versailles, detailing his plans for returning to Isle de France by the end of 1788. Resupplied with wood and fresh water, the ships left Australia on 10 March 1788 and were never heard from again. Their fate was of deep concern in French maritime, scientific, and public circles, and several rescue attempts were launched. While La Pérouse's expedition had set off in an atmosphere of optimism, even jubilation—which was initially borne out by the impressive list of new territories explored and the numerous trading opportunities identified in the Americas, Asia, and Russia—the loss of both vessels without any trace was a severe blow, dashing immediate hopes of further expansionist voyages.

Even though these voyages enjoyed huge popularity, the Versailles monarchy was moribund. During the turbulent years of the Revolution, French seafaring entered a lull. Still, one voyage stands out: a rescue mission dispatched to search for La Pérouse, about whom no news had been heard for years but whose fate remained of great interest. The naval officer and colonial governor Antoine Reymond Joseph Bruny d'Entrecasteaux was chosen to lead the expedition. He departed from Brest in September 1791 with two ships, the second one captained by Jean-Michel Huon de Kermadec.[36] As they sailed toward Australia, the expedition's scientists collected and cataloged hundreds of new species. D'Entrecasteaux also reconnoitered Nouvelle-Amsterdam Island, which had first been seen by a Castilian navigator in 1552 and which would be claimed by France in 1843. But while d'Entrecasteaux's ships came tantalizingly close to the site of La Pérouse's disappearance, he did not realize it and found no trace of the lost Frenchmen or their ships. And the expedition, ambitious and hurried, ultimately claimed the lives of both captains: Kermadec died of consumption and exhaustion in early March 1793, while d'Entrecasteaux died of scurvy and dysentery four months later. The ships subsequently made it to Surabaya, where they were seized by the Dutch, who were at that point at war with France. The men were imprisoned and, upon their release, had to find their own way home. While the many crates of scientific specimens gathered on the voyage were confiscated, the well-known British botanist Joseph Banks was able to secure the return of most of the specimens to France.

The disappearances and deaths of Marion Dufresne, La Pérouse, d'Entrecasteaux, and Kermadec were by no means exceptional: navigators Surville (drowned off Peru), Saint-Aloüarn (tropical disease), and Baudin (tuberculosis) also perished on their austral expeditions.[37] Quite apart from the likes of Marion Dufresne and his men, who were killed by the inhabitants of the lands they visited, French seamen of the era (like those of other countries) fell ill and died at a high rate from a combination of disease, spoiled food, and exposure. The unceasing cold endured on searches for Terre Australe, and the heavy humidity of the tropical waters that separated France from the cold southern seas, were unkind to the sailors, who worked and slept in damp clothes. Food stores were often wet and spoiled from leaks in the wooden ships, and the water in the hold was frequently contaminated with excrement. The lack of fresh fruit and vegetables onboard exacerbated the situation as entire ships fell ill due to lack of vitamins. Malaria, dysentery, typhus, yellow fever, and venereal diseases, too, often decimated crews with no regard for rank. While efforts were made to conquer scurvy during the revitalization of the French Navy after the Seven Years' War, the path to understanding this illness was neither linear nor swift.[38]

The Opening of Antarctica

Despite Cook's pessimism, it did not take long for the Antarctic waters to emerge as a commercial opportunity. As Napoleon led France into war, sealers swarmed toward the Antarctic, eager to exploit the frigid southern seas for profit. Between 1780 and 1820, private entrepreneurs slaughtered millions of seals in the vicinity of the Falkland Islands, the South Georgia and South Sandwich Islands, and the Chilean coast.[39] The seal populations of the French possessions of Kerguelen and Crozet were likewise ravaged. Whalers followed the sealers in pursuit of whales and elephant seals, valued for their oil.[40] Driven by growing rivalry over resources, territory, and trade, sealers, sailors, and surveyors ventured farther and farther south until, in 1820–1821, three parties, from Russia, Britain, and the United States, all sighted the Antarctic Continent (at that time, not yet known to be continental in nature). The first to do so, almost in unison, were Russia's Fabian Gottlieb von Bellingshausen, a naval officer acting on behalf of the state, and Britain's Edward Bransfield.[41]

While France was absent from these first sightings of the Antarctic Continent, this was still one of the great eras of French navigation. During the Restoration, from 1814 to 1830, and the July Monarchy, from 1830 to 1848, France embarked on a striking series of expeditions to the Pacific.[42] During the first part of this era, from 1814 to 1840, the French state sponsored eleven major voyages for the purposes of discovery, expansion, and scientific investigation—many more than Britain (five) and the United States (three), and a hair's breadth more than Russia (ten). Given the French political and economic situation of the time—following the upheavals of the Revolution and defeat in the Napoleonic Wars—this investment demands explanation. France was a country defeated, physically drained, choked by rampant social and political divisions, and forced to pay a huge war indemnity and accept 150,000 occupiers from Britain, Russia, Austria, and Prussia. The crushing loss at the Battle of Trafalgar in 1805 had left the

French fleet in tatters. But France's defeat in the Napoleonic Wars did not mean the end of aspirations to power and prestige, especially as represented by science. The navy, certainly, was in dire shape both materially and financially, but maritime scientific voyages were still seen as a means of building reputation and standing. There was a desire to perpetuate the tradition of impressive (if often ill-fated) expeditions under the Ancien Régime (and even through the Revolutionary period), and especially to build anew on the Ancien Régime's scientific legacy. Like in 1763, in 1815 many good naval officers found themselves inactive and looked to scientific voyaging as a means of advancing their careers at a point in time when the navy was weakened. The Pacific was chosen as a venue for rebuilding and projecting French power since it was a theater in which France had enjoyed previous successes, a region of the globe with much left to discover and explore, and an ideal location for resuming rivalry with Britain.

There was also a clear geopolitical dimension at play: between the loss of Isle de France (renamed Mauritius) in 1810 and growing British influence in the region, resentment of the French-British power imbalance grew. Isle de France had long been a key Indian Ocean naval base and shipbuilding center, as well as a regular supply depot, for French navigators. As one of the few colonies retained after 1763, its loss was felt sharply. At the same time, the French also resented British colonial activity in Australia and New Zealand, which was seen as profiting from France's defeat in the Napoleonic Wars to capture a decisive advantage in the South Pacific. The British, lamented Hyacinthe de Bougainville (son of Louis-Antoine de Bougainville), were poised to gain control of the entirety of Australia despite previous French landings in the region.[43] The British annexation of New Zealand similarly antagonized the French. To the French after 1815, preventing Britain from extending its sphere of influence over the entire Pacific was paramount.

It was thus with glory, rivalry, and pride in mind that the restored monarchy took to Pacific voyaging with zest. Louis XVIII gave his patronage to expeditions including those of Louis-Claude de Freycinet and Louis Isidore Duperrey, who circumnavigated the globe in 1817–1820 and 1822–1825, respectively, and Bougainville the son, who set out to establish diplomatic and commercial relations with the Far East in 1824. While Freycinet's ship was lost in the Falkland Islands, the crew and most of the scientific work, including almost five hundred previously unknown plant specimens, were rescued, a huge morale boost to those who followed in his wake. And in the 1830s, with the reign of Louis-Philippe, political ends—namely, commerce and empire—took on a larger role in the pattern of French southern voyaging.[44] It was on one of these voyages, Jules Sébastien César Dumont d'Urville's 1837–1840 expedition to the southern seas, that France became an Antarctic nation.

2

AN UNEXPECTED TERRITORY

Near the end of the remarkable post-Napoleonic series of Enlightenment-inspired voyages to the south seas came the one that would place France's name on the Antarctic map: that of the seasoned explorer and naval officer Jules Sébastien César Dumont d'Urville in 1837–1840.

Born in Condé-sur-Noireau, Normandy, in 1790, the eighth child but only surviving son of Gabriel Charles François Dumont d'Urville, a bailiff, and Jeanne Françoise Julie Victoire de Croisilles, Dumont d'Urville was an intelligent but sickly boy.[1] After his father's death, the family settled near Caen on the banks of the Orne and Dumont d'Urville was tutored by his maternal uncle, Father Jean Jacques François de Croisilles, who offered the young boy a classical education. With a bursary, Dumont d'Urville then entered Caen's Lycée Malherbe. When he turned seventeen in 1807, he joined the French Navy. But this came at a bad time: just two years earlier, the navy had been humiliated at the Battle of Trafalgar, and with the British still blockading French ports, Dumont d'Urville found himself inactive, only able to dream of the faraway voyages that had initially drawn him to service. He put this time to use by nurturing his intellectual interests: classical languages, mathematics, and natural sciences. The more he immersed himself in his studies, the more he gained a reputation as a difficult man, sullen and taciturn, to the point that he was turned away from the first French grand scientific voyage after the end of the blockade, that undertaken in 1817 by Louis-Claude de Freycinet aboard the *Uranie*. In these years of disappointment, Dumont d'Urville's world was lightened by his relationship with Adèle Dorothée Pépin, the daughter of a watchmaker, whom he married in 1815.

Dumont d'Urville finally found his long-awaited opportunity to travel in 1819, when he was named to the *Chevrette* expedition, which was assigned to map the islands of the eastern Mediterranean. It was on this voyage that his scientific career and public profile took off. When the *Chevrette* called on the Greek island of Milos, Dumont d'Urville went ashore, as always, in search of plants and insects. A farmer showed him a stone statue, a female figure, broken into pieces. Awed by its beauty, Dumont d'Urville identified the statue as likely representing Venus of the Judgement of Paris. He had to leave it behind, however, when his captain decided that their ship had no suitable storage place for such a find. Upon arrival in Constantinople, Dumont d'Urville recounted the whole story to the French ambassador, who promptly sent men to purchase the statue. The transaction was complicated by competing bids—but, from the French point of view, it was ultimately successful: the statue was soon the center of attention at the Louvre, where it was considered the quintessential example of the classical female nude.[2] Today, it is one of the most famous statues in the world. For his part in the Vénus de Milo affair, Dumont d'Urville was awarded the *Légion d'honneur* and promoted to lieutenant—and he also became a household name in France. Less spectacular but more personally satisfying was his appointment to the Linnean Society in recognition of his collection and study of botanical and entomological specimens from the voyage.

A year later, the navy, newly reorganized, was eager to send a major expedition to the south seas. Under experienced officer Louis Isidore Duperrey, with Dumont d'Urville as his second-in-command, the expedition left Toulon in mid-1822 for a three-year circumnavigation. Their ship, *La Coquille*, had a huge capacity for stocking fresh water, victuals, and scientific specimens—the last particularly pleasing to Dumont d'Urville, who had tasted success and had big scientific ambitions. The significant time spent around the islands near Australia and New Zealand was an El Dorado for Dumont d'Urville, again responsible for botany and entomology. During the voyage, which covered more than twenty-one thousand leagues and crossed the equator six times, he collected vast numbers of specimens, including four hundred previously unknown plants and seven hundred previously unknown insects. Although the men did not know it, their ship also passed very close the site of La Pérouse's wreck of 1788—something that would later become of great importance to Dumont d'Urville. *La Coquille* returned to France in early 1825, full to the brim with scientific discoveries, hugely celebrated for having spent nearly three years at sea with no loss of life.

Dumont d'Urville was again promoted and assigned command of *La Coquille*, which he was instructed to take back to the South Pacific to further explore its islands, and specifically the region in which it was thought that La Pérouse's ships had been lost. Decades after his disappearance, La Pérouse's fate still mystified and intrigued the French, so much that Dumont d'Urville rechristened his ship the *Astrolabe* in honor of one of La Pérouse's lost vessels. Dumont d'Urville left Toulon in the spring of 1826 and made his way to the Pacific via the Cape through terrible storms. His men spent most of the following year exploring the islands to the north and east of Australia. In Hobart, where they came for rest and resupply, Dumont d'Urville heard stories of Peter Dillon, a merchant trader who claimed to have found evidence of La Pérouse's ships.[3] Born in Martinique to an Irish father, Dillon was a disreputable adventurer. Nonetheless, the French navigator decided to pursue the lead—a good instinct, as Dillon had been correct. In February 1828, Dumont d'Urville found the wrecks of La Pérouse's ships among reefs in Vanikoro. His men labored to bring up anchors, a cannon, and a blunderbuss, all encrusted with coral, proof of the discovery. The wreck had been located, even if its circumstances and the fate of La Pérouse and his men will never fully be known. The Frenchmen paid homage to their lost compatriots with a twenty-one-gun salute from the *Astrolabe*. They also built a monument of stone and wood and inscribed it with the words "To the memory of La Pérouse and his companions!—*Astrolabe*, 14 March 1828."[4] Dumont d'Urville then turned his ship back to France, where it arrived in the late spring of 1829, full to the brim with a precious cargo of specimens including sixteen hundred plants and nine hundred rocks.

Hailed in France for unraveling the mystery of La Pérouse's disappearance, Dumont d'Urville found acclaim in official and public spheres. In the summer of 1829, Charles X approved his promotion to captain and the *Académie des sciences* lauded his expedition's scientific results. The next year, Dumont d'Urville took the deposed king into exile after the July Revolution. As well as the massive official account of the *Astrolabe*'s voyage, comprising twelve volumes and five albums, Dumont d'Urville wrote the popular "Voyage pittoresque autour du monde" ("Picturesque Journey Around the World") for a public audience.[5] A lavishly illustrated account of French and foreign maritime expeditions, the "Voyage pittoresque" enjoyed huge success and many reprintings, propelled by the navigator's rising fame.[6]

As he finished writing his accounts of the *Astrolabe*'s voyage, Dumont d'Urville was already on the lookout for a new expedition: he wanted to sail through the Strait of Magellan to the Pacific—something no French vessel had done since Bougainville's circumnavigation of the 1760s—and then on to the Solomon Islands, New Zealand, and the Philippines. With this voyage, he planned to fill in blank and little-known parts of maps, fly the French colors in the region, and continue his ethnographic and natural scientific studies— ambitions that spoke to him as much as for the advancement of scientific knowledge as for building on his life's work.

But when news reached France that both the United States and Britain were preparing new voyages of discovery to the Antarctic, it was received with alarm. In face of the two foreign expeditions, King Louis-Philippe intervened directly in Dumont d'Urville's plans, adding a second ship and altering the voyage to include an Antarctic component. Dumont d'Urville was instructed to follow and extend the British sealing captain James Weddell's route near what is now known as the Antarctic Peninsula and, ultimately, to penetrate farther into high southern latitudes than anyone had done before.[7] Weddell's record of sailing to a latitude of 74°15' south, achieved in 1823, was at that time unbeaten. Louis-Philippe also ordered Dumont d'Urville to bring honor and glory to France by attempting to reach the South Pole.[8]

With the British (under James Clark Ross) and the Americans (under Charles Wilkes) also preparing to head to the Antarctic, the element of national ambition and pride imbued in Dumont d'Urville's voyage—his third and last to the Pacific—was unmistakable. His initial reaction, however, was far from enthusiastic: "I would prefer three years of navigation under burning equatorial skies to two months in polar climes," he wrote.[9] But Dumont d'Urville soon saw a glittering opportunity to enhance his public profile, increasingly important to his self-image, writing that "I finally recognized that an attempt to reach the South Pole would, in the eyes of the public, have a character of novelty, *grandeur* and even wonder, which would not fail to draw attention."

All three expeditions were also motivated by a desire to win one of the great remaining scientific firsts: the south magnetic pole. At the beginning of the nineteenth century, there was intense interest in Earth's magnetic field. Sailors and scientists alike saw the magnetic poles as key to solving navigational problems and better understanding the physics of the globe. "In the humanist tradition of the West few artefacts are as revered as the magnetic compass," writes Granville Mawer: "It is regarded as an invention that made it possible to spread the influence of Western civilization across the face of the globe. . . . More important, the desire to understand magnetism as a natural phenomenon—the better to exploit it—was a powerful stimulus to the development of Western scientific method."[10] In what has been termed the "Magnetic Crusade," the 1830s and early 1840s saw a series of expeditions to locate the magnetic poles and chart Earth's magnetic fields. After James Clark Ross—the British naval commander, naturalist, and Arctic explorer—located the north magnetic pole in 1831, the search for its southern counterpart was on. As the three national expeditions prepared to head to the Antarctic, there was for France the chance to best both Britain, its adversary of old, and the United States, the emerging commercial rival, by being the first to the south magnetic pole. Even having been defeated in the Napoleonic Wars not long before, by the 1830s France was the second most powerful naval presence in the Pacific and winning the magnetic race seemed entirely possible. Doing so would be proof of national reascendency.

Dumont d'Urville to the Antarctic

In preparation for the voyage, Dumont d'Urville's two ships—his well-loved *Astrolabe* and the *Zélée*—were reinforced in anticipation of passing through Antarctica's ice fields: their prows were strengthened with wood and bronze and their hulls with copper, and giant ice saws were installed.[11] And given the lack of specific knowledge of the Antarctic waters in France, Dumont d'Urville himself traveled to London for ten days in the spring of 1837, where he purchased maps and books and spoke to navigators, hydrographers, and naturalists familiar with some of the waters in which he would travel. His encounters with the British at this time of Franco-British rapprochement (which would culminate in a military alliance during the Crimean War) were a far cry from his early days in the navy, when British ships were blockading French ports. Still, while John Washington, secretary of the Royal Geographic Society, and Francis Beaufort, Royal Navy hydrographer, greeted him warmly, privately they considered the Frenchman an unwelcome intruder into a British area of expertise.[12]

As summer changed to autumn, Dumont d'Urville guided his ships away from Toulon on his third long voyage to the southern oceans.[13] While he was eager with anticipation, his wife was not, dreading yet another long separation. Dumont d'Urville commanded the *Astrolabe*, and his good friend Charles Hector Jacquinot the *Zélée*. Following the king's instructions, they headed first toward the Antarctic Peninsula, crossing through the Strait of Gibraltar and then sailing across the Atlantic to the eastern coast of South America. This early part of the voyage was fraught with troubles. In Tenerife, crew members were arrested by the Spanish authorities after a drunken brawl, and a stop was necessary in Rio de Janeiro to disembark a sick midshipman, who was left in the care of the French consul. And the crew was weakened by the rotten meat they were regularly ingesting—a harbinger of the troubles that would plague the men for the next three years.

The ships encountered their first icebergs in December, and on New Year's Day 1838 pack ice blocked them from venturing any further south. Over the following two months, the crews worked to find a passage through the ice, but their efforts were in vain. Where Weddell had found open sea fifteen years previously, Dumont d'Urville found only ice. Despite being reinforced, his ships were not adequate to the task: a warship, the *Astrolabe*'s sides bore gun holes, weakening the structure of its hull and, consequently, its handling in ice fields.

Wind, fog, snow, and ice battered the ships, exhausting the men until so many suffered from hypothermia that Dumont d'Urville was forced to turn back despite not having penetrated as far south as he had hoped.

Escaping the ice, the ships sailed to the South Orkney Islands and then to the tip of the Antarctic Peninsula. Through thick fog, the men spotted land that was only roughly sketched, if shown at all, on their maps. Dumont d'Urville named the coast Terre Louis-Philippe for the king who had sponsored his voyage, and the land to the east of this coast he named Terre Joinville for the king's son, the prince of Joinville. In 1902, the Swedish explorer and geographer Otto Nordenskjöld showed that Terre Joinville is actually a group of islands and named the northernmost of them for Dumont d'Urville: it is now known as D'Urville Island.[14] Dumont d'Urville, wrote Nordenskjöld, "must be esteemed the real discoverer of the whole of this coast."[15]

But conditions on the ships were rapidly worsening. Between the unending fog, rain, and cold and the onset of scurvy, by February 1838 dozens of men were bedridden. At the end of the month, Dumont d'Urville abandoned his efforts and headed for Chile. By the time the ships reached Talcahuano, both captains and two-thirds of the crew were showing signs of scurvy, and one sailor had died from it. The sick men were taken ashore and tended to, and the ships were reprovisioned with fresh fruit, vegetables, and meat. Dumont d'Urville also managed to find copper to repair the ice-damaged sheathing of the ships' hulls.

Further up the coast, in Valparaiso, Dumont d'Urville received a distraught letter from his wife, Adèle, telling him that their youngest son, Emile-Jules-Léon, had died of cholera only a month after his departure from Toulon.[16] Emile-Jules-Léon's death came one year and one day after their daughter Sophie had succumbed to cholera at the age of two. In fragile health, alone in France and mourning the loss of her son, unable to contemplate her future, Adèle begged her husband to come home. While he did not heed her request, and instead "composed himself" and chose to continue with his voyage, Dumont d'Urville was devastated by the news and increasingly ill in its aftermath, suffering frequently from gout and incapacitating stomach pains.[17]

The expedition then sailed to the South Pacific and spent a year among the Pacific islands. Dumont d'Urville guided his ships to the site of La Pérouse's wreck, which he had located ten years earlier. On that voyage, the captain had been too sick with malaria to visit the wreck in person; this time, he was able to search the seabed for more remnants of La Pérouse's ships and go ashore to look for traces of the lost men. While Dumont d'Urville's men conducted wide-ranging scientific and ethnographic investigations during this year in the islands, illnesses continued to plague the ships. Seventeen men died of dysentery and tropical fevers, including five within a single week, and dozens more were incapacitated with violent diarrhea. No one was spared, from cooks to officers to the captains themselves.

In mid-December 1839, two years and three months after leaving France, the two ships arrived in Hobart. There, and in Australia more widely, interest in Dumont d'Urville's voyage was high since almost a year earlier Vandemonian and Australian newspapers had reported—incorrectly but to great curiosity—that the French expedition had discovered an austral continent to the south of the South Shetland Islands.[18] While these articles were corrected a few months later, the interest they generated in Dumont d'Urville's expedition was palpable.[19] As the sick men received treatment at the hospital in Hobart, Dumont d'Urville set himself to the task of uncovering information about the path and results of his rival American expedition, the United States Exploring Expedition under Charles Wilkes. He met first with Sir John Franklin, the governor of Tasmania, "who had such a grand and honorable reputation since his discoveries in the north of America" and whom the French captain, as he wrote, "passionately wanted to meet."[20] But at their first meeting, Franklin could offer no information on Wilkes's expedition. From others, Dumont d'Urville learned that Wilkes was in Sydney, having once already been blocked from venturing south by pack ice, and making ready to again set sail toward the Antarctic—news that the Frenchman took as a challenge. While Dumont d'Urville's instructions had been to penetrate toward the Antarctic on the other side of the globe, he decided to try again south of Hobart: preoccupied by the knowledge that Wilkes and Briton James Clark Ross were planning to push southward, Dumont d'Urville did not want to leave the honor of discovery to his rival captains. "What I have heard here [in Hobart] has converted a venture into an obligation. The American expedition, which is now in Sydney, and the James Ross expedition, which is expected here at any moment, are ardently in pursuit of the same objective, and each thinks only to penetrate into the Antarctic regions as far as possible. In the same spirit, it would be regrettable if a French expedition was obliged to hold itself back," he wrote to the minister of the navy on the last day of 1839.[21]

In preparation, Dumont d'Urville inspected and repaired his ships and recruited men (including several deserters from a French whaler berthed in Hobart) to replace the many he had lost to death or sickness. Given the decimation of his crews, Dumont d'Urville wanted to push south with only one ship, the *Astrolabe*—but when this decision prompted a feud with Jacquinot, the *Zélée*'s captain and his good friend, Dumont d'Urville acquiesced. He himself was so afflicted with gout that he was unable to accept all the dinner invitations he received in Hobart, instead sending Jacquinot to represent the French expedition. "Our crews were so weak, with so few healthy men," he wrote, lamenting that the preparations were taking much longer than he wanted.[22] And pressure was on: the ships needed to leave by New Year's Day to make the most of the austral summer season before the waters were barred by ice. Given the time they had already been away from France and the weakness of the crews, this was not to be a lengthy campaign, but a short and focused one. Dumont d'Urville's path was dictated by what he calculated to be the most direct route toward the magnetic south pole, one of the era's scientific holy grails.

The ships set sail south in the wee hours of the New Year. On the corvettes were enough live pigs and sheep to provide fresh meat for three weeks, as well as gallons of lime juice—efforts to counter the sicknesses that continued to plague the expedition. Fifteen days later, on 16 January 1840, the men spotted their first iceberg, an immense mass stretching for nearly half a kilometer and rising over twenty meters out of the sea, an unworldly and ethereal specter. Soon the ships were surrounded by pack ice. When they crossed the Antarctic Circle on 20 January 1840, the men showered rice and beans from the mastheads in a polar parallel to equatorial baptism; given the freezing temperatures and precarious state of health onboard, Dumont d'Urville had expressly forbidden any rituals involving water.[23] Later that same day, sailing through heavy snow, surrounded by icebergs, they spotted land—rocky islets covered in black dots, which upon closer inspection turned out to be small penguins (figure 3). Since Dumont d'Urville forgot to add a day in his journal when his ship passed the 180th meridian from the east, this is recorded in his own diary as 19 January 1840, a source of some confusion and controversy in the following years.[24]

The next day, the ships each sent a yawl toward the islets. A small group of men disembarked on an islet they aptly named *Rocher du Débarquement*. The landing parties stayed for half an hour, observing the penguins, collecting rock samples—proof of their debarkation—and searching in vain for lichens and shells.[25] Between the churning waters and rocky slopes, climbing out of the yawls and onto the rocks was no mean feat; one man fell into the water and subsequently developed hypothermia and died of a respiratory infection. While ice prevented the ships from reaching the Antarctic mainland—Rocher du Débarquement was about five hundred meters away—the coast was visible from the ships. Dumont d'Urville claimed the territory, islets and mainland, for France, and his men unfurled the tricolore on the top of the islet, the red and blue bands providing a sliver of color in an otherwise monochrome environment (figure 4). "We took possession in the name of France, including the neighboring coast, which the ice prevented us from approaching. Our enthusiasm and our joy were such that it seemed to us that we had added a province to French territory by this peaceful conquest. . . . In this case, we believed our actions to be sufficiently founded in law to maintain the old custom in favor of our country: we did not dispossess anybody, and our titles were indisputable. Thus we

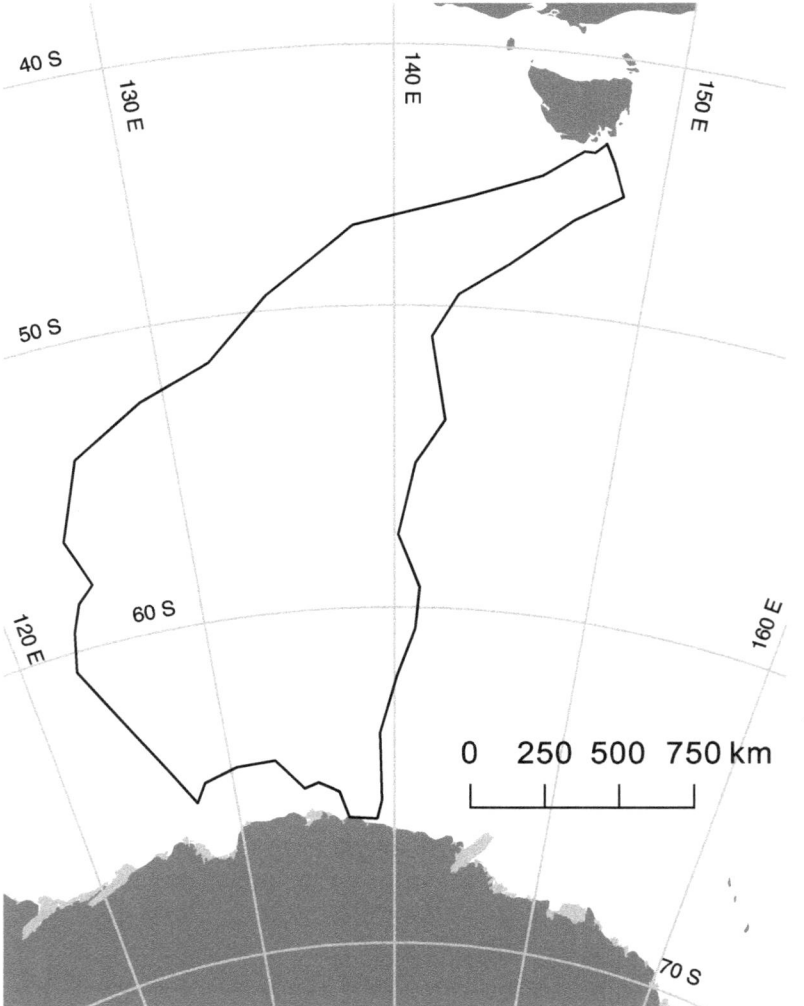

FIGURE 3. Path of the Dumont d'Urville expedition between Hobart and the Antarctic, 1840. Map by Richard Martin-Nielsen.

then saw ourselves as being on French soil," Lieutenant Joseph-Fidèle-Eugene Dubouzet wrote soon after.[26] The only other witnesses to the *prise de possession* were the penguins, whose antics and facial expressions greatly amused the men. The sense of accomplishment and honor is clear: "The ceremony ended as it should, with a libation. We drank to the glory of France which filled us completely, a bottle of the best of her wines, which one of our companions had the presence of mind to bring with him. Never has Bordeaux wine been called

FIGURE 4. Léon Jean Baptiste Sabatier, *Prise de possession de la Terre Adélie le 21 janvier 1840, parages Antarctiques* (Taking possession of Terre Adélie on 21 January 1840), 1846, lithograph, 34.5×54.5 cm (National Library of Australia).

upon to play a more worthy role; never has a bottle been more satisfactorily emptied."

When the yawls returned to the ships and Dumont d'Urville saw the rock samples for himself—samples that appeared to be granite, indicative of continental geology—all doubts about the discovery left him, and he began to name the nearby land.[27] Having honored the king and prince on the expedition's first foray south, this time Dumont d'Urville chose to recognize his own family. For the mainland, he chose *Terre Adélie* for his wife, who had endured many long separations from her husband over the course of his explorations and who had suffered greatly in his absence. "Adélie" was the affectionate diminutive by which Dumont d'Urville called his wife, born Adèle Dorothée Pépin. The land the men first sighted was named *Cape Découverte*, and the mainland point closest to Rocher du Débarquement was named *Pointe Géologie*. Two other promontories were named *Cape Jules*, for Dumont d'Urville's surviving son, and *Cape Pépin*, for Adélie's family. And, later, the expedition naturalists Jacques Bernard Hombron and Honoré Jacquinot named the penguins that dotted the islets of the region for Adélie as well: still today they are known as *Gorfou d'Adélie*, or Adélie penguins (*Pygoscelis adeliae*).[28] That many of the names chosen were personal, reflective of family and not of nation, is indicative of the human toll of separation.

When Dumont d'Urville guided his ships away westward, he had no idea that it would be over a century before the French would return to the territory he had claimed for his country. Over the following days, the ships zigzagged back and forth in front of towering ice cliffs as their captains tried to guide them safely to the coast, but all efforts were stymied by ice, heavy snow, and wind (figure 5). The compass needle spun wildly and enticingly, indicating proximity to the south magnetic pole. While the French expedition did not locate the pole, the cartographer and hydrographer Clément Adrien Vincendon-Dumoulin and his assistant amassed significant magnetic data—enough, Dumont d'Urville hoped, that they would later be able to precisely determine its position.

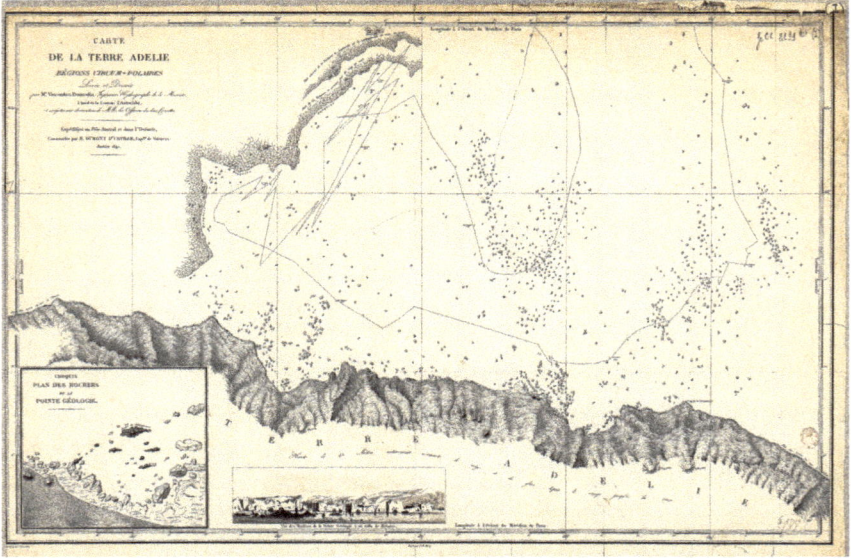

FIGURE 5. Clément Adrien Vincendon-Dumoulin, *Carte de la Terre Adélie et Régions circum-polaires. Levée et Dressée par Mr Vincendon-Dumoulin Ingénieur Hydrographe de la Marine à bord de la Corvette l'Astrolabe et assujettie aux observations de MM. les Officiers des deux Corvettes. Expédition au Pôle Austral et dans l'Océanie Commandée par M. Dumont d'Urville Capne. de Vaisseau, Janvier 1840* (Map of Terre Adélie and circumpolar regions. Surveyed and drawn by Mr. Vincendon-Dumoulin, hydrographic engineer of the Navy aboard the Corvette *Astrolabe* and in accordance with the observations of Messieurs the Officers of the two Corvettes. Expedition to the Southern Pole and Oceania, commanded by Captain Dumont d'Urville, January 1840), 1840, ~1: 288 000 (Bibliothèque nationale de France).

On 28 January, eight days after the Frenchmen spotted land, a ship appeared out of the fog and raised the American flag. Dumont d'Urville recognized it as the *Porpoise* under Commander Cadwalader Ringgold, part of the United States Exploring Expedition. What happened next is unclear. While Ringgold's records suggest that Dumont d'Urville deliberately put on sail to avoid meeting with the *Porpoise*, Dumont d'Urville's records show that, after hoisting the French flag, he reset his sails to keep up with the other ship, hoping to facilitate communication—but, Dumont d'Urville wrote, Ringgold misinterpreted this maneuver and bore off to the south.[29] The captains agree that the ships failed to meet. Afterward, censure was volleyed in both directions: Dumont d'Urville criticized the Americans for shrouding their expedition in a cloak of secrecy, both in port and on the seas, while Ringgold accused Dumont d'Urville of ungentlemanly and even dangerous conduct. While Dumont d'Urville was largely exonerated from wrongdoing in France, the *Zélée*'s surgeon, Élie Le Guillou, suggested that the French captain's actions might have been taken deliberately to keep his discoveries secret.[30] This disagreement over the encounter between the *Porpoise* and the *Astrolabe*, however, paled in comparison to the feud between the two expeditions over first sighting.

Dumont d'Urville's ships continued sailing westward and French lookouts again spotted the coast, or so they thought. Dumont d'Urville named this part of the coast *Côte Clarie*, using Jacquinot's diminutive for his wife Clara. This land has never been refound: it was an illusion, floating ice seen through fog, illustrative of the difficulty of perception in polar waters. For Dumont d'Urville, the advantages of continuing to explore were rapidly diminishing. He had sighted land in the Antarctic and had the rock samples to prove it, and his men had disembarked and claimed territory for France. Little more was to be gained, especially given that the crew were suffering from cold, tired, and falling sick. Aware of Wilkes's ships roaming the area, Dumont d'Urville also wanted to publicize his discovery and preempt any American claims. On 1 February, a month after leaving Hobart, he turned his ships north and headed back to port.

Upon arrival in Hobart seventeen days later, Dumont d'Urville immediately wrote to Paris with a detailed report and charts of his Antarctic explorations: the expedition, he emphasized, had sighted land, disembarked, and claimed possession for France. These communications were entrusted to the *Calcutta*, an English ship setting sail for Europe. Dumont d'Urville also called on the Franklins at Government House and described his discoveries to them in person, and further circulated a short report to newspapers throughout Tasmania and Australia. In these papers, the French captain profusely thanked the Vandemonians, and especially Sir and Lady Franklin, for their warm welcome and declared that his expedition had found land in the Antarctic: on 19 January, he wrote,

"We observed land stretching from the S. to the W.S.W. as far as the eye could reach either way."[31] Soon, his expedition was fêted as having discovered land—both islets and coast—and collected rich geological samples. "The exertions of the French Commodore have been crowned with success," announced one newspaper.[32] In accordance with the procedures of the era, the discovery and *prise de possession* were announced in the *Moniteur*, the official journal of the French government, and the *Annales maritimes et coloniales*, the official monthly periodical published by the Ministry of the Navy.

After repairing, repainting, and resupplying their ships, the French crews made to depart Van Diemen's Land and start on the long journey back to France. Two of the crew, too ill to make the voyage, were left in hospital in Hobart. The return journey took them first to New Zealand, where they stopped to make more geomagnetic observations, and then on a course past New Caledonia to the Indian Ocean, around the Cape of Good Hope and north to Saint Helena, where Dumont d'Urville ordered the ships to pause to allow his men to visit Napoleon's tomb. It was the last such pilgrimage as shortly thereafter Napoleon's remains were brought back to France. Finally, the *Astrolabe* and the *Zélée* entered Toulon harbor in early November 1840, after a voyage of three years and two months and more than twenty-five thousand leagues. Despite the pouring rain, all men were on deck for the ships' arrival, representing one of the most remarkable voyages of discovery under the French flag.

Upon return, Dumont d'Urville, suffering from debilitating gout and exhaustion—"no more than a spectre, a worn body"—was reunited with Adélie and spent some much-needed downtime in Toulon before attending to official duties in Paris.[33] Promoted to rear admiral, he was awarded the *Société de géographie*'s gold medal, fêted as the guest of honor at the Parisian Literary Society, and invited to dine with the king at the Tuileries Palace. The expedition was lauded for its scientific contributions and for its discovery of land in the Antarctic. Despite these successes, the heavy loss of men continued to weigh on Dumont d'Urville, as did his own health problems and his wife's depression, fueled by the deaths of her children and her failing physical health. "We have these polar discoveries to console us a bit [un peu] of the loss of thirty men to dysentery, of 160 people on the expedition," he wrote to his close friend Isidore Lebrun.[34]

Competition and Rivalry in the Ice

Far from having been conducted in an uncontested space, Dumont d'Urville's discovery of Terre Adélie was intimately linked to two other exploratory voyages of the era: those of US Navy lieutenant Charles Wilkes and Briton James

Clark Ross.³⁵ In the years immediately after Dumont d'Urville's return to France, Wilkes challenged the French captain's claim to the first sighting of land in the vicinity of Terre Adélie—a challenge that played out in a court-martial stateside, in newspapers and books, and in public. Ultimately, however, the United States' decision to not claim any territory in the Antarctic meant that it had no long-term political repercussions.

Under Wilkes's command, the United States Exploring Expedition set out in mid-1838 with six ships and 350 men.³⁶ Motivated by a desire to expand US influence, diplomatic presence, and commercial opportunities around the globe, it was one of the largest Western voyages of discovery (in terms of numbers of men and ships) ever to set sail. Wilkes and his men spent four years exploring and surveying the Pacific, Atlantic, and Indian Oceans as well as penetrating toward the Antarctic. The last fully sail-powered circumnavigation of Earth, the expedition covered nearly twenty-six thousand leagues, during which geographic surveys and cartographic work were supplemented by scientific studies, especially in botany and ethnography, by the handful of civilian scientists onboard. Despite Wilkes's disdain for the natural scientists on his expedition—he often refused to let them leave the ships until surveying and charting had been completed, much to their fury—the expedition brought back tens of thousands of floral and faunal specimens, which came to form the basis of many of the Smithsonian Institution's collections.³⁷

Concerning the Antarctic, Wilkes's instructions were to explore as far as possible to the south of both Tierra del Fuego and Van Diemen's Land. After a first failed effort near the Antarctic Peninsula, the expeditions' lead ships arrived in Sydney in late 1839. The Americans spent a month repairing the ships and preparing for another encounter with the ice, setting sail again on 26 December, six days before Dumont d'Urville. Wilkes's aim was to sail south until blocked by ice and then turn westward and search for open paths. The ships spent nearly two months battling the ice, sailing and charting land for fifteen hundred kilometers near the Antarctic coast, naming many individual features. To Wilkes's immense frustration, his men were never able to disembark, except on an iceberg—denying them physical proof of discovery.

When Wilkes arrived back in Sydney on 11 March 1840, he was unimpressed to be met by newspapers announcing Dumont d'Urville's discovery of land on 19 January. Despite his ships' logbooks not showing any land sightings on or before that date, Wilkes began to build a claim for an earlier sighting. In his first report to the US secretary of the navy, he asserted that his expedition had spotted land just hours before Dumont d'Urville. While Wilkes's instructions swore him to secrecy about his expedition's results, upon hearing of Dumont d'Urville's proclamation he decided to speak out.³⁸ In the *Sydney Morning Herald*, Wilkes claimed the first sighting of land in the region: "On the morning of the 19th of January we saw land to the south and east, with many indications of being in its vicinity, such as penguin, seal, and the discoloration of the water; but the impenetrable barrier of ice prevented our nearer approach to it," he wrote.[39] This edition of the newspaper also contained, on the same page, a report of the French sighting, a hint of the dispute that was about to erupt. As other Australian newspapers took up the story, they were divided between trumpeting Wilkes's "glorious result" and circumspection on the basis that Wilkes failed "to take possession of the territory, or to effect a landing at any point."[40]

The United States Exploring Expedition returned home in the spring of 1842 with only two of the original six ships, the *Vincennes* and the *Porpoise*.[41] By the time they arrived stateside, tensions onboard had reached a breaking point. Wilkes, whose arrogance and temper were legendary, was all but at war with his officers. Far from a triumphant return after an arduous four-year voyage, the expedition descended into open hostility. The secretary of the navy was soon flooded with complaints and accusations. Wilkes himself was court-martialed on charges of illegal punishment and of altering written records so as to be able to claim priority over the French in the discovery of land in the Antarctic. "Lieut. Wilkes never thought of claiming this discovery of land on the 19th, until after his arrival at Sidney, when he found that another nation had claimed to have made such discovery on the afternoon of the 19th," read the official charge.[42]

The court-martial took place aboard the ship *North Carolina*, berthed in New York Harbor, in the summer of 1842. As witnesses gave evidence and documents were produced, the case laid bare the rifts between Wilkes and many of his officers. While Wilkes had announced in Sydney that his expedition had discovered land on the morning of 19 January, the ships' logbooks showed the first sighting as taking place on 28 January. When personal journals, possibly modified, and draft reports were added to the slew of evidence, the date on which Wilkes's men first sighted land was muddied further.[43] The officer of the watch for the morning in question and the *Porpoise*'s captain both told the court that they had heard nothing to support Wilkes's claims and did not believe land had truly been sighted prior to 28 January.[44] While Wilkes was supported by two officers from the *Peacock*, no clear evidence was produced to substantiate earlier sightings. Confronted with this messy testimony, the court found that the charges of falsifying his discoveries and doctoring his journals were not proved, and thus that the verdict had to be not guilty. Wilkes was, however, convicted on two charges of authorizing improper punishment and sentenced to public reprimand.

Priority of discovery within the Antarctic Circle became mired in controversy on both sides of the ocean. French opinion was, unsurprisingly, strongly in Dumont d'Urville's court. While preparing the expedition narrative for publication after Dumont d'Urville's untimely death in 1842, Vincendon-Dumoulin appended a blunt repudiation of Wilkes's claims. "Ultimately, it is certain that Lieutenant Wilkes, on his own testimony, did not see Terre Adélie, and did not undisputedly establish its existence, until several days after us," he wrote: "It is thus difficult to understand why he is seriously claiming in his favor the honor of first discovery of the *austral continent*, upon which we were the first to have disembarked."[45] That there was, in fact, still no proof of the continental nature of the land is representative of both a long history of hope and the high stakes at play. On both sides of the Atlantic, all agreed that the French set foot on land in the Antarctic but the Americans did not—something held up as a clear victory in France.[46] That the disembarkation was only on an islet and was enabled by a matter of chance—the weather shone favorably on Dumont d'Urville's ships that day—was acknowledged but not seen to distract from the success. In the United States, the media initially heralded Wilkes's discovery with great fanfare, but this enthusiasm quickly faded as Wilkes's reputation was tarnished by the charges and publicity they attracted, especially as US newspapers printed the court-martial transcripts and the confusion of evidence they brought to light in lurid detail.[47]

The controversy over Wilkes's claims persisted well into the twentieth century. The French remained prickly on this point even after World War II, consistently emphasizing Dumont d'Urville's priority over his rivals and not infrequently exaggerating the French navigator's role, calling him the "true discoverer" of the Antarctic Continent.[48] US sources came to shy away from claiming "first sighting" or said outright that Dumont d'Urville had preceded Wilkes.[49] An exception, but a vocal one, was Wilkes's most strident supporter of the interwar period, William Herbert Hobbs. A US geologist and former director of the University of Michigan Greenland Expeditions, Hobbs embarked on a mission to win recognition for American Antarctic exploration. In an article pointedly titled "Wilkes Land Rediscovered," he attempted to prove Wilkes's priority of discovery over Dumont d'Urville and credited Wilkes with "establishing the existence of an Antarctic Continent, one of the great discoveries in the history of geography."[50] Ego, honor, and reputation all hung in the balance.

Evaluating the evidence from the time, Wilkes's claim to first sighting is almost certainly untrue. That Wilkes's own words and actions "raised as many questions as they answered," in Granville Mawer's assessment, is itself condemnatory.[51] Ultimately, however, in terms of long-term geopolitical consequences, that Dumont d'Urville claimed land for his country with the backing of his king has made all the difference. Wilkes made no such claim for the United States, something that has been explicitly recognized by the US government. While Wilkes's expedition was sponsored by his government, he had no authority to make territorial claims, in line with broader US policies of the time. Still, the United States consistently points to Wilkes's achievements as part of the historical activity on which the country reserves the right to make claims in the Antarctic.[52]

The third expedition into the ring was that of the veteran British explorer James Clark Ross. Ross's British Antarctic Expedition of 1839–1843 was more focused than the French and US expeditions: Ross's primary aim was to locate the south magnetic pole; his instructions "made no mention of colonial acquisition and said little about geographical discovery."[53] For the British and for Ross particularly, having won the north magnetic pole, the southern one beckoned. While its position had been calculated, most famously by Carl Friedrich Gauss, setting foot on the pole was considered both one of the great scientific firsts and an exploratory jewel. Of the three rival expeditions, Ross's was by far the best equipped. HMS *Erebus* and HMS *Terror* were former bomb vessels, enormously strong, built to withstand the powerful recoil of their mortars—a boon in the Antarctic pack ice that could crush weaker ships. The ships were also reinforced to enable them to push and break through ice in ways in which Dumont d'Urville and Wilkes could only dream of. Ross may have been third on the scene, but he was much better prepared to handle the conditions, and he also had the advantage of John Balleny's journal from his 1838–1839 voyage aboard a sealing schooner, which he studied meticulously.

Ross set off for the Antarctic from Chatham in September 1839, making stops en route to erect magnetic observatories across the southern region. This included the French territory of Kerguelen, where he landed in May 1840 and installed an observatory despite the ferocious winds that nearly carried the entire contraption away. The *Erebus* and the *Terror* arrived in Van Diemen's Land in mid-1840 when Dumont d'Urville was already on his way back to France. During his first season in the ice, Ross deliberately pursued a more easterly route than the other two expeditions so as to not retrace their steps. The British ships met the Great Icy Barrier (now called the Ross Ice Shelf) and followed it eastward, searching for a way to penetrate further south. While Ross failed to set foot on the south magnetic pole, he came very close. When pack ice stopped his ships just off the coast, Ross and Francis Crozier, his close friend and commander of the *Terror*, calculated that the pole was 260 kilometers inland. They hoped to find a safe harbor for the winter from which parties could strike out in the spring for Mount Erebus and the magnetic pole, but they were stymied by the ice.

When Ross retraced Wilkes's route following a map provided by the US captain, he found only water and ice in many places where Wilkes's charts showed land. Ross declared that Wilkes had been deceived by glacial reflections and by low-hanging clouds, mistaking ice shelves for coast. To Ross, this threw doubt on all Wilkes's claims of land sightings and on all his maps: "The sky has been dull, but the horizon quite clear; we could have seen land at a great distance, yet none has been in sight, and thus once and for all we have definitely disposed of Wilkes Land.... After reading Wilkes's report again, I must conclude that these places are non-existent."[54] Backed by the British Admiralty, Ross's public denunciation of Wilkes further tarnished the US navigator's reputation. The British press was quick to pick up on Ross's comments, soon calling Wilkes's accounts of his voyage "quite untenable."[55] Ross was also unimpressed with the French and US captains for other reasons. "That the commanders of each of these great national undertakings should have selected the very place for penetrating to the southward, for the exploration of which they were well aware, at the time, that the expedition under my command was expressly preparing, and thereby forestalling our purposes, did certainly greatly surprise me," he wrote in his expedition narrative in 1847.[56] To the Hydrographic Office, Ross reported that the two other expeditions had produced only meager results.

While Ross's accusations and criticisms wounded Wilkes deeply, Dumont d'Urville did not live to hear them. His untimely death in the spring of 1842, just a year and a half after returning from the Antarctic, marked the end of the journey for one of France's great navigators. With his discovery of Terre Adélie, the crowning jewel on a voyage he had initially been reluctant to undertake, France took an unexpected and unanticipated place in the Antarctic arena. While Dumont d'Urville's discovery would be largely ignored through the rest of the nineteenth century, it grew increasingly consequential as rivalry over the Antarctic intensified in the twentieth century.

3
APATHY AND NEGLECT

Just a year and a half after returning to France from his third grand voyage, Dumont d'Urville died in entirely unexpected and horrendous circumstances along with his wife, Adélie, and son, Jules. On the second Sunday of May 1842, the family spent the day at Versailles, taking in the *Grandes Eaux* festival and admiring the splendor of the palace's many fountains. Late that afternoon, they boarded a steam train to return to Paris. Then, catastrophe: the first locomotive broke an axle and collapsed, causing the train to crumple in on itself and derail. As the coke from the fireboxes ignited, the wooden carriages caught fire. Unable to escape through the carriages' locked doors, the passengers were trapped, victims of smoke and flames. The horror and the toll were high: as many as 250 people died in excruciating and terrifying conditions, including Dumont d'Urville, his wife, and their son. The rail accident and the subsequent efforts to identify victims from immolated body parts was described in all its awful detail in newspapers even in the smallest French regions.[1] It was the worst rail accident in Europe to that day.

Dumont d'Urville's funeral befit his status as a celebrated explorer and navigator, indeed a national hero. The cortege, pressed in on all sides by sailors, included several companies of grenadiers as well as a regimental marching band. Hundreds of members of the public, too, lined the streets, kept back a respectful distance by the municipal guard. The list of dignitaries attending the funeral, from naval minister admiral Guy-Victor Duperré to representatives from scientific academies to deputies from the National Assembly, was as impressive as was to be expected. After the service at the Church of Saint-Sulpice, Paris's second-largest church, Dumont d'Urville, Adélie, and Jules were buried in the Montparnasse Cemetery.[2] The tomb, designed by architect Simon-Claude Constant-Dufeux and paid for in part by the government, still stands: it is a tall, tapered limestone column with bas-relief scenes from Dumont d'Urville's expeditions. One scene shows the *Astrolabe* and the words "Voyage autour du monde Pôle Sud—Terre Adélie."

Dumont d'Urville's death, both tragic and sensational, was talked about across the country. The predominant sentiment was one of shock that a valiant explorer who had survived so many risks on his far-flung voyages could die in such a ghastly and needless way so close to home. "After having escaped the most horrendous dangers, after having sailed all the seas, having made immense contributions to science, the brave rear admiral Dumont d'Urville has perished at the edge of Paris with his wife and young son," read a typical newspaper.[3] Held up as "one of the most illustrious navigators to have pushed back the boundaries of the Earth and enriched the universe with a new continent," as astronomer Gustave de Pontécoulant declared at the unveiling of a statue of the navigator in 1844, Dumont d'Urville was praised for his courage, his perseverance in face of adversity and personal tragedy, and his triumphs in distant seas.[4] His taciturn manner and cantankerous nature were forgotten. In the aftermath of his death, the attention was on the man himself, cast as a heroic figure: Dumont d'Urville was seen and celebrated as one of France's leading nineteenth-century navigators, a scientifically erudite captain whose voyages illuminated the ethnography of the Pacific islands, solved the mystery of La Pérouse's fate, and discovered the treasured Vénus de Milo statue.[5] In comparison, Terre Adélie attracted little attention: Dumont d'Urville's Antarctic discovery would only come to define his legacy much later.

Through the rest of the nineteenth century, Terre Adélie appeared regularly in French geography textbooks and atlases, where it was listed along with other austral lands but rarely singled out. Other than brief descriptions along the lines of "buried under heaps of snow and ice," these works offered no discussion of the territory—a lacuna attributable to the economic and human focus of geography teaching in the school system at the time.[6] This focus prioritized the populated and productive lands of France's growing colonial empire. Further, in line with the toponymic norms of other countries, these books labeled the territory "Terre Adélie or Wilkes Land," an appellation that intimated ambivalence about discoverer, putting more weight on international consistency than on the French claim.[7] At the university level and even in geographical societies, study and knowledge of the polar regions was minimal and Terre Adélie played no important role, again owing to the primacy of the colonial project.[8] In public life and the cultural sphere of the mid- to late nineteenth century, too, the territory was only rarely a topic of genuine interest or conversation; indeed, Jean Robert's comment that Terre Adélie was almost forgotten after Dumont d'Urville's death is fair.[9]

Terre Adélie did find a small slice of fame in the literary world through Jules Verne's writing. Verne's admiration for Dumont d'Urville comes through in his science fiction adventure *Vingt mille lieues sous les mers* (Twenty Thousand Leagues Under the Seas), originally serialized in 1869–1870 in the periodical *Le magasin d'éducation et de récréation* and published as a lavishly illustrated book the following year.[10] "This d'Urville was one of your great sailors," said Captain Nemo to the story's narrator, scientist Professor Pierre Aronnax, "one of your most intelligent navigators. He is the Captain Cook of you Frenchmen." Nemo and Aronnax then dream of Dumont d'Urville's expeditions, "his circumnavigations, his double attempt to find the South Pole which brought about the discovery of the Adélie and Louis-Philippe Lands." Through the story, Verne uses accounts of Dumont d'Urville's voyages as source material to craft geographic descriptions, narrative content and structure, and even wording and literary devices.[11]

In this period, too, Terre Adélie was absent from French national ambitions. No French explorers voyaged to the Antarctic for the rest of the nineteenth century, nor was Terre Adélie on the political radar. Under Napoleon III and the Third Republic, the country had other priorities. France's overseas efforts, driven by commerce and a desire for influence and guided by the *mission civilisatrice* (the "civilizing mission"), focused on Africa, the Far East, and the South Pacific. In addition to the existing colonies, this new empire eventually included Algeria and other parts of North Africa, a large swath of West Africa, Madagascar and the Comoros, Indochina, and a number of archipelagos in the Pacific. By the end of the nineteenth century, France's colonial empire was second only to Britain's in terms of size and wealth.[12] While the French were deeply interested in their colonial lands, Terre Adélie lay outside this interest and no geopolitical or strategic significance was ascribed to the Antarctic territory. Terre Adélie stood apart from the French colonial project, offering neither profits and revenues, valuable raw materials, nor a market for French goods, and from French cultural exploration, lacking as it was in Indigenous inhabitants. Unlike in Britain, where the Antarctic was seen to be an integral part of empire, Terre Adélie did not fit into the French imperial fabric. Neither did Terre Adélie and the Hexagon share any of the geographic, geological, environmental, or emotional connections that linked the Antarctic to Australia, Argentina, and Chile.[13] The lack of direct competition for Terre Adélie also contributed to the absence of any sense of urgency surrounding the Antarctic territory: unlike the British-Argentine dispute over the Falkland Islands, Terre Adélie faced no external threat and there was no impetus forcing the French state to act there.

Sub-Antarctic Challenges

Through the same period—the long second half of the nineteenth century—French interest and activity in its sub-Antarctic possessions was likewise low. These uninhabited possessions comprised four sets of islands: Îles Saint-Paul and Nouvelle-Amsterdam and the Crozet and Kerguelen archipelagos (figure 6). While Crozet and Kerguelen had been discovered and claimed by French navigators in 1772, the other two islands were not discovered by the French. Nouvelle-Amsterdam was first sighted in 1552 by Juan Sébastien Elcano, a Castilian navigator who accompanied Magellan on his famous voyage, and Saint-Paul sometime before 1559 by Portuguese navigators. France laid claim to these islands in 1843, when the governor of Bourbon (Réunion)[14] sent Captain Martin

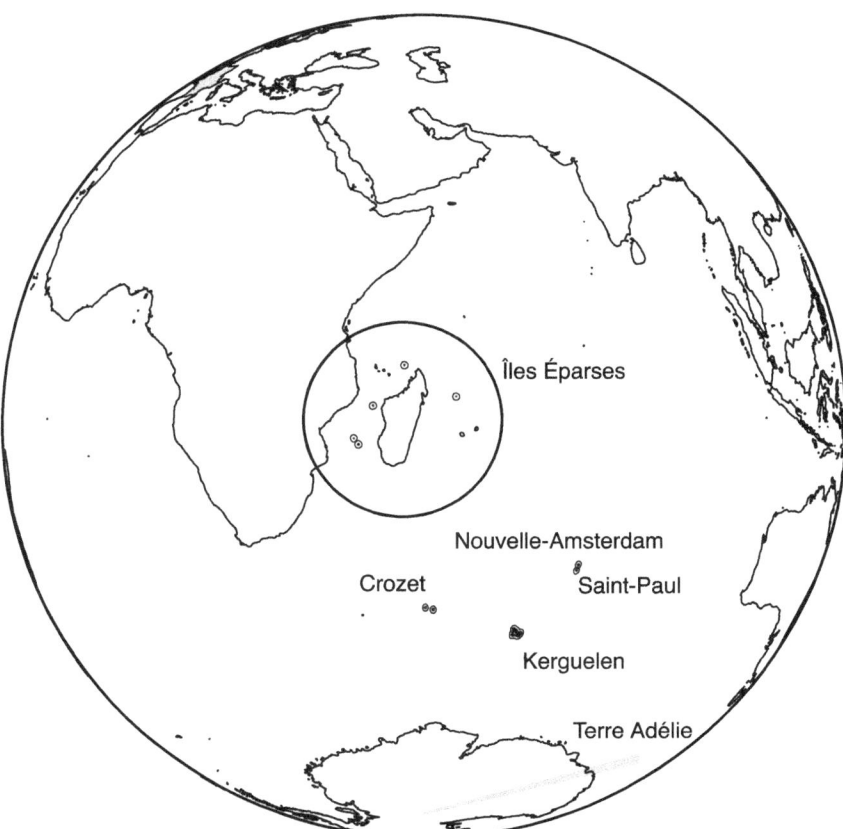

FIGURE 6. France's Antarctic and sub-Antarctic possessions. In 2007, the Îles Éparses (Scattered Islands) were joined administratively to the other austral possessions. Map by Richard Martin-Nielsen.

Dupeyrat to take formal French possession of the islands, which he did on 1 July (Nouvelle-Amsterdam) and 3 July (Saint-Paul), hoisting the tricolore and firing a gun salute. The governor had been acting on the interests of fishermen from Bourbon, who were increasingly active in the vicinity of the islands.

France's interest in these possessions was sparked by the imperial division of the globe, when the European powers were eager to take even remote and uninhabited territories for their expanding empires, but sovereignty over the islands was not well defined. While *prises de possession* took place and were duly announced, actual control was nonexistent. During the second half of the nineteenth century, small numbers of French fishermen frequented and occasionally lived on Saint-Paul and Nouvelle-Amsterdam, where they made unsuccessful attempts to found small stations and colonies. And French astronomers aboard *Le Fernand* visited Saint-Paul in 1874 to observe the passage of Venus in front of the sun, at which time the geologist Charles Vélain undertook a geological study of the islands.[15] But the most numerous visitors in this period were British and US whalers and sealers. Austrian and German scientists and British troop transporters also used the islands unchallenged. In a particularly telling incident, when French sailors were shipwrecked on Crozet in 1887, their only means of rescue was to attach a tin label to the neck of an albatross, which eventually came ashore in western Australia.[16] The Australians informed the French about the situation, but by the time France sent a ship to investigate, the men were gone.

Given the lack of French control over the islands, Britain twice considered making a play for Kerguelen, in 1841–1842 and again in 1886–1887. In the first instance, James Clark Ross reported to his government that Kerguelen (which he had visited on his way to the Antarctic in 1840) would be valuable as a coal depot given its position on the route between the Cape, India, and Australia.[17] Its interest piqued, the Foreign Office consulted with the Queen's Advocate as to Kerguelen's legal status. Weighing the exigencies of sovereign possession, the Queen's Advocate argued that France's failure to undertake "a real occupation of it [Kerguelen], within any reasonable space of time" nullified the title claimed on the basis of discovery and *prise de possession*.

A similar situation arose a half century later when two men representing the Indian Ocean Guano Company of Melbourne applied for a concession "to enable them to export guano and other exports and products from an island named the 'Island of Desolation,' or 'Kerguelen's Land'."[18] The men, Bruce Smith and J. Brougham Drummond, emphasized the strategic advantages of their proposition for the British Empire: "We need not point out to you the advantages which would accrue to your Government (in the event of valuable coal or shale deposits being discovered) by the possession of an additional coaling station which would be about midway between the Cape of Good Hope and the Australian

Continent; nor need we mention the value which such a depot would be to the merchant shipping of Great Britain, the vessels of which are frequently passing in or about the latitude of the island."[19] Investigating the situation, the British government again concluded that by abandoning the islands after discovery, the French had likewise abandoned their territorial rights. The parchment left by the French did not, the British concluded, support "de facto occupation" since "during the whole of that time [the past 114 years], they [the French] had not (so far as is known here) revisited the island, nor had any Frenchman ever occupied any portion of it."[20] Ultimately, however, despite what seems to have been a practical and legitimate questioning of French rights in Kerguelen, and potential advantages to the British, these challenges to rights and resources were not acted on.[21] They did, however, raise questions that would become more urgent in the early twentieth century, especially for Terre Adélie: Was discovery alone sufficient for maintaining a territorial claim, and if so for how long? Could France hold onto remote possessions without effectuating some degree of occupation and control? What legal standards and precedents were at play? And did the political will exist in France to make the commitment and investment necessary to uphold the claims under international law and forestall annexation?

Despite the clear weakness of the French claims, the lack of real threat—after all, the British twice chose not to pursue a challenge—gave the French government leeway to continue to neglect its sub-Antarctic possessions without repercussions. Until the very end of the nineteenth century, these possessions were all but ignored in Paris. While there was discussion of sending a French vessel to Kerguelen in 1870, the outbreak of the Franco-Prussian War quickly put an end to that idea. Various schemes, from the practical to the outlandish, were from time to time proposed: fishing, hunting, and livestock raising (despite the myriad practical impediments); a naval resupply station for victuals and coal (championed by Vice Admiral Charles Jules Layrle as a precaution in case navigation via the Suez Canal was interrupted); and even a penal colony.[22] Finally, in 1892 the Ministry of the Navy ordered French ships to the islands. The aviso *La Bourdonnais* was tasked with raising the French flag on Saint-Paul and Nouvelle-Amsterdam—but upon arrival at the islands in October 1892, bad weather made debarkation impossible, and the ceremony took place aboard the ship in the outlying waters. Soon afterward, the ship *L'Eure*, sailing from Madagascar, visited Kerguelen's Port Christmas. This time, the men were able to disembark, and on 2 January 1893 they renewed the French claims made in the early 1770s. Led by Commandant Louis Édouard Paul Lieutard, the men erected a mast topped by a metallic flag and mounted a copper plaque with the inscription "Eure—1893." The officers presented arms, sounded the bugle, and saluted to twenty-one blasts of the ship's cannons.[23] They then continued on to

Saint-Paul and Nouvelle-Amsterdam, where they renewed the claim made by the men of *La Bourdonnais*.[24] There were no challenges to these moves from Britain or from other countries, a sign the French took as indicating that their sovereignty over the islands was secure.

The renewed *prises de possession* captured the imagination of brothers René and Henry Bossière, private entrepreneurs from Le Havre, who solicited and received a concession from the French state to work the Kerguelen archipelago.[25] Valid for fifty years from 1893, the concession allowed the brothers to breed sheep and to build facilities for fishing and commerce, but the government offered no financial or material assistance. Leaving behind their family whale oil business in Patagonia, the brothers brought sheep from the Falklands to Kerguelen. The enterprise soon failed and by 1901 they were forced back to Le Havre.

As the Bossière brothers toiled with little success on Kerguelen near the end of the century, a quiet challenge arose from Australia. In 1899, Henry Copeland, a member of the New South Wales Legislative Assembly, published a pamphlet titled *Kerguelen Island and Australian Commerce*. Noting Kerguelen's position as a strategic waypoint between Australia and South Africa in an otherwise largely empty ocean, Copeland argued that Kerguelen's future could be imagined in two starkly different ways: as a location for a naval base to protect Australian shipping interests or as "a den from which sea-wolves could sally forth to prey on our unarmed vessels."[26] Copeland proposed that Australia occupy and colonize the archipelago to avoid having it fall into the hands of a future enemy. With Australia on the verge of becoming an independent Dominion, and the consequent growing interest in establishing a broad regional presence, Copeland's message would gain traction in the following decades.

To Antarctica for Science and for France

The absence of French ships from the Antarctic through the second half of the nineteenth century is representative of a broader lull in exploration at the time: between 1843 and 1895, no official expedition from any country ventured to the white continent. During this half century, only sealers and whalers roamed Antarctica's waters.[27] Despite the many questions raised by the Dumont d'Urville, Wilkes, and Ross expeditions—among them, the extent and shape of Antarctic lands, their geography, and their insular or continental nature—no answers proved quickly forthcoming. As the end of the century approached, the outline of Antarctica's coast was only roughly sketched and its interior completely unknown.

This lull ended abruptly at the turn of the century. In 1895, the 6th International Geographical Congress, held in London, identified the Antarctic as a major void in human knowledge and pointed to the exploration, mapping, and naming of that furthest region as the most important outstanding project facing geographers. As geographical, commercial, and scientific curiosity turned eyes south, a series of expeditions took shape.[28] For the explorers, Antarctica was a virgin territory, an uninhabited and icy land, hostile and forbidding—but also full of promise, beckoning with glory and fame. Beginning with Adrien de Gerlache de Gomery's Belgian Antarctic Expedition of 1897–1899, the first to overwinter in the Antarctic, this era of exploration took shape as a race to fill in blanks on the map and—the ultimate prize—to reach the South Pole. While de Gerlache's overwinter was unplanned (his ship, the *Belgica*, became trapped in ice in the Bellinghausen Sea in late February 1898 and only broke free seven months later, costing several expedition members their sanity and lives), the Anglo-Norwegian explorer Carsten Borchgrevink's Southern Cross Expedition, a private venture, executed a planned overwinter on the Antarctic mainland in 1899.[29]

Antarctic explorers of this era came from many countries, including Britain, Belgium, Norway, Germany, Sweden, Australia, Japan, and indeed France. "Its goal was as abstract as a pole, its central figures were romantic, manly and flawed, its drama was moral (for it mattered not only what was done but how it was done), and its ideal was national honor," writes Tom Griffiths of what is often called the "heroic age" of Antarctic exploration.[30] These expeditions brought back copious amounts of geographic and scientific data about a virtually unknown part of the world, capturing international attention for their remarkable feats of physical and mental endurance as much as for the many lives claimed by the ice. Central to this era, of course, was the race to the South Pole, which saw humans penetrate deeper than ever before into the continent, smoothing the way for explorers to secure funding and bringing the Antarctic into the public imagination. When Robert Falcon Scott and Roald Amundsen set out for the pole in 1911, the first to die trying and the second to emerge victorious, national pride and one of the last great exploratory firsts were on the line. By World War I, the continental nature of the Antarctic was confirmed, most of its coastline was mapped, and exploration of its interior had begun.[31]

French involvement in turn-of-the-century Antarctic exploration was spearheaded not by the state but by a private individual, the explorer, physician, and sportsman Jean-Baptiste Charcot. Born in Neuilly-sur-Seine in 1867, Charcot soon developed a love of the sea and of adventure.[32] As a young boy, he was captivated by the novels of Jules Verne and revered Christopher Columbus for his exploits in the Americas. He excelled in sports, at rugby and as a yachtsman. But at his father's urging, he put these dreams to the side and studied medicine. The elder Charcot, Jean-Martin, was an eminent physician and pioneering neurologist and expected his son to follow in his footsteps. Charcot the younger studied at Paris's La Salpêtrière Hospital from 1890 to 1894, then worked in a clinic for diseases of the nervous system and at the Pasteur Institute. Charcot's first loves, however, continued to call to him, and soon he was both training for the Summer Olympics of 1900, where he won two gold medals in sailing, and beginning to sketch out plans for expeditions to the polar regions. Freed from the need to practice as a physician by his inheritance—his father's death left him well off—Charcot cast his eyes to the furthest reaches of Earth. To Charcot, the Antarctic represented an immense scientific laboratory, the vastest and most unknown of the world—and one in which he desperately wanted to play a part. Like the Olympics, the Antarctic also appealed to Charcot as a means of winning prestige through gentlemanly competition.

Charcot began his exploring in the north with expeditions to the Shetlands, Hebrides, Faroe Islands, Jan-Mayen Land, and Iceland in 1901–1902. These were, in his mind, preliminary voyages designed to build his experience, confidence, and name before embarking on a major polar expedition. Charcot organized and financed these expeditions himself; they were private, not state, endeavors. Satisfied with this experience, Charcot then turned to the Antarctic. His choice to head south was rooted in his desire for France to play a part in the trailblazing explorations taking place there, for the French flag to fly in Antarctica at a time when so many other countries were mounting expeditions to that great land. "The history of foreign polar expeditions is so long that volumes are required to recount it, but ours can be summarized in a few notes," he wrote in a pamphlet pointedly titled *Pourquoi faut-il aller dans l'Antarctique?* ("Why Must We Go to the Antarctic?").[33] In it, Charcot begs France to wake up, to escape its "extraordinarily ignorant" posture about the southern reaches of the globe, to "win the esteem and respect of other nations" by playing an active part in the discovery of the Antarctic. For Charcot, an Antarctic expedition was also a way of rebuilding France's national cohesiveness and international image in the aftermath of a period of social and political disharmony as well as the deeply divisive Dreyfus affair. Indeed, to Charcot, the expedition was necessary for the glory of France, offering an opportunity for his country to reaffirm its vitality and reassert its rightful place on the world stage. Charcot also hoped to lend assistance to the search for the Swedish explorer Otto Nordenskjöld, missing after an overwinter on Snow Hill Island off the coast of the Antarctic Peninsula.[34]

To Charcot's scientifically trained mind, the Antarctic represented a region of unparalleled possibility for discovery. There, he wrote, "all is unknown, everything presents with a strange aspect, unexpected, and the efforts made to date to understand the mysteries of the large white patch that the twentieth century cannot leave undefined on its maps have only made their illumination more passionate, more necessary."[35] Charcot was particularly intrigued by the glaring blanks on turn-of-the-century maps: with only a few small exceptions, everything inside the south polar circle was completely unknown, and even outside that circle there were still vast unknown regions. While the Antarctic was almost always described as a continent, he noted, at the opening of the century there was still no proof that it did not consist of islands separated by vast expanses of water and ice, or two or more large landmasses with outlying islands. These questions gripped Charcot, whose natural curiosity shone strongly, and propelled him to assemble a group of scientists to join him on his voyage.

With the Antarctic in his sights, Charcot ordered the construction of a thirty-two-meter-long steamship, *Le Français*, in Saint-Malo, and petitioned the French government for funding. He found sympathetic ears in intellectual circles, including those of Henri Froidevaux, a historian and geographer and the director of the *Société de géographie*'s library, who was hopeful that Charcot's plans would light a fire under the French state and convince the government to build on "the heritage of Bouvet and Kerguelen and Dumont d'Urville."[36] But Charcot's and Froidevaux's hopes proved empty as the government declined to grant financial support. Even though French president Émile Loubet endorsed the expeditions, Charcot was forced to raise most of the funds privately, an indication of the continued lack of state interest in the white continent. Drawing largely on his own funds, he put together four hundred thousand francs, barely sufficient for his plans. Charcot was forced to rely on in-kind donations and buy much of his equipment secondhand; as a result, *Le Français* was a maddening ship to handle. "The engine, the best we could get for our money, was not strong enough for the work to be done, and its defects had to be made good by the skill and energy of men and officers," Charcot wrote, resulting in a slow and tedious voyage interrupted frequently by the need to stop for repairs.[37] Charcot was deeply disappointed by the lack of support from his country, but not overly surprised: after all, as he noted, France had entirely neglected the Antarctic for more than sixty years. That his expedition was by necessity a "poor, small, modest" private initiative was something he was willing to endure in the hopes that it would become a launching pad for future French Antarctic exploration.[38]

His ship ready, Charcot and his men set out from France for the Antarctic Peninsula in mid-1903. His choice of destination was influenced both by Nordenskjöld's last known coordinates and by a desire to build on de Gerlache's cartographic work in the region. The peninsula was diametrically opposite Terre Adélie, and Charcot felt no compunction to return to the territory Dumont d'Urville had claimed for France some sixty years previously. Between 1903 and 1905, Charcot and his men explored and overwintered "as far south as possible" in the peninsula region, as Charcot told the Royal Geographical Society upon his return, naming some of the lands they saw but making no territorial claims.[39]

The team collected vast quantities of scientific data and the expedition's second-in-command, Lieutenant André Matha, drew the best maps of the region to date. With specialists in cartography, botany, zoology, gravity, magnetism, and hydrography, the expedition had a serious scientific tone set by Charcot himself. During the overwinter, when *Le Français* was frozen into the ice, the men used skis and sleds to conduct overland raids. In 1905, with his men suffering from scurvy, Charcot left the Antarctic and took *Le Français* to Buenos Aires, where he sold it to the Argentinian government to cover the expedition's debts.

French newspapers and periodicals covered Charcot's expedition in minute detail and in glowing terms, often accompanied by resplendent photographs of the explorer, his men, and his ship against the gleaming Antarctic ice fields. Charcot was held up as a hero in the tradition of Jules Verne, at once visionary, patriotic, and adventurous.[40] The expedition was hailed as a triumph for all of France despite the state having refused to assist Charcot. France was now part of a small and distinctive club, that of countries whose men had spent a full year in Antarctica's ice. Thanks to this coverage, Charcot returned home a national hero. And when the minister of the navy greeted him in Paris and presented him with the *Légion d'honneur*, Charcot's hopes rose that the French government might now be receptive to his vision of a state committed to the white continent. With his newfound fame and a pressing desire to continue his scientific work in the Antarctic, Charcot was in a stronger position to push the French government to support a second expedition. This time the government agreed, providing seven hundred thousand francs, significantly more than the entire cost of the first expedition.

Having sold *Le Français* in Argentina, Charcot procured a more robust ship, the *Pourquoi-Pas?*, and set sail again in 1908, "pour la science, pour la France" (for science, for France).[41] Upon arrival in the Antarctic Peninsula region, he continued the cartographic and geographic work of his first voyage. Pushing south of 65° into an unknown region and discovering Côte des Fallières (which he named for new French president Armand Fallières), Charcot expressed his joy for having "penetrated into a region considered by explorers and geographers as being of the highest interest, but heretofore impenetrable."[42] The men overwintered and then set course through a vast unexplored area, discovering over 3,200 kilometers of new coastline and drawing maps southward to 70°—maps that remained authoritative for decades afterward.[43] Indeed, in 1939 the US geologist William Herbert Hobbs, a notoriously harsh critic of Dumont d'Urville, commented that the best existing maps of the Antarctic Peninsula were based on "Charcot's careful surveys."[44]

With his two expeditions, Charcot gave France a place at the table of countries that had undertaken significant work in the Antarctic. In Britain and the

United States, especially, his scientific work was highly lauded. France had "take[n] her part with the other great nations in the peaceful struggle against the unknown," as Charcot was immensely proud to declare to the Royal Geographical Society.[45] Charcot never again returned to the Antarctic, instead rising steadily in the navy during and after World War I and then pursuing scientific voyages from the Mediterranean to the North Atlantic to Greenland. In 1936, his ship was hit by a violent storm near Iceland and battered against rocks. All the men aboard save one died as the ship sank. Charcot's body was recovered and returned to France, where he was mourned as a national hero and honored with a state funeral at Notre-Dame de Paris. In the ensuing decades, the story of Charcot's shipwreck was well-known in France, but his Antarctic exploits were largely forgotten—something that would have been devastating to the man himself, should he have known.

Like Dumont d'Urville, Charcot discovered lands in the Antarctic Peninsula region but never claimed them for France. Today these lands form part of the overlapping British, Argentinian, and Chilean claims. While he did name many of the features he saw, claiming territory was never part of Charcot's plans or intentions.[46] He was driven not by a desire for territory but by a desire to renew French prestige and conduct the most exhilarating scientific work he could imagine. Given the state's disinterest in his first expedition, too, any claim he might have made then would have been evaluated weakly in international law: he was certainly under no official instruction to claim land for his country. Charcot's disinterest in territorial claims is also evidenced by his choice of location: on neither of his expeditions to the Antarctic did he choose to visit Terre Adélie, where he could have reinforced Dumont d'Urville's earlier claim. Nor did Charcot attempt to reach the South Pole, at that time an object of the utmost fascination. Though he toyed with the idea, ultimately he considered the pole a goal at odds with his scientific focus.

British Claims and French Apathy

Even as Charcot drew attention to the white continent, the French state continued to all but ignore its Antarctic and sub-Antarctic possessions—to the extent that France nearly ceded Crozet to the British out of indifference. In 1905, having received an application from a private individual for mining rights in Crozet, the British government concluded that the archipelago's status was unclear given the inchoate nature of France's title. The Foreign Office approached the French government and inquired about the islands.[47] While the British emphasized that "H. M. Government had no intention of asking for the abandonment of any

French rights or for any arrangements which could be considered as requiring the surrender of an equivalent on their part," the French response was vague and unconsidered. The French ambassador in London told the British that France would be willing to consider renouncing its claim to Crozet if it were to receive something in return; recognition of the neutrality of the Minquiers Islands in the English Channel was mooted.[48] This response shows how little value the French state placed on its sub-Antarctic possessions at the time: far from ringing alarm bells, the British inquiry did not even merit serious debate in government. But Britain declined to pursue the matter, and when the French decided almost ten years later that the entire exchange had been badly handled, France was able to retain possession of Crozet.

As for the Bossière brothers, despite the failure of their enterprises at the end of the nineteenth century, they were still determined to make a go of Kerguelen. The brothers joined forces with a Norwegian company and established a small whaling factory and a seasonal settlement at Port Jeanne d'Arc in 1908. They also expanded their activities to Saint-Paul and Nouvelle-Amsterdam in 1911. But sheep rearing proved to be in vain and whaling was not much more successful. By 1914, only the two brothers remained; their employees had all fled to France and their many appeals to the French government for assistance were ignored or rejected. Even when the brothers asked for official help in supporting France's claim to the islands, they were rebuffed. When the minister for colonies suggested to his naval counterpart, Théophile Delcassé, that he send a warship to renew the French claim to Kerguelen, replenish the previously established supply stocks, and police fishing in the region, Delcassé was uninterested, replying that he had no ship available for such a difficult task.[49]

In the Antarctic, the situation began to change as whaling, the race to the South Pole, and dreams of mineral riches drew attention to the political lacuna on the white continent. In 1908, the year Charcot set out on his second expedition, Britain issued Letters Patent to formalize its first Antarctic claim. The Falkland Islands Dependencies included Antarctic mainland territory (Graham's Land) as well as the South Georgia Islands, the South Orkneys, the South Shetlands, and the Sandwich Islands. The 1908 Letters Patent were intended to perfect Britain's inchoate title to the region by providing elements of administration and oversight: attached to "Our Colony the Falkland Islands," the territories were placed under the governance of the governor and commander in chief of the Falklands.[50] The British claim was motivated in large part by the economics of whaling, which had exploded around the Antarctic Peninsula in the early years of the twentieth century, and the desire to control the activities of Norwegian whalers in the area.[51] The Letters Patent were also meant to secure British rights in the face of possible challenges from the French, the Argentinians, and the

Chileans.[52] British authorities began to exercise jurisdiction in the area, requiring whaling companies to apply for British licenses and pay British taxes. That the claim included lands seen and explored by Dumont d'Urville and Charcot did not cause any protest in France, as the French explorers had not made any territorial claims in the Antarctic Peninsula region and the French state did not consider discovery alone to be a valid basis for sovereignty. The abject lack of discussion about these territories in government, however, exemplifies just how little importance France ascribed to the Antarctic at this time. Indeed, only a few years earlier, as the French geographer and explorer Charles Rabot lamented, the French state had destroyed almost all of its accounts of Dumont d'Urville's voyage to Terre Adélie.[53]

Three years later, the British turned their interest to the one part of the continent for which there was an existing French claim. Wanting to increase administrative control over the southern seas and to regularize the issuance of whaling licenses near Terre Adélie, in late 1911 the Foreign Office instructed Sir Francis Bertie, the British ambassador in Paris, to ascertain the status of France's Antarctic claim. Noting that Dumont d'Urville had landed in the region and taken formal possession of "Adelie Land" in 1840, but that there had been no further French activity there, Bertie was instructed to "enquire of the French Government whether they claim that portion of the Antarctic continent."[54] Days after receiving the instructions, Bertie approached Justin de Selves, the French foreign minister.[55] Within the French government, alarm bells finally started to ring. That the British were sounding out the French on this question was correctly interpreted as a nascent challenge to France's inchoate title over the territory—and suddenly the lack of any French presence, administration, or even government interest in Terre Adélie for more than seventy years took on new significance.

During a flurry of meetings and consultations early in the new year, Albert Lebrun, the French minister for colonies, urged de Selves to assert France's rights to Terre Adélie.[56] The navy, too, spoke out, arguing that Dumont d'Urville's *prise de possession* of 1840 meant that these rights were secure and offering the navigator's records as evidence.[57] Lebrun also advocated direct action, pushing his naval counterpart to send a ship to the "lands previously recognized by Dumont d'Urville" to support the French claim.[58] Likewise, he again called for an official visit to France's sub-Antarctic possessions to head off similar challenges. It was at this time that France came to regret offering to renounce its claim to Crozet several years earlier. The worry that a foreign power—most likely Britain—might displace France in these possessions spread through several sections of government: in addition to the two ministries and the navy, Raymond Poincaré (président du Conseil and future president of France) and Louis Barthou (garde des Sceaux) urged the government to reassert France's claims over its austral possessions without delay.

Soon, Poincaré, who had succeeded de Selves as foreign minister, told the British in unequivocal terms that the French claim to Terre Adélie was valid and secure. Dumont d'Urville had taken possession of Terre Adélie "in the usual way for the era," Poincaré asserted, and his *prise de possession* was widely published and circulated at the time.[59] The French state, he concluded, had no intention of renouncing its rights over any of France's Antarctic or sub-Antarctic possessions and was taking steps to reinforce those claims. The British quickly acquiesced, informing the French government that Britain recognized the French claim to the land seen by Dumont d'Urville—specifically, the land of "about 150 miles, lying between 66° and 67° south latitude and 136° and 147° east longitude"—and that future British claims to Antarctica would avoid this area.[60] The limit of 147° east was in fact an error, a misprint made by a Hobart typesetter in 1840 and propagated over time. The limit claimed by Dumont d'Urville himself was 142° east, and the discrepancy would come to have interesting repercussions in the late 1930s.

This response, with its assurance that Britain was not planning to annex Terre Adélie, quieted the flurry of voices that had been calling for France to reassert sovereignty over its Antarctic and sub-Antarctic territories. With the immediate threat gone, so too the sense of urgency disappeared—and the territories again slid out of government interest. It took a full year for France to send a ship to its sub-Antarctic islands: in 1913–1914, Captain Raymond Rallier du Baty, a veteran of Charcot's first Antarctic expedition, surveyed Kerguelen aboard *La Curieuse*. But with the outbreak of World War I, the Antarctic was pushed to the back burner. In the end, no French expedition set out for Terre Adélie at all at this time.

Douglas Mawson and the Australian Challenge

At the same time as the British were quietly testing France's hold over Terre Adélie, the Australian geologist and explorer Douglas Mawson set out on an ambitious expedition that would also serve to underline the insecure nature of the French claim. Trained as a mining engineer and geologist, Mawson joined Ernest Shackleton's British *Nimrod* expedition of 1907–1909, when he delighted in reaching the south magnetic pole and climbing Mount Erebus. Inspired by these exploits, Mawson envisioned an explicitly Australian expedition to what he called Adelie Land, the unexplored portion of the Antarctic Continent to the south of Australia, which included Terre Adélie. Known as the Australasian Antarctic Expedition, it took place from 1911 to 1914.[61]

The political dimensions of Mawson's expedition were clear from the beginning. The region of the Antarctic south of Australia, Mawson explained to the *Sydney Morning Herald* in 1910, "is the nearest part to Australia, and it should be Australia's special duty and her obligation to contribute to the world at large whatever store of secrets this land holds. Whatever material of economic value—gold and mineral wealth, whale oil, seal oil, or anything else it may contain—will of course be to the advantage of Australia."[62] And when he formally announced the expedition at the Australasian Association for the Advancement of Science early the next year, Mawson made clear his desire to secure the region he called "Australasian Antarctica" for his country. For Mawson, territory and science were intimately linked; science was both an objective unto itself and a means for Australia to build territorial legitimacy in the Antarctic. His expedition, he said, would "take possession of that area between Cape Adare and Gauss Berg, and hoist the Australian flag upon it"—a pressing task, he continued, to ensure that the region would not "have to be abandoned to a foreign nation, several of which are already pressing upon the Australasian Antarctic."[63] Critically for France, the area Mawson described included Terre Adélie.

After setting off from Hobart aboard the whaling steam yacht *Aurora* in late 1911, Mawson established his main base at Cape Denison, just a sliver east of the edge of Terre Adélie as defined by Dumont d'Urville. Mawson's men conducted an ambitious scientific program, collecting data about a region for which, as Mawson emphasized, "only the most scanty information was at hand."[64] Despite extreme winds which made life unbearable and work often impossible, sledding teams penetrated deep into Terre Adélie: a party led by Edward ("Bob") Bage traversed five hundred kilometers into the French territory and Frank Wild's group detailed Terre Adélie's coastline. While the expedition's scientific results are striking, it is best known for the tragic deaths of Belgrave Ninnis, who fell (along with six of the team's best dogs, most of their rations, and their tent) into a crevasse on a sledding traverse, and Xavier Mertz, who died on the return journey of the same traverse, possibly from hypervitaminosis A (the excessive intake of vitamin A, which is found in high levels in the livers of the sled dogs the men were consuming).[65] Mawson's subsequent punishing solo trek back to Cape Denison, where he arrived after the *Aurora* had departed, forcing him to spend an extra year in the Antarctic, secured his legacy as one of the heroic Antarctic explorers of the early twentieth century.

Mawson's position on the French claim to Terre Adélie was one of diplomatic nicety on the French and international stages, especially before his expedition, combined with nationalist exigency on the Australian stage, particularly in the expedition's aftermath. Before leaving Australia to embark on his expedition, Mawson courteously wrote to Charcot, the French figure most closely associated with the Antarctic at that time, formally announcing his intention to debark in Terre Adélie, which he explicitly described as having been "discovered by Dumont d'Urville."[66] That the French had been the first to sight Terre Adélie was something Mawson repeated frequently, along with his admiration for the French captain's abilities and courage. The respect Mawson evidenced toward Dumont d'Urville was emulated by his men, and particularly by John King Davis, the *Aurora*'s captain. Prior to their setting out, Charcot had gifted the Australian team bottles of Bourgogne wine. In early 1912, Davis wrote to Charcot to say that he and his men had brought the wine to Terre Adélie and drunk it in honor of Dumont d'Urville. "We found Terre Adélie, discovered by Dumont d'Urville, exactly as he had described it," wrote Davis: "Having seen this coast myself, I have more admiration than ever for Admiral Dumont d'Urville. He must have been a magnificent sailor to have accomplished what he did without steam and without any of the progress of the modern era."[67]

Given the location of Mawson's explorations, he was drawn into the long-standing controversy over the rival French and US claims to first sighting. In this, Mawson was solidly on the side of the French navigator, writing that Dumont d'Urville had preceded Wilkes to the region by seven days. In Mawson's mind, the veracity of Wilkes's account was fatally tarnished by its inaccuracies and inconsistencies. "Land was reported [by Wilkes] almost daily, but, unfortunately, subsequent exploration has shown that most of the landfalls do not exist," wrote Mawson, further underlining that Wilkes's expedition "did not once set foot on Antarctic shores, and, possibly on account of the absence of the scientific staff, his descriptions tend to be inexact and obscure."[68] Mawson's position on the issue is epitomized by his choice to name the stretch of navigable waters to the north of Terre Adélie the D'Urville Sea. The naming of geographical features is ipso facto political; in this case, Mawson made clear his position on the Wilkes-Dumont d'Urville controversy.

But upon return, Mawson's stance hardened. In the book of the expedition he published in 1915, called *The Home of the Blizzard: Being the Story of the Australasian Antarctic Expedition 1911–1914*, Mawson accentuated the weaknesses of Dumont d'Urville's expedition: his men never set foot on the Antarctic mainland, and they too were tricked into seeing and naming land that was, in fact, only a mirage.[69] Mawson then cited the Antarctic scholar Hugh R. Mill's unflattering summary of Dumont d'Urville's expedition, which called his discoveries "of but little account" and complained that the French captain only gave the "vaguest account" of the lands he saw. Building on these ideas, Mawson began to articulate a different future for Terre Adélie.

Mawson's emphasis on the weaknesses of France's claim to Terre Adélie went hand in hand with his desire to secure for Australia the Antarctic sector he ardently believed to belong to his country. He repeatedly pointed out that there had been no French presence in Terre Adélie whatsoever since Dumont d'Urville's discovery of 1840—a choice on the part of successive French governments that, to Mawson, negated any rights to the territory.[70] As such, Mawson continued, France's inchoate title was superseded by his own explorations. He urged the Australian Commonwealth Government to advance a claim not only to Terre Adélie but also to France's sub-Antarctic islands, which suffered from similar weaknesses to title.[71] Mawson's argument—that these sub-Antarctic islands could, in the future, provide Australia with critical strategic naval bases and communications facilities—was one that would recur regularly over the next half century.

Mawson took a very different line when he traveled to France in 1914, where he was much admired for his exploits and received a very warm welcome. At a reception hosted by the *Société de géographie* in Paris, Mawson praised Dumont d'Urville and took pains to explain that the Australian expedition had not "debaptized" Terre Adélie, but rather focused its efforts in the adjacent region—a portrayal of the expedition massaged for his audience.[72] The French press reported widely on Mawson's visit, painting him as a larger-than-life figure who had survived against the greatest of odds, but said nothing about the implicit and explicit challenges his expedition posed to France's Antarctic claim. Newspapers, journals, and even scholars focused on the dangers and near misses, on Mawson's perilous solo trek and the tragic deaths of Nennis and Mertz.[73] In government, too, there was all but no discussion of Mawson's challenge to the French claim. In contrast to Britain, which had made its ambitions in Antarctica well-known, the French Third Republic showed little interest in engaging in Antarctica in the early twentieth century, even in the face of rising and ever more explicit challenges.

4

FORMALIZING SOVEREIGNTY

By the end of World War I, nearly eighty years had elapsed since Dumont d'Urville had claimed Terre Adélie for France—eighty years in which no French citizen had returned to the territory and in which the French state had shown all but no interest in it. This began to change in the interwar years, when Britain and its southern Dominions made clear their long-term intentions for the white continent. By the 1920s, France had no choice but to act if it wanted to retain its Antarctic territory.

Britain made the first move, modifying the wording of its 1908 Antarctic claim to explicitly state that the Falkland Islands Dependencies stretched all the way to the South Pole. This was done using the sector principle (that is, the extension of territorial claims to a pole along meridians) in 1917.[1] Despite the unclear legal standing of the sector principle, there was little international reaction to the British declaration, even by countries that might have considered the British claim to infringe on their own rights in the region. Soon, the extent of Britain's ambitions became clear: no less than painting the Antarctic pink. Leading this charge was Leopold S. Amery, the undersecretary of state at the Colonial Office, who declared that "the whole of the Antarctic should ultimately be included within the British Empire [and] while the time has not yet arrived that a claim to all the continental territory should be put forward publicly, a definite and consistent policy should be followed of extending and asserting British control with the object of ultimately making it complete."[2] By 1920, this was official government policy. To claim more territory, Britain next acted through its southern Dominions. In 1923, Britain took possession of the Ross Dependency (originally claimed by James Clark Ross in 1841) and put it under New Zealand's charge. Situated southeast of New Zealand, the Ross Dependency again stretched to the South Pole along meridians. The sector principle would later be used by other Antarctic claimants, including France.[3] While an Australian claim was also discussed at this time, British authorities were apprehensive about how the French would react to territorial challenges in the vicinity of Terre Adélie, and held off.

As Britain upped its game, France was forced into action. Australian voices calling for the annexation of Terre Adélie grew louder, too, pointing out that the French state had entirely neglected Terre Adélie for nearly a century. Finally, the French government sensed a real threat. While Dumont d'Urville and Charcot had both explored the Antarctic Peninsula region, neither had made any claims there, leaving Terre Adélie as France's only possible Antarctic territory.[4] Should the Australians convince the British to make a move, France could well find itself shut out of the white continent altogether. France was also motivated by the need to protect fishing, whaling, and sealing rights around Terre Adélie and around its sub-Antarctic possessions, as well as by a desire to secure coal and mineral resources in those possessions. These resources were of increasing interest to both the French and the British, as evidenced by a growing series of requests for permits to exploit them.[5] Just as the British Antarctic claim of 1908 had been prompted in part by whaling, so too did questions of resources push the French decisions of the 1920s. "Scientific missions effected at the beginning of this century in the austral seas have established that these dependencies of our overseas domain, for a long time neglected, can offer extremely precious resources to the fishing industry: whales, seals, and elephant seals are abundant in these neighborhoods," declared the Ministry for Colonies—but only with state involvement and administrative authority could France ensure control over these resources.[6]

Acting on these concerns, in 1924, eighty-four years after Dumont d'Urville discovered Terre Adélie, France formalized its claim to the Antarctic territory, as well as to its sub-Antarctic possessions, with a series of decrees. The first, issued on 27 March, reserved hunting, fishing, and mineral rights in and around Terre Adélie and Crozet to French citizens, and announced that the minister for colonies would have authority over "every concession of any nature" in the territories.[7] Shortly thereafter, on 2 April, Terre Adélie was placed in the surveillance zone of French naval units in the Pacific, while Kerguelen, Crozet, and Saint-Paul and Nouvelle-Amsterdam were assigned to France's Indian Ocean patrols.[8] The most important of the decrees came on 21 November, when France further consolidated its claims to Terre Adélie and the sub-Antarctic islands and placed these possessions under the jurisdiction of Madagascar's colonial government.[9] Finally, on 30 December, another decree regulated whaling, sealing, and the exploitation of other cetaceans in the coastal regions and territorial waters of the austral possessions, and made all but a small part of Kerguelen into a national refuge park with specific protections for certain species of birds and mammals.[10] The refuge park initiative had been sparked by Étienne Peau, a naturalist, pioneering underwater photographer, and assistant curator at the Muséum du Havre, who visited Kerguelen in 1923. Peau's criticisms of whaling practices there and his arresting photographs of the slaughter, reprinted in French newspapers, struck a note with the French public.[11] Rather than a means of articulating authority in and control over distant possessions, however, the park initiative was a bureaucratic response to the public outcry. It had little effect on whaling, in part because no map existed showing the area under protection.[12] Following the normal cartographic practices of the time, these decrees spoke of "la Terre Adélie ou Wilkes," an appellation that, despite its undertones, seems to have generated no discussion in France.

From the perspective of sovereignty, the French government hoped that by attaching the austral possessions to an existing colonial government, they would be incorporated into a preformed administrative structure, thereby perfecting their inchoate titles. The intention, as the Ministry for Colonies wrote to the president of the Republic, was to exercise "effective and continued control" over the possessions through administrative organization.[13] Madagascar was chosen based on its location: it seemed "naturally designed, by the geographical situation of this colony and the means of action within its power to ensure the sovereign authority of France for this part of our colonial possessions." While Madagascar was certainly closer in proximity to the austral possessions than was the Hexagon, it was still very far away, and in practical terms it was a weak choice for establishing effective occupation—a situation that would grow more problematic in the following decades.

Soon after the 1924 decrees, the government of Madagascar took some concrete steps toward establishing administrative and protective structures over Terre Adélie and the sub-Antarctic islands. Judicially, the territories were attached to the *tribunal de paix* in Tuléar (now Toliara, on Madagascar's southwestern coast). And toward the control of natural resources, the government named a game and fish warden for the territories, a role initially held by Commandant Fontaine, the captain of the steamer *Lozère*.[14] While they provided a veneer of sovereign power, however, these actions were weakened by the realities of the situation: with no means of reaching Terre Adélie, the government in Madagascar had no capacity to exercise the powers it claimed via legislation. Moreover, with no on-the-ground administrative presence in any of the austral possessions, it was hard to argue that France exerted any real authority over those possessions.

Even in Kerguelen, where private attempts at resource exploitation had been underway for decades, cost, distance, and remoteness served to undermine efforts to install state presence. In 1930, the Ministry for Colonies urged Madagascar's governor general to send a functionary to Kerguelen to establish an administrative office, keep an eye on fishing and hunting, and maybe even open a customs outpost. And in preparation for the Polar Year of 1932–1933, discussion swirled around the idea of installing a meteorological station in Kerguelen. But in face of the sheer impracticalities of access and supply, nothing came of these ideas. In the 1930s, official French presence in the austral territories was limited to two brief naval visits to the sub-Antarctic islands: the *Antarès* sailed to Kerguelen, Crozet, and Saint-Paul in 1931, and the *Bougainville* visited Kerguelen and Crozet in 1938–1939. Even communication was essentially nonexistent. In Saint-Paul, neglect turned tragic in 1930 when a relief ship did not arrive to evacuate the employees of a failed spiny lobster cannery and five people, including a young child, died from starvation and scurvy.[15] And when another group attempting to exploit crustaceans ran out of coal and food on the island eight years later, their shortwave radio distress calls were picked up not by the French officials in Madagascar they were trying to reach but by a twelve-year-old amateur radio operator in California. In these circumstances, it is surprising that these French possessions were not annexed by the British, Americans, or Australians.

In France, the 1924 decrees attracted only polite, brief attention. There was general agreement among those with any interest that the decrees were necessary to protect French rights, especially as Britain was beginning to aggressively assert its presence in the region.[16] But they were legal instruments, utilitarian and practical; they were accompanied neither by expeditions nor by presence. While the empire had a strong hold on political, intellectual, and cultural imagination in interwar France, this conception of empire was still centered on the populated and economically viable colonies and did not stretch to include remote and uninhabited possessions in the Antarctic and sub-Antarctic.

Australian Ambitions

In Australia, the French decrees of 1924 were received with a mixture of alarm and outrage. The Australian press judged the French claim to Terre Adélie based on discovery to be secondary to the territory's geographic, historical, and emotional ties to Australia. "Adelie Land should be ours, from every point of view—patriotic, sentimental, and economic," wrote *The Register*, noting that Australia's leading geologists and explorers considered the entire swath of the Antarctic Continent to the south of Australia to belong to that country.[17] Of particular resentment was what in Australia was seen as the French claim's lack of geographic justification. "France aims at making Adelie Land a dependency of Madagascar, although Madagascar is separated from Adelie Land by almost a quarter of the earth's circumference," wrote Brisbane's *The Daily Mail*: "On the other hand, Adelie Land is not only well within the 'Australian Quadrant' of the Antarctic Continent, but is actually nearer to Hobart than Hobart is to Perth."[18] The dearth of French presence in Terre Adélie since Dumont d'Urville's brief insular landing of 1840, together with the Australasian Antarctic Expedition's extensive exploration of the territory, too, rankled.[19] Mawson thundered against the French decrees, declaring that "the French cannot uphold their claim" and that "the mere planting of the flag has no significance in international law."[20] While emotions on this issue ran high in Australia, the opposite was true in France. By dint of geographic proximity, the Antarctic mattered to Australians in a way it did not matter to the French. As Rohan Howitt points out, this was a case of the "vernacular Australian understanding of sovereignty that presumed that proximity to the Antarctic bestowed implicit territorial rights clashing with a French understanding that emphasized discovery, proclamation, and nominal administration."[21]

The press, the Australian National Research Council, and prominent geologists and explorers all pressured the Australian government to act. Only by speaking out against the French claim to Terre Adélie, these voices argued, could Australia secure control of the much larger slice of the Antarctic pie that "on geographical and historical grounds, it is thought, should belong to Australia."[22] In response, the Australian government pushed the British Colonial Office to take up the issue, recommending that the "Australian quadrant" be immediately annexed and France's claim to Terre Adélie explicitly challenged. The Australian argument was centered on geographic and historical considerations that pointed to Australia as the rightful claimant. While Australia's request seemingly fit into Britain's long-term Antarctic policy—to eventually annex the entire continent—still Britain treated the so-called Australian quadrant cautiously, guided not by emotion or nationalism but by big-picture strategic interests. The Colonial Office was less rash than the Australians, more attuned to the broader premises on which the empire rested. Thanks to the French decrees of 1924, the British realized, Terre Adélie could not be wished away, but needed to be dealt with diplomatically—and, in particular, in a way that did not open any doors for potential challenges to British holdings anywhere around the globe. Until that happened, the Australian claim was put on ice.

At Australia's request, the Antarctic was discussed at the 1926 Imperial Conference, one of a series of meetings of government leaders from the British Empire held periodically between 1887 and 1937. To the dismay of Australian Antarctic proponents, British officials concluded that France had an indisputable claim to Terre Adélie. As to Australia's geographic proximity argument—that countries situated near the white continent should have priority rights to territorial control—the British government rejected it outright, since any acceptance of this argument would give credence to Argentina's interests in the Falkland Islands and their Dependencies. For Britain, in comparison to the maintenance and defense of the empire as a global entity, Australia's hunger for Antarctic territory ranked a distant second. Further, British officials judged that the French would react badly to any proposal to exchange Terre Adélie for another territory such as the New Hebrides. The result was a severe setback for Australian Antarctic hopes—a setback that only intensified the Australian desire to make a claim and to deny France its title to a sliver of the continent. Soon, Douglas Mawson was sent back to the Antarctic to lead a new expedition with express instructions to make territorial claims at every opportunity.[23]

Finally, in early 1933 Britain made its move, claiming a huge sector of the Antarctic to the south of Australia, but explicitly excluding Terre Adélie. A few months later, Australia legislated to accept administration of this vast swath of Antarctica, which is known as the Australian Antarctic Territory. Covering 42 percent of the white continent, the Australian Antarctic Territory both surrounds and dwarfs Terre Adélie (figure 7).[24] With this move, Britain and its Dominions had now laid claim to about two-thirds of the continent. That Terre Adélie was excluded from this new claim was clear from the Australian Antarctic Territory Acceptance Act, which read: "That part of the territory in the Antarctic seas which comprises all the islands and territories, *other than Adelie Land*, situated south of the 60th degree south latitude and lying between the 160th degree east longitude and the 45th degree east longitude, is hereby declared to be accepted by the Commonwealth as a Territory under the authority of the Commonwealth, by the name of the Australian Antarctic Territory."[25]

For the French, the exclusion of Terre Adélie from the Australian claim was both a relief and a victory: a relief because it ended years of niggling uncertainty, and a victory because the state construed this exclusion as explicit recognition and acceptance of France's title. But Terre Adélie still lacked clear boundaries. Neither France's 1924 decrees nor the Australian Acceptance Act specified its precise extent, a touchy issue that would prove tricky to resolve.

Negotiating Boundaries

With the creation of the Australian Antarctic Territory, the lack of clarity over Terre Adélie's boundaries came to the fore. The French decrees did not specify whether the claim consisted of only the coastal region seen by Dumont d'Urville

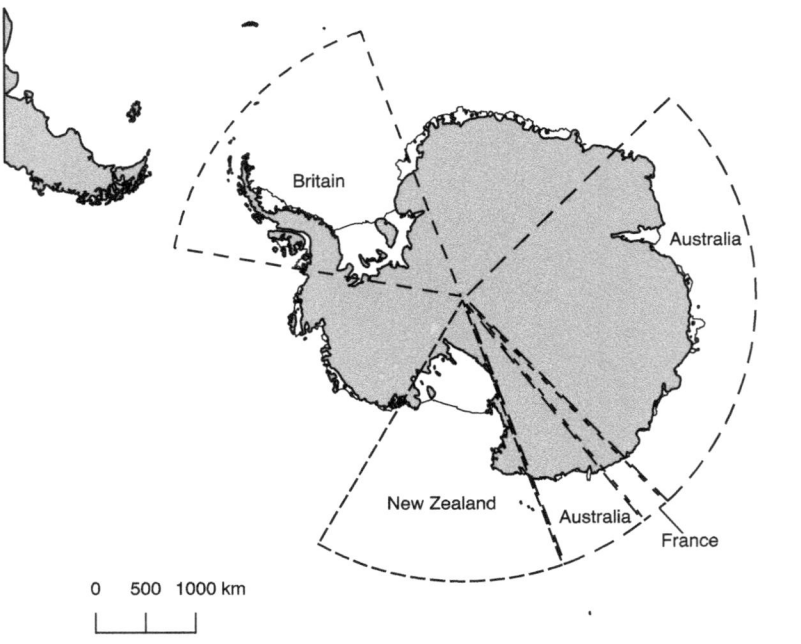

FIGURE 7. Claimed territories in the Antarctic, 1933. Map by Richard Martin-Nielsen.

or of a pie-shaped sector stretching to the pole—and nor was it clear where exactly the territory's eastern and western limits lay. Now, fixing Terre Adélie's boundaries could only be done in negotiation with the British.

As negotiations opened, the French government looked to take advantage of the lack of consistency between different maps and documents to maximize the extent of the possession. They began cheekily, proposing limits of 136° east and 147° east longitude, a choice which almost doubled Dumont d'Urville's original claim of 136° east to 142° east, but which was consistent with an official British note from 1913.[26] When the French ambassador in London, Charles Corbin, wrote to British officials proposing these boundaries in October 1933, he also made clear that France's claim extended over the entire pie-shaped sector stretching to the South Pole.[27] Any lingering Australian hopes that the two sections of the great Australian Antarctic Territory might be connected south of the coast were dashed by this use of the sector principle.

The British countered that the mention of 147° east in their 1913 note had been a mistake—and it stemmed, indeed, from an error made by a Hobart typesetter in 1840 and perpetuated over the decades—and declared themselves unable to accept the French proposal. They countered with the narrower limits "given on Commandant d'Urville's own chart as published by your Government, and dated 1840." "In view of the tremendous amount of work and expenditure that has already been undertaken by His Majesty's Governments in connection with the exploration of the whole of the coastline and portions of the interior of the Australian Antarctic Territory, and also of Adelie Land, and of the fact that the only French effort which has been directed toward this area of the Antarctic has been the extremely brief visit of Commodore d'Urville in 1840, the suggestion of the French government that the eastern boundary of Adelie Land should be fixed to the east of the 142nd meridian of longitude east of Greenwich cannot be accepted," the British explained patiently to the French government.[28] By bringing up the lack of any French presence in the territory since 1840, the British probed France's weak spot. Fully aware of the realities of the situation, French diplomats quickly abandoned the push for 147° east. But they were still not satisfied with being restricted to 142° east. They then argued for a limit of 143° east, this time justifying the extra degree with a map published by the British Admiralty. But the British again pushed back, pointing to the activity of Mawson's Australasian Antarctic Expedition between 142° east and 143° east. The French negotiators knew they were defeated but saw a way to save face, declaring it proper that the monument in memory of Australian Antarctic explorers conveniently erected a hairsbreadth east of 142° east be situated in the Australian, and not the French, sector.[29]

As these negotiations were advancing, Australia spoke out, upset about France's use of the sector principle. Australia pushed Britain to challenge this usage since a Terre Adélie which stretched to the South Pole would split Australia's Antarctic territory into two distinct wedges joined only at the pole. Dumont d'Urville's men, the Australians emphasized, had only landed on an outlying islet, and no French citizen had ever actually set foot on the continental part of Terre Adélie, let alone explored its interior. But the British were well aware that denying the use of the sector principle to the French would jeopardize the Falkland Islands Dependencies, the Australian Antarctic Territory, and the Ross Dependency, all of which were dependent on that principle. Allowing the French to claim a pie slice of the Antarctic, British authorities contended, was necessary for broader imperial interests.[30] On this, Britain was also influenced by Canada's needs, since the sector principle was important to Canadian territorial integrity in the Arctic. The British did, however, recognize Australia's concerns and suggested asking the French government to permit free passage between the two Australian sectors.

Terre Adélie's boundaries were formalized on 1 April 1938 with a presidential decree declaring that "the islands and territories situated to the south of the

60th parallel of south latitude and between the 136th and 142nd meridians of longitude east of Greenwich are under French sovereignty."[31] From the French point of view, the result was slightly disappointing but not unexpected; after all, the French had been absent from Terre Adélie for nearly a century and had no answer to Australia's twentieth-century expeditions in the region. And from the British point of view, the negotiations were a success: France had been restricted to the smallest possible slice of the Antarctic pie.[32]

The British suggestion concerning free passage between the two sectors of the Australian Antarctic Territory was acted on quickly as it offered advantages to both parties. After a brief exchange of notes between Sir Eric Phipps, the British ambassador to Paris, and Georges Bonnet, the French foreign minister, an agreement on aerial navigation was signed in October 1938. It allowed Commonwealth aircraft unfettered overflight rights over Terre Adélie and, conversely, French aircraft unfettered overflight rights over the British, Australian, and New Zealander Antarctic territories.[33] For the British and Australians, this was a means to tie together the otherwise split Australian Antarctic Territory. For the French, it served a different purpose: the agreement represented formal Commonwealth recognition of Terre Adélie's boundaries. That the French had no capacity whatsoever to act on this agreement—no French ship had sailed to Terre Adélie in nearly a century, let alone had a French aircraft penetrated Antarctic space—was beside the point; ultimately, for the French, this agreement was about recognition.

The War Interrupts

At the opening of World War II, French administration of its Antarctic and sub-Antarctic possessions was embryonic and control was only theoretical. The government of Madagascar had no means of accessing Terre Adélie or exercising any real authority over that territory. At this time, the French claim to Terre Adélie was recognized by Britain, Australia, and New Zealand. France also considered Norway to recognize the claim, but here the circumstances were less clear: while Norway had given de facto recognition to the French claim in 1939 when its minister of foreign affairs declared that Norway would not lay claim to any territory already in the possession of another nation, this recognition was not explicit.[34] But it was the United States' refusal to recognize the claim that most perturbed the French state. As well as protesting the 1924 decrees with an official complaint to the French Ministry of Foreign Affairs, the US State Department swiftly protested the 1938 aviation agreement, informing both the French and the British that "the United States reserves all rights which it or its citizens may have with respect to the question of aerial navigation in the Antarctic as well as to those questions of territorial sovereignty implicit therein."[35] And later the same year, the United States lodged a complaint with the French government asserting that since no French citizen had ever set foot on the continental portion of Terre Adélie, the claim was invalid under international law.[36]

Led by Bonnet, the French government reacted swiftly to these challenges, underlining the "unquestionable sovereign rights which France has acquired over Adelie Land" and pushing back against the American position.[37] Bonnet pointed out the various official publications, notices, and decrees supporting the claim, writing that "under these circumstances, I take pleasure in thinking that the reserves formulated by the United States Government do not concern Adelie Land, over which the rights of the French Government have, for nearly a century, been regularly established and have never given rise to contention." Bonnet's closing remark exaggerated the situation—in the first instance, far from having "regularly" supported its title to Terre Adélie, the French state had ignored the territory for nearly eighty years, and in the second, France's claim to Terre Adélie had indeed been contested by Australia—but it was a necessary exaggeration to bolster the strength of the French position. This aggrandized identity narrative, designed to pull distant territories closer to the French collective consciousness, was built on over the following decades and persists to the present day.

But just as it seemed that the French government was beginning to defend its interests in Terre Adélie more vigorously, war broke out and the Antarctic was again shunted to the background. Terre Adélie and France's sub-Antarctic possessions were all but forgotten as the Hexagon was invaded and occupied. Terre Adélie means "almost nothing" in France, stated *Paris-Midi* in 1940, accurately and concisely summarizing the situation in both political and public discourse.[38] In late April 1940, Jules Marcel de Coppet, Madagascar's governor general, did pass a decree "urgently" reserving the right to explore for mineral resources in Terre Adélie and the sub-Antarctic islands to the colony, a formal act building on Bonnet's earlier protestations.[39] But this decree was meaningless given the complete lack of access and presence. Just months later, de Coppet was dismissed by the Vichy regime for his pro-British policies.

During the war, a few voices in France called attention to Terre Adélie's potential strategic value but, while prescient, at the time they were very much in the wilderness. These voices were by and large collaborationist, concerned by the implications of the American naval officer and explorer Richard E. Byrd's Antarctic expedition for the continent's political future. The paper *L'union française*, for example, saw growing American activity in the Antarctic as a threat to French interests there and pushed France to position itself advantageously in the Antarctic sphere.⁴⁰ These ideas were underpinned by a belief, deeply felt but vague in detail, that Terre Adélie would in the future be important for aviation routes and might even offer mineral riches.⁴¹

The war did demonstrate the strategic importance of France's sub-Antarctic islands. In October 1940, the British ship HMS *Neptune* visited the Kerguelen and Crozet archipelagos in search of a German surface raider that was preying on Allied ships off the western coast of Africa. Midshipman Nigel Fawcett described the islands as "deserted but beautiful in a rough and unspoilt way."⁴² While they did not find the raider, there was no mistake: German auxiliary cruisers, including the *Atlantis*, the *Pinguin*, and the *Komet*, visited Kerguelen in 1940 and 1941.⁴³ As the islands were uninhabited, the Germans were able to repair their boats, replenish fresh water supplies, and hunt and forage for rabbit, mussels, and Kerguelen cabbage without interference. The Germans even considered establishing a weather and radiotelegraphy station in Kerguelen, going so far as to load the necessary supplies onto the *Charlotte Schliemann*, but the mission was never carried out. In late 1941, Australia, concerned that Kerguelen's deep, sheltered inlets could easily hide Axis commerce raiders and submarines, sent a naval ship to the islands. Finding traces of German presence, the Australians planted mines to deny the Germans further use of the harbors.⁴⁴ In this way, the war brought both the austral islands' strategic value and vulnerability to the fore.

Law, Title, and Territory

What did international law say about France's hold over Terre Adélie?⁴⁵ Standards and conditions for territorial claims and sovereignty are neither static nor immutable; they have changed and evolved over time, and they are still in flux today.⁴⁶ While prior to the sixteenth century, papal grants formed the basis for European territorial acquisition, in the sixteenth and seventeenth centuries, the British, French, and Dutch refused to recognize Castile's and Portugal's papal grants in the New World. As explorers sailed into the New World without encountering real opposition, the claims of the Iberian powers were delegitimized. Soon, discovery and *prise de possession* (typically, raising or displaying a royal ensign or other symbol) by a person authorized by a king or government to acquire territory, as well as public notification of the discovery, came to form the basis for European territorial claim. Later, the concept of effective occupation took hold as a necessary follow-up to discovery. While the use of occupation to claim new territory can be traced to ancient Rome, in the eighteenth century effective occupation became increasingly important for Western powers looking to acquire land outside Europe. The insufficiency of discovery alone for acquiring territory is seen, for example, in the contests for the Pacific Ocean's Sulu Archipelago (which was awarded to Spain in 1885 over Britain and Germany owing to Spanish presence on some of the islands), for Nootka Sound (Vancouver Island), and for Navassa Island (Caribbean Sea). The effective occupation criterion was codified during the late nineteenth-century partition of Africa, and particularly the 1885 Treaty of Berlin, where it was enshrined as necessary for a European state to acquire rights over African territory. By the early twentieth century, occupation in some guise—usually permanent, under the sanction of a state, and including official acts of administration—was widely considered essential to determining the legal status of disputed territories.

Prior to the 1924 decrees, France's claim to Terre Adélie was based solely on Dumont d'Urville's discovery, *prise de possession*, and official notifications of 1840. At that time, in legal terms, this was generally regarded as creating only an inchoate title that needed to be perfected within a reasonable time period. Without some formal administration or occupation, the act of discovery, even of uninhabited lands, was considered to gradually lose its validity. By the interwar period, France's absence from Terre Adélie reached eighty years—a time span that pushed at the limits of acceptability, as Australia was quick to point out. Given the growing Australian aspiration to annex Terre Adélie, it became clear to the French government that discovery alone was no longer sufficient to support its claim to sovereignty. With the interwar decrees, France aimed to perfect its inchoate title over the territory by integrating it into an existing colonial administration. But no state personnel were sent—and, moreover, the government of Madagascar had no means of accessing Terre Adélie. Territorial control was entirely fictional, as was the actual exercise of sovereign rights.

Despite these weaknesses, a legal decision about East Greenland, taken in 1933, provided a useful precedent for France, as it suggested that more lenient legal standards for effective occupation could apply in regions that were uninhabited, geographically remote, or with harsh natural environments. In the Greenland case, Norway challenged Denmark's claim to sovereignty over the eastern portion of that great island on the basis that Denmark had no established presence there. The International Court of Justice in The Hague ruled that Denmark could not be expected to continuously occupy and exert authority over all of Greenland because of its inaccessible nature and harsh Arctic environment. Instead, the court decided that Denmark's limited governmental functions in connection with Greenland were sufficient to award that country full sovereignty over the vast island, a decision that suggested that effective occupation in polar environments demanded little in the way of the actual exercise of sovereign control and rights. The functions the court cited included legislation regulating hunting, fishing, and navigation; the administrative division of Greenland into provinces; and state-authorized and -sponsored resource, exploratory, and scientific activity.[47] It was Denmark's "intention and will to exercise such sovereignty and the manifestation of State activity," the court concluded, that gave the country a valid title to sovereignty over the entirety of Greenland.[48] This case suggested that effective occupation should be measured against more lenient standards in the Antarctic than in more typical regions, and that countries could in some cases exercise sovereignty over distant territories through symbolic administration alone.[49]

In the interwar years, France used precisely this diluted form of effective occupation to justify its claims to Terre Adélie and the sub-Antarctic islands: it issued administrative decrees and regulations, tied the territories into the country's colonial judicial apparatus, and appointed nonresident officials. But, as Malcolm Shaw points out, in order to claim sovereignty over *terra nullius*, states must demonstrate a relatively stronger title than that of competing states, "one that may take into account issues such as geography and international responses."[50] And in this respect, Australia posed a genuine threat: not only could Australia point to geographic proximity, but Mawson's expeditions—with their bases, scientific activities, and monuments, representing presence, the creation of new terrain knowledge, and a physical stamp on the natural environment—provided the basis for a competing legitimacy. That Mawson and his compatriots had sailed to, landed at, camped on, and explored parts of Terre Adélie while no French citizen had ever set foot on the continental portion of the claim gave particular weight to Australia's position. In comparison, France's legal decrees looked increasingly archaic. And loss of title by discovery in face of the exercise of other sovereignty rights by another state was not unknown: in 1928, the Permanent Court of Arbitration awarded the Island of Palmas to the Netherlands over the United States in precisely such a situation, asserting that sufficiently developed displays of state authority over territory "prevail over an inchoate title derived from discovery, especially if this latter title has been left for a very long time without completion by occupation."[51] With such precedents, the French claim to Terre Adélie looked weak as the centenary of Dumont d'Urville's discovery approached with no further French activity or presence. This was resolved in France's favor only in 1933 with the explicit exclusion of Terre Adélie from the Australian Antarctic Territory, itself a product of British imperial calculations.

Also problematic for France, as for all claimant states, was the lack of recognition of Antarctic claims in the international arena. While Britain, France, Australia, and New Zealand recognized each other's claims by the late 1930s, other countries—including most notably the United States—did not. Sovereignty is inseparable from the recognition of legitimacy of a state's authority over territory by other states. It is not only declared but also bestowed by mutual recognition at the state level. That France's claim to Terre Adélie was only recognized by a very small number of other countries pushed at the limits of sovereignty, however conceived.

This lack of recognition was at the heart of the increasingly important American position. Indeed, the United States was the only other country that might have made a claim to Terre Adélie in the interwar years. After all, Charles Wilkes had explored the same area in the same time frame as Dumont d'Urville, and despite the problems with the veracity of his accounts, he was still staunchly defended in some quarters. The lack of an American claim to Antarctic territory at this time is especially curious in the context of the British claims of 1908, 1917, and 1923, which included many islands and regions that had been earlier discovered and explored by Americans, as well as the French claim to Terre Adélie.

In the closing decades of the nineteenth century, the United States paid little attention to the distant and unwelcoming Antarctic, preoccupied as it was with post-Civil War domestic development. This continued into the early twentieth century. By the early 1920s, as Britain's intentions for the Antarctic were becoming clear and just as France was readying its decrees, the US government still had no coherent policy for the white continent. While the US Navy Department was antagonized by the French decrees and expressed some interest in pursuing territorial claims around Terre Adélie, "particularly in view of the possibility of the discovery of fuel and other mineral deposits," the matter was soon dropped—something Barry Plott attributes to the sheer impossibility of exploiting mineral resources in the Antarctic at the time.[52]

In the interwar years, the American decision to not pursue an Antarctic claim was based on two principles, both enunciated by Secretary of State Charles Evans Hughes. The first declared that in the case of *terra nullius*, discovery and *prise de possession* alone were not sufficient to support a claim to sovereignty; rather "actual settlement" was also required—and Hughes stipulated that there could be no dilution of this requirement for regions "where for climatic or other reasons actual settlement would be an impossibility," such as Antarctica.[53] The second said that since the US government had not officially endorsed the early Antarctic discoveries made by its citizens, the State Department was reluctant to recognize territorial rights based on their expeditions. Made in the spring of 1924, these statements came to be known as the Hughes Doctrine. The first of these points—the lack of settlement—provided justification for the United States' refusal to recognize the French claim. But conversely, the Hughes Doctrine was also a saving grace for France, since the United States applied it equally to its own potential claims. Hughes noted explicitly that he could not recommend that the United States claim the territory seen by Wilkes in the vicinity of Terre Adélie because of the lack of American settlement in the region and because Wilkes had not been instructed by Congress to acquire territory.[54] With this, the possibility of an explicit American challenge to the French claim was greatly diminished: while the United States did not recognize France's claim, nor was it going to enter the fray with a counterclaim.

With the declaration of the Australian Antarctic Territory in 1933 and the entry of Argentina and Norway into the claims race, even the theretofore disinterested State Department began to take the continent, and possible American rights there, more seriously. Concern escalated stateside in 1938 when the German Reich launched a third Antarctic campaign, intended to secure whaling resources in order to reduce dependence on imported oils and fats.[55] President Franklin D. Roosevelt took up the matter of the Antarctic personally, directing the State Department to "conduct a study on the manner in which the United States might protect such territorial rights as it possessed in these regions."[56] In 1939, Roosevelt himself signed a letter of instructions for Byrd, directing him to establish two bases in Antarctica and to explore the regions of the continent where the basis for American claims was the strongest. "Members of the Service may take any appropriate steps such as dropping written claims from airplanes, depositing such writing in cairns, etcetera, which might assist in supporting a sovereignty claim by the United States Government," read Roosevelt's letter.[57] But the pressures of the war soon ended these activities. Byrd was recalled to serve in the Office of the Chief of Naval Operations in the spring of 1940, his new bases were abandoned, and the expedition's last members returned to Boston in early 1941. The status quo established in the interwar period persisted and continues to the present day: while the United States reserved and continues to reserve the right to make Antarctic claims, it has neither made a claim to any part of the continent nor recognized any claims made by other countries.

While neither of the two potential interwar challenges to France's claim to Terre Adélie—Australia's desire to annex the territory and an American move based on Wilkes's explorations—came to fruition, they were sharp reminders that France still had a long way to go to perfect its title. The French state needed to show possession of the territory, effective control and not merely the publication of legal decrees, in order to defend its claim to sovereignty both legally and morally. But this need was not recognized until the very end of the 1940s.

5
SCIENCE AND PRESENCE

Douglas Mawson's declaration that the Antarctic contained great deposits of uranium, made in the autumn of 1946, was sensational in the burgeoning postatomic world. Soon after Mawson's comments, the *New York Times* ran a story describing a six-nation race to find and exploit this uranium.[1] Despite the famed aviator and polar explorer Richard E. Byrd's subsequent denial of any American pursuit of uranium on the white continent, the idea of the Antarctic as a source of uranium was fanned by the media, particularly in France. While Terre Adélie had long been considered worthless, the journalist and translator Gustave Aucouturier wrote, everything had changed now that the continent was thought to have economic and strategic value.[2] In this new situation, he continued, France ought to be wary of American intentions and particularly of Byrd's new Antarctic expedition, called Operation Highjump—especially given the refusal of the United States to recognize France's claim to Terre Adélie. The liberation paper *Combat*, too, urged the French state to "not abandon the 'few acres of frozen land' that remain ours"—a reference to the still-bitter loss of France's colonies in Canada to the British in the eighteenth century.[3] And, drawing a parallel between the nineteenth-century partition of Africa and the twentieth-century partition of the Antarctic, *Le Monde*, the newspaper founded at Charles de Gaulle's request after the liberation of Paris in 1944, dangled the possibility of finding uranium in Terre Adélie as the next chapter for France's Antarctic story.[4] While these calls for action went unanswered by the state, their general tone—both vis-à-vis France's relationship with the United States and the desire to retain French possessions in a rapidly changing world—would persist for decades to come. The French state's lack of engagement with Terre Adélie in the immediate postwar years reflected the overwhelming need for reconstruction at home as well as the political instability of the Fourth Republic, whose revolving-door governments allowed only the most urgent tasks to be tackled.

While in France the Antarctic was off the political agenda at the end of the war, in the United States government interest in the white continent surged. In 1946, the US Navy launched Operation Highjump, bringing 4,700 men, thirteen ships, and thirty-three fixed-wing aircraft and helicopters to the Antarctic under Byrd's command—the largest and most organized operation the white continent had ever seen. It aimed to photograph extensive areas of the continent from the air, train thousands of troops in polar environments, and test equipment in polar conditions. Byrd's operation also built a shore base, known as Little America IV, and an airstrip at the Bay of Whales, and conducted extensive scientific investigations. Operation Highjump's mission, confidential at the time, spoke directly to the sovereignty question: it was responsible for "consolidating and extending United States sovereignty over the largest practicable area of the Antarctic Continent."[5] In early 1947, just days after the expedition's forward group reached the Antarctic, the *New York Times* published an article outlining the American strategy: "The United States plans to claim a big share of the 6,000,000-square-mile Antarctic continent, officials disclosed today. The strategy for clinching the claims will be considered upon the return of Rear Admiral Richard E. Byrd. . . . United States policy now, as restated this week by Under Secretary of State Dean Acheson, is to rest on the claims made by individual American explorers and surveyors and to recognize none of the claims advanced by Britain, Chile, Norway, France, Argentina and other countries."[6] Alarming as this should have been, the French government—far too preoccupied by domestic reconstruction and European politics—made only the weakest of diplomatic protests.[7]

Paul-Emile Victor and Expéditions Polaires Françaises

But even as the French Fourth Republic showed no interest in Terre Adélie, the territory was championed by a private individual: the ethnographer and polar explorer Paul-Emile Victor. Born in Geneva in 1907, Victor grew up in the Jura region of eastern France, with its rolling, forested mountains.[8] His boyhood was spent immersed in the worlds of Jack London, Jules Verne, and Rudyard Kipling, fueling in Victor dreams of exploring the furthest ends of Earth. As a young man, however, he had difficulty choosing his path. After leaving the *École Centrale de*

Lyon, a *grande école* for engineering, without a diploma, Victor went south to the port city of Marseilles, where he attended the *École nationale de la navigation maritime* as a student officer from 1928 to 1930. He found his military service in the French Navy disappointing and again changed direction, moving to Paris in 1933 to study at the *Musée d'ethnographie du Trocadéro*, housed in the impressive Trocadéro Palace, built for the Paris World's Fair of 1878. There, Victor tutored under Marcel Mauss, a sociologist who taught his students to reject geographical determinism, to question traditional conceptions of race, and to immerse themselves in Indigenous societies.[9] Mauss's interest in the Arctic drew Victor's eyes north.

Just a year after arriving at the Trocadéro, Victor's long-held dreams of exploration were realized when he spent the winter of 1934–1935 in Angmagssalik (now Tasiilaq), a community in southeastern Greenland. The following year, Victor and three companions used dogsleds to cross Greenland's great ice sheet from west to east, an arduous forty-nine-day traverse covering more than seven hundred kilometers. "We have arrived tired but enchanted," they wrote in a telegram to Paris at the end of the crossing: "Numerous dogs are dead."[10] Victor remained another fourteen months in Greenland, living with an Indigenous Greenlandic family. Upon return to France, his forceful personality and eloquent recitations of his adventures captured the media's attention, while his ethnographic articles, lectures, and drawings gathered praise in the scientific world. He also entered the public eye with two popular books, *Boréal* and *Banquise*.[11] This ability to make a name for himself would underpin his ensuing decades of work in both the Arctic and the Antarctic.

With the Fall of France in 1940, Victor—who had been assigned to the French naval attaché in Stockholm—left Europe for Morocco and Martinique. There, he was unsettled, unhappy with his inaction in face of the war but at the same time reluctant to join the Gaullists in wake of the Allied invasion of Vichy French-controlled Levant. In 1941, he arrived in the United States, where he applied for citizenship and enlisted with the US Army Air Forces. Thanks to his experience in Greenland, Victor was assigned to the Arctic section of the Arctic, Desert, and Tropic Information Center, which had been created to study the challenges posed to military personnel by hostile natural environments.[12] There, he wrote manuals for polar travel and survival, conducted cold environment training camps in the Rocky Mountains, and commanded an air search-and-rescue center in Alaska.[13]

Victor's wartime experience with the US military opened his eyes to more efficient ways of interacting with polar environments. "Here I became familiar with parachuting techniques and the performance of aircraft and Weasels [motorized tracked vehicles] under northern conditions," he wrote, seeing in these technologies the solution to all the problems which had plagued his earlier dog-sled travels.[14] As the war ended, Victor set his sights on building France into a leader in polar science and logistics. With years of experience in Greenland in the 1930s, his new knowledge, and a thirst for polar affairs, Victor dreamed of a new age of polar exploration: one that left the lone, struggling heroic explorer far behind and capitalized on technological innovations to conduct large-scale, systematic campaigns. The era of polar exploration focused solely on survival was over, he believed, and a new era of scientifically oriented, precisely planned expeditions was dawning.[15]

Victor returned to France at the very end of 1945, eager to embark on a new expedition to Greenland. While he initially focused only on that great island, which he called "the land of my dreams," he soon expanded his plans to include the Antarctic.[16] Victor was persuaded to look to the white continent by the French alpinists Jacques-André Martin, Yves Vallette, and Robert Pommier. In 1946, the three young men spent several months mountaineering on the Norwegian island of Spitsbergen, where they discovered a high mountain peak they named Mont Général-Perrier (now Perriertoppen) after Général Georges Perrier, the president of the Paris-based *Société de géographie* which had funded their expedition. On their way home, however, the men were perturbed to see a Norwegian newspaper article questioning France's right to Terre Adélie.[17] Since no Frenchman had set foot in the territory since 1840, the article argued, it could hardly be considered to belong to France. At the time, Norway's strategic interests in the Antarctic, propelled by the need to support its whaling fleets, were well-developed. While Martin, Vallette, and Pommier were eager to head to Terre Adélie themselves to fly the French flag over the territory, they had neither the funding, reputation, nor connections needed. Instead, they brought their concerns to Victor, already France's dean of polar exploration, asking him to support France's claim to Terre Adélie by launching an expedition to the territory.

After initial reluctance, Victor agreed to add the Antarctic to his agenda and his fledgling polar organization, *Expéditions polaires françaises—Missions Paul-Emile Victor*, took on new significance. Victor's plans for dual expeditions to Greenland and the Antarctic were ambitious and technologically intensive, much too expensive to be funded privately. As Victor wrote, "There was no question of undertaking such a program . . . with dog sleds and walking;" rather, the expeditions were to be "essentially scientific" in both intent and execution—ideas that would form the core of Expéditions polaires françaises' narrative for decades to come.[18] To gain state support, Victor emphasized the role of scientific expeditions in performing sovereignty in Terre Adélie—a territory in which no Frenchman had set foot for over a century. "We must not lose this land for which French possession is already deeply contested," Victor wrote in 1947—an exaggeration, but an effective one.[19] The clear weakness of France's title gave Victor the ammunition he needed. "Since its discovery more than 100 years ago, no Frenchman has returned, while several foreign expeditions have been there," he repeated, reminding the French political class of Mawson's earlier challenges to Terre Adélie—and adding that an expedition was urgently needed "if France wants to defend her rights to this territory."[20]

On this point, Victor was supported by international law. Even with the administrative decrees of the interwar years and taking into account judicial decisions about other remote territories, French effective occupation in Terre Adélie hung by a thread. Real control over its slice of the Antarctic pie (or, in French parlance, Camembert) was nonexistent. The territory was only sustained because no other country chose to mount an active challenge. The two countries that might have done so, Australia (via Britain) and the United States, had both backed off before the war. Still, the United States represented an ongoing, niggling uncertainty given Operation Highjump's aims. To add to this, the meaning of effective occupation in the polar arena shifted in the 1940s. With new developments in polar logistics, as Peter Beck writes, "a *permanent* Antarctic presence through a scientific base and associated administrative arrangements came to be regarded as essential for the satisfaction of the effectiveness criteria, and during the 1940s governments were subject to pressures to maintain their claims in this manner."[21] Britain responded to these pressures with Operation Tabarin, a late-war operation that established several bases and post offices on the Antarctic Peninsula, and its peacetime extension, the Falkland Islands Dependencies Survey.[22] Chile and Argentina, too, opened permanent continental bases in 1947–1948 and in 1951, respectively.[23] Even the United States, which claimed no territory and recognized no claims, reestablished the suggestively named Little America base in 1946. But France still had nothing. Even worse, as American voices were eager to remind the French, Dumont d'Urville's men had never set foot on the continental portion of the claim, but only on an outlying islet.

Victor pointed, too, to growing strategic interests in the Antarctic. "Since the war, the principal nations of the world have recognized the strategic, economic, technical, and scientific importance of the polar regions," he wrote in 1947—but France was too preoccupied by domestic and European concerns to look to the poles.[24] France risked, Victor continued, being eclipsed by the long list of other countries—the United States, Canada, Great Britain, the USSR, Denmark, Norway, Sweden, Australia, New Zealand, Chile, and Argentina—already active in one or both polar regions. And should the Antarctic prove to be a bonanza of natural resources, he added, France needed to be present both to capitalize on them and to keep Terre Adélie French. As he pled his case, Victor only found a modicum of public support: while some newspapers called for France to reassert itself in the Antarctic, French society by and large ignored (or was ignorant of) Terre Adélie in the immediate postwar years.[25]

The French government, too, was not initially receptive to Victor's ideas: the enormous costs and difficulties of postwar reconstruction dominated all other considerations. But the sovereignty argument ultimately won the day. Soon, the government agreed to support Expéditions polaires françaises' planned expeditions to Terre Adélie and Greenland. On 2 July 1947, the French president, Vincent Auriol, a moderate Socialist, granted Victor's fledgling polar organization his patronage, writing personally to Victor to give him the good news.[26] Funding was channeled through the Ministry of Education and the *Centre national de la recherche scientifique*. The presidency also instructed the French military to assist Victor as necessary, by loaning equipment and personnel, emphasizing the potential strategic and military value of France's Antarctic territory.[27] As well as the need to assert French sovereignty in Terre Adélie, the government was swayed by strategic thinking suggesting that in the future, Terre Adélie might be located on the shortest aviation routes between South America, South Africa, and Australia, and might even provide a tactical base in times of war.[28] As the Antarctic gained international attention, its strategic and resource value—whether imagined, wished for, or real—glittered brightly enough for the government to devote some money even as other, more urgent, needs pressed.

The government's decision to support Terre Adélie was also a reaction to American activity in Antarctica. In January 1946, not even eighteen months after the liberation of Paris, the polar explorer Lincoln Ellsworth announced a terrestrial and aerial cartography campaign on the white continent. In the same month, First World War fighter ace Eddie Rickenbacker proposed that the United States drop an atomic bomb on the Antarctic ice cap to gain access to the gold, copper, iron, coal, and other riches he thought to be hidden below.[29] And Operation Highjump's unambiguous aim to gather as much information about the continent as possible before new claims were made added fuel to the fire. Politically weakened by the war and dependent on the United States for aid, France was eager to push back against American hegemony where it could—and the Antarctic was an area in which this seemed possible.[30] This was wrapped up in broader fears of encroaching American culture and control, widespread in French politics and society at the time.[31] And this French concern about American intentions for Antarctica was far from misplaced: as soon as the French government agreed to support an expedition to Terre Adélie, the United States lodged an official protest.

It needs to be emphasized how extraordinary the commitment of state money for Terre Adélie and Greenland in 1947 was: newly liberated after World War II,

France was a country ruined, in dire need of reconstruction. Cities, roads, and ports were devastated from years of bombing and from German sabotage in the closing days of the war. One-quarter of the country's housing stock was destroyed. Rationing was still in effect. The country's scientific establishment was in tatters, directionless, and short of resources.[32] Politically, France was preoccupied not by adventures to far-flung regions of the world but by the practical matters of putting things to right after a shattering war: rebuilding the country, physically and emotionally; reviving democratic institutions and governance after Nazi occupation and Marshal Pétain's rule; punishing collaborators; and an ideological struggle with Communism.[33] Tensions in Europe, especially concerning the future of Germany, and the need to rebuild France's place in the European sphere post-Pétain also preoccupied the government.

For all these reasons, it was not the right time to mount expensive missions to the polar regions, especially not to Greenland, where France had no territorial interests. In another way, however, the expeditions were a means of alleviating some of the emotional effects of the war. Victor's plans offered an apolitical way to boost the nation's esteem after the humiliation of occupation, part of a broader faith placed in the idea of the overseas as a vector to rebuild France into a great nation. As Victor remarked during a visit to Washington in 1956, "It is simply that precisely at that moment France needed a 'lift.' Even such a strange thing such as a successful polar expedition would help in its way to revive our national prestige."[34] Victor's desire for France to take a leading place in polar science—a place that would bring economic and technological advantages as the polar regions grew in importance—also spoke to the country's ambitions in the early Cold War and offered a much-needed way of raising morale, part of what Gabrielle Hecht calls the broader "metaphysical and physical (re)building of the French nation."[35] With his polar plans, Victor became part of a small group of postwar French hero-explorers who gave the public a chance to dream amidst the devastation. Together, Victor, Jacques Cousteau (oceans), Maurice Herzog (mountains), Norbert Casteret (caves), and Haroun Tazieff (volcanoes) broke seemingly impenetrable barriers, encapsulating youth, risk-taking, adventure, and success. Apolitical heroes, admirable to all, these men gave the country something to be proud of at a time when pride was greatly needed.

Victor's success in gaining government funding in an unpropitious political climate owes to his connections and sheer force of personality. Indefatigable, he met with the French president, pressed ministers and military personnel, lobbied the media, and gave public lectures to draw attention to his cause. But it was his friendship with André-Frank Liotard that clinched it. Before the war, Liotard had emigrated to the United States, where he worked as a professor of French language and literature and as a pastor. Drawn together by their mutual fascination with the Arctic, Victor and Liotard shared an apartment in Washington in 1941. After the war, Liotard came back to France, where he was close to André Philip, the minister of the economy: they had served together in Algeria in de Gaulle's Free French Forces and both belonged to the Reformed Church of France. By convincing Philip to support Victor's polar plans, Liotard brought the government on board. He was rewarded by leading Expéditions polaires françaises' first expeditions to Antarctica, leaving Victor to focus on his main interest, Greenland.[36]

The vehicle through which France was to assert its claim over Terre Adélie, Expéditions polaires françaises, was a private organization, not a government body, led by a private man, not a government employee. This setup underlines the lack of French government interest in the Antarctic in the postwar era and foreshadows future strife, when private and official agendas would clash. Given the private nature of Expéditions polaires françaises, it was not fully funded by the government. Victor raised significant funds and in-kind donations from the private sector, especially from companies eager to associate themselves with polar adventures and daring. Food giant Nestlé, for example, supplied Victor's expeditions with Nescafé and Nescao: "strong comforts in difficult moments," the company's advertisements read, highlighting its relationship with France's Arctic and Antarctic heroes.[37] "In Greenland, in Terre Adélie, all the members of the Paul-Emile Victor expedition use Lafuma Super-Camping bags," read another advertisement, showing two underdressed members of Expéditions polaires françaises apparently about to embark on a polar hike with the company's backpacks.

State involvement with Expéditions polaires françaises in its early years was minimal. Other than creating a scientific commission, guided by members of France's most prestigious scientific and research academies and responsible for elaborating scientific programs, the government imposed little supervision. Far from being a government initiative or priority in the postwar years, Terre Adélie was a private endeavor. In some cases, this went exceptionally far. When the United States proposed a "condominium" for the Antarctic in 1948, the French Ministry of Foreign Affairs was not the least bit interested—and it fell to Expéditions polaires françaises to conduct bilateral meetings with other countries on the subject.[38] The lack of state political interest in the Antarctic was a source of unending frustration for Liotard and Victor in these years.

Mission: Terre Adélie

With funding secured, Victor immediately began making plans for expeditions to both Terre Adélie and Greenland.[39] For the Antarctic, his aims were ambitious: he wanted to establish a permanent base and maintain continual French presence in Terre Adélie, explore and map the coastal and inland regions of the territory, and undertake a comprehensive program of scientific research. And he wasted no time: Expéditions polaires françaises launched its first expedition to Terre Adélie in late 1948, not even a year and a half after winning government support. Given the lack of French experience in the Antarctic, Victor sent Frenchmen to participate in British and Australian Antarctic expeditions in order to gain experience and know-how. As Victor set his plans in motion, Yves Vallette (one of the three Spitsbergen mountaineers) joined the Australian National Antarctic Research Expedition for the 1947–1948 austral summer, where he was overjoyed to meet his hero, Douglas Mawson. And Liotard joined the Falkland Islands Dependencies Survey in 1948, visiting Britain's Antarctic meteorological stations aboard the *John Biscoe*. France's planned reassertion of sovereignty over Terre Adélie was, by necessity, launched with foreign help.

But how was France going to access Terre Adélie, given that the country had no ship capable of breaking through pack ice and reaching the Antarctic coast? The solution, again, was to look abroad. Victor used his wartime connections to purchase an American ship in San Francisco, which he rebaptized the *Commandant Charcot* in honor of the French polar explorer with whom he had sailed to Greenland in the 1930s.[40] Paid for by the French government, the former US Navy netlayer was brought first to Saint-Malo, where it was reinforced in anticipation of the icy Antarctic waters. Much of its hull was doubled and covered in iron at the waterline; the bow strengthened with tar, sheet metal, and more wood; and the diesel tank doubled in size. The interior, too, was overhauled to allow the small ship to accommodate sixty men, thirty dogs, and a huge quantity of supplies. The *Commandant Charcot* was then moved to Brest to be kitted out for the voyage by the French Navy. Purchasing a ship for this first voyage, as opposed to the cheaper option—leasing an icebreaker from another country—was both deliberate and symbolic: the presence of a French ship in Terre Adélie was meant to be a display of France's hold over the territory. Indeed, in attestation to the expedition's sovereignty objective, the navy was assigned responsibility for the sea voyage to the Antarctic and for officially reaffirming French sovereignty in Terre Adélie—missions that, in the government's eyes, needed to be undertaken by an official, not a private, body.[41]

But en route from Saint-Malo to Brest, the *Commandant Charcot*'s two motors broke down and the ship had to be towed to port. The motors then had to be completely disassembled and repaired, a task that took weeks, eating through vital time and making it unlikely that the ship could reach Terre Adélie before the end of the precious austral summer season in which the Antarctic waters are navigable. Expéditions polaires françaises blamed the navy for these delays, for not having properly checked the motors before the departure for Brest, an inauspicious beginning to the partnership. The ship was not ready until late November, leaving little time and hope for reaching Terre Adélie during the 1948–1949 season. Still, spurred by political developments in the Antarctic, Victor pushed forward, not willing to wait an entire year for a better opportunity—even though he thought their chances of success minimal.[42] The US State Department had made it known that it wanted the claimant countries to come together and reach an agreement on the Antarctic's political future. It was clear that without presence in Terre Adélie, France would find itself in a weak position at the negotiating table. The *Commandant Charcot* had to leave and try to reach the territory that season.

Under the command of Captain Max Douguet, one of the only French naval officers with polar experience, the *Commandant Charcot* departed from Brest on 26 November 1948, over a month later than planned. Hailing from a long tradition of sailors, the Brittany-born Douguet had spent eleven months around Greenland during the Second International Polar Year of 1932–1933. The *Commandant Charcot* called at Casablanca, Durban, and Hobart before reaching the Antarctic ice floes on 11 February 1949 (figure 8). It was, however, as feared too late in the season: the ship was unable to handle the tremendous pack ice near

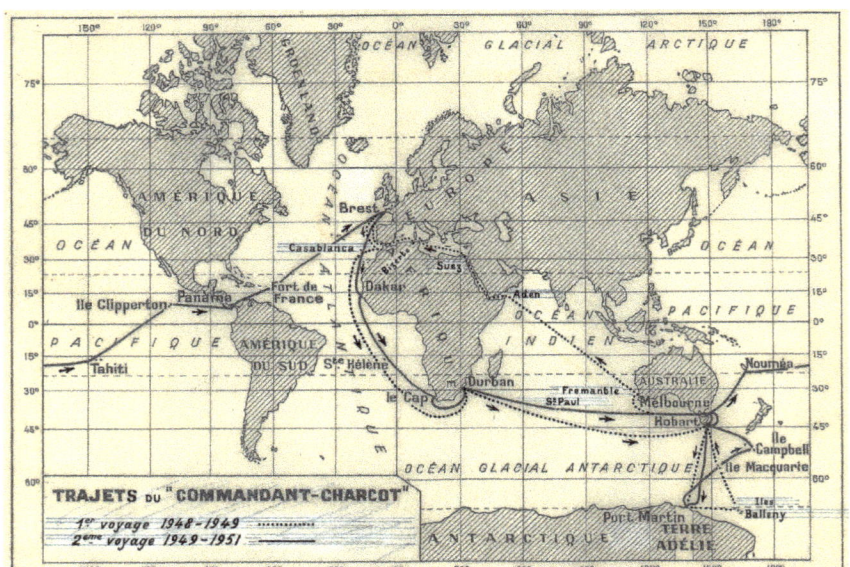

FIGURE 8. Path of the *Commandant Charcot*: first voyage 1948–1949, second voyage 1949–1951, 25×33 cm (Expéditions polaires françaises, Archipôles, IPEV).

Terre Adélie. After two weeks of fighting the ice, Douguet took the decision to turn around and head back to France empty-handed. The stops to explore the Balleny Islands and Macquarie Island en route back home were small consolation for the Expéditions polaires françaises team. Perhaps most disappointed were the three mountaineers who had originally inspired the expedition, all of whom had been included on the team.

The failure to reach Terre Adélie also exposed a rift between Expéditions polaires françaises and the navy. For its part, Expéditions polaires françaises blamed the navy for the motor problems that delayed the ship and ultimately ruined the expedition. And the navy, which saw the Antarctic expedition as a narrow political venture to reaffirm sovereignty, grew increasingly frustrated with Expéditions polaires françaises' elaborate scientific program. While for the navy, science was a peripheral component of the Terre Adélie project, for Victor and Expéditions polaires françaises, the case was reversed: science was front and center, the expedition's raison d'être, a goal unto itself and tool for reaffirming sovereignty. The French Navy was never as attuned to Antarctic affairs in the early postwar period as was the US Navy, with its major operations driven by the nascent Cold War. In the US military, environmental knowledge of the polar regions was seen to have direct strategic relevance to the East-West divide.[43] But in the French military, the collapse of the colonial empire, and not the growing antipathy between the superpowers, was all-consuming. As a private organization, Expéditions polaires françaises did not feel compelled to align itself with the navy's perspective, while the navy shared the government's lack of interest in Terre Adélie—fissures that would soon widen and lead to divorce.

As the *Commandant Charcot* slowly made its way back to France having failed to reach Terre Adélie, the National Assembly took up the question of France's Antarctic and sub-Antarctic possessions. Just as American interest in the Antarctic had forced Expéditions polaires françaises' hand in late 1948, foreign interest in the sub-Antarctic islands was beginning to raise alarm bells in France: the British wanted to erect a meteorological and radio station in Saint-Paul, while the Australians and the Americans were itching to install themselves in the Kerguelen archipelago. The strategic position of these possessions was increasingly clear: they were well-situated to provide meteorological information for maritime and aerial navigation, to study the little-understood general circulation of the atmosphere, and to link South Africa and Australia. These two countries had been pushing France to install meteorological facilities on its sub-Antarctic islands for a number of years, as had the International Civil Aviation Organization. In light of this, a group of deputies led by the long-serving politician Louis Rollin asked the government to act. "The requirements of international law in matters of sovereignty command us to assert our rights over the southern islands by effectively occupying them on a permanent basis and by establishing an administrative unit there," they told the National Assembly: "It is important that France choose without delay: either she will respond . . . or else she will lose territories whose economic value is certain."[44] Other countries, the deputies continued, "consider our titles and our rights precarious"—a warning underscored by the Australian group that spent three months in Kerguelen in the spring of 1949. France had no independent means of knowing that the Australians were on French territory, no means of observing their actions there, and no means of controlling their access or length of stay.

In France, it was agreed that action needed to be taken to prevent annexation.[45] The government in Madagascar, which officially administered the austral possessions, however, had few tools and little money at its disposal. While it did unite Terre Adélie and the sub-Antarctic islands into an austral district and attach them administratively to the province of Tamatave in 1949, this legal move—reminiscent of the decrees of the 1920s—did little to strengthen the French position.[46] Any real exertion of control over the territories would be expensive, requiring expeditions and presence. This time, the threat of annexation was strong enough to push the French government into action. In the autumn of 1949, an expedition finally left France for the sub-Antarctic possessions, installing permanent stations in Kerguelen and Nouvelle-Amsterdam—the most significant sign of effective occupation to that date.[47]

The state did not need to organize a similar expedition to Terre Adélie as Expéditions polaires françaises was already setting its second attempt to reach the Antarctic territory in motion. During the summer of 1949, the *Commandant Charcot*—battered from its first battle against the ice—was repaired in Brest. A second expedition to Terre Adélie, again captained by Douguet, departed France on 20 September 1949, much earlier in the season than the previous year. The ship followed the same route, around the Cape to Australia where, at a cocktail party thrown in their honor, the French team met Douglas Mawson. Starstruck, the Frenchmen listened, rapt, to the veteran Australian explorer as he recounted tale after tale from his expeditions. Gone, at least for that evening, was any hint of Mawson's previous opposition to the French claim to Terre Adélie.

Having learned the hard way about the ice conditions near Terre Adélie, this time the *Commandant Charcot* carried a bright red Stinson Voyager seaplane to guide it through the pack ice. Aided by the plane, which made ten reconnaissance flights over fifteen days to chart a path to the coast, the expedition arrived successfully in Terre Adélie in early 1950.[48] On 18 January 1950—110 years almost to the day after Dumont d'Urville had reached Antarctica and claimed the territory for France—the French team carefully stepped out onto Terre Adélie's icy banks under the gaze of hundreds of curious penguins. They were the first French citizens to ever set foot on the continental portion of the claim. "Our hearts overflowed with inexpressible joy," wrote Liotard, the expedition's leader and the man who had been so instrumental to winning government support: "The long months of effort and waiting, the successive trials faded in the jubilation of this first victory."[49] In a ceremony intended to reaffirm French sovereignty, Captain Douguet hoisted the tricolore in the presence of a navy honor guard. The blue, white, and red flag flapped violently in the Antarctic winds.

The flag hoisting was one of a series of symbolic, legal, and administrative acts designed to strengthen France's claim over the territory. The Council of Ministers appointed Liotard as the government's official representative in Terre Adélie, giving the expedition a clear political raison d'être.[50] While in practice this appointment raised a number of questions to which there were no simple answers (Should Liotard carry a service or diplomatic passport? Did he need to stop in Madagascar on his way to the Antarctic?), the intent to buttress sovereignty was clear. Liotard was also personally instructed by the overseas minister to report confidentially on anything that might strike him as relevant to national defense or the security of the state.[51] In his official capacity, Liotard established an administrative unit in the territory. "In accordance with the instructions given to me," as he wrote later, "I then proceeded with the material installation of the permanent postal establishment of Terre Adélie."[52] The Terre Adélie post office, which was in principle open for sending and receiving regular and registered mail, as well as for official and private telegraph services, is representative of a common and inexpensive way of demonstrating sovereignty in remote territories.[53] The men also installed a copper plaque on Rocher du Débarquement, where Dumont d'Urville's men had set foot 110 years earlier. And in another performance of sovereignty, France overprinted stamps with the words "Terre Adélie—Dumont d'Urville"—the sale of which, Victor hoped, would provide additional funding for his expeditions.[54] The Overseas Ministry legally affixed a time zone to Terre Adélie—namely, that of Greenwich +9 all year long.[55] Finally, the French government went to great efforts to route radiotelegraphy transmissions between Terre Adélie and Paris through French territories (at first, New Caledonia and, later, Kerguelen), not wanting to rely on a foreign country (namely, Australia) for communication purposes. Taken together, these performances of sovereignty built a basis for effective occupation in line with legal decisions about other remote territories and the actions of other claimant countries. While the French government knew there was no hope of convincing the Americans to recognize the claim to Terre Adélie, it was finally beginning to do the work necessary to be able to defend that claim in the future.

Overwintering in the French Antarctic

As the ship was slowly unloaded, Liotard and his men found themselves surrounded by the hundreds of tons of materials that would keep them alive over the next year in one of Earth's harshest natural environments: food rations, medical equipment, tents, fuel, and a prefabricated wooden base, designed to resist extreme cold and winds (figure 9). Scientific instruments, sleds, and motorized snow tractors called Weasels, too, lay on the rocky shore. The Weasels, central to Victor's vision of modern polar exploration, had been purchased used from the United States. In keeping with more traditional polar travel, the team also brought thirty sled dogs to Terre Adélie, including a much-loved puppy named Tuffiau who had been born on the *Commandant Charcot*. Three weeks after arriving, the *Commandant Charcot* departed and Liotard's team of eleven men entered a full year of isolation. The team overwintered through twenty-four-hour darkness and ferocious weather, their days and nights dictated by an ambitious scientific program as well as by the technical challenges of supporting life in the Antarctic.

A site was soon chosen for France's first Antarctic base, named Port-Martin in honor of Jacques-André Martin, one of the original three mountaineers who had suggested adding the Antarctic to Victor's agenda. Martin died of a heart attack on the trip south and was laid to rest in South Africa. Port-Martin's main

FIGURE 9. At the Port-Martin site in Terre Adélie, 1950: before the base was built, the men lived in tents (Robert Pommier, Archipôles, IPEV).

building, a wooden cross-shaped hut forty meters long by nine meters wide, was nestled on uneven bare rock and appended by smaller huts for scientific work. It took the men more than two months to build the base and install their scientific equipment—two months defined by ferocious storms and howling winds, fatal in the case of some of the dogs, and often overwhelming for the men. "This was the establishment of a veritable French village, the most isolated, the furthest from all civilized places," declared Liotard.[56]

In 1950, Terre Adélie was still virtually entirely unknown and unexplored. Only part of its coastline and a very small portion of its interior had been mapped, by Dumont d'Urville's expedition in 1840, by Mawson's expeditions of 1911–1914 and 1929–1931, and by the British Royal Research Ship *Discovery II*, which sailed near the territory in 1931 and 1938. But many of these observations were made from a fair distance away and the maps were imprecise and incomplete. Operation Highjump's aerial photos from 1947, too, proved all but useless because of the lack of coordinating observations from the ground—something that, while immediately frustrating, was in fact a comfort to the French: in this case, at least, American technological superiority in the Antarctic had fallen flat. When the Expéditions polaires françaises team arrived, then, their best map showed only a scallop-edged coast with promontories vaguely indicated, and in their best photos it was impossible to distinguish floating ice from coast. Of Terre Adélie's weather the team was better informed through Mawson's written accounts of his time in the territory, which he discomfortingly called "the home of the blizzard."[57] The French team pored over Mawson's accounts on their voyage south and accosted the man himself with questions during their stop in Australia—but still they were taken aback by the first blizzard they endured, on 18 February 1950, whose 140 kilometer per hour winds made the sea smoke and froth under a sky the color of ink and whipped snow horizontally across the ice with unfathomable violence.[58] A portentous beginning, this storm claimed one victim, Reine, Tuffiau's dam and one of the team's favorite dogs.

From the moment their ship docked, the men were surrounded by great numbers of Adélie penguins, thousands upon thousands of the small black and white birds, gorging themselves on krill, noisy to the point of being deafening. Like their compatriots of 1840, the men were delighted and entertained by the penguins, quickly anthropomorphizing them and attributing human emotions and temperaments to their physical appearance, facial expressions, and movements. "We were struck by the resemblance of these extraordinary birds to middle-aged burghers in frock-coats. Their very gait has something about it of the self-satisfied man of property. And the sight, not just of one or a handful, but literally thousands of these creatures in their native habitat, smug in appearance, and exuding an air of conservatism and traditionalism, rooted in a long past of established institutions, is fraught with comic overtones," wrote Luc-Marie Bayle and Pierre Dubard.[59] While penguin eggs and steaks featured regularly on Port-Martin's menu, and sled dogs at play killed the penguins by the hundreds, the Adélie penguins also provided emotional comfort for the men, identifiable living creatures in an otherwise desolate land, disappearing for the winter and reappearing in the spring, almost as if announcing the imminent arrival of the supply ship.[60]

During their year in Terre Adélie, Liotard's team undertook twelve traverses by dogsled and Weasel, covering over two thousand kilometers of sea ice and of the Antarctic Continent itself.[61] Among these traverses, the discovery of one of the largest known Emperor penguin rookeries stands out—a rookery that was later celebrated in the Oscar-winning film *La marche de l'empereur* (*March of the Penguins*, 2005) and which has come to symbolize Antarctica's climactic fragility (figure 10). Another traverse took the men to Cape Denison, where they found the huts that Mawson had erected forty years earlier on his Australasian

FIGURE 10. Procession of Emperor penguins and chicks, Pointe Géologie archipelago, 1957 (Archipôles, IPEV).

Antarctic Expedition. When the Frenchmen arrived at Mawson's base after a two-day-long sled journey, "with emotion, we contemplated this place which it seemed we had known forever, so many times we had read and re-read about it."[62] While Mawson's astronomy hut had survived the elements, the rest of the buildings were partially destroyed, and the huge cross erected as a memorial to Belgrave Ninnis and Xavier Mertz, who perished on the Far Eastern Party sled expedition, had lost its crosspiece. Breaking into the collapsed living quarters with sledgehammers, the French team enjoyed a veritable feast: plum pudding, French-style peas, rhubarb, and strawberry jam. Before returning, they repaired the cross and lashed Mawson's Nansen-style sled—still in perfect condition—to their dogsleds to bring back to Port-Martin.

Expéditions polaires françaises maintained continual presence in Terre Adélie from January 1950 until January 1953 with three successive expeditions.[63] Each austral summer, a new team and new supplies arrived by ship, and the old team rotated out and returned to France. The goals of the expeditions were fourfold: to reassert French sovereignty over Terre Adélie, to establish and occupy a French base, to explore and map the coastal regions and border of the ice sheet, and to conduct scientific research in the territory. This represents the first French effort to use presence and science to strengthen its Antarctic claim. In addition to the scientific program at Port-Martin, the teams covered over seven thousand kilometers with dogsleds and with the Weasels that had so captured Victor's imagination during the war, pushing as far as three hundred kilometers into the continent's interior. By naming each expedition leader as an official representative of France, the government, too, lent political weight to the expeditions. After Liotard returned to France, this position was conferred on Michel Barré, René Garcia, and Mario Marret in turn. As such, France's territorial claim in the Antarctic was reinforced by three years of continual presence and the knowledge that scientific discoveries, investigations, and expeditions bring. From the point of view of international law, the manifest interest shown by France in the territory, as evidenced by the deployment of state authority in the form of funding, official representatives, postal and telegraphic services, and environmental authority all worked together to demonstrate effective occupation.

Following Victor's vision of modern polar work, the Expéditions polaires françaises teams were designed to prioritize scientific work: there was a separation of roles between the scientists, whose job it was to focus on their research, and the polar technicians, who were there to make everything go smoothly for the scientists. "Not so many years ago, the only polar problem was survival," wrote Marret, the last expedition leader, in 1953: "Today, the role of polar technicians is to make the scientists forget about this vital problem."[64] This extended far beyond the mechanics of making things work: Expéditions polaires françaises also put time and effort into those details that make life in a remote and difficult environment less demanding. Particular attention was paid to meals, which were prepared to French standards by a dedicated cook. In the winter of 1951, the cook, Raoul Desprez, went so far as to make a cake decorated with a sugar model of the Port-Martin base (figure 11). By providing not only proper meals but also using pleasures of the palate to boost morale, Desprez and the other cooks who served in Terre Adélie in the early 1950s were seen by the scientific personnel as critical to maintaining good relations among the overwinterers. Still, technological progress was far from an unbroken line: while Victor was using airplanes to support his expeditions in Greenland at this time—as he had dreamed of doing at the end of the war—this proved less feasible in Terre Adélie, an example of geography and logistics limiting the use of technology.

FIGURE 11. Raoul Desprez (cook) and Michel Barré (expedition leader) contemplating a cake decorated with a sugar model of Port-Martin, 1951 (Roger Kirschner, Archipôles, IPEV).

But in the early hours of 23 January 1952, Port-Martin's workshop caught fire. Unable to tame the flames, the men could only watch as gale-force winds fed the raging fire. Flames and black smoke engulfed the main building, bursting out the windows and pushing through the roof (figure 12). In just thirty minutes, the living quarters, workshop, garage, and machine shelter were destroyed: the base was reduced to metal frames, blackened and heaped on the rocks, a large oven leaning drunkenly atop. No men or dogs were injured, and the men managed to save their scientific results, but little else could be salvaged from the wreckage. In this, the team was lucky: fire was a huge and often fatal risk at wooden Antarctic bases of the era, and just a few years earlier two men had been killed when a British base on the tip of the Antarctic Peninsula burned down. In a second stroke of luck, the supply ship *Tottan*, which had brought the third team just weeks before, was still nearby and was able to evacuate most of the men. Expéditions polaires françaises had been forced to lease the *Tottan*, a trawler, from Norway after falling out with the French Navy. Small, cramped, and without much in the way of cargo space, the *Tottan* was ill-suited in all ways except cost: at 60 million francs, it was much less expensive than any other option. The men from Expéditions polaires françaises quickly grew fond of the

FIGURE 12. The Port-Martin base burns, 23 January 1952 (Roger Kirschner, Archipôles, IPEV).

Norwegian crew, whose taciturn manner and liberal consumption of aquavit they admired. That the Norwegians had none of the French Navy's disgruntlement with the Antarctic mission, too, helped. While Victor pointed out the disadvantages of relying on a foreign ship to access a French territory from the perspective of sovereignty, the French government was preoccupied by more acute problems.[65] It was only later that lack of independent access would come to be seen as a threat to French sovereignty over the territory.

Even with the base in ruins, the idea of losing the overwinter was anathema to many of the men, and especially to experienced polar hand Mario Marret, who saw presence in Terre Adélie as the linchpin for the legitimacy of France's claim. Marret was also repulsed by the idea of failure: "Morally, the image of our return to France, the mission not accomplished, leaving in place a base razed by fire, seemed intolerable to me," he wrote.[66] After all, this was a time when the French still felt it necessary to emphasize Charles Wilkes's dishonesty in his claim to first sighting.[67] Still, with Port-Martin demolished, means were limited. While the bulk of the third expedition team was forced to leave aboard the *Tottan*, seven men led by Marret remained for a full year at a secondary base on Île des Pétrels, seventy kilometers away from Port-Martin in the Pointe Géologie archipelago. The island had been named during an earlier overwinter for the many snow petrels that nested there, and a small base had deliberately been situated there so as to be near the Emperor penguin rookery discovered in 1950. The wooden base, built and provisioned for four men, was cramped and uncomfortable with seven, but Marret proved to be an exceptional if unconventional leader. A young anarchist, during the war he served in the Resistance as a radio operator for the US Office of Strategic Services in Algeria before being infiltrated into France, where he was captured in the spring of 1944. Four months later, he was exchanged for two Abwehr agents. Marret joined Expéditions polaires françaises as a radio operator, first venturing to the polar regions during the 1948 summer campaign in Greenland. He then joined the first French expedition to Terre Adélie and, with the death of the cinematographer Jacques-André Martin at sea, he took over the filming tasks and found a calling. His first short film, *Terre Adélie*, which narrated the overwinter of 1950, won a prize at the 1954 Venice Biennale.[68] Another film, recorded during the Île des Pétrels overwinter, focused on the Emperor penguin rookery: documenting the penguins' life cycle, detailing their social and breeding habits, and capturing their sounds—the first time their extraordinary full winter breeding cycle had been recorded.[69] Marret was also uncannily skilled in polar techniques, able to repair just about any piece of broken equipment, a skill he put to good use during his year on Île des Pétrels.

When Marret and his men left Terre Adélie at the end of their overwinter in January 1953, there was no team to replace them: the government had declined to provide money to rebuild the Port-Martin base. After three years, French presence in Terre Adélie ended. With no idea when France might mount another Antarctic expedition, Marret and his men arranged some dried flowers, candles, and a welcoming note in their small base before leaving abroad the *Tottan*. The funding promise of 1947 had been on a one-time basis, and the government had neither the inclination nor desire to extend it.[70] This underlines the general lack of interest in Terre Adélie in France at the time. Victor's lobbying efforts—he met with the French president, arranged elaborate public welcomes for each returning ship, and hosted film soirées in France, Britain, and the United States—did not bear fruit this time.[71] This was because of other, significant pressures on the government as well as growing resentment in the upper echelons of the navy toward Expéditions polaires françaises. The navy had never been enthusiastic about the Antarctic mission, only coming on board reluctantly in 1947, and was particularly unhappy with the mission's broad scientific remit. This attitude was incomprehensible to Expéditions polaires françaises, which remained prickly toward the navy, the result of simmering resentment over the time it took to repair the *Commandant Charcot*'s motors in the autumn of 1948. When the rise of hostilities in Indochina put pressure on the military's budget in 1950–1951, the Antarctic fell off the bottom of the navy's priority list.[72] The Ministry of National Defense concurred, arguing that all Antarctic funding should be shifted to Vietnam.[73] The lack of any urgency on the part of the government was also due to the absence of any clear or direct threat to Terre Adélie. Never did the French find themselves in the same situation as the British expedition that arrived at the Antarctic Peninsula's Hope Bay in 1952 to find an Argentinian naval party already present, firing guns over their heads and ordering them to leave.

Already at odds over the failure of the first mission and the costs of the *Commandant Charcot*, the navy sought to end its partnership with Expéditions polaires françaises on the basis that sovereignty had been reasserted in Terre Adélie and thus that the mission was complete. This way of thinking was antithetical to Victor, who saw continual presence as the only method of ensuring that sovereignty. Soon, tensions between the Expéditions polaires françaises team and the naval personnel were palpable. It did not help that Victor lost one of his best contacts in the armed forces, General Delaye, when he was sent to Indochina.[74] In August 1951, the *Service hydrographique de la marine* ordered the navy to stop all work for the Antarctic expeditions and to recuperate the navy's instruments and equipment from the *Commandant Charcot*.[75] The navy then disposed of the

Commandant Charcot and refused to put any more personnel to Expéditions polaires françaises' disposition. More broadly, the armed forces as a whole began turning down Victor's requests for equipment, explaining that they had to put Indochina and French North Africa first and no longer had excess capacity for the Antarctic. From then on, for decades, Expéditions polaires françaises would lease foreign ships to access Terre Adélie.

Victor and Expéditions polaires françaises had other critics, too. In the early to mid-1950s Victor found himself in a feud with R. Pierre Lejay, an influential Jesuit geophysicist. The son of a navy rear admiral, Lejay entered the Society of Jesus in 1915 and was ordained in 1926; he also earned a doctorate in mathematics at the Sorbonne. Soon, Lejay left France for China, where he worked at and then directed the ZiKaWei observatory near Shanghai. Operated by the Jesuit Fathers of the French Province, ZiKaWei was at the time the largest private meteorological organization in the world, connected to a network of stations spanning from Siberia to Manila to Guam.[76] There, Lejay's interests included geodesy, meteorology, the high atmosphere, and radiotelegraphy. Most ambitiously, he conferred with General Chiang Kai-shek about the feasibility of mapping the whole of China, something Lejay thought possible to accomplish within five years owing to his technical inventions.[77] After the war, Lejay returned to France and became active in Parisian scientific circles: he was named director of the Ionospheric Bureau and president of the National Center for Gravimetric Studies, and elected as a member of the prestigious Academy of Sciences. He was deeply unimpressed with Victor and Expéditions polaires françaises, which Lejay thought spent too much money, were poorly organized, and conducted inadequate scientific work. When he was named president of Expéditions polaires françaises' scientific commission, Lejay became an opponent close to home. This conflict would come to a head during France's preparation for the International Geophysical Year of 1957–1958.

Even in the period from 1948 to 1953, it was a struggle for Expéditions polaires françaises to access the funds it had been promised. The second and the third expeditions were on-again, off-again as funding transfers were repeatedly delayed, and the navy's growing disinclination toward the enterprise caused enormous stress within Expéditions polaires françaises.[78] The revolving door of Fourth Republic governments did not help, either: soon after Auriol granted Expéditions polaires françaises his patronage in 1947, the ministerial instability of the postwar political system became clear. Government coalitions were undisciplined and insecure, and the actions of the Communists after they left government led to social unrest, strikes, and violent clashes with the police. Steep rises in the cost of living further inflamed social conflict and unleashed riots. Sabotage on the Paris-Tourcoing rail line in late 1947 killed nearly twenty people.

Between political instability, social upheaval, labor disruptions, and the situation in Indochina, the Antarctic was far from the minds of the French political class. It was quiet threats such as that Liotard made in 1951 that kept the money flowing: in that year, Liotard wrote directly to the president, saying that his Australian counterparts were showing interest in operating in Terre Adélie themselves and would fill any vacuum left by the French.[79] The threat of annexation, it seemed, had not disappeared.

Likewise, there was no sustained interest in the Antarctic in the public sphere in the early 1950s. This was despite Victor's efforts to publicize (and raise money for) Expéditions polaires françaises through film soirées, some of which were even attended by the president of the Republic. Brief spikes of interest, spurred by specific events, were the exception to this rule. There was a spike of public interest when Dumont d'Urville's route logs from his Antarctic voyage were discovered in a private library in Isère. Dumont d'Urville, who died in the Versailles rail disaster of 1842, had left the logs with Clément Adrien Vincendon-Dumoulin, his hydrographer. Vincendon-Dumoulin used the logs to compile the expedition's official publications when he took over responsibility for documenting the voyage after Dumont d'Urville's untimely death. Left among his effects when he died in 1858, the logs resurfaced in late 1948, drawing a brief flurry of attention.[80]

There was a second spike of interest when Expéditions polaires françaises sought adoptive families for the sled dogs used in Terre Adélie. In late 1952, when it became clear that no funding was forthcoming for a new base and that French presence in the territory would have to end, Victor radioed Marret, asking him what he wanted to do with the dogs. Marret's response was immediate: "Refuse to slaughter dogs which we will bring back STOP have confidence in you to find solution."[81] The men were attached to the dogs, one of whom had been born on the *Commandant Charcot* and was bottle-fed at Port-Martin after its dam died in a storm, and dreaded the possibility of having to kill them. Victor launched an appeal on the radio and in newspapers throughout France to find adoptive homes for the dogs. "Lack of funding: The 25 Esquimo dogs of the Liotard expedition threatened with slaughter," read the headlines. Twenty-four hours after the appeal went out, three thousand volunteers came forward: the problem was not finding new homes for the dogs but choosing among the many options. When Marret received the good news, it was, he wrote, "one of the happiest moments of our entire stay!"[82]

But this interest was only sporadic. For the French public, activity in Terre Adélie was seen as a series of exciting but intermittent and discrete events, ones that generated intense but short-lived interest.[83] This interest was spurred primarily by media reports, themselves only irregular and fleeting. Reporter François

Courtet's description of the French attitude toward Terre Adélie at the time as one of "total disinterest" was accurate.[84] Still, the actions taken in this era laid the groundwork for supporting France's claim to Terre Adélie: putting men on the ground, erecting bases, establishing an on-the-ground administrative presence, and building geographic and scientific knowledge about the territory. Together, these elements provided a foundation for legitimating the French claim in a geopolitical environment that was about to become much more heated.

6
GROWING MATURITY

While Terre Adélie had been administered by Madagascar since 1924, by the mid-1950s this was no longer tenable. Between Madagascar's move toward independence and a growing desire to reaffirm French sovereignty over its most distant possession, Terre Adélie needed to be pulled closer to the Hexagon. The link with Madagascar had always been tenuous at best. While legal decrees tied the Antarctic territory to the Indian Ocean colony, in practice it was a fictional link: there was no geographic, historical, nor economic connection. Neither did Madagascar have the financial, logistical, or technical means to access Terre Adélie or to establish an administrative presence there. After World War II, it became harder to maintain with a straight face that Madagascar contributed to any real effective authority over Terre Adélie. The crux of the matter was made clear by Robert Bargues, the inspector general for Overseas France: "The administrative attachment to Madagascar could seem, to a certain extent, theoretical," he asserted in a speech in late 1950.[1] With Expéditions polaires françaises' expeditions of 1949–1953, it became clear that Terre Adélie's future lay not with an island off Africa's eastern coast but with polar experts in Paris. Madagascar's Representative Assembly recognized the inherent problem and soon announced that it was in favor of the austral territories being detached from Madagascar and administered directly from the Hexagon.[2]

In Madagascar, too, the political situation was in flux. In late 1945, the *Mouvement démocratique de la rénovation malgache* (Democratic Movement for Malagasy Rejuvenation) began to push for independence in an early postwar challenge to France's colonial empire. By the spring of 1947, the nationalist movement was spreading across the island. It was violently repressed by eighteen thousand French forces who drew on weapons of terror—including torture, rape, and mass executions—to quash the uprising. Officially, 11,200 people were killed, but historians have estimated the real number to be much higher, possibly as high as two hundred thousand.³ By early 1949, the nationalists were defeated and their leaders imprisoned. For a short while, it seemed that Malagasy independence had been thwarted. But with the Việt Minh victory in Indochina in 1954—after an eight-year war, financially and morally devastating for France—the potential independence of other French colonies became a political reality. France's Socialist government passed the *loi-cadre Defferre* in 1956, transferring powers from Paris to French colonies in Africa. Named for Gaston Defferre, the overseas minister, the law introduced almost-universal suffrage: while Africans living in French colonies had become French citizens in 1946, the vast majority were deprived of the right to vote until the new law. The law also devolved power toward territorial assemblies and abolished the different electoral colleges for Europeans and non-Europeans. Still, it was designed not to encourage equivalence or decolonization, but as an "active attempt to renegotiate imperial policy and perpetuate French influence overseas" by transferring direct administration but retaining ultimate control.⁴ Regardless, the law's reforms built the framework for Madagascar's independence. The Malagasy Republic was declared in October 1958 and full independence was achieved in 1960.

Taken together, these events pushed the French government to question Terre Adélie's attachment to Madagascar. Noting the growing international interest in the Antarctic and sub-Antarctic regions, Bargues, the inspector general, called for the government in Paris "itself to directly exert its authority over these faraway lands."⁵ While the overseas minister, Louis Jacquinot, introduced legislation to this effect in 1951, the instability of Fourth Republic governments meant that nothing happened quickly. Finally, on 6 August 1955, Terre Adélie, together with France's remote and uninhabited sub-Antarctic possessions (Crozet, Kerguelen, and the Îles Saint-Paul and Nouvelle-Amsterdam), were folded by law into a *Territoire d'outre-mer*, or overseas territory.⁶ The new territory, called *Terres australes et antarctiques françaises* (French Southern and Antarctic Lands, or TAAF), was headquartered in Paris.⁷ A legal entity with administrative and financial autonomy, funded through the Overseas Ministry, TAAF was managed by a chief administrator (*administrateur supérieur*) named by the Council of Ministers and charged with the powers of the Republic in the territory.⁸ The chief administrator was assisted by a consultative council made up of members named by the implicated ministries for periods of five years. This political and administrative setup was expressly designed for possessions with neither Indigenous nor permanent populations. Since TAAF's four districts had no electors, TAAF had no elected representatives in the French parliament.

The TAAF districts were linked by neither history nor geography nor climate: they included a slice of the Antarctic and a handful of archipelagos scattered in the southern Indian Ocean, some discovered by French and some by Castilian and Portuguese navigators. They were, however, linked by isolation and a lack of Indigenous inhabitants and permanent populations, as well as by their previous attachment to Madagascar. In terms of France's overseas empire, they represented the ends of Earth. As François Garde, TAAF's chief administrator from 2000 to 2004, has noted, they were grouped together in 1955 as a marriage of convenience: given the need to transfer their attachment from Madagascar to Paris, it was simplest from an administrative point of view to keep the group of uninhabited possessions as one.[9] Over the ensuing decades, the districts posed very different logistical, administrative, and legal challenges. Being grouped with the other districts in a single administrative bracket would later prove problematic for Terre Adélie, when it was singled out as having the least economic potential.

The creation of TAAF in 1955 was also prompted by growing concern about France's hold over its austral possessions. In an era of increasing international interest in the Antarctic and sub-Antarctic, as well as sweeping geopolitical changes affecting the region and France's overseas presence more broadly, the Fourth Republic felt compelled to reaffirm sovereignty over these districts for several reasons.

First, the wartime use of Kerguelen as a supply and rest station by the Germans highlighted the vulnerability of the austral districts. Early in the war, Kerguelen was visited by German auxiliary cruisers, which took advantage of the lack of human presence in the archipelago to repair their boats and replenish fresh water and food supplies. These incursions were only discovered when Australia sent a naval ship to the islands in late 1941. After the war, Australia openly declared its interest in Kerguelen, prompted by the security implications of leaving a vacuum. Starting in 1947, Australian scientific expeditions landed in Kerguelen, where they made magnetic observations and visited the abandoned French whaling station.[10] The political rumblings of the previous decades resurfaced. France needed to make a choice: establish permanent presence in Kerguelen or risk Australian annexation. The belief among high-ranking French officers that Kerguelen was strategically important pushed France to decide to establish presence there. These officers saw Kerguelen, situated equidistant between South Africa and Australia, as a strategically valuable waypoint for ships in an otherwise empty expanse of ocean.[11] "The role of Kerguelen in controlling Atlantic-Pacific lines of communication in case of conflict will be essential," wrote Robert Genty, a French Air Force colonel seconded to the Ministry of National Defence: "He who possesses Kerguelen will become master of sea and air links between the two big oceans and will control traffic in the southern Indian Ocean."[12] If France did not establish presence in Kerguelen, the French government realized, either the Australians or the Americans would step in and take over. In 1949, France announced its intention to build a base in Kerguelen. Named Port-aux-Français, the base saw its first overwinter in 1951 and has been occupied ever since. For similar reasons, a base, named Camp-Heurtin, was built on Nouvelle-Amsterdam to serve both Nouvelle-Amsterdam and Saint-Paul.[13]

Second, the rapid loss of overseas territory during decolonization also pushed France to affirm sovereignty over its remaining possessions, including the remote and unpopulated ones. As the colonial system was dismantled, it slowly became clear that the future of France's overseas ambitions was going to look very different from the past. With Hồ Chí Minh's decisive victory at the Battle of Điện Biên Phủ in 1954, France withdrew its forces from all its colonies in Indochina and relinquished all claims to territory on the Indochinese peninsula. In the same neighborhood, Laos and Cambodia had gained full independence a year earlier. In Africa and the Maghreb, where French influence had likewise reigned, the situation was similar. Pro-independence fighters in French Cameroun began a guerrilla war in 1955, leading to independence in 1960, while Morocco regained its independence from France in the spring of 1956. Of pressing concern to the Fourth Republic was the Algerian War, which began in 1954 and sparked a series of political crises in France, consuming the country for eight years.[14] This war led to the collapse of the Fourth Republic and the return of Charles de Gaulle to power in 1958 before Algeria won its independence in 1962—political events that would directly affect Terre Adélie. As these conflicts grew and their ramifications became clearer in the early to mid-1950s, there was a desire to pull together France's remaining overseas territories, regardless of their size, remoteness, or population, and reaffirm sovereignty over them. For Terre Adélie and the sub-Antarctic islands, this meant a new administrative structure, governed from Paris, and legal attachment to the Hexagon, all of which was achieved through the creation of TAAF. While they did not form a large or politically significant portion of France's overseas presence, the TAAF districts did, in their own modest way, help maintain France's prestige and place in the world when its colonial empire was collapsing. By virtue of being devoid of Indigenous inhabitants, too, the TAAF districts floated above the thorny problem of how to reconcile the Algerian War with the idea, so intrinsic to French identity, of the *mission civilisatrice*.

Finally, rising international interest in the Antarctic after World War II also forced France to reconsider Terre Adélie's status. Beginning with Operation

Highjump in 1946–1947, the United States made clear its ambitious plans for the white continent. Operation Highjump provided Expéditions polaires françaises with thousands of aerial photos of Terre Adélie—photos that, while not of practical use due to technical problems, were still a sharp reminder that France lacked any aerial capacity in Antarctica. Being outperformed by the United States in terms of creating maps and developing terrain knowledge did not bode well for France's claim to sovereignty. The sheer scale, ambitious nature, and technological superiority of Operation Highjump and its successor, Operation Windmill, made the French expeditions of the early 1950s seem small and insignificant.[15] This American activity in Antarctica, coupled with concurrent Argentine and Chilean expeditions as well as the British Falkland Islands Dependencies Surveys, drew attention to the continent and the uncertain state of its sovereignty claims. By the mid-1950s, Norway, Sweden, Australia, and the USSR were also active in the Antarctic, and South Africa and New Zealand were making plans for the continent. While the French claim to Terre Adélie had been reinforced by the expeditions of 1949–1953, there was still a need to pull Terre Adélie closer to the Hexagon and to make clear France's intention of retaining sovereignty over its slice of the Antarctic—and the creation of TAAF in 1955 served these ends.

In line with the motivation for its creation, TAAF had four principal missions: assuring French sovereignty, conducting scientific investigations, providing meteorological services, and inventorying and exploiting natural resources in its districts. As France had already formally claimed the districts and linked them administratively to the Hexagon, the next step in the assertion of sovereignty was presence: TAAF aimed to establish permanent French bases in every austral district. From the outset, these were envisioned as scientific bases in recognition of the role of science in performing sovereignty in remote and uninhabited lands—something that had been encouraged by earlier international legal decisions about other remote territories and that other claimant states, especially Britain, were making matter in the Antarctic. In Nouvelle-Amsterdam and Kerguelen, bases had existed since 1949–1950, providing homes for small, rotating teams of scientists. TAAF continued to support and expand these bases, including setting up meteorological stations in conjunction with the *Direction de la météorologie nationale*. These stations relayed daily observations to France and to countries with interests in the Indian Ocean (namely, Australia and South Africa) and also conducted research in climatology and high-altitude physics.[16] But when TAAF was founded in 1955, neither Terre Adélie nor the Crozet archipelago had bases or, indeed, any French presence at all. In Terre Adélie, presence was soon reestablished thanks to the International Geophysical Year of 1957–1958, while Crozet had to wait until early in the following decade. With regard to TAAF's resource mission, there was no discussion of resource exploitation in Terre Adélie during TAAF's early years. At this time, TAAF's resource outlook focused on the sub-Antarctic districts, where it included the exploitation of marine resources (algae, spiny lobster, and fish), attempts at sheep and reindeer farming (with reindeer imported from Lapland, in addition to the sheep that brought earlier from the Falklands by the Bossière brothers), and plans to harvest sea elephants for oil and bonemeal.[17]

The creation of a new administrative structure for Terre Adélie meant changes for Expéditions polaires françaises. Until 1955, Expéditions polaires françaises had a large degree of freedom in its activities. It was a private polar organization, something that differentiated it from all big polar programs in other countries. While Expéditions polaires françaises was reliant on government funds—it did raise funds privately, but its bipolar programs were too expensive to be sustained with private funding alone—it had been largely free from political considerations from its inception in 1947. This changed with the creation of TAAF. In 1955, TAAF became responsible for Terre Adélie, taking charge of the district's administration, facilities, budget, and planning, while Expéditions polaires françaises was transformed into a contractor carrying out work in the Antarctic. All funding for Terre Adélie now passed through TAAF, which exerted oversight over Expéditions polaires françaises' budget. Expéditions polaires françaises was required to keep TAAF "constantly informed" about its activities and spending.[18] With respect to science, TAAF became responsible for conceiving of and developing annual scientific campaigns and long-term scientific projects in the Antarctic and sub-Antarctic. Expéditions polaires françaises' remit was to execute those programs by providing the necessary logistics, organization, transport, and infrastructure.[19] As Expéditions polaires françaises became drawn into TAAF's political orbit, its role, as the American Antarctic scientist and naval officer Leonard LeSchack wrote, "changed from that of constituting essentially the entire French Arctic and Antarctic program to its present function of supplying the logistics for a larger, more developed, permanent program."[20] Paul-Emile Victor chafed at the new administrative structure, resentful of the divide between what he saw as Expéditions polaires françaises' demotion within France and the organization's stellar international reputation: in the mid-1950s, for example, both Japan and Belgium expressly used Expéditions polaires françaises as a model when designing their own national polar organizations, and the US military even called on Expéditions polaires françaises to help solve scientific and technical problems.[21] Tensions came to the surface as Victor pushed back against the new supervisory structures, repeatedly complaining to the French presidency.[22] While Expéditions polaires françaises remained a private organization, it no longer enjoyed the freedoms of its first eight years, and became more and more entangled with government structures.

New Impetus: The International Geophysical Year

When TAAF was created in 1955, France had no base and no presence in Terre Adélie. After Port-Martin burned, there was no money forthcoming to build a new base and Victor's dream of continual French presence in Terre Adélie was cut short. For TAAF, this presented a problem: without presence, there was no way of securing French sovereignty. TAAF saw science, and the presence and authority imparted by scientific bases, expeditions, and knowledge generation, as the chief means of performing sovereignty in its districts. Before long, a solution came in the form of the International Geophysical Year (IGY) of 1957–1958, which gave new impetus to French state interest in the Antarctic.

The IGY was an unprecedented global program of scientific data collection and observation, a cooperative effort of sixty-seven countries and thousands of scientists.[23] Envisioned as a successor to the First and Second Polar Years, which took place respectively in 1882–1883 and 1932–1933, the idea for the IGY was first raised in the United States in the early 1950s. With the advent of computing, radar, and rockets, the scope of the project was expanded from the polar regions to encompass the geophysics of the globe as a whole. The timing—from 1 July 1957 to 31 December 1958—was chosen to coincide with an expected maximum in solar activity. The Antarctic, a region of exceptional geophysical and geographical interest, formed a major component of the IGY: twelve countries were active on the white continent during the project. Britain, Argentina, the United States, and the USSR all installed seven or more stations. Hundreds of men and thousands of tons of material were brought to the Antarctic by ship and by plane, representing massive financial and logistical investment, one of the largest and most expensive scientific projects ever envisaged to that point.

The IGY's chief aim was a coordinated, open, civilian program of concurrent data collection, analysis, and exchange across the globe to study geophysical phenomena on a large scale. Equally, however, it was an international scientific enterprise operating outside of politics at a time of tension across East and West, an audacious project with deep implications for the production, circulation, and exchange of scientific data as well as for international relations. With the Korean Armistice Agreement in July 1953 and Joseph Stalin's death earlier that year, the way was paved for scientific cooperation between the West and the USSR, and the IGY emerged as a respected and unifying project in the early Cold War. While this ideal was certainly not perfectly realized in practice, the level of international cooperation seen during the IGY (such as friendly exchanges of scientific personnel between the Americans and Soviets in Antarctica) was impressive given the geopolitical climate of the era.[24] Particularly noteworthy was that the Antarctic claimant states allowed other states unimpeded access to work in, and even build bases in, claimed territories—something almost unthinkable in other parts of the world. Political tensions were, unsurprisingly, not completely erased, something seen in particular in the depiction of territorial claims on maps. The location of many Antarctic bases, too, was motivated not by scientific considerations but by political ones.[25]

While tensions over the Antarctic were in principle put to the side for the duration of the IGY, in France the political reality of mass activity on the white continent could not be ignored. "It has been announced that the Americans will equip 50 boats, an air and submarine fleet, with an expeditionary corps of 10,000 men, as well as colossal vehicles built to roll over the ice despite its cracks and chasms," *Revue des deux mondes*, a respected cultural, literary, and current affairs periodical, announced in 1955: "It is thus an enterprise that seems as political as it is scientific."[26] Describing the IGY as a combination of "cooperation and rivalry" in *Le Monde*, Paul-Emile Victor pointed out that France needed to join the "crowd" making its way to the Antarctic or risk being excluded from the continent's future.[27] And as the writer Xavier Reppe reminded his country, France had a poor record of conserving the fruits of its explorers, having already lost Bouvet, Prince Edward, and Marion Islands, and having failed to protest when the British annexed the Antarctic Peninsula.[28] As other countries made their interest in and ambitions for the Antarctic visible, the French government came to realize that France could scarcely stay out and hope to retain a claim to authority over a slice of the Antarctic pie. The lack of French presence in Terre Adélie since early 1953 took on new meaning: only with presence could France demonstrate sovereignty over this territory. Soon, the government committed almost 1.5 billion francs for the IGY, of which 900 million were earmarked for bases in Terre Adélie.[29] This amount was widely criticized by scientists and in the media as being too low, leaving France at risk of being eclipsed by other countries with higher budgets, but it was grudgingly accepted as the best possible outcome given the enormous financial pressures of the situation in Algeria.[30]

In France, the Academy of Sciences took charge of preparations. These efforts were led by R. Pierre Lejay, the Jesuit geophysicist who had long been a vocal opponent of Victor and Expéditions polaires françaises. Lejay soon recruited Bertrand Imbert to head France's Antarctic program for the IGY. During the war, Imbert had joined the Free French Navy, operating in North Africa and landing on the Normandy coast in June 1944, where his frigate, *La Surprise*, protected the American battleship *Augusta* from German attack. After a brief postwar stint in Indochina, Imbert was seconded from the navy in order to participate in Expéditions polaires françaises' expeditions to Terre Adélie. When he was contacted by Lejay, he cut short a hydrographical expedition in Morocco to return to France. It was immediately clear to Imbert that only one organization in France had the logistical know-how to operate in the Antarctic: Expéditions polaires françaises. But for years Lejay had been combative toward Victor and his organization, criticizing them in Parisian political and scientific circles, accusing them of scientific and logistical shortcomings and of wasting public funds.[31] Given his eminence, Lejay's words carried weight, especially in the Academy of Sciences, where he found sympathetic ears. There was also a feeling in the upper echelons of the academy that the private nature of Expéditions polaires françaises was problematic as it meant that the government lacked control over the organization. But practicalities settled the matter quickly: as Imbert pointed out, only Expéditions polaires françaises could get the job done. A contract was soon signed stipulating that the Academy of Sciences would define the scientific work to be done while Expéditions polaires françaises would be responsible for operations and logistics. The French Army was involved, too, lending Imbert heavy tracked vehicles for transport in Terre Adélie, the protracted negotiation of which made clear that Expéditions polaires françaises' previous dispute with the navy colored the way the entire French armed forces saw Antarctic endeavors.[32]

Imbert planned three expeditions to Terre Adélie for the IGY: a preparatory expedition in 1956, followed by two scientific expeditions from 1957 to 1959. In October 1955, the first team left France aboard the *Norsel*, packed to the brim with materials to build and supply two bases, as well as five tracked vehicles, an enormous tractor, and sleds. Wooden crates were piled every which way on the deck and no space, however small, was left empty. On the day of departure, gray and overcast, hundreds of family and friends lined Rouen's concrete dock, the men dressed formally in suits and long coats, the women wearing hats, and the children stiff in school uniforms.[33] As the *Norsel*'s Norwegian captain, Guttorm Jakobsen, sounded the ship's horn three times, all the men assembled on the bridge for the departure. Robert Guillard, the leader of the preparatory expedition, was struck by the enormity of leaving his wife and infant son, Thierry, for over a year.[34]

Expéditions polaires françaises had been forced to lease the *Norsel* from Norway after the split with the navy and the loss of the (in any case largely inadequate) *Commandant Charcot*. The *Norsel* had originally been built as an icebreaking tug for the *Kriegsmarine* by the German occupiers of Norway but was not finished before the end of the war. After the war, it was purchased by a Tromsø-based company and fitted out for sealing. Before being chartered by the French in 1955, the *Norsel* had visited the Antarctic as part of the Norwegian-British-Swedish Antarctic Expedition (1949–1952) and the Falkland Islands Dependencies Survey (1954–1955). Known as *Polarbussen* (the Polar Bus), the ship was scarred from its many encounters with the ice, neglected and sad in appearance.[35] But Imbert knew that its captain and his Norwegian crew had a stellar reputation. Still, that France was leasing a foreign ship to access Terre Adélie was a point of contention: why, Reppe asked, when the Americans, the Soviets, and the British owned massive polar icebreakers, did France "need to relegate herself to the last rank, by continuing to lease a foreign ship of 600 tons [which can only] transport twenty-five people and less than 200 tons of cargo?"[36]

After leaving Rouen, the *Norsel* called at Algiers, Aden, Melbourne, and Hobart en route to Terre Adélie. Through the Suez Canal, it had a military escort due to ongoing tensions between France and Egypt. And when the ship reached the Red Sea, Captain Jakobson stopped to allow his passengers to bathe in the biblical waters. This preparatory expedition also marked Paul-Emile Victor's first trip to the Antarctic. Victor, who had flown to Australia to avoid the months-long sea journey, joined the ship in Melbourne. Previously, Victor had been too involved in Expéditions polaires françaises' work in Greenland to travel to Terre Adélie.

The *Norsel* arrived in Terre Adélie on New Year's Day 1956, almost three years to the day since the last French presence in the Antarctic territory. The fourteen-member team, led by Guillard, was tasked with building two bases and preparing them for the opening of the IGY on 1 July 1957. A veteran of the Resistance, Guillard had assisted in the liberation of Lyon and the campaign in Alsace. After the war, he entered the *École militaire de haute montagne*, where he specialized in the maintenance of tracked vehicles. During a sojourn in Austria to practice high-mountain parachuting, he met Victor. Recognizing Guillard's technical aptitude, Victor asked the young man to join Expéditions polaires françaises. Between 1948 and 1951, Guillard spent nearly all his time in Greenland—but still he found time to become a national bobsleigh champion and compete for France at the 1952 Winter Olympics in Norway. Between his close friendship with Victor, his vast experience in polar environments, and his unparalleled technical know-how, Guillard was a natural choice to lead the preparatory team to Terre Adélie.

It took Guillard and his men two weeks to unload supplies from the *Norsel* by hand, laboriously, one item at a time, until a mountain of wooden crates sat upon the exposed rock, each one labeled in black stenciled lettering, an edifice of great curiosity for the many penguins who crowded around. Rather than rebuild at the hellishly cold and windy Port-Martin site, the new main base was situated at the site of Mario Marret's old hut on Île des Pétrels, near the Emperor penguin rookery, a location with marginally calmer weather. The base was named Dumont-d'Urville in honor of the French explorer who had discovered the territory. Upon arrival at the site, Guillard and Victor found Marret's hut still intact, with the welcoming note, candles, and dried flowers left three years earlier, all atop a checkered green tablecloth. Thanks to the lessons of the Port-Martin fire, Dumont-d'Urville was built from prefabricated metal buildings erected on scaffolding over the irregular rock surface: fireproof, lightweight, and able to withstand the weight of snow accumulation. The base consisted of living quarters, a workshop, a kitchen, a mess, a bathroom, a darkroom, a laundry room, and sleeping quarters, all kept warm—or at least tolerably warm—by fuel oil generators. In anticipation of the base being buried by snow, the windows were almost all in the roof (figure 13). Surrounding the main base were eleven small wooden shelters for scientific work, as well as a garage for maintaining the tracked vehicles and sleds.[37]

The preparatory team then transported a second, smaller base over the ice sheet to a site near the magnetic south pole, 320 kilometers south of the Dumont-d'Urville base, in preparation for two three-man overwinters to take place during the IGY. The base and supplies (including 360 kilograms of flour, 35 kilograms of lentils, 15 kilograms of carrots, 1,200 packs of cigarettes, and one game of Monopoly), a total of more than forty tons, were mounted on long skates and towed by Sno-Cats and Weasels, tracked vehicles specially built for polar conditions. The team of seven men, led by Guillard, left Dumont-d'Urville in early October 1956 and only arrived at their destination at Christmas: ferocious weather prevented them from traveling for 100 of the 120 days of their traverse.

FIGURE 13. The first two buildings for the Dumont-d'Urville base, built for the International Geophysical Year, 1956 (Archipôles, IPEV).

One-meter-deep sastrugis—snow dunes, as smooth as marble and as hard as rock, easily capable of breaking Caterpillar tracks—reduced the average speed to five kilometers an hour and the vehicles struggled to stay upright in the howling winds and uneven terrain.[38] Guillard's years of experience maintaining and repairing tracked vehicles proved essential to the traverse's success. The immense difficulty of this overland traverse highlighted the lack of French aviation capacity in the Antarctic: Imbert would have preferred to establish the inland base with air support, but he could secure neither an airplane nor the help of the Armée de l'air.[39] This lack of aviation capacity would become a recurring theme over the following decades.

Arrival: snow as far as the eye could see in all directions, a white desert stretching to the horizon, not smooth but ridged and sculpted by the wind, rough edges throwing shadows helter-skelter, no indication other than from the sextant that they were in the right place. To the Frenchmen, it was at once nothing and everything: the blankest of slates, the riskiest of endeavors, and the most necessary. Exhausted from the arduous traverse, the men still needed to build the base from prefabricated semicylindrical sections of sheet metal, a form designed to withstand the pressure of snow accumulation, and dig out a 130 cubic meter hole by hand to accommodate it.[40] When this was completed, the base, named Station Charcot, was slid gently into the hole by two Sno-Cats. During the first night, a blizzard hit, whipping snow like froth and completely burying the base. The following morning, only the two ventilation shafts and the radio masts, which reached several meters up into the air, were visible. Station Charcot looked like a submarine frozen into the ice (figure 14). Atop one of the masts flapped the French flag, a declaration of France's presence in the deep interior of Terre Adélie. For the entirety of the IGY, the base could only be accessed via trapdoors in the roof.

Early in 1957, the second French team arrived in Terre Adélie. The voyage, again aboard the *Norsel*, had been long and dull: with the nationalization of the Suez Canal by Egyptian president Gamal Abdel Nasser, the ship was forced to take the long route around, passing through the Panama Canal.[41] The team of twenty-three men, led by Imbert, found their quarters uncomfortable, smelly, and cramped, and many suffered from weeks of seasickness. Upon arrival in Terre Adélie, they installed scientific equipment at the Dumont-d'Urville base and, with the official launch of the IGY on 1 July 1957, began a year of data collection and studies. Their work was continued by the third team, which arrived in 1958, led by Gaston Rouillon, an alpinist and veteran of three expeditions to Greenland. The French scientific program included extensive work on high-altitude circulation, katabatic winds, snow accumulation, ice thickness, magnetism, the high atmosphere and ionosphere, and south polar auroras.[42] In the

FIGURE 14. Station Charcot buried in the snow, 1957 (Archipôles, IPEV).

spirit of the IGY, the team at the Dumont-d'Urville base was also in daily radio contact with the Soviet teams at Mirny and the American teams at McMurdo, and weekly contact with the British, New Zealanders, and Australians.

Of the twelve countries who built bases in the Antarctic during the IGY, only three—France, the United States, and the USSR—dared to overwinter in the continent's interior. For Imbert, the two overwinters at Station Charcot were not debatable: France *needed* to be present in the continent's interior, a need as essential for political considerations as for scientific ones. It was a risky endeavor with no chance of rescue should something go wrong over the long austral winters, with their extreme cold temperatures, ferocious winds, and powerful blizzards. Overwintering in the interior was meant to prove French capability on the great ice sheet, to demonstrate the success of made-in-France polar technologies, and to send a clear message about future ambition. Acutely aware that the United States and the USSR were investing much more heavily in the Antarctic, Imbert and the Academy of Sciences saw Station Charcot as an essential symbol of France's commitment to the white continent.[43] The choice of location, too, was symbolic. By situating Station Charcot near the magnetic south pole, Imbert carved out a place for France in the landscape defined by the two superpowers: the American interior station, Amundsen-Scott, was located at the geographic South Pole and its Soviet homologue, Vostok, at the southern pole of inaccessibility.[44] Indeed, Station Charcot provides the quintessential example of what Aant Elzinga calls the "siting of new research stations [based on] the political need to demonstrate a presence."[45] Entirely cut off from the rest of the world with no possibility of relief, escape, or help, the two teams of three Frenchmen endured twenty-four-hour darkness and temperatures that plunged to minus 40°C in their laboratory.[46] Indeed, the project was so risky given the limited means at Imbert's disposal that he had a hard time convincing his superiors to give it the green light. He did so by taking preparatory measures to the extreme: among other precautions, the men who were to spend the year at Station Charcot had their appendixes removed before they left France.[47]

Station Charcot was very much the poor man's effort: whereas the United States and the USSR used airplanes and enormously long trains of tracked vehicles to transport large teams of men and thousands of tons of material into the interior from their respective coastal bases of McMurdo and Mirny, the French effort was small and entirely dependent on small-scale land transport. These arduous traverses saw their passengers imprisoned for days on end in the vehicles while storms raged outside. With the motors off to save fuel, the cold was biting, and between the lack of visibility and howling blizzards, the men endured extreme discomfort when venturing outside to relieve themselves. The French traverses were mentally trying—as were the overwinters at Station Charcot. Near misses included carbon monoxide poisoning and the only man with extensive medical training falling seriously ill. A windmill, which was supposed to generate electricity for lights and radio contact with Dumont-d'Urville, also failed catastrophically during the first winter. When he had not heard from Station Charcot in weeks, Imbert, who was overwintering at Dumont-d'Urville, had to decide between sending out an overland rescue team in the heart of the polar winter—by any estimatation, an extremely risky proposition—or asking the Americans or Soviets for help. In the end, he did ask the Soviets for a reconnaissance flight over Station Charcot, but with no radio contact and perpetual darkness, there was no chance of finding the station from the air. Even given the spirit of the IGY, this reliance on a foreign country to come to the help of Frenchmen in a French territory did not bode well for sovereignty. All this was a far cry from the American and Soviet interior stations with their sophisticated facilities, creature comforts, and air links to the coast. At Amundsen-Scott, located at the South Pole, the Americans enjoyed barracks, a galley and mess hall, a photography lab, a chapel, a garage, and several buildings for scientific work.[48] There, the eight scientists were supported by another eight naval personnel. Still, the men at Station Charcot found ways of alleviating the harsh conditions of their overwinter: at midwinter, on 21 June 1957, they enjoyed a special dinner including Tahitian punch, asparagus and ham, vol-au-vent, chicken, chocolate biscuits, fruit tart, coffee, and cognac.[49]

FIGURE 15. A stamp issued by France for the International Geophysical Year—note Terre Adélie highlighted in the bottom left.

Even though the IGY was designed to be apolitical, and there was tacit agreement among the participating nations that political arguments over Antarctica were to be put to the side for its duration, still performances of sovereignty were common. In addition to flying the tricolore over the two bases, the French also issued several new postal stamps declaring their presence in Terre Adélie, erected plaques and monuments, and printed postcards and other paraphernalia highlighting the "French Antarctic" (figure 15). And in 1958, the French president, René Coty, received and congratulated Imbert and the members of his Antarctic expedition, decorating them with the *Étoile noire du Bénin* for their contributions toward *rayonnement* and France's influence in the world.[50] The choice of this award was carefully made, and represented Terre Adélie's rising importance to France's overseas stature in a time of rapid territorial loss.

French scientific work during the IGY cemented the country's reputation as a powerhouse in Antarctic science—something that would bring benefits for decades to come. Most immediately, this status was recognized when, upon the creation of the Scientific Committee on Antarctic Research (SCAR) in 1957–1958, the French geographer Georges Laclavère was elected as its first president.[51] But despite France's scientific successes during the IGY, it ended in tragedy on 7 January 1959 when, just hours before the *Norsel* was due to arrive and transport the third expedition team back home, the meteorologist André Prud'homme disappeared in a blizzard while taking measurements only two hundred meters from the Dumont-d'Urville base. He was presumed drowned.

Toward the Antarctic Treaty

Far from being an isolated event, a self-contained year and a half of intense scientific work, the IGY ultimately transformed Antarctic politics and laid the groundwork for the continent's future management. At its best, the IGY offered a vision of Antarctica as a cooperative laboratory for scientific inquiry, a place of mutual advancement of human knowledge, even of friendship and peace. The idea of returning to the pre-IGY state of rising tensions in the Antarctic, especially given the enmity of the Cold War and the impact of the East-West divide on geopolitics, was far from desirable. The Antarctic stood out as a pristine environment, one of the least touched places on Earth, and there was a growing desire to protect it from becoming yet another site of military buildup.

Even before the IGY officially opened, there was already debate about what would follow. In December 1956, six months before the IGY got underway, the United States proposed a one-year continuation, and many participating countries readily agreed to extend their work and international cooperation for an additional year. In France, the possibility of an additional year led to a heated debate: Expéditions polaires françaises and many French scientists were in favor, but the government—the holder of the purse strings—was hesitant. There was also opposition from some scientists, led by Lejay, who were still unhappy with Victor's hold over French polar science. With Lejay's death in 1958, however, this opposition foundered. While the government had committed to fund France's participation in the IGY itself, it had little interest in extending this support, especially given the financial burden of the war in Algeria. The funding for the Dumont-d'Urville base and Station Charcot had been intended to support expeditions between 1956 and 1959, full stop. Indeed, the plan for the third and final expedition explicitly included closing the two bases and ending French presence in Terre Adélie. This was part of a broader state disregard for Terre Adélie, underpinned by a belief that the territory lacked the prestige of France's other overseas possessions.[52] Victor, still fuming from the abandonment of Terre Adélie after the Port-Martin fire, was furious at the thought that it might again be left bereft of French presence. He lobbied the government, arranging for meetings with the president and pressing his case, all in pursuit of an extended mandate.[53] But it was not until pressure was applied from outside that Victor got his way.

By the time of the IGY, the political situation in the Antarctic had changed significantly from the interwar years. While Britain, its Dominions, France, and Norway all made claims to Antarctic territory in the interwar period, the massive logistical difficulties of operating in such an inhospitable place meant that they installed no permanent facilities and conducted little or no activity in the claimed territories. Indeed, in France, the sheer difficulty of accessing Terre Adélie was seen to justify complete absence from the territory. But this vision of the Antarctic Continent began to change during the war. The IGY then saw the installation of bases (some very sophisticated), the construction of ice runways and complex radio networks, and regular incursions of icebreakers and large cargo planes. Antarctic logistics, while still difficult, were no longer in the realm of the impossible. As such, the standards for effective occupation also changed. The closure of the French bases, Victor knew, would greatly weaken the claim to sovereignty over Terre Adélie.

At the same time, US president Dwight Eisenhower proposed an international conference to discuss the future of the Antarctic. Eisenhower addressed the eleven other countries active in Antarctica during the IGY: France, Britain, the USSR, South Africa, Belgium, Japan, Australia, Chile, New Zealand, Norway, and Argentina.[54] "It would be desirable for countries who participated in the IGY Antarctic program to agree on a program to assure the continuation of successful scientific cooperation," said Eisenhower: "Such an agreement could also have the advantage of avoiding political rivalries, needless and undesirable on this continent, the waste of funds intended to defend isolated national interests, and the return of frequent international disagreements in this territory."[55] In this, the United States was strongly influenced by a desire to limit Soviet activity in the Antarctic, and saw internationalization as a peaceful and effective means of doing so. American officials were also motivated by the lack of any major minerals findings (or indeed any findings of economic significance at all) in the Antarctic during the IGY, which suggested that the United States would not be missing out on an economic bonanza by pushing for internationalization.

From mid-1958 to mid-1959, at the height of the Cold War, the twelve countries—including the two rival superpowers—embarked on a marathon of over fifty meetings in Washington to define Antarctica's political future.[56] Rather than solving the thorny political problems facing the continent, the United States proposed freezing the legal status quo: no country would have to renounce its historic rights or claims and no country would be able to make new claims or accrue rights from its activities on the continent for the duration of the treaty. This careful structure protected the interests of all countries at the table despite a tripartite division of views on sovereignty. This division consisted of those countries with mutually recognized claims to parts of the Antarctic based on discovery and territorial acquisition (Britain, France, Australia, New Zealand, and Norway); those countries with mutually recognized claims based on inherited territorial rights from the Treaty of Tordesillas of 1494, as well as geographical proximity and continuity and related "natural rights" (Chile and Argentina); and those countries who had not made formal claims but who reserved the right to do so or were interested in possibly doing so.[57] The United States and the USSR, in particular, saw the continent as a *terra nullius*, a land that belonged to no one. That the Argentinean and Chilean claims overlapped with the British claim further complicated matters.

In order to prevent the continent from being pulled toward militarization, the United States also proposed to make the Antarctic a nonmilitarized and nuclear-free region—something that both supported long-term American interests and spoke to broader international concerns about the white continent. These proposals were deeply pragmatic: the two superpowers saw them as the best possible way of avoiding confrontation and, simultaneously, preventing the other from gaining any strategic advantage.[58] The claimant countries saw the proposals as a solution to the impossibility of defending their claims by conventional military means, should tensions reach that point. Further, an agreement among the twelve, and especially an agreement built on science as a cohesive and unifying force, was a means of keeping outsiders (such as the United Nations) out of the continent's management. In short, the twelve countries involved came to believe that their interests in the Antarctic, disparate as they might be, would be best protected by a treaty along the lines of that proposed by Eisenhower. This is perhaps best summarized by the British diplomat John A. Heap, who wrote that the treaty was propelled not by altruism but by practical judgments: "The parties gained little from [the Antarctic Treaty] but what they all, variously, have stood to lose without it made the exercise worthwhile."[59]

With this stance, the United States made it clear that it was not going to pursue any claim to territory in the Antarctic. By the 1950s, the United States only had two possible courses of action toward a claim: making a claim to the unclaimed sector of the continent, widely seen as the least valuable region, or challenging other nations' claims, all of whom were partners in important Cold War defense and security alliances. Further, if the United States were to make a claim, the Soviets would inevitably follow suit—not something the Americans wanted to encourage. And after the IGY, when the Soviets declared their intentions to remain active in the Antarctic, the United States saw internationalization as a solution to both the Soviet problem and American scientific aspirations.[60] In the balance of things, an agreement that the Antarctic would be used only for peaceful purposes and guaranteeing free access to the continent to American scientists offered distinct advantages over a troublesome claim to the United States.

The American decision to not pursue a claim was also a reaction to the escalating dispute between Britain (on one hand) and Argentina and Chile (on the other), whose Antarctic claims overlapped. Argentina laid formal claim to land in the Antarctic in 1942, when a military expedition placed a copper cylinder containing an official notice and a flag on Deception Island. This claim added a new dimension to the long-standing British-Argentine dispute over the Falkland Islands, leading to an increasingly acrimonious bilateral relationship and opening the door to a complete breakdown in the Antarctic Peninsula region. The United States was left in the uncomfortable position of potentially having to choose between a significant European ally and important Latin American relationships. As the dispute deepened, the specter of military confrontation in the Antarctic loomed. In this context, internationalization offered a peaceful solution to the British-South American dispute in which the United States could maintain its desired neutrality.

The potential of a treaty for the Antarctic—something long-term and carrying international weight—changed the debate in France. In mid-1958, the Conseil de Cabinet decided, on recommendation from the Overseas Ministry, to permit one more year of work in Terre Adélie to coincide with the extension of the IGY. But the government's commitment was restrained: it did not provide any substantial funding. Rather, money for the additional year came from Expéditions polaires françaises, which had raised funds privately since its inception in 1947, primarily from the sale of photographs and books and from tickets to exhibitions, films, and speeches. The subsequent year was a reduced campaign with the simple goal of continuing the momentum of the IGY and hopefully bridging to permanent presence in the territory. The additional expedition, decided on at the last minute, had to be put together in a rush. A team of twelve men under the leadership of René Merle arrived in Terre Adélie in late January 1959. Their overwinter was difficult, defined by maintenance tasks and fixing the scientific instruments that had been used continuously for two years, but they also managed to conduct some territorial reconnaissance and draw a geological map of Terre Adélie's coastline.[61]

TAAF, too, was pushing for continued French presence in Terre Adélie, seeing presence as the kingpin for maintaining French sovereignty over the district. TAAF joined Victor's lobbying effort, pressuring the government to commit to permanent presence. The left-wing media also called for the government to not pull out of the Antarctic so that, as *Le Monde* put it, "France [would] have a stronger position during the discussion on the future of the Antarctic."[62] The esteemed law professor René-Jean Dupuy summarized a growing feeling when he wrote that France could only defend its claim to Terre Adélie by keeping the Dumont-d'Urville base open and demonstrating "real occupation" of the territory.[63] Together, these voices argued that, with the continent's future under intense scrutiny, French sovereignty over Terre Adélie could not be assured by sporadic presence; rather, to guarantee its rights in Terre Adélie, morally, legally, and politically, France needed to commit to permanent presence.

With the return of Charles de Gaulle as prime minister in mid-1958 and then as president soon afterwards, these advocates found the political opening they needed.[64] With its implications for prestige, overseas reach, and relations with the United States, French activity in Antarctica fit neatly into the Gaullist worldview. Soon, motivated by the negotiation of the Antarctic Treaty and by growing American activity on the continent, de Gaulle committed France to continued and continuous presence in Terre Adélie.[65] This decision was both a concrete step toward rebuilding France's prestige and *grandeur* and part of his broader, systematic effort to distance France from the United States while remaining Cold War allies—a balancing act designed to underline France's independence.

De Gaulle's obsession with independence had its roots in both his complete dependence on Britain during the war and France's dependence on the United States for postwar credit and reconstruction. It also stemmed from resentment of his treatment by Eisenhower and Roosevelt during the war and by the great powers immediately after the war. The allies took time to recognize the legitimacy of de Gaulle's provisional government and France was invited neither to the September 1944 meeting of the new United Nations Security Council nor to Yalta in February 1945. Determined to rebuild a stronger, autonomous France, de Gaulle pushed for an independent nuclear deterrent, which would ensure France's place as a permanent member of the UN Security Council and make a strong statement about French capability and sovereignty. It was also the basis for his 1966 decision to withdraw France from the North Atlantic Treaty Organization's integrated command structure and to demand that the United States remove its thirty bases and nearly thirty thousand troops from French territory.

In the wake of the Suez Canal crisis, de Gaulle was primed to distance his country from the United States as far as practically possible given the Cold War in all spheres, whether they be political, military, economic, or cultural. In the Antarctic context, de Gaulle deplored the idea of depending on the United States to affirm French rights in Terre Adélie—and the only way to prevent this, he agreed with Terre Adélie's advocates, was with continual French presence. At the same time, de Gaulle was motivated by the desire for France to keep pace with other countries in the Antarctic: "France, which possesses Terre Adélie, cannot remain absent in a land where all her neighbors maintain numerous and permanent bases," as one of his secretaries of state declared.[66] In this respect, too, de Gaulle was concerned about the United States' immense financial and technological advantages in the Antarctic arena. Similar forces were at work when it became clear that the USSR would not vacate the Antarctic after the IGY. In practical terms, de Gaulle's decision meant that the Dumont-d'Urville base would remain open and continually occupied by teams of French scientists and technicians, managed and operated by TAAF and Expéditions polaires françaises.

Of central importance to de Gaulle was to restore France's honor, *grandeur*, and rank among the great powers. While the idea of "grandeur" radiates through France's past, the war and its aftermath—and especially decolonization—called into question the future of French identity.[67] The gap created by the Vichy regime during the war and the revolving-door governments of the Fourth Republic, beset by ministerial instability and political crises, threatened France's status on the world stage—a status that was dear to the political landscape advanced by de Gaulle. And the winding down of the second empire forced the country to confront the tight link between *grandeur* and domination, to find new ways to showcase French prestige globally. During the war, the empire contributed in no small way to the liberation of the Hexagon, in strategic terms and by supplying colonial troops—and after the war, when France was so weakened at home, the empire provided a basis for the country to reclaim its status as a world power. This is why, as soon as the war in Europe was over, France looked to rebuild its imperial presence in the Levant, Indochina, and Africa. But when de Gaulle returned to power in 1958, that idea of France was finished. With the independence of significant former French colonies in the 1950s, and with the path set for Algerian independence, de Gaulle's vision of France as a *puissance mondiale moyenne* (midsized world power) demanded a stronger hold over France's remaining overseas possessions.

By the end of the 1950s, it was clear that the vision of the French state as a territorial entity that reached around the world—something intrinsic to the Fifth Republic's 1958 constitution—was now dependent on smaller and more remote possessions such as Mayotte, Martinique, Djibouti, Réunion, New Caledonia, French Polynesia, and Terre Adélie.[68] As Jean Chesneaux reminds us, these lands were "no longer seen as mere French possessions in the old colonial tradition but as intrinsic parts of France itself; they stand as *terres de souveraineté*, lands under French sovereign jurisdiction, a term dating back to the expansionist policies of Louis XIV."[69] More and more, they became central to France's influence and presence internationally. In this context, the four TAAF districts, with no Indigenous populations, stood out as secure overseas regions: remote, often overlooked, and yet increasingly relevant to demonstrating France's presence far from the Hexagon and to providing a basis for rebuilding French prestige unmarred by a colonial past. Indeed, as TAAF's former chief administrator François Garde has written, "In a deserted continent where the great tide of decolonization will never reach, the assertion of the tricolore is a discreet form of revenge on history."[70] By committing to continual French presence in Terre Adélie, de Gaulle offered a boost to his country's national pride at a time of immense change, a way forward from what were widely seen in France as humiliating failures in Indochina and Algeria. In this context, Terre Adélie gained importance "in the eyes of all who want France to remain *grande*."[71]

Victor capitalized on the sympathetic mind he found in de Gaulle, meeting with him several times to push his case and writing to him on a regular basis. De Gaulle was warm toward the dean of French polar exploration, disposed to his cause and also of practical help, pushing other ministries to do Victor's bidding and even occasionally conjuring up more money in response to Victor's frequent requests.[72] De Gaulle also personally met with members of Expéditions polaires françaises at the Elysée palace and wrote letters to Victor and his teams at least annually congratulating them and showing his support for French Antarctic presence.[73]

Negotiating a Future

During the negotiation of the Antarctic Treaty, which took place from mid-1958 until the end of 1959, France's interests were represented by Pierre Charpentier, who headed the French delegation in Washington. Trained in law, Charpentier joined the diplomatic service in 1929, serving in London, Moscow, and Rabat before the war. A Resistance fighter and member of the *Forces françaises de l'intérieur* (French Forces of the Interior) during the war, Charpentier was again posted to Moscow in 1944. Over the next decade, he worked at France's embassy in Romania and led the French delegation to the Organization for European Economic Co-operation as well as France's trade negotiations with the USSR before being named ambassador to Greece. By the time the Antarctic Treaty negotiations opened, Charpentier was a senior diplomatic adviser to the French government.

Led by Charpentier, France came out fully in favor of military neutralization and scientific cooperation in the Antarctic. Military neutralization appealed to France for the same reasons it appealed to the other countries at the table: it removed both a set of potential threats to Terre Adélie and the intractable question of how the territory might be defended militarily. For France, too, whose Antarctic presence had essentially never had a military component, a demilitarized continent was a hedge against any future Operation Highjump. And the idea of Antarctica as a continent dedicated to science was appealing to France given the country's scientific successes in the early 1950s and during the IGY: with science as currency, the French would be rich in Antarctic terms, able to project authority and command respect. Charpentier pointed, too, to the political will in France to increase scientific cooperation in the Antarctic, another means of pushing back against American hegemony. In this respect, Expéditions polaires françaises' focus on science in the early 1950s was vindicated, while the French Navy's position seemed ill-thought-out.

More difficult for the French negotiators was the concept of sovereignty in Antarctic space. For Charpentier and his political masters, French sovereignty over Terre Adélie was written in stone, stretching back to Dumont d'Urville's discovery of 1840. Pointing to de Gaulle's commitment to continual presence, Charpentier noted that "the French Government is proud, in addition to having indisputable historical claims, to be able to rely on a permanent occupation."[74] The idea of relinquishing or weakening that sovereignty was anathema to the government, which saw France's slice of the Antarctic pie in the larger context of French overseas possessions and ambitions. But it was equally clear that any treaty would have to balance the positions of claimant and non-claimant states, something that could only be done by acknowledging but not fully recognizing existing territorial claims.

Tasked with winning the French over to the idea of "freezing" sovereignty claims, the US State Department legal adviser Herman Phleger and diplomat Paul C. Daniels spent considerable time negotiating with their French counterparts in the months leading up to the conference. Determined not to weaken France's claim to Terre Adélie, the French remained resolute.[75] Three days before the Washington Conference on Antarctica opened, Charpentier called on Phleger and Daniels and declared that France would "under no circumstances" agree to an article that inhibited the recognition of France's claim to Terre Adélie: "On the highest levels it had been decided that French sovereignty in Antarctica should not be prejudiced by any treaty which provided that the other parties reserved their position that such claims were not recognized," declared Charpentier.[76] Charpentier delivered the same message to Richard Casey, the Australian minister for external affairs and head of Australia's delegation to the conference.

As the negotiations progressed, Charpentier maintained this stance, calling for the freezing of sovereignty claims proposed in the draft treaty text to be diluted since it "implied a legal negation of France's rights in Antarctica and was, therefore, unacceptable to France."[77] On this, however, he found himself alone: other national representatives, including from Britain, the United States, Australia, Norway, and the USSR, believed that altering the draft text would upset the delicate balance between claimant and non-claimant states—a balance being tested on other fronts at the same time.[78] France's intransigence was due to both an unyielding position on sovereignty and uncertainty over the constitutionality of signing a treaty weakening any claim to sovereignty. France, the state with the smallest claim, was proving the least flexible of the participants. As he wrote in his diary, Casey feared the French position would "destroy the conference and treaty."[79]

When Charpentier privately made it clear that any change in the French position would have to be taken up at the highest levels of government, Casey did just that. Complaining personally to the French foreign minister, Maurice Couve de Murville, Casey warned him that by proving the least flexible of all the participating countries, France was playing at ruining the entire treaty conference.[80] His case was helped by the chief of Soviet Antarctic expeditions and president of the USSR's geographical society, who chose that moment to describe French sovereignty over Terre Adélie as "imagined."[81] Indeed, it was the Soviet threat that finally won the French over: as Casey pointed out to Couve de Murville, a freezing of claims was the best way of countering Soviet ambitions in the Antarctic, which might include claims to any sector, including Terre Adélie. Australia was especially provoked by the USSR's decision to open research stations in the Australian Antarctic sector, which stoked fears that the Soviets would establish secret missile bases from which they would be able to threaten major Australian cities—fears Casey enunciated clearly to the French.[82] As other countries piled on, ultimately isolating the French, the die was cast. Couve de Murville wanted neither to lose out to the Soviets nor for France to be blamed for a failed treaty conference. Charpentier's instructions were reversed and, after insisting on small changes to the article's language, he announced that France was willing to agree to a freezing of claims. France also succeeded in having French included as one of the four official treaty languages, along with English, Russian, and Spanish—a reassurance of prestige with which Norway, also a claimant state, had to do without.

The Antarctic Treaty was signed in Washington on 1 December 1959 and entered into force in June 1961. The treaty banned all military measures, including bases, fortifications, maneuvers, and weapons tests south of the 60th parallel (with an exception for logistical presence). It also enshrined Antarctica as a land of open scientific investigation and maintained the legal status quo of sovereignty claims in their present state for the duration of the treaty. The article pertaining to sovereignty, Article IV, reads as follows:[83]

1. Nothing contained in the present treaty shall be interpreted as:

    (a) a renunciation by any Contracting Party of previously asserted rights of or claims to territorial sovereignty in Antarctica;

(b) a renunciation or diminution by any Contracting Party of any basis of claim to territorial sovereignty in Antarctica which it may have whether as a result of its activities or those of its nationals in Antarctica, or otherwise;
(c) prejudicing the position of any Contracting Party as regards its recognition or non-recognition of any other State's right of or claim or basis of claim to territorial sovereignty in Antarctica.

2. No acts or activities taking place while the present treaty is in force shall constitute a basis for asserting, supporting or denying a claim to territorial sovereignty in Antarctica or create any rights of sovereignty in Antarctica. No new claim, or enlargement of an existing claim, to territorial sovereignty in Antarctica shall be asserted while the present treaty is in force.

This article is often called the "miracle" of the Antarctic Treaty, as it allows states with conflicting interests to interpret its meaning to suit their purposes. It is precisely on this basis that France was able to accept it: France has consistently interpreted Article IV as in no way weakening its claim to Terre Adélie. Charpentier made this point clearly at the end of the negotiations, asserting that "on the occasion of signing the Antarctic Treaty, the Republic of France reaffirms the sovereignty that she exerts over Terre Adélie."[84] In France, the treaty was also interpreted as respecting the historical actions of Antarctica's early discoverers, in particular Dumont d'Urville, and hence as lending support to France's claim.[85] Since signing the treaty, France has consistently maintained that "in signing and ratifying the Antarctic Treaty the claimant States have in no way renounced their sovereignty and that this is especially true of France in respect of Terre Adélie," as the government put it to the United Nations in 1984.[86] In this narrative, the major discontinuities in France's Antarctic activity (which reached 110 years between discovery in 1840 and the next visit in 1950) do not figure at all; rather, in the French perception of the territory, the country is seen as having a long, proud, historic Antarctic tradition. This construction of an identity narrative is enabled by the lack of any competing narrative: Terre Adélie has neither an Indigenous population nor direct territorial competitors offering an alternative view.

In practice, France has held that continual presence in Terre Adélie is the third essential step, after discovery and formal claim, for sustaining and justifying the territorial claim.[87] With this in mind, France has maintained continual occupation at the Dumont-d'Urville base from 1956 to the present day. This occupation has focused on scientific research, illustrative of the ways in which science has become the lens through which Antarctic legitimacy and influence are measured.[88] Nonetheless, the treaty has had practical impacts on France's governance of Terre Adélie, including preventing the French state from enacting regulations affecting foreign nationals. Since signing the treaty, France has been actively engaged in the Antarctic Treaty System, assuming a leadership position, determined to maintain an authoritative voice in Antarctic affairs and particularly in shaping how Terre Adélie is perceived internationally.[89] The ATS is paramount to French national interests in the Antarctic: it offers France a political structure through which its claim is stabilized and protected, and it is the mechanism by which France feels best able to wield authority over Terre Adélie itself and the management of the continent more broadly. The ATS also gives France another power base in Antarctic affairs, one that in some senses counteracts France's lack of geographic connection to the continent.

The Calm before the Storm

Underpinned by new commitment, the 1960s saw a steadiness and maturity in French Antarctic affairs. The Antarctic Treaty provided a path for the continent's future, making it clear that science would play a predominant role, and science was one of France's strengths in the region. Activities in Terre Adélie shifted from individual scientific projects and campaigns to long-term plans, from temporary facilities to a better-built and -equipped base. But the decade was also marred by tensions over logistics and Terre Adélie's administrative situation.

Designed for the IGY, the Dumont-d'Urville base was originally built with a three-year lifetime in mind. It was adequate for those purposes, but by no means suited for larger groups over longer periods. Once the stamp of permanence was given to French presence in Terre Adélie, the base needed to be rethought. Improved unloading facilities, including a road between the ship's docking place and the base, were urgently needed: through the IGY, the supply ships were loaded and unloaded by hand over rocky, unprepared terrain, a time-consuming, arduous, and inefficient affair. Victor quickly drew up detailed, long-term infrastructure plans for proper dockside facilities, a road, a quay, a vehicle garage, larger living quarters, and new scientific laboratories.[90] He envisioned a base capable of comfortably hosting forty people over the winters and twice as many during the austral summer crossovers, suited for the climate, pleasant rather than utilitarian—all in keeping with his view that polar expeditions had entered a modern scientific age, one that left the hardships of the earlier era of adventuring behind.

Victor's plans were soon approved by his government masters and work began in earnest in the summer of 1962. That season, the scientific program was reduced in order to maximize progress on infrastructure. Priority was given to new generators to more than quintuple the base's power capacity and to scientific facilities for the upcoming International Years of the Quiet Sun (1964–1965). Over the following two years, new laboratories were built for meteorology, magnetism, seismology, cosmic rays, and natural radioactivity. A bar, foosball table, discotheque, and library (complete with comfortable leather chairs and thousands of books and magazines) were added, and the inadequate unloading facilities were transformed with a wharf, five-ton crane, and proper road.[91] Aware of the challenges of isolated overwintering in small groups in a harsh climate, Victor also capitalized on physical infrastructure decisions to improve mental health on the base through the long, dark winters—for example, designing the living quarters to be homey rather than institutional and calling for the personnel to have individual bedrooms. Expéditions polaires françaises had also long insisted that overwinterers be able to be in telegram contact with their families back home at minimal expense.[92] In late 1966, a sleek, modern kitchen was installed, part of a broader effort to make meals a source of pleasure. The stainless-steel kitchen, with humungous ovens, neatly stacked crockery, and copper pans hanging from wall hooks, was the domain of a dedicated chef. "Everyone knows that in France, appetizing meals are indispensable for maintaining morale," wrote the newspaper *Le Monde* in an approving article, noting that suppers at Dumont-d'Urville included gratin dauphinois, veal marengo, and Camembert.[93]

On the ground, this infrastructure work was overseen by Christiane Gillet, Expéditions polaires françaises' chief engineer and one of the first women to participate in expeditions to both polar regions. Gillet, who designed the French Jarl-Joset station in Greenland as well as much of the new construction at Dumont-d'Urville, had both the technical aptitude and mechanical abilities to hold her own in an otherwise exclusively male environment. While other countries forbade women from the Antarctic at this time (the British Antarctic Survey, for example, took until 1983 to allow women to participate in its field programs), Gillet's presence in Greenland and Terre Adélie was not so much a result of French gender or workplace policy as of the fact that Victor and Expéditions polaires françaises considered her indispensable.[94] But while Gillet headed Expéditions polaires françaises' technical section from 1956 until 1998, still she was forbidden from overwintering in the Antarctic, something only opened to Frenchwomen in the 2000s.

Through the 1960s, the maturation of France's place in the Antarctic can be seen through funding, science, logistics, international cooperation, and administration. Economic growth at home meant that money was available to support extensive work at the Dumont-d'Urville base—even if the amount provided was

128   CHAPTER 6

never enough to satisfy every want. The improvements made to the base in this decade were not just about the comfort of its inhabitants; they were also a physical stamp of French presence in Terre Adélie, a tangible statement about the French claim. Expedition teams grew in size and scope. In the austral summer of 1963, the Dumont-d'Urville base played host to seventy people, a number unimaginable in the days of the early expeditions. Increased means meant bigger projects, such as the launch of Dragon sounding rockets in 1966–1967 by a team of nearly thirty researchers from the *Centre national d'études spatiales* (figure 16).[95] The French conducted joint expeditions with the Soviet Academy of Sciences, including a 1,500-kilometer traverse from Vostok to Mirny led by French glaciologist Albert Bauer. While the Soviets were impressed by Bauer's scientific expertise, the French were equally impressed by Soviet polar logistics.[96] Bauer and his compatriots were transported directly to Vostok aboard a Soviet Ilyushin aircraft. The Ilyushin, flown by the polar aviation branch of Aeroflot, landed on a four-kilometer-long snow runway at Vostok. Unlike the Americans,

FIGURE 16.   With penguins in the foreground and the Astrolabe glacier in the distance, a Dragon rocket rises in a plume of combustion gases, 1967 (Jean-Clair Loison, Archipôles, IPEV).

who used jet rockets to enable their planes to take off from snow surfaces, the Russians "just opened the throttles and waited, apparently unconcerned by the time and the distance it took to get lifted by the thin air."[97] This logistical feat underscored France's lack of heavy aviation capacity in the Antarctic and presaged a push for air access to Terre Adélie.

Performances of sovereignty, too, were common through the decade. In 1966, TAAF's chief administrator, Pierre Rolland, inaugurated an official mapping and toponymy commission, the *Commission de toponymie des TAAF*, intended to systematize the giving of historically significant French names to locations in the TAAF districts.[98] The inclusion of Gaston Rouillon as one of the commission's four members underscores Expéditions polaires françaises' influence on French Antarctic affairs at the time. Through this decade, French authorities also pushed back when they sensed that any aspect of France's hold over Terre Adélie was in jeopardy, such as protesting when the Soviets wanted to take over the radio frequency already in use in the territory.[99] More broadly, France hosted the Antarctic Treaty's fifth consultative meeting in Paris in November 1968, at which the French minister of foreign affairs, Michel Debré, made clear his country's commitment to the white continent.[100]

With the Antarctic Treaty, credibility and a strong voice in the Antarctic depended on scientific work and logistical capacity. France excelled at the first but suffered from logistical shortcomings and—contrary to de Gaulle's desires—was not infrequently forced to rely on help from other countries. At the end of the 1968–1969 austral summer campaign, the supply ship *Thala Dan* got stuck in pack ice eighty-five kilometers from Dumont-d'Urville. Purpose-built for polar waters by Danish company J. Lauritzen Lines in 1957, the red-and-white *Thala Dan* was the *Norsel*'s successor. The lease of a foreign ship itself was an indication of France's logistical weaknesses: despite claiming a portion of the Antarctic pie, France still did not have its own polar ship and relied on foreign vessels to access its own territory. After several days of effort, it became clear that the *Thala Dan* could not make it to the rocky shore of Terre Adélie that season. With forty-two men waiting to be repatriated to France and insufficient provisions at the base to sustain them through another austral winter, France was forced to ask the Americans and the Australians for help.[101] Australia stepped up and, together, the teams used helicopters to ferry all the men, scientific documents, provisions, and materials between the *Thala Dan* and the Dumont-d'Urville base. This incident, combined with earlier failures and near misses, made it clear that France could not assure the security of the Dumont-d'Urville base alone—a significant problem for the sovereignty mission. The French were also embarrassed when an American team conducting observations of Antarctic bases under Article VII of the Antarctic Treaty in 1963–1964 could not land and properly inspect Dumont-d'Urville because of the lack of landing facilities at the French base.[102] Air access to Terre Adélie, in the form of a long prepared snow or tarmac runway, was increasingly seen as essential.

There was also trouble on the administrative and management front through the 1960s. With Expéditions polaires françaises now answering to TAAF, Victor found himself in a new and uncomfortable position, with diminished control over French Antarctica. Victor appealed to officials at all levels of government to clarify the lines of demarcation in order to—as he saw it—prevent TAAF from encroaching on his remaining authority. Victor was particularly insistent that the name "Expéditions polaires françaises" appear on all data, photographs, and articles published from French scientific work in Antarctica, demanding retractions and corrections from offending publishers and scientists.[103] Those who published material without Expéditions polaires françaises' explicit consent, too, found themselves at the receiving end of long, legal reprimands.[104] Expéditions polaires françaises also pushed its own agenda by promoting its films and books in school classrooms and reaching out to teachers via pedagogical magazines, as well as holding public lectures and film soirées. None of these efforts were well received by a growing group of young scientists who thought Victor's iron grip over scientific work in Terre Adélie unreasonable.[105] In 1965, they rebelled, alerting the Academy of Sciences of Victor's demand that his own name be included on all publications. Government authorities agreed that the practice was inappropriate and put an end to it.

Nonetheless, the 1960s were the calm before the storm. At the very end of the decade, on 21 July 1969, the twenty-seven-member French team at Dumont-d'Urville—deeply ensconced in the Antarctic winter—listened intently as Neil Armstrong made history by setting foot on the moon. The radio broadcast was staticky and in English, a language with which many of the overwinterers struggled, but the emotion they felt was deep: "The moon, always extraordinary in the Antarctic, seemed close to us, and, paradoxically, in our isolation, we felt more at one with the three astronauts than with the other Earthmen," recalled overwinterer Jean-Pierre Jacquin.[106]

7

CRISIS AND CHOICES

After a period of calm through the 1960s, in the following decade Terre Adélie became mired in troubles. Budgetary and management problems, compounded by intragovernmental disputes and an economic crisis, threw France's commitment to its Antarctic territory into crisis. Soon, the fundamental national interest of retaining Terre Adélie was openly questioned at high political levels. The strategic and political advantages the territory offered to France were difficult to measure and hard to explain in concrete terms. As French scientists struggled to work in the Antarctic through the 1970s and 1980s, the tight link between science and authority began to unravel. This was a period of soul-searching for French polar aficionados, one that forced the country to confront the hard truths of Antarctic presence.

The proximate cause of this crisis was the onerous cost of chartering ships to service France's Antarctic and sub-Antarctic districts. By 1979, well over half of TAAF's budget went to leasing the French-owned *Marion Dufresne* to service the sub-Antarctic islands and the Danish *Thala Dan* to service Terre Adélie.[1] While the *Marion Dufresne* was property of the French state, TAAF still needed to pay to use it, and leasing a foreign vessel was necessary for accessing Terre Adélie since France had no polar ship of its own—a fact that weighed heavily both on the balance sheet and on perceptions of sovereignty. The *Thala Dan* was Expéditions polaires françaises' workhorse through the 1970s. By the middle of the decade, however, much-needed renovations—including an enclosed bridge, extra cabins, and a helicopter pad—increased the cost of the lease to the breaking point. In 1978, Expéditions polaires françaises sent Jean Vaugelade, its director following Victor's retirement two years earlier, to Norway on an urgent mission to find a cheaper ship.[2] Costs also piled on from other directions: fuel prices rose sharply and, citing economic pressure, the Armée de l'air drastically increased what it charged to provide helicopter pilots for Terre Adélie.[3]

By the late 1970s, TAAF was in serious financial trouble. Even with emergency infusions of money, at the end of 1978 TAAF's debt was just shy of 10 million francs, and in 1979 unpaid bills from the previous year piled up.[4] TAAF's oceanographic campaigns, a vital part of its scientific research program, had to be canceled for lack of money. For Terre Adélie itself, the combined costs of ships and salaries for personnel exceeded the territory's budget allocation. These problems meant that Expéditions polaires françaises' upcoming overwinter at Dumont-d'Urville had to be reduced by a third, from thirty-five to twenty-four people, severely affecting the planned scientific program.[5] On TAAF's bases, infrastructure work was postponed and living conditions—already difficult— worsened, leading to unhappy personnel isolated and far from home. The Dumont-d'Urville base, in dire need of repairs, was far from the seamless, modern polar installation Victor had envisioned in the late 1940s. Even Victor's personal efforts to remedy the situation were blocked by the lack of money: retired and living in French Polynesia, Victor wanted to travel to Terre Adélie and use his media aptitude to bring attention to the territory—but Expéditions polaires françaises did not have the money to pay his passage.[6]

Apart from limited emergency infusions, the broader economic situation in France meant that there was no room to provide TAAF with real financial relief. By the late 1960s, France's long period of strong economic growth had begun to falter. The franc was devalued against the West German mark and the US dollar in 1968, and with Richard Nixon's suspension of the Bretton Woods system in 1971 the franc entered a decade of instability. The 1973 oil crisis and subsequent economic stagnation across the Western world hit France hard, reliant as it was on imported oil. As energy and production costs increased, social upheaval was rife and the era of the *Trente glorieuses* (Glorious Thirty) came to a sudden end. Valéry Giscard d'Estaing's government, in power from 1974 to 1981, was marred by rampant inflation and economic instability and had little extra money for TAAF's remote territories.

Incapable of fulfilling its missions and operating its bases in a safe manner, TAAF was in crisis. Unable to pay bills, Vaugelade took the exceptional step of writing to Prime Minister Jacques Chirac, warning that Expéditions polaires françaises might be forced to abandon the Dumont-d'Urville base since it could no longer afford to continue leasing ships to access the territory.[7] Vaugelade's threat had clear implications for sovereignty: continual presence at Dumont-d'Urville was critical to France's claim to effective occupation in the territory, to French polar legitimacy, and to the country's status in the Antarctic Treaty System. TAAF's administrators built on these themes to make their case, adroitly combining self-preservation and strategic arguments. If TAAF did not receive more money, and soon, its chief administrator Roger Barberot wrote, the Dumont-d'Urville base would have to close—"a blow against the interests of France's future."[8] "It must be remembered that the ultimate purpose of the French presence [in the TAAF districts] is the affirmation and maintenance of our sovereignty over these lands," continued Barberot: "But this sovereignty only makes sense because it is accompanied by scientific and economic activities and a permanent presence." France's future as an Antarctic player, Barberot argued, was linked to questions of scientific priorities and prestige: Was Antarctic science a field in which France wanted to be competitive on the international scene? While French scientific work in Terre Adélie had long been well regarded, TAAF's budget was no longer sufficient to support a robust and internationally competitive program of inquiry. By linking science and sovereignty, Barberot tried to position TAAF as critical to maintaining possession of France's Antarctic territory. Three years after Vaugelade wrote to Chirac, TAAF's consultative council brought this to a head by addressing the new prime minister, Raymond Barre, warning explicitly that France would have no choice but to close the Dumont-d'Urville base, pull out of the Antarctic altogether, and cede the Crozet archipelago to a friendly nation if more money was not forthcoming.[9]

Alarmed, the Overseas Ministry ordered an official inspection of TAAF. Bernard Vinay, the inspector general for overseas affairs, traveled to TAAF's three sub-Antarctic districts but not as far as Terre Adélie, which was significantly more difficult to access. His report was broadly supportive of TAAF and the austral possessions.[10] The Antarctic was increasingly a place of international competition, Vinay wrote, attracting interest from the two superpowers—and as such it was "inconceivable" for France to give up on its Antarctic base despite its high cost. As more and more countries built up bases and activity on the continent—activities that were in principle scientific but that in practice had present and future political implications—French influence and authority in Antarctica were at stake. Given the particularities of the Antarctic, supporting Terre Adélie meant supporting Antarctic science: science was both at the heart of French presence in Terre Adélie and central to the international conception of the white continent. The choice facing the government was simple, Vinay concluded: either more money needed to be committed or the Dumont-d'Urville base would be shuttered—and with it, France's role in the Antarctic would end. In this, TAAF also found support at the Ministry of Foreign Affairs, where the prestige and influence associated with Antarctic presence were seen as beneficial in a global context. At a time when many countries were turning their attention to Antarctica, that ministry insisted, "it would be regrettable if the French presence in this region be questioned because of a lack of funds."[11]

As inspector general, Vinay was a politically neutral party, but his personal experience made him naturally supportive of Terre Adélie. Born in the French protectorate of Tonkin, Vinay (1921–2018) studied Oriental languages and overseas administration before embarking on a series of diplomatic appointments. He began on home ground as an administrative liaison for the Far East immediately after the war, and then moved to Paris, where he took part in the Pau conference on Indochina and worked on France's fragmenting African interests. When he was named to the Office of the Inspector General for Overseas Affairs, he soon found himself entangled in Terre Adélie's problems. Having been struck personally by the loss of French Indochina, Vinay was a natural ally of TAAF, sympathetic to both the specific challenges faced in Terre Adélie and the broader desire to secure France's remaining overseas possessions.

But not all in government saw TAAF and Terre Adélie as the victims of too little funding. At the Overseas Ministry, TAAF's problems were seen to be the result of poor leadership and management. The ministry's opinion was scathing: TAAF's lack of administrative competency is "particularly worrying," wrote ministry official Jean Chaussade in 1979, listing a litany of problems: the secretary general is not being informed about the territory's files, the technical service is understaffed, the bases are inadequately managed, the rules governing finances are being ignored, no long-term budget plan is in place, and so on.[12] TAAF is no longer "being managed in any real sense of the word," he concluded. The relationship between the ministry and TAAF became increasingly strained when TAAF stopped replying to Chaussade's requests for information, claiming to be overwhelmed, and Chaussade responded by accusing TAAF's staff of incompetence. The minister himself weighed in, blaming TAAF's financial problems on its broader administrative failings and arguing that TAAF's scientific research, while of high quality, did not focus sufficiently on economic opportunities.[13] The ministry gave TAAF an ultimatum: TAAF needed to reorganize its administration, search for budgetary savings, focus on resources of economic value, and assure sovereignty in its districts, or face the consequences.[14]

This focus on economic value represents a different assessment of TAAF's priorities. By telling TAAF to prioritize economy- and resource-based science, the ministry both emphasized the three sub-Antarctic districts, which had more resource potential than Terre Adélie, and underlined the importance of the upcoming Antarctic minerals convention negotiations to France. That French geological research in Terre Adélie was not sufficiently advanced to contribute usefully to those negotiations was another black mark for the territory.[15] From the ministry's point of view, in economic terms Terre Adélie paled in comparison to the sub-Antarctic possessions, which offered an abundance of krill, fish, algae, and alginates.[15] Even Vinay, the inspector general who was otherwise supportive of France's Antarctic mission, thought that TAAF's scientific program demonstrated a lack of forethought about the territory's long-term goals and the country's overseas priorities. "The results obtained after more than twenty years of research, while they have permitted better comprehension of certain phenomena important to national or international science, do not seem to have brought answers to questions of great importance for TAAF," wrote Vinay, "not because the research did not produce results, but simply because the desirable research was either not undertaken or only partially undertaken (cf. economic mission)."[17] Vinay, too, wanted TAAF to focus on research with potential links to economic activity—that is, geology and the movements and nature of fauna and flora. The science-sovereignty link, so important in the Antarctic sphere, had more than one interpretation.

TAAF pushed back against these criticisms, appealing directly to Prime Minister Barre, demanding to know why its repeated requests for more money had been ignored and again pointing to the closure of the Dumont-d'Urville base and the end of France's role in the Antarctic as natural consequences of the ongoing situation.[18] For TAAF, this "nuclear option" was never thought of as a real possibility, but rather as a threat intended to spur action on the part of the government. But outside of TAAF, the idea of abandoning France's Antarctic territory was being seriously considered. The questions raised by the Overseas Ministry were broad and strategic: How much emphasis should be given to each of TAAF's four primary missions? Did it make sense to focus on economy and resources in a frozen territory? In a period of economic hardship at home, was Terre Adélie worth the expense, or should resources be focused on other, more economically promising overseas districts? What benefits did Antarctic presence bring to France, and at what cost should it be maintained?

Aware of the depth of these problems, TAAF turned to an outsider—an accomplished polar scientist, not a government official or administrator—to turn things around. In 1980, Bernard Morlet, a high atmosphere physicist and veteran of several campaigns in Terre Adélie, was named head of TAAF's research mission. With his decades of experience in the Antarctic and his immense scientific competence, the hope was that he could turn a new page for the austral territories. Morlet took to his new role with enthusiasm and energy. He soon reassessed TAAF's research mission, created scientific and environment committees, and reorganized Expéditions polaires françaises, all with the aim of better evaluating scientific priorities and budgets—a deliberate effort to respond to the Overseas Ministry's concerns.[19] Morlet's scientific committee, independent of TAAF, consisted of twelve scientists and experts appointed by the Ministry of

Research and charged with evaluating, organizing, and coordinating all scientific research in TAAF's districts. Morlet also spearheaded conferences bringing together France's polar and subpolar scientists and promoted French polar research internationally. His efforts made waves in government, and soon the Ministry of Foreign Affairs named Morlet both as its scientific adviser for the Antarctic and as the country's scientific representative to the Antarctic Treaty meetings.

Born on Valentine's Day 1932 in Paris, Morlet was educated at the *École normale supérieure*, a prestigious French *grande école*, in physics, specializing in radioastronomy. Upon graduation, he became involved in the preparations for the International Geophysical Year. He was rewarded with an overwinter in Terre Adélie, where he took charge of high atmosphere studies and ionospheric research. This year opened his eyes and his heart to the Antarctic, a place that came to define the rest of his life. After a break for military service in Algeria, Morlet once again set his eyes on France's southern territories: through the early 1960s, he led atmospheric and ionospheric studies in Kerguelen, including coordinating global efforts to study nuclear fallout from the American Johnson Island atomic bomb test of 9 July 1962. Morlet then set up ionospheric stations in Kerguelen and Terre Adélie, as well as in the Hexagon, and again overwintered in Terre Adélie, this time as chief scientist. In the 1970s, he led four more summer campaigns in Terre Adélie and coordinated extensive high atmosphere, magnetospheric, and ionospheric studies throughout TAAF's districts.

But one thing Morlet could not do was secure more money for TAAF. Despite his interventions, TAAF's budget woes continued to worsen. As TAAF ran deficits year after year, the territory was forced to impose austerity measures, and maintenance of and presence at its bases continued to decline.[20] By 1985, Expéditions polaires françaises hit bottom: unable to afford to lease a ship for the entire austral summer season, the estival scientific campaign in Terre Adélie was shortened by a month, cutting it to a bare minimum.[21] Permanent staff at Expéditions polaires françaises' Parisian headquarters were let go, too, falling from thirty in 1976 to only nineteen in 1988. Among the remaining personnel, morale was low. Things only worsened at the end of the decade when a fire on the *Marion Dufresne* immobilized it for two months. Since TAAF could not afford to lease another ship, both servicing of the sub-Antarctic districts and planned oceanographic campaigns were cut.[22]

Ship problems were not restricted to the *Marion Dufresne*, either. In 1988, France finally purchased a polar ship of its own to service Terre Adélie. The ship had been built in Britain two years previously, intended for servicing offshore oil platforms in the Canadian Arctic. But with the collapse of oil prices, this expensive source was abandoned. France was able to purchase the ship, still unused, for 25 million francs. It was renamed the *Astrolabe* in honor of two older, celebrated *Astrolabes*, those of La Pérouse and Dumont d'Urville.[23] With a steel-reinforced hull designed to withstand thick pack ice, the Lloyds-certified polar ship was symbolically important: France was no longer dependent on foreign nations to access Terre Adélie. For the first time in nearly four decades, the French flag was to fly above a French ship in France's Antarctic territory. But it was not smooth sailing: soon, the *Astrolabe* was forced to remain in port in Hobart because Expéditions polaires françaises could not afford to pay for fuel. When it finally sailed, it became imprisoned in pack ice, trapped fifty kilometers from Terre Adélie with sixty people and a year's worth of supplies on board.[24] Over the ensuing years, the ship proved to be slow, cramped, and expensive to operate, guzzling enormous quantities of fuel. The *Astrolabe*'s rocky journey was representative of TAAF's situation more broadly at the end of the 1980s: trapped, pressed in on all sides, and with an uncertain future.

Throughout this decade, TAAF's financial problems were compounded by the deteriorating relationship with its parent ministry. Incensed with TAAF, the Overseas Ministry steadily decreased its funding, from 103 million francs in 1980 to only 75 million francs at the end of the decade (all in 1990 francs, with inflation taken into account).[25] The 1990 research season was only saved when TAAF and Expéditions polaires françaises diverted money from other sources, but by the end of that year those sources, too, were exhausted. Between the very high fixed costs of running an Antarctic base and the rise in fuel prices due to the Gulf War, almost nothing was left for scientific research. TAAF protested these reductions each year, pointing out the dangers of the devolving situation. "It is illusory to think that this privileged situation [France's position in Antarctica] can be maintained in the face of growing international pressure, with decreasing means," wrote squadron vice-admiral Claude Pieri, TAAF's chief administrator, in 1985, warning that the present situation meant "a significant step backwards for French presence in Antarctica in terms of sovereignty as well as in terms of scientific research."[26] A veteran of World War II and the Indochina War, Pieri (1922–2002) ascended the ranks of the French Navy in the 1970s, ultimately assuming overall command of France's submarine fleet, including the naval component of France's nuclear force de frappe. In 1982, he was named chief administrator of TAAF, a position he held until his retirement five years later. Tough, confident, and accustomed to getting his way, Pieri was a fierce defender of Terre Adélie throughout his tenure. But Pieri's pleas fell on deaf ears. The extent of the ministry's frustrations with TAAF was never fully appreciated by the territory.

By the end of the 1980s, TAAF's problems had persisted for nearly two decades. The Overseas Ministry ordered a full audit of the territory. The auditors' report, released in the early spring of 1989, was damning.[27] Between budget problems and rising expenses, the auditors wrote, TAAF was no longer able to fulfill its missions. The auditors emphasized that TAAF's spending was not properly accounted for—a red flag for the territory's financial management. It also became clear that Expéditions polaires françaises did not document its spending properly and its accounts were a mess—to the extent that experts had to be called in to decipher the books.[28] Even more seriously for Morlet, the auditors questioned TAAF's legal basis for conducting scientific research. The territory had assumed research responsibilities, the auditors argued, that were not explicitly given by its founding legislation. For Morlet, alarm bells were ringing: the inadequacy of TAAF's founding texts of 1955 vis-à-vis the territory's actual research activity gave its critics a legal mechanism for taking research responsibilities away. Here was, very possibly, the beginning of the end of TAAF.

For Morlet, responding to the auditors' report had to be done carefully: he needed to shape the narrative or risk being sidelined (or worse) and convince the Overseas Ministry of TAAF's value and utility. At the same time, he needed to take the auditors' complaints seriously and not ignore them, as TAAF had been doing to its critics for over a decade. Morlet agreed with the auditors that, read narrowly, TAAF's legal texts were incompatible with the modern conception of research that was being practiced in Terre Adélie.[29] Changing the 1955 legislation, however, was not an option as it would require reaffirming France's sovereignty over Terre Adélie, something that was now complicated by the Antarctic Treaty. Presciently, Morlet worried that the ministry would respond to the auditors by creating a new polar organization to supersede TAAF. Concerned that TAAF would be deprived of control over its scientific mission, he argued that the legal issue was not enough to warrant this step. After all, TAAF was already feeling pushed out of the Antarctic sphere in other ways, such as being denied a representative at the Antarctic minerals convention negotiations of the mid-1980s.[30] By linking science to sovereignty, Morlet sought to argue that scientific research was the most certain expression of sovereignty in the otherwise unoccupied austral districts, and especially Terre Adélie—something he hoped would guarantee TAAF's survival.

But TAAF's fortunes only continued to worsen. By early 1991, its reserves were empty. Exasperated, the financial controller refused to approve the territory's draft budget.[31] TAAF was unable to transfer money to Expéditions polaires françaises, threatening the entire 1991–1992 Antarctic program: the situation was "catastrophic to the point of compromising the activity of the Antarctic base," as the newspaper Le Monde put it in a scathing article.[32] Morlet, for his part, took the issue public, telling the paper Libération that, at this rate, the Terre Adélie base might have to close.[33] This had long been TAAF's trump card, but only rarely was it used in the public sphere. Expéditions polaires françaises also spoke out publicly, complaining that its scientific program was in jeopardy for lack of funds.³⁴ In the end, the overwinter went ahead, but only because money was moved between accounts, against the rules—a maneuver reminiscent of those that had previously been flagged by the auditors.

Terre Adélie in Political Context

For the Overseas Ministry, the strategic, economic, or political utility of most of France's possessions was clear. Building French societies overseas, and in particular *rayonnement* (the diffusion and influence of French language and culture), was a priority for the ministry—but this only applied to populated possessions. Some possessions offered economic advantages, such as nickel in New Caledonia and marine resources more broadly. Others provided the basis for regional cooperation and alliances. And French Polynesia was a critical geostrategic asset as the location of French nuclear testing after Algerian independence. But Terre Adélie was an outlier. With no population, no electorate to push its interests, and no clear economic potential, Terre Adélie was fundamentally different from France's other overseas possessions. The strategic and political advantages Terre Adélie offered to France were difficult to measure and hard to explain in concrete terms. In all these ways, the Antarctic territory held little cultural, diplomatic, or economic importance at the ministry. In the 1970s and 1980s, too, the Overseas Ministry was consumed by unrest in the French Pacific territories, including a militant nationalist movement in Melanesia and rebellions that twice brought New Caledonia to the brink of civil war. These urgent problems shunted the Antarctic to the far back of the ministry's concerns.

The Overseas Ministry's attitude toward Terre Adélie was an extension of a long history of state disinterest toward the territory, especially by conservative governments. In what was a strongly political ministry, Terre Adélie held little sway. In 1954, in a telling example, the finance commission complained publicly that Terre Adélie was home to only a few Frenchmen posted there temporarily, and some penguins—hardly a view conducive to investment.³⁵ That France's strategic priorities did not include the Antarctic is evident from budget comparisons, which show that France's Antarctic budget was half or less than that of the other Antarctic Treaty consultative parties.³⁶ "We are not taken seriously" and "Antarctic research doesn't interest anyone at the DOM-TOM [the Overseas Ministry]," complained Expéditions polaires françaises, lamenting the reality of the situation—that with no voters and no clear political raison d'être, Terre Adélie had no political clout.³⁷ This disinterest was not challenged by the French public, for whom the Antarctic attracted only sporadic attention.

On the other hand, Terre Adélie did contribute to *grandeur*, to France's prestige and global reach, which have long been central to its self-image. France's early overseas activities were motivated by the search for strategic, commercial, and political benefits to boost its global power—objectives shaped as much by a desire for wealth and knowledge as by competition and cultural influence. In the eighteenth and early nineteenth centuries, France was the predominant force in Europe. As France subsequently lost authority and territory in Europe, it expanded its overseas interests to counteract those losses—an approach that was felled by decolonization after World War II.[38] With France's overseas presence greatly reduced, the remaining possessions provided credibility to France's self-defined desire to be a midsized world power—a concept central to the French collective imagination and to de Gaulle's grand design. As the former prime minister Barre (himself from Réunion) put it, "Whatever the cost, our overseas possessions assure us of a global dimension which is fundamental to us."[39]

In this context, despite the Overseas Ministry's lack of enthusiasm for TAAF and Terre Adélie, still Terre Adélie played an important role for France—not an economic or cultural role, but something more subtle. France's remaining overseas territories, Terre Adélie included, provided a physical basis for France's claim to international reach and global presence. The French ambition to retain presence in all the world's major oceans, as Jean Chesneaux reminds us, is not to be underestimated:[40] it carries influence comparable to that of the Cold War American containment doctrine and Soviet Brezhnev intervention doctrine.[41] Supporting this ambition, he continues, "does not need to be justified in terms of profits and losses, any more than France's army and navy, the French state museums, or the diplomatic service." It was precisely these ends that sustained Terre Adélie through the 1970s and 1980s despite the Overseas Ministry's censure. Terre Adélie and the sub-Antarctic possessions were also connected to the larger Pacific arena, with which France has strong historical, ideological, and emotional ties—and which has long been used to help justify the global nature of French ambitions. In this way, the austral possessions helped resolve the dilemma of how to maintain *grandeur* even after the end of the empire. The lack of Indigenous populations in these possessions, too, was pointed to by their supporters as a benefit: they were one part of France's overseas history arguably entirely untainted by colonial wrongs.[42]

TAAF's case was also helped by growing economic interest in living marine resources in the Antarctic and sub-Antarctic waters. As commercial interest in these resources grew through the 1970s, the Antarctic Treaty System consultative parties set out to define a convention to manage them.[43] The Antarctic Treaty had been silent on the question of resources since the treaty negotiations were sensitive enough without bringing to the table a fraught issue with tight links to ownership, control, and title. But by the 1970s there was pressure to act. New understandings of environment and conservation arose from the 1972 UN Conference on the Human Environment as well as the 1974 Law of the Sea Conference, highlighting questions of sovereignty and control over living marine resources in coastal waters and beyond. Increased fishing in the southern oceans, too, led to the prospect of radical declines in krill stocks.[44] For the consultative parties, there was a feeling that if they did not manage (and were not *seen* to manage) these resources properly, the international community would gain leverage in its burgeoning challenge to the Antarctic Treaty System's monopoly over Antarctica's management. Propelled by a sense of urgency, the Convention for the Conservation of Antarctic Marine Living Resources (CCAMLR) negotiations took place rapid-fire between 1978 and 1980.[45] In order to protect their dominance and minimize challenges from the international community, the consultative parties conducted the negotiations in secret. For TAAF, the negotiations drew attention to the economic potential of the austral districts, which was viewed positively by the Overseas Ministry.

During the negotiations, French authorities, especially military authorities, were deeply concerned about the convention's proposed application north of 60° south, a zone that included the Kerguelen and Crozet archipelagos. They worried that, were France to agree to allow these islands to be governed by the convention, it risked creating a slippery slope by which the provisions of the Antarctic Treaty would creep northward and threaten French sovereignty interests in the sub-Antarctic.[46] France demanded, and obtained, a special covenant: measures already adopted by France for the conservation of marine living resources in the waters adjacent to Kerguelen and Crozet remained in force even after the convention came into being, and France reserves the right to decide whether those waters will be included or excluded from each of the convention's measures (including new ones) for as long as it remains in force.[47] This demand went against the trend of the negotiations and the desires of the other consultative parties, almost leading to the collapse of the talks—a sign of France's determination to put sovereignty and control over its possessions first.

This entire episode cast France in a bad light, especially given the secrecy surrounding the negotiations. France's assertiveness was taken as a sign that it was "unambiguously . . . prepared to prevent Convention conservation measures applying within the EEZ [Exclusive Economic Zone] of its sub-Antarctic islands, thus considerably reducing the ambit of the ecosystem approach"—a black mark on France's already-poor environmental record.[48] The French were also seen, not for the first time, as being unnecessarily prickly about sovereignty issues. But from France's point of view, it was a triumph: the special covenant explicitly demonstrated international recognition of French rights over its sub-Antarctic possessions.[49]

From the point of view of the Antarctic Treaty System, too, the convention was regarded as a success: by quickly and firmly agreeing on a convention to fill a gap in the Antarctic Treaty, the consultative parties demonstrated both their capacity to manage resources responsibly and their responsiveness to pressing concerns. Similar forces would soon be at work during negotiations over Antarctic minerals.

Shortly after the living marine resources negotiations, with the 1982 UN Convention on the Law of the Sea (UNCLOS), French worldwide territorial power took on a new aspect. France's far-flung and remote possessions were now anchors for its extensive Exclusive Economic Zones and continental shelves, areas where France enjoys sole exploitation rights over all natural resources (with certain limitations).[50] Given the widespread geographic nature of those possessions, France has one of the largest Exclusive Economic Zones in the world, an enormous area of nearly eleven million square kilometers, two-thirds of which are in the Pacific.[51] With UNCLOS, France's austral possessions cemented the country's oceanic status, giving the previously marginal possessions new value. While Terre Adélie's political situation means that the Antarctic territory has not yet been included in France's UNCLOS submissions, the territory's potential future strategic and economic value took on new meaning.[52]

In the 1980s, the Antarctic Treaty System (ATS) was facing other challenges, too. The ATS had long been criticized for being a "club of the rich," exclusive and undemocratic. This came to a head in the autumn of 1982 when Malaysia's prime minister, Mahathir bin Mohamad, put the issue to the United Nations General Assembly. Since substantial scientific research in Antarctica—a very costly endeavor—was required for a country to gain voting rights in the ATS, Mahathir argued, developing countries were all but banned from having a voice in Antarctic affairs. He called for the Antarctic to be deemed "common heritage of mankind" and for the Antarctic Treaty to be replaced by an international authority that would administer the continent based on majority consensus—and ensure that developing countries would benefit from the profits of any future mineral activity.[53] The Antarctic was too important to the world as a whole to be controlled by a small number of states, he continued, advocating the UN as a multinational body capable of democratizing the continent's management.

Malaysia pushed this issue in bilateral diplomacy, gaining the support of many developing countries. At the UN, Antigua and Barbuda called for the rectification of historical injustices: "The world has vastly changed since the Antarctic Treaty was signed in 1959. There are now 159 Member States of the United Nations, most of which are developing countries. In 1959 they had neither the opportunity nor the sovereign competence to participate in events in Antarctica. It is not only unfair, it is unjust to suggest that we should abide by decisions made without our involvement.... It is in the interests of global peace and stability to address the democratization of Antarctica now."[54] By treating the Antarctic as *terra communis*, this position denied the validity of existing territorial claims. The continent's political and legal landscapes were facing their most significant challenge since the negotiation of the Antarctic Treaty. "These uninhabited lands do not legally belong to the discoverers, just as the colonial territories do not belong to the colonial powers," Malaysia asserted in a statement that rang alarm bells in France: "[They] belong to the international community. The countries presently claiming them must give them up so that either the United Nations administers these lands or the present occupants act as trustees for the nations of the world."[55]

To the French government, this clash between opposing perspectives of legitimacy and management posed a serious threat to Terre Adélie.[56] While behind closed doors, French authorities worried that the Antarctic Treaty System—and thus France's position in the Antarctic sphere—would be weakened by these challenges, in public France vigorously defended the ATS. Pointing out that mechanisms existed in principle for any state to accede to the Antarctic Treaty, and that the ATS had grown from the original twelve signatory states in 1959 to thirty-two states in 1984, France's representative to the United Nations argued somewhat unconvincingly that the Antarctic system "ensures the representation of States of all political and economic categories from all regions of the world."[57] France also emphasized the Antarctic Treaty's success in providing a lasting solution to the claims problem and in preventing a reescalation of international rivalries. If the treaty were to fall, French diplomats told the UN, disputes and even open conflict over territorial claims could well arise. Through the decade, challenges to France's position in Antarctica and hold over Terre Adélie came from all sides, internal and external, and the territory's future seemed far from clear.

France as a Polar Nation

In the 1980s, there was among French polar aficionados a great pining for the heroic days of French polar adventuring—a feeling that France had once been a polar giant and was now reduced to a bit player, with all the fault resting squarely on its own shoulders. French polar explorers of the past—Jules Poret de Blosseville, Philippe d'Orléans, Jules Sébastien César Dumont d'Urville, Jean-Baptiste Charcot, and Paul-Emile Victor among them—were revered as men who charted new paths in the coldest regions of Earth and brought deep pride to their country. But by the 1980s, this age of heroism was long over: France's

Antarctic interests were suffering and the country was all but absent from the Arctic.

For French polar scientists, the effects of TAAF's financial problems and the state's lack of commitment to the polar regions were acute. The successes France had enjoyed in polar glaciology, atmospheric studies, and biology in the 1970s and 1980s were increasingly hampered by money woes. French polar scientists worried constantly about funding, personnel, logistics, and facilities; they had neither the money needed to conduct vigorous, wide-ranging scientific programs nor the funds to build modern laboratories at the Dumont-d'Urville base. Even the wildly successful 905-meter-long ice core drilled by French glaciologists in the interior of Antarctic in the late 1970s, which allowed for the reconstruction of climate over almost fifty thousand years, was colored by the paucity of French logistics: the operation would not have been possible without American air support, again underlining France's inability to act independently in Antarctica—something that was embarrassing to a nation that saw itself as one of the big Antarctic powers.[58] Every time French scientists had to rely on their American counterparts to transport them to or in the Antarctic, they were reminded of their own country's lack of logistical infrastructure and capacity. While the French continued to debate air access, the Americans were landing ski-equipped C-130 Hercules aircraft directly at Dumont-d'Urville on temporary snow landing strips.[59]

Through the 1980s, French Antarctic scientists grew increasingly frustrated. Their grievances were legion. Contractual terms for scientists working in Terre Adélie left much to be desired. The biological science building at the Dumont-d'Urville base did not have running water and support for Antarctic biology was insufficient, complained the biologists Pierre Jouventin and Alain Guille.[60] French astronomers and astrophysicists saw Terre Adélie as an ideal observation site and wanted to come to the Dumont-d'Urville base, but, as Morlet lamented, TAAF did not have the financial or logistical means to support them.[61] A team from the Nice observatory went instead to an American Antarctic base for its research, again emphasizing the gap between the United States and France. As France's lack of support for Antarctic science impinged on the work of its researchers, international partners began to turn away, abandoning France and moving their activities to the other side of the continent. There was a widespread feeling among French Antarctic scientists that their research could only be resurrected with a new station in the continent's interior—but at the time, TAAF had neither the logistical capability nor the money to build such a station.

Victor, by then retired, was appalled at the situation. The edifice he had worked so hard to build, he wrote to the French government, was crumbling, and France's privileged place in polar research—Victor's life work—was being lost. Victor had, after all, devoted his entire career to building Expéditions polaires françaises. Through Victor's work, France was the first country to organize civilian research expeditions in both the Arctic and Antarctic after World War II. In the first four postwar decades, Expéditions polaires françaises led more than forty expeditions in Antarctica as well as twenty expeditions in the Arctic with almost three thousand scientific and logistics personnel, covering hundreds of thousands of kilometers, producing thousands of scientific publications, and developing innovative new polar techniques and materials. But by the mid-1980s, this was in decline. "Expéditions polaires françaises is in the process of dying, asphyxiated," Victor wrote, calling for "an SOS" to revive French polar research.[62] This feeling that France was losing its "polar greatness" also came across in French newspapers, which expressed outrage at the idea of France's only Antarctic base being closed.[63] All these voices came together to call for an airstrip near the Dumont-d'Urville base. The airstrip project, which stretched from the late 1960s to the early 1990s, consuming well over 100 million francs despite ultimately failing, was long seen as a panacea for the host of problems facing Terre Adélie: the onerous cost of ship servicing, the limitations to scientific campaigns dictated by Terre Adélie's natural environment, the safety of personnel on the ground, French competitiveness in Antarctic affairs, and the legitimacy of France's claim to the territory.

For Morlet, these aggrieved voices represented a grave concern: French research in Antarctica was already dwindling and suffering and would continue to do so—perhaps even to the point of no return—unless French capacity in Terre Adélie was strengthened. For France to contribute to solving major global problems in the fields of climate research, glaciology, paleoclimatology, and physical chemistry and dynamics of the atmosphere, Morlet concluded, the country needed to take ownership of its work in Antarctica—and that meant renewed investment and commitment.[64] If French Antarctic research was to get a new wind, then scientists and government officials needed to come together and build a stronger system; there needed to be consensus on objectives and solidarity in terms of means. But the political backing for this was lacking through the 1970s and 1980s.

The situation was even worse in the Arctic, where France claimed no territory and had no body corresponding to TAAF to support French research at all. While French explorers and scientists had been active in the Arctic earlier in the twentieth century, by the 1980s France conducted essentially no independent Arctic research. French work in Greenland through the middle of the century, in particular, had hinged on Victor's personal interest in the island, and with Victor retired and living in the South Pacific, the Arctic fell off France's radar. But still a feeling of connection, even of entitlement, endured, resurfacing during

France's fight to be included in the International Arctic Science Committee (IASC).

In late 1988, the eight Arctic border countries (Canada, the United States, the USSR, Denmark, Finland, Norway, Sweden, and Iceland) proposed to join together to form a committee for Arctic scientific research. From the get-go, France was deeply concerned about being excluded from this new Arctic "club."[65] Despite France's lack of territory in the Arctic, there was still a perceived relationship stemming from the country's earlier activity in the region, and particularly from Expéditions polaires françaises' successes in developing polar technologies in Greenland. But given France's low activity in the Arctic sphere, it was hard to make the argument that France ought to be included. French commitment to the Arctic was something of the past, not the present. The parallel with the Antarctic was crystal clear: unless France succeeded in being admitted to IASC, the country would find itself in the position of an outsider in the Antarctic Treaty System, denied decision-making power, an unequal status that would be a blow to French pride and historical memory.

The threat of being left out of IASC came as a wakeup call to the French state. The response was swift: France must, the government asserted, rebuild its Arctic strengths and look to capture a stronger place in the Arctic world—goals that could, given France's lack of territory in the region, only be accomplished through scientific research. "While France has for a long time been a country engaged in polar Arctic research, her interests [now] seem to be poorly defended," wrote the Ministry of Research and Technology: "There exists no structure that can support and endorse the actions of French scientists, nor that assures the coordination and follow-up of their research."[66] A plan was quickly laid out to bolster France's status in the Arctic with the hope of ultimately gaining admittance to IASC.[67] It was nothing short of ambitious: to turn France into a significant player in Arctic science, to create permanent Arctic research structures with guaranteed funding, and to establish a new organization to coordinate research programs in both polar regions.

The broad-scale and long-term geopolitical implications of being excluded from Arctic affairs rang alarm bells in other parts of government, too. For the Ministry of Foreign Affairs, IASC membership represented a crossroads: if France did not succeed in being admitted, the country would likely never refind a path to participation in the Arctic region—an outcome that was anathema to a ministry that so valued French influence and presence across the globe. "Without rapid action on our part, we risk finding ourselves separated from a strategic region in which France has a long history with the expeditions of Cdt Charcot and Paul-Emile Victor," agreed the *Centre national de la recherche sci-*

entifique, emphasizing the weight of historical memory.[68] This appeal to the exploits of a small number of individual explorers, too, was linked both to the collective memory of a prouder past and to uncertainty about the future of France's place in the Antarctic.

As it became clear that France alone did not have a strong enough voice to push into IASC, it joined forces with three other European states (Germany, Britain, and the Netherlands) in an effort to gain entry. They immediately encountered resistance and named themselves the "quatre exclus" (the "four excluded").[69] The main sticking point was territorial sovereignty: as the Finnish government pointed out bluntly to French diplomats, the Arctic is different from the Antarctic in that the North is exclusively comprised of territories over which a limited number of countries exert full sovereignty.[70] The Finns patiently explained that, since France was not one of those countries, France had no place in Arctic projects. This simple point had a big impact on the government's thinking. In the Arctic, France's voice was weak *precisely because* it claimed no territory in the region. If France were to give up on Terre Adélie, as was being considered, it would find itself in the same position in Antarctic affairs: excluded, with no voice and no power. France's privileged place in Antarctica was dependent on Terre Adélie. When put so bluntly, this point boosted ministerial support for French Antarctic presence.

A month after France was rebuffed in Helsinki, the "quatre exclus" made a joint démarche to the Arctic border countries.[71] While the United States hinted that it was sympathetic to France's desire to participate in Arctic affairs, Canada and the USSR took a harder line. All interested scientists, regardless of nationality, would be able to participate in IASC's scientific activities, the Canadians said, but the Arctic border countries had special responsibilities and thus would retain special authority in IASC. This was, of course, precisely what France had been maintaining in the Antarctic Treaty System for decades; it was precisely the reasoning that gave France its privileged place in Antarctic affairs. Being on the other end of the stick hurt.

Ultimately, France's lobbying paid off and it was invited to IASC's founding meeting in Resolute Bay in 1990—not as a full or founding member, but as a participant. French government officials were surprised and pleased with this outcome—it was more than they had hoped for given the negative reaction to their diplomatic efforts.[72] Early the following year, France was admitted as a new member of IASC in Oslo. Pride was redeemed and a lesson learned: France could no longer remain absent from Arctic science and still expect a voice at the table—and, similarly, France needed to invest in Antarctic science if it wanted to maintain its voice in the Antarctic sphere.

8

ENVIRONMENTAL AUTHORITY

As Terre Adélie was engulfed by crises, one idea above all stood out as a panacea for all the problems facing French Antarctica: air access. The effort to build an airstrip in Terre Adélie stretched from the late 1960s until the early 1990s—a massive and costly endeavor that ultimately ended in failure as the continent's political dynamics evolved.

When France became active in Terre Adélie after World War II, the only way to access the territory was by ship: first the French-owned *Commandant Charcot*, which despite its reinforced hull could not reliably make it through thick pack ice, and then leased Norwegian, Danish, and Canadian ships. Reliance on foreign vessels to access a French territory did little to support France's sovereignty agenda. Moreover, frustration soon grew with the formidable expense of the leases, as well as with the ships' propensity for getting stuck—often for weeks on end—in the pack ice near Terre Adélie. The French had, by mischance of discovery, been cursed with one of the least accessible sections of the Antarctic coast. Given the limitations, unreliability, and onerous expense of the ships, the French government and Expéditions polaires françaises soon identified air access as the solution to the many problems plaguing Terre Adélie. With the Americans and Soviets already using aircraft in the Antarctic, the idea did not seem farfetched.

While the airstrip project was first discussed in the 1960s, nothing happened quickly. For more than a decade, Expéditions polaires françaises undertook preparatory studies and government ministries debated how to fund the project. After consultations with the French Air Force, who would ultimately be responsible for providing the planes, and the Americans, who were vastly more experienced in polar aviation, a plan was set: to build a long hard-rock airstrip near the Dumont-d'Urville base, capable of supporting Transall C-160s, a medium tactical transport plane codeveloped by France and West Germany, flying in from Tasmania or New Zealand.[1] In early November 1982, the secretary of state for Overseas France, Henri Emmanuelli, announced that France would build an 1,100-meter-long airstrip in Terre Adélie.[2] It would take another eleven years before the airstrip was completed. Five main arguments underpinned the project.

First, calculations showed that air access would reduce the cost of servicing Terre Adélie. The high cost of ship leases weighed heavily on TAAF's budget, leaving the territory in financial distress from the early 1970s on. Little money was left to support scientific personnel at the Dumont-d'Urville base. As France was forced to reduce, and reduce again, the number of overwintering personnel at Dumont-d'Urville, questions began to be raised about the compatibility of minimal presence with the sovereignty mission in the Antarctic.[3] With an airstrip, ship transport would only be needed for fuel oil and heavy machinery; all passenger and supply transport would be accomplished by air. The cost issue was taken further by Paul-Emile Victor, the Ministry of Foreign Affairs, and senior members of the government, who argued that with ship servicing alone, presence in Terre Adélie was too expensive to maintain and France would be forced to abandon its Antarctic claim.[4]

Second, air access would allow for longer scientific campaigns and more sophisticated scientific work in Terre Adélie. Given the direct link between science and authority in Antarctica, this was seen as a means of boosting France's status in both Antarctic research and politics.[5] As the continent's political situation normalized with the Antarctic Treaty, competition between states for territory was replaced by competition to unearth the continent's scientific secrets. Strong scientific work has long engendered the justification of political control in the Antarctic and moral claims to Antarctic sovereignty.[6] It was precisely this relationship between scientific research and authority that the French were eager to capitalize on with the airstrip project: the airstrip was envisioned as a conduit through which French science, and thus France's position, in the Antarctic would be strengthened. With air access, summer campaigns could be more than doubled in length, from two months to five months. A coastal airstrip was also the first step toward facilitating interior travel and building a permanent scientific station deep inland—something French scientists and politicians saw as paramount to France's future in Antarctic research. Reliance on mechanized overland transport, Victor and his deputy Jean Vaugelade noted as early as 1962, was severely limiting France's operations in Terre Adélie; only the airplane, they continued, "offers an efficient and affordable solution to the problems of traveling across the interior of the Antarctic continent."[7] The use of airplanes to open scientific doors, too, was representative of Victor's view of technological modernism as central to the conquest of the polar worlds in the postwar era, and he was already putting them to use with great effect in Greenland.[8]

Third, air access would improve the safety of personnel in Terre Adélie, as with sea servicing alone it was impossible to evacuate personnel during the long austral winters. Since France was maintaining continual presence at Dumont-d'Urville, the inability to rescue ailing or injured personnel was an ongoing concern. In 1951, this came to a head when Claude Tisserand, the radio operator, suffered from an intestinal occlusion. It was a matter of life and death, and evacuation was impossible. Surrounded by all the station's men, who assisted as they could with the finicky anesthetic gas, expedition doctor Jean Cendron operated twice on Tisserand, placing an artificial anus in his abdomen as a patch until he could be evacuated the following austral summer (figure 17). Despite the successful outcome for Tisserand, it was not a situation the French wanted to repeat. But the danger was underlined by a second near fatality when, during

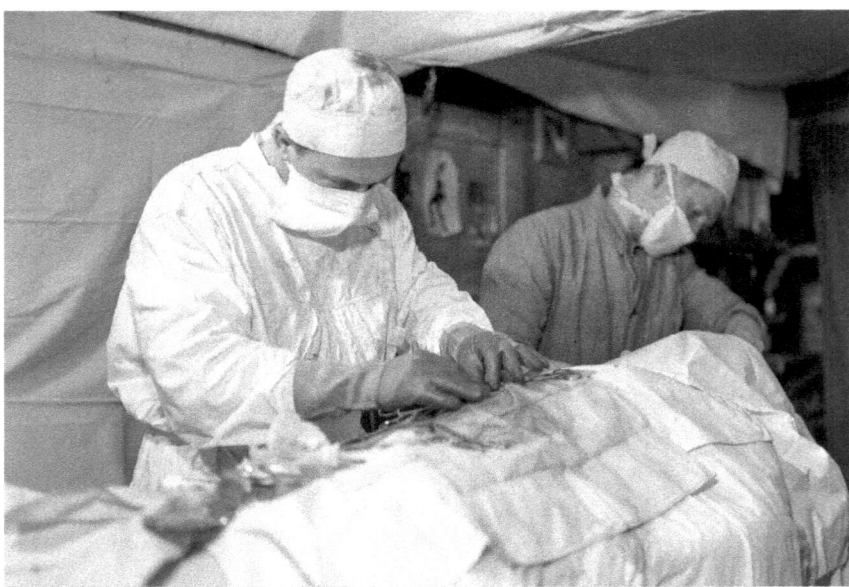

FIGURE 17. An emergency surgical operation in the improvised operating room in Terre Adélie: Jean Cendron prepares to operate on Claude Tisserand, 1951 (Archipôles, IPEV).

the International Geophysical Year, geophysicist Andre Lebeau needed an emergency appendectomy.

Fourth, air access would allow the French to be more competitive in the Antarctic. As it stood, France was at a distinct disadvantage compared to other countries who already operated aircraft in the Antarctic. When the United States proposed a transport network to connect all Antarctic bases with American ski-equipped C130s in the early 1970s, the link between logistical capacity and political weight came to the fore.[9] Concerned that France risked becoming dependent on the United States for logistics in the Antarctic, Expéditions polaires françaises wrote to the minister of defense warning that "the realization of this project would inevitably lead to a situation in which the US has a monopoly over air transport to and in the interior of Antarctica."[10] A decade later, the French deficit in Antarctic aviation had not abated: "France could soon be the only country that has not yet taken the turn toward air links," complained Bernard Vinay, the inspector general for overseas affairs.[11] France also felt threatened by increasing international interest in the Antarctic as represented by other access technologies such as West Germany's new polar icebreaker, an expensive symbol of commitment from a country with no territorial claim on the continent. That France did not have an icebreaker of its own was long a source of embarrassment. It did not help that the seasoned New Zealander diplomat George Laking pointed out publicly that his country's air access to its Antarctic territory was a marker of superiority over France.[12] Falling behind in the Antarctic was particularly worrisome to France: an airstrip would at once enhance France's presence and show its desire to retain its voice in Antarctic affairs.

Fifth, and lastly, an airstrip would be a concrete representation of France's presence in Terre Adélie, a physical symbol of French sovereignty over the territory. Just as Antarctic science has always been a geopolitical performance, as Peder Roberts reminds us, so too have Antarctic logistics and infrastructure.[13] In a place where the traditional norms of sovereignty do not hold, in a continent so remote and difficult to access, investing in logistical capability is a key way of performing sovereignty. The French decision to build an airstrip in the middle of an important bird nesting site speaks to the strategic import of the project: a primary belief that an airstrip was not only desirable but indeed necessary to support France's claim to territory. Further, an airstrip would boost France's polar legitimacy at a time when the Antarctic Treaty was being challenged by developing countries and environmental NGOs (ENGOs).[14] The airstrip soon became symbolic of a new chapter in human interaction with Terre Adélie's environment, one that integrated technology, science, and sovereignty.[15]

Construction and Controversy

The Terre Adélie airstrip proved a beast to build. It quickly became clear that there was no suitable site near the Dumont-d'Urville base. On the inland side, icy cliffs towered thirty meters in the air, an impenetrable wall of white. On the other side, rocky islands and archipelagos, free of ice and close to the coast, dotted the sea. None of them, however, were long enough to accommodate an airstrip. To solve the problem, Expéditions polaires françaises decided to connect a group of islands with a rock causeway. The islands would be leveled with dynamite and the rock thus obtained used to fill the spaces between them (figure 18). In all, over 720,000 cubic meters of rock were to be blasted and moved.[16] After preliminary studies suggested that this plan would succeed, construction began during the austral summer of 1982–1983.

Quickly, however, the airstrip project met with opposition from ENGOs who argued that the work would destroy important nesting grounds for Adélie penguins, snowy and giant petrels, Cape pigeons, and fulmars, and disrupt the nearby Emperor penguin colony. Greenpeace maintained steady direct action

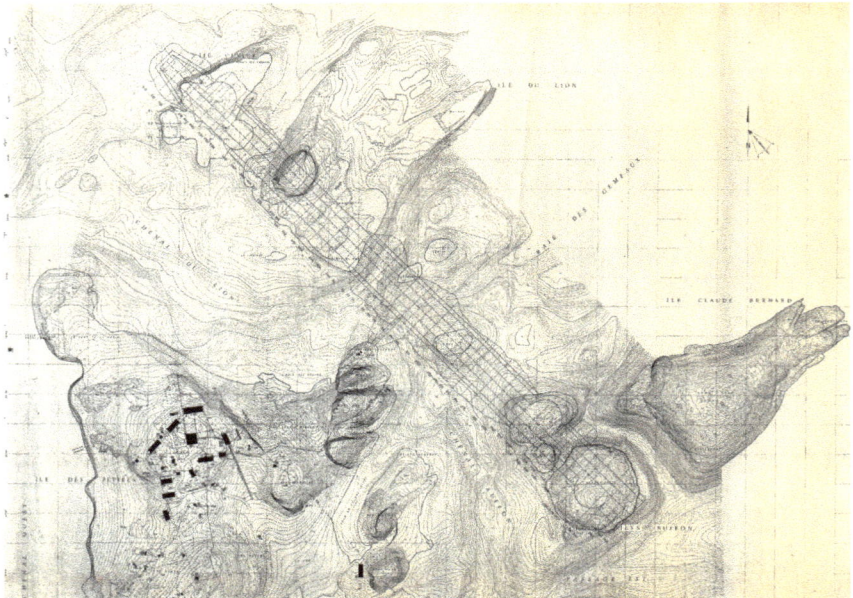

FIGURE 18. Airstrip plan, 1983: The rectangular grid shows where the airstrip will be built; the outlines of the islands to be razed are seen underneath. The small black rectangles in the lower left are the buildings of the Dumont-d'Urville base (Archipôles, IPEV).

with activists in penguin costumes occupying government buildings in Paris and others blocking the *Polarbjørn*—the Norwegian ship leased to bring construction materials to Terre Adélie—from leaving Le Havre.[17] Later, Greenpeace confronted the *Polarbjørn* with a twenty-ship protest flotilla in Hobart.[18] Greenpeace's aim was to attract international attention to the airstrip and pressure the French government to suspend construction until an environmental impact study could be carried out—a study that, as Greenpeace pointed out, was required by French law. Greenpeace's concerns were echoed by other ENGOs, including the Antarctic and Southern Ocean Coalition, which emphasized that the islands the French were blasting and leveling were one of the richest sites for fauna in the whole of Antarctica.[19] The French Academy of Sciences joined these voices, unanimously passing a resolution highlighting the danger of the airstrip for the area's avifauna, demanding a rigorous environmental impact study, and arguing that the construction violated both national law and the Antarctic Treaty.[20] In contrast, the Antarctic Treaty consultative parties took no action, even when evidence of harm to penguin colonies was presented—representative of a broader lack of willingness within the Antarctic Treaty System to impose sanctions or reprimands for environmental infractions.[21]

The French law referred to by Greenpeace and the Academy of Sciences was a 1976 law requiring all big projects affecting the environment to conduct impact studies. Since their introduction by the United States in 1970, environmental impact statements and assessments have played a central role in environmental management in the Antarctic.[22] While French law required environmental impact studies from 1976 on, the efficacy of this legislation left much to be desired: the law was neither well enforced nor held to high standards.[23] There was widespread mistrust of the law and the studies were seen as something to be worked around rather than constructively engaged with.

In face of outside pressure, France was forced to carry out an environmental impact study for the airstrip. The study, undertaken by Expéditions polaires françaises, concluded that the airstrip's impact on bird life, landscape, and ice circulation would be minimal to null.[24] It is clear from the study that the idea of "impact" had been politicized: the airstrip's impact on access to Terre Adélie and scientific research in Antarctica was given more weight than its impact on bird life and the environs. The study was approved by TAAF but strongly criticized by ENGOs as well as by the Ministry for Industry and Research. In response, the overseas minister named an expert committee, led by Louis Thaler, to reassess the project's environmental impact. Thaler (1930–2002) was a natural choice: perhaps the most influential French evolutionary biologist of his time, by the early 1980s he was widely called upon as an authoritative voice on controversial subjects. As a student in the United States in the 1950s, Thaler had been captivated by the ideas of George Gaylord Simpson, one of the fathers of the modern synthesis of evolutionary theory. Over the following two decades, Thaler's research brought together methods from paleontology, ecology, molecular biology, and genetics to shed light on the mechanisms of evolution. A brilliant speaker and interlocutor, his ideas—often radical in France at the time—soon made him well-known in scientific circles. With respect came duty: from 1978 to 1983, Thaler served as president of Montpellier-II University and frequently adjudicated in various capacities.

Thaler's report described the initial environmental impact study as "unsatisfactory in procedure and depth" and painted the airstrip project in a negative light but did not go so far as recommending that it be stopped.[25] The technical underpinnings of the project were insufficient, Thaler wrote, adding that human activity was already having negative consequences for the Pointe Géologie archipelago. Unsurprisingly, his report failed to please anybody. On one hand, Greenpeace thought that Thaler's report did not criticize the project strongly enough, and other ENGOs argued that the project should be terminated on the basis of the report.[26] On the other, Claude Pieri, TAAF's chief administrator, complained that Thaler's report neither understood nor represented the project correctly.[27]

Rather than openly distribute Thaler's report—a concept at the heart of environmental assessments—the French government chose to withhold it, drawing rebuke from Australia and New Zealand.[28] The Australian government was sensitive to the difficulties the airstrip controversy was causing for the Antarctic Treaty System: at a time when the ATS was being increasingly challenged, Australian politicians argued, it was not wise to open doors to criticism, especially with regard to the environment. Tasmanian State MP Bob Brown led this fight against the project, calling on the federal government to refuse the *Polarbjørn* entry to Hobart port and accusing the French of egregious environmental breaches, including "plann[ing] to inject hundreds of Adelie penguin eggs with poison to stop breeding" and dynamiting Adélie penguin nesting sites.[29] While the Australian government did not go so far as closing the port to the French, Brown's outspokenness drew attention to the airstrip. In private, furious French authorities accused Australia and New Zealand of egging on the environmental protesters in the hope that France would be forced to abandon the airstrip and pull out of the Antarctic altogether.[30]

Brown's accusations, while inflammatory, were not far off the mark. French government documents make it clear that nests were disturbed and displaced, eggs were destroyed, and birds (both chicks and adults) were killed during the airstrip construction. In some cases, eggs were removed from nests to encourage adult birds to vacate a certain area. In other cases, eggs were replaced with artificial ones (often, potatoes painted white); the real eggs were then transported to other colonies in the archipelago, where they were redistributed into the nests of unsuspecting penguins. Adélie penguin chicks in the construction zone were also deliberately killed in the months corresponding to the incubation and hatching phases. Adult penguins, too, were killed by explosions (approximately twenty in 1984, for example), but it was difficult to determine how many because of the nature of the debris.[31]

In both Australia and New Zealand, the airstrip tensions added to what was already a difficult political relationship with France. As well as a serious falling-out over French nuclear tests in Polynesia, in the 1980s the countries clashed over the future of New Caledonia, which led France to eject the Australian consul general in Noumea.[32] While Australia worried about the long-term ecological consequences of nuclear testing and about French military presence in Australia's sphere of influence, in France there was steadfast unanimity on the need for the tests to guarantee an independent nuclear force de frappe. The low point came in July 1985 with the *Rainbow Warrior* bombing, when French agents blew up the Greenpeace ship in a New Zealand port as it was about to embark on a protest against the tests. Bilateral protests against the airstrip were not limited to Australia and New Zealand: around the world, French embassies were so inundated with letters from governments, environmental groups, scientists, and individuals that Paris had to draft talking points to help the embassies craft their replies.[33]

Faced with these differing views, the Overseas Ministry hesitated, requesting a second environmental impact study. At the same time, the French Ministry for Industry and Research, which had given 12 million francs toward the airstrip in 1982–1983, pulled its funding, arguing that both the cost and the environmental risks were too high. An interministerial dispute broke out, with the secretary of state at the Ministry of the Interior accusing the Ministry for Industry and Research of jeopardizing not only French scientific research but also French sovereignty in Terre Adélie.[34] Exasperated by these disputes, the overseas minister halted work on the airstrip in the spring of 1984 and asked for a high-level ruling on whether the project should go ahead.[35]

Senior figures in the French government lost no time making their case, arguing that the airstrip was essential to France's claim to Terre Adélie. Their position was stark and simple: either the airstrip went ahead or France would be forced to abandon its Antarctic claim. Diplomats appealed directly to the prime minister, writing that "the construction of this airstrip constitutes, in effect, the condition *sine qua non* for the maintenance of our presence in Antarctica."[36] And an interministerial group addressed President François Mitterrand, stating bluntly that "stopping the construction of the airstrip would lead to the closure of the base and, by consequence, the end of French presence in Antarctica. This departure from Terre Adélie would question (1) our sovereignty, (2) our strategic position, and (3) our participation in international conferences on the Antarctic which is critical at a moment when the mineral resource treaty is being negotiated and when the question of common human heritage in Antarctica is being raised at the UN."[37] They were supported by Paul-Emile Victor, now retired but still very much the dean of French polar science: "Without this airstrip," he wrote, "France's presence in Antarctica will be seriously compromised and will probably quickly disappear."[38] The airstrip was also wrapped up in larger dreams of national pride and polar legitimacy. "At a time when India and Brazil are making considerable efforts to establish permanent bases in Antarctica, and just now China too," the Ministry of Foreign Affairs pointed out, "it is inconceivable that France, a pioneer in the discovery and exploration of the continent, gives up for lack of means."[39]

These arguments carried weight and there was broad cross-party agreement on the airstrip's necessity. The French state took the decision to restart construction unofficially in 1986 (by providing funding and allowing construction materials to be sent to Terre Adélie) and officially in 1987.[40] With Expéditions polaires françaises' director Michel Engler at the helm, the aim was to complete the airstrip by 1991. One hundred million francs were authorized for the project, to be provided jointly by the Overseas Ministry, the Ministry for Research and Higher Education, and the Ministry for Transport.[41]

As soon as the decision to proceed was made, Greenpeace upped its campaign against the project. Its ships stopped at Terre Adélie as part of the World Park movement, during which Greenpeace installed a base near Robert Falcon Scott's hut at Cape Evans and pressured the consultative parties to ban commercial exploitation and pollution in the Antarctic.[42] When Greenpeace's activists disembarked in Terre Adélie, they were met by signs in French and English declaring that access to the airstrip site was prohibited "to all people foreign to the site, due to the risks linked to the operation of such a site and in particular to the movement of heavy public works machinery."[43] These signs had been carefully worded by the French government in order to comply with the Antarctic Treaty's observer rules while also giving the on-the-ground personnel justification for denying the activists access to the site. But those personnel had been expressly forbidden from confronting the activists, who simply bypassed the signs and chained themselves to the heavy construction equipment (figure 19).[44]

French authorities were at a loss for how to deal with the protesters, especially given the nebulosity of legal jurisdiction in the Antarctic. What should, and what could, be done if protesters conducted illegal acts in Terre Adélie? The Ministry of Foreign Affairs spilled much ink on this question, ultimately proposing that

FIGURE 19. Greenpeace activists blocking construction equipment at the airstrip site, 1990 (Patrice Fauquemberg, Archipôles, IPEV).

arrested protesters could be brought to Hobart and dealt with there—an unsatisfactory solution from the point of view of sovereignty—but also instructing the construction teams on the ground in no uncertain terms to avoid confrontation.[45] Arresting foreign national protesters in Terre Adélie would open a legal Pandora's box and highlight the uncertainties of jurisdiction in the Antarctic, something French authorities were determined to avoid. Greenpeace's activists made the most of the French restraint, scoring a victory with photos showing penguins running from heavy machinery, as well as the cadaver of a penguin killed during the earthworks: "irrefutable proof," Greenpeace argued, that the French authorities were minimizing the real impact of the project.[46] While France was impotent to push back against this direct action, it did retaliate by calling for Greenpeace and other ENGOs to be banned as observers at the Commission for the Conservation of Antarctic Marine Living Resources meetings, and certainly feared that ENGOs might succeed in pushing their way into Antarctic Treaty meetings, creating what French diplomats called "an effect of contagion within the Antarctic system."[47]

Greenpeace's tactics, which stretched from Europe to Australia to Antarctica, drew the ire of the French government, forcing General Bernard Norlain, the chief of the prime minister's military cabinet, to spend time and energy countering the environmentalists.[48] The police were summoned several times to TAAF's headquarters, to ports where the *Polarbjørn* called, and even to Expéditions polaires françaises' fortieth anniversary celebrations, all targets of the activists.[49] But the French had little success against Greenpeace's public relations strategy. The airstrip became a cause célèbre for ENGOs. "France deliberately broke the eggs of a hundred birds' nests and is ready to displace 5,000 penguins, contravening the provisions of international agreements of the protection of the environment," reported the spokesperson for the Antarctic and Southern Oceans Coalition.[50] With these protests came media coverage: "France dynamites Antarctic penguins" read a provocative headline in the *New Scientist*.[51]

Australia, too, was unhappy, complaining to the French embassy in Canberra that "by restarting construction, France risks to find itself again committing infractions against agreed measures as the project constitutes a danger for the survival of the Emperor penguin colony."[52] This tense meeting was part of two years of ongoing discussions between Australia and France as to whether France was contravening its obligations under the Antarctic Treaty System (ATS). While the French maintained that they were within their rights under the treaty, the Australians were uncomfortable with the immediate environmental consequences of the construction and with the longer-term implications for the stability of the ATS. The Australian concerns, however, were ultimately without teeth. While the Australian government initially considered closing the port of Hobart to France, in the end it not only kept the port open but also allowed the French to charter the Australian ship *Nella Dan* to transport heavy equipment to Terre Adélie. To France's advantage, Australia chose to prioritize unity within the ATS and its own Antarctic airstrip ambitions.[53] And Australia never did follow through on its veiled threat to come inspect the construction site under the auspices of the Antarctic Treaty, although it is unclear whether this was due to the high cost of such an inspection or to the French counterthreat to retaliate by inspecting the ice runway the Australians were proposing for their Casey Antarctic base.[54]

Environmentalism in France

While international ENGOs led a charge against the airstrip, there was less in the way of local or national protest against the project—a reflection of the state of environmentalism in France at the time.[55] In the 1960s, the environmental movement spread from the United States to Europe, making tentative inroads in France. French scientists, local politicians, and members of the public who lived close to sites of industrial degradation (such as the southern port zone of Fos-sur-Mer and the Breton coast, where the *Torrey Canyon* oil spill devastated the shore) began to speak out. Jean Dorst's 1965 book, *Avant que nature meure* (*Before Nature Dies*), one of the first French treatments of human impacts on nature, was widely read.[56] Still, the French public was largely unconcerned about and unengaged with environmental issues up to and after the events of 1968.

During the May 1968 civil unrest, protesters saw environmental problems as a secondary issue, a reflection of broader problems with France's political elite and consumer society. Still, May 1968 marks a turning point: before then, French environmentalism had been restricted to a small number of intellectuals, whereas the protests brought more attention, albeit not sustained, to the cause.

The French government responded to these burgeoning concerns by creating a Ministry for the Environment and Protection of Nature in 1971. This ministry, however, was weak, poorly funded, and unable to control its agenda. It struggled to take a holistic approach to the environment as large swaths of nature, such as forests, wildlife, and waters, were already under the control of other ministries who saw the newcomer as a rival. Other major issues with environmental aspects, such as energy, health, and planning, were also controlled by other, stronger, ministries. It was no secret that environmental policy was expected to be subservient to economic development: Valéry Giscard d'Estaing, then minister of the economy and finance, made it clear that the environment ministry should cost the state nothing. Soon, the new ministry's first leader, Robert Poujade (who was only a *ministre délégué*, or junior minister, and not a full cabinet minister—another indication of the ministry's lowly status), declared that it was "the ministry of the impossible" and resigned.[57]

As Jacques Theys writes, in the 1970s French environmental politics "was conceived of and institutionalized more as a short-term and technical response to a political problem (the crisis of May 1968) than as a real political choice."[58] It was a concession rather than representative of genuine political desire for change, favoring intellectual debate over action. Instead of tackling environmental problems, the new ministry sought to gain leverage over the environmental movement. "By hiring and directly engaging the movement's leadership, the ministry in some sense co-opted and silenced the political ecologists," notes Stephanie Pincetl: "Their issues became the state's issues, only to be relegated to intellectual debate."[59] For two decades, French environmental politics suffered from a persistent lack of legitimacy.

In French society, too, environmentalism was inchoate through the 1970s: the French public was less concerned about environmental issues than was the case in other western European countries. After the oil shock of 1973, the French government intensified the construction of nuclear power plants. The plan was met with ardent opposition: militant demonstrations against nuclear power, growing doubt about the state's ability to manage resources, and protests over industrial pollution raged through the middle of the decade, culminating with the sixty- to eighty-thousand strong protest at the Creys-Malville reactor site near Grenoble in the summer of 1977. As protesters threw Molotov cocktails, riot police responded with truncheons and tear gas, killing one man and seriously injuring more than one hundred others. But the antinuclear protests were not representative of any broader environmental movement; indeed, through the decade environmental issues were taken up by only a small minority.[60] ENGOs such as Greenpeace likewise had little success gaining members in France. The sinking of the *Amoco Cadiz* off the coast of Brittany in 1978, with its catastrophic oil spill, highlighted the fragility of coastal environments and the dangers of transporting petrol through those environments—but the ultimate lesson the French public learned from the sinking was that the idea of making polluters pay rarely works in practice, another obstacle to the take-up of environmental ideas.

As the 1980s opened, there was still no broad public concern over the environment in France, and what vitality had been present in the 1970s was drained by the stresses of another economic crisis. The French antinuclear movement receded as the impact of its protests proved minimal. The movement had lost the nuclear power battle, and not even the Three Mile Island (1979) and Chernobyl (1986) accidents did much to revive it.[61] While some environmentalists wanted to enter the political arena, they were not able to come together, agree on platforms, and run effective campaigns. When the left came back to power in 1981, environmentalists were initially optimistic, but the *Rainbow Warrior* bombing severed all bridges between the environmentalists and the left in power. As such, French environmentalism remained weak, especially in comparison with other western European countries.[62] With regards to the airstrip, while the Ministry of the Environment initially expressed concerns, it was swayed by the strategic arguments in favor of the airstrip and soon indicated that it would not oppose the project.[63]

That there was little in the way of protests against the Terre Adélie airstrip in France is part and parcel of this broader context. The Academy of Sciences and the small group of French biologists who spoke out against the project were exceptions to this rule. Among them, the animal biologists Yvon le Maho and René Groscolas wrote to French government officials and published an open letter in *Le Monde*: "The risks are unacceptable for scientific reasons as well as for the simple preservation of a wildlife capital and the protection of one of the Antarctic's most beautiful sites," they argued.[64] They were incensed over the environmental impact study, which they described as "particularly naive, especially concerning the consequences of the project on the mortality of birds." Terre Adélie held a deep place in Le Maho's heart—he had first overwintered at the Dumont-d'Urville base in 1971—and he firmly believed that the biological impacts of the project were being willfully ignored. Biologist Patrice Robinson, too, argued that the work was having dire consequences for Adélie penguins, cutting off their normal migration route and destroying an important nesting and reproduction site.⁶⁵ This was part of a wider conflict between disciplines in French Antarctic science, where biologists found themselves in the minority on a number of issues. In the airstrip context, their voices had little impact.

The Airstrip in Political Context

Why was the airstrip so strongly defended in France over the years, even as international opposition to the project grew? Through the 1980s, ENGOs won media coverage and harangued the French government, but they were unable to make the airstrip's environmental context matter at a high level. Bilateral complaints at France's embassies around the world, too, failed to resonate in government. For French authorities, the issues that drove the airstrip—strategic interests, national ambition, and sovereignty—trumped concerns for the environment. Throughout the 1980s, the airstrip's proponents were dismissive of environmental concerns, arguing that the construction would have minimal detrimental effects on bird life and that any damage would be eclipsed by the airstrip's benefits. Moreover, they simply refused to meaningfully engage with critics. The airstrip's opponents, Pieri thundered, were conducting "false and partisan campaigns."⁶⁶ Victor wrote bluntly that "all the numbers advanced by the project's adversaries [about the loss of bird life] are *false*."⁶⁷ He also ridiculed the concerned biologists, going so far as to accuse them of abusing their scientific responsibility, calling them "*tout feu tout flamme*" (all fired up).⁶⁸ While the minister of the environment did send a biologist, Vincent Bretagnolle, to mitigate disruption to bird populations, this was only after French biologists openly published data showing that the Emperor penguin colony close to the construction site had decreased in size by 60 percent between 1962 and 1989.⁶⁹ Bretagnolle ringed more than seven thousand birds, built barriers to prevent birds from nesting on the work site, and lured birds away from the construction zone by painting rocks white to imitate guano deposits.⁷⁰

The airstrip retained an aura of importance, indeed of necessity, to its supporters because the very idea of sovereignty over Terre Adélie had become embedded into the project. As Christy Collis and Quentin Stevens have written, Antarctic spaces are actively produced by physical practices and infrastructure: the installations built in the Antarctic are a means by which claimant countries exert control over distant possessions.⁷¹ For France, the airstrip was, from the get-go, construed as a potent symbol of French sovereignty over Terre Adélie. Despite occupying a small area at the very edge of the territory, the airstrip's imagined impact on France's Antarctic space was huge. Representing increased territorial control via improved access, it came to embody France's future in the

Antarctic; indeed, the airstrip and the claim to Terre Adélie became inseparable. In an era where technological and scientific achievements increasingly supported geopolitical power, the airstrip was a modest but pointed means of demonstrating France's political intentions in Antarctica. And as a way through which the government articulated its political intentions, the airstrip became entrenched in the production of France's Antarctic space.

Support for the airstrip was also connected to a wider lack of interest in environmental protection in government. While every French political party of the 1980s spoke about the importance of environmental protection, in practice environmental concerns did not greatly influence policy- and decision-making. The lack of high-level interest in the environment was exemplified by the aftermath of the sinking of the *Rainbow Warrior* in July 1985. The Greenpeace ship was in port in Auckland, about to lead a protest against French nuclear testing near the Mururoa Atoll, when French operatives bombed the ship, killing one man, the Portuguese-Dutch photographer Fernando Pereira. Tellingly, after finally admitting culpability, the French government expressed more regret over the arrest of its agents and the forced resignation of high-level officials than over France's position on nuclear testing.[72] Indeed, just months after the bombing, President Mitterrand visited Mururoa to show support for nuclear testing, and France resumed nuclear testing in the South Pacific the following year. While in the Pacific region the bombing aroused intense emotions and triggered protests against violations of rights, morals, and international law, in France there was an explosion of patriotic solidarity toward the two arrested agents, whose incarceration was seen as harassment, not justice. In French society, the state's use of violence to stymie Greenpeace's campaign, even in the waters of a friendly country, was entirely acceptable. This instinctive reaction is representative of a broader national solidarity surrounding France's worldwide status: when it comes to *grandeur*—and nothing embodies *grandeur* as much as an independent nuclear deterrent—the ends always justify the means.[73] High-level disregard for the environment was again visible in 1986 when, in the aftermath of the Chernobyl disaster, the French government deliberately concealed the domestic fallout in order to protect the French nuclear program. While other European countries panicked, in France the authorities calmly explained that the radioactive clouds had lost all their noxiousness by the time they arrived at the French border.[74] Independent tests showed otherwise. As Gerry Nagtzaam writes, by the mid-1980s France had developed a reputation as being "among the least interested states when it came to global environmental protection."[75]

This poor environmental reputation was accentuated by the government's position on the airstrip. Greenpeace and the Academy of Sciences argued that the construction violated the Agreed Measures for the Conservation of Antarctic

Fauna and Flora since it was wounding, killing, and interfering with the living conditions of native birds.[76] Adopted at the 1964 Antarctic Treaty Meeting in Brussels, the Agreed Measures aims to protect fauna and flora from the impact of human activity on the continent. Outside commentators agreed: the historian and polar expert Peter Beck, among others, argued that the airstrip construction "appeared to constitute a clear breach of the Agreed Measures" and certainly did not comply with the spirit of the safeguards.[77] The secretary of state for Overseas France responded forcefully to these accusations, making it clear that the French state was not going to allow the Agreed Measures to restrict its freedom to act in Terre Adélie: "Planning for air access does not constitute a violation of the treaty because it falls in the framework of necessary operations for the establishment, supply and exploitation of stations," he argued.[78] Allowing the Agreed Measures to interfere with the airstrip plans, he continued, would represent an unacceptable infringement on France's claim to Terre Adélie. To the government, the physical transformation of the Antarctic environment caused by the construction was justified by the strategic transformation of the space for France's benefit. In this context, the airstrip was seen as a means of boosting the legitimacy of the claim: a physical symbol of France's intention to remain in Terre Adélie despite the efforts by developing countries to dismantle existing claims. The physicality of the airstrip and its attendant structures (hangar, road, and control tower) were a stamp on the environment, a concrete sign of human, and specifically French, engagement in an otherwise almost entirely desolate territory.

This reaction is also indicative of the limits of France's policy of positive engagement with the Antarctic Treaty System. For France, the ATS is of appreciable value; it is the mechanism through which France wields power and influence in the Antarctic sphere, and it protects Terre Adélie at minimal cost to the French state. The French attitude toward the ATS has generally been one of positive, even eager, cooperation. But this has one important reservation: France has consistently defended its sovereignty interests in Terre Adélie and its sub-Antarctic possessions to the point of breaking with the consensus-based norms of the ATS when those interests are perceived to be threatened.

Minerals, Sovereignty, and Environment

While sovereignty over Terre Adélie was at the heart of the airstrip project through the 1980s, at the end of that decade France's geopolitical strategy for Antarctica shifted—with unexpected consequences for the airstrip. These changes were driven by the negotiation of a minerals convention for the Antarctic.

Like in the case of living marine resources, the Antarctic Treaty made no explicit reference to mineral exploration and exploitation—what is often called the "resource gap."[79] The sovereignty implications of minerals were simply too touchy to deal with at the end of the 1950s. In the 1970s, the question of Antarctic minerals came to the fore, propelled by the *Glomar Challenger* expedition, which uncovered potential traces of hydrocarbons in the Ross Sea, and the Arab oil crisis. But it was still unclear whether the Antarctic offered viable mineral resources, and, if so, how feasible it would be to extract them.

Within the French government, ministries jostled to bring attention to the Antarctic minerals question through the mid-to-late 1970s. Anxious to strengthen France's petrol politics, the Ministry of Scientific and Industrial Development saw the Antarctic as one ingredient in the diversification of hydrocarbon resources and pushed for the continent and its waters to be opened to prospecting and exploitation.[80] With technological progress, the ministry thought, French companies would be in a strong position to exploit hydrocarbon resources in Antarctic sedimentary deposits. Given that the chance of discovering hydrocarbons in Terre Adélie was thought to be zero, the ministry wanted France to obtain assurances from the other claimant states that French companies would have free access to more promising areas. This thinking was strategic but also speculative: no exploitable mineral resources had yet been discovered in Antarctica despite centuries of "treasure island" visions. The Ministry of Foreign Affairs partially concurred, instructing the French delegation to the 1974 Antarctic Treaty consultative meeting to announce that France was disposed to opening Antarctica to mineral exploration.[81] France's top diplomats were, however, more attuned to the sovereignty implications of resources, and made it clear that their first priority was to keep Terre Adélie as "a territory where her sovereignty is whole and entire."

In 1982, the Antarctic Treaty System consultative parties began negotiations to regulate mineral resources on the white continent.[82] At the same time, the ATS was being increasingly challenged by outsiders. Soon, the consultative parties saw the minerals question as a potential tipping point, an issue that, if not handled correctly, could destabilize or even destroy the ATS. The negotiations were tense and complex as the claimant states tried to balance the jurisdictional implications of mineral resources with the need to accommodate other parties in order to make the regime widely acceptable and forestall efforts to establish an alternative framework for Antarctica's management. And pressure was on: as Christopher Beeby, the New Zealander chair of the negotiations, wrote, "The most important reason for deciding to do the job quickly was that, for so long as the minerals question remained unresolved, it presented a *political* threat to the Antarctic Treaty and the Antarctic Treaty system."[83]

During the negotiations, France found itself in a difficult position, frustrated by the competing interests of the parties around the table. Bombarded with telegrams and instructions from Paris, the French negotiators were on the losing end of many debates, including veto powers over mining activity, which France wanted to disallow, fearing that they would be deployed for political purposes.[84] But ultimately the Ministry of Foreign Affairs instructed the French negotiators to not let specific issues stymie cooperation, judging that failure to reach an agreement quickly would weaken the ATS, potentially fatally.[85] In this respect, the presence of observer states such as India and Brazil at the meetings, as well as increasing pressure on the ATS from the developing world, swung the balance in the French position. For France, the negotiation of a strong agreement to show the collective character of the ATS's management and maintain control over Antarctic space proved more important than the details of the convention itself.[86]

The Convention on the Regulation of Antarctic Mineral Resource Activities (CRAMRA) negotiations lasted for six years, until June 1988. Despite being forced to accept significant compromises, as the convention took its final form the French negotiators sent a telegram to Paris recommending that it be accepted as it was the best possible deal for France under the circumstances.[87] The Overseas Ministry concurred, arguing that the convention was positive for French interests in Antarctica since it reinforced France's position at the heart of the "Antarctica club," it awarded France an important role on the regulation committees, and it kept the balance of power over Antarctica with the claimant states. France's main aim—strengthening "the credibility of the Antarctic system, its coherence and its operational character," as the envoy François Senemaud wrote—had been achieved.[88] Before the convention could come into force, it still had to be ratified by the sixteen consultative parties to the Antarctic Treaty.

In mid-1989, however, President Mitterrand declared that France would not ratify the minerals convention for environmental reasons—a death knell for the convention. Mitterrand's decision was a volte-face from a country that had long been considered one of the least pro-environment members of the Antarctic Treaty System, and an entirely unexpected decision given both how intensely France had been involved in the mineral rights negotiations and the strength of normative consensus-based decision-making in the ATS. Mitterrand's decision caught France's allies and outside commentators off guard.[89]

Concerned about the implications of the minerals protocol for its territorial rights in the Antarctic, Australia likewise declined to ratify it.[90] Together, the two countries published a joint communiqué declaring their desire to instead establish a comprehensive environmental protection regime for Antarctica.[91] After fierce negotiations, this came to fruition just two years later, in 1991, when the Protocol on Environmental Protection to the Antarctic Treaty was signed in Madrid, designating Antarctica as a "natural reserve, devoted to peace and science." Known as the Madrid Protocol, it came into force in 1998.[92] The Madrid Protocol prohibits all activities related to mineral resources in the Antarctic, other than scientific research, until 2048; this can only be changed with the unanimous consent of the consultative parties and if a binding legal regime on Antarctic mineral resource activities is in force.[93] With regard to sovereignty concerns—always a sticky issue in the Antarctic—the Madrid Protocol's ban on mining acts to prevent potential disputes over the ownership of any exploitable mineral resources.

Why did France change its mind on the minerals convention and pursue the Madrid Protocol? And how did this connect to the Terre Adélie airstrip? In 1989, two widely publicized oil spills highlighted the fragility of the polar regions: the *Exxon Valdez*, which spilled 10.8 million US gallons of oil in Alaska's Prince William Sound, and the *Bahia Paraiso*, which unleashed 170,000 US gallons of oil when it sank in Antarctica's Arthur Harbor. Both resulted in environmental catastrophes. Images of the devastation, broadcast by media around the globe, gave ammunition to ENGOs in their fight against the minerals protocol. Together with growing interest in ozone depletion over the Antarctic and awareness of the white continent's importance for climate change, these oil spills fueled a global turn toward the protection of Antarctica's environment. While in 1982, when the minerals negotiations began, global warming and ozone depletion were hardly on the radar, by 1989 they were major international issues and the Antarctic was considered critical to understanding them. In that year, a "green fever" erupted: *Time* magazine chose planet Earth as its "person of the year" and in France the popular television station TF1 declared that human damage to the natural environment was endangering the planet's future. As the environment came to the fore in Antarctic geopolitics, the mineral protocol's credibility suffered a blow. Mineral exploration and exploitation of any kind would engender environmental risks that were now much less defensible.

In France, the oceanographic explorer and conservationist Jacques Cousteau (1910–1997) took up the Antarctic minerals cause. A pioneer of modern underwater diving and filmography, Cousteau also had strong environmental interests that grew from his successful publicity campaign against the planned dumping of radioactive waste in the Mediterranean Sea by the *Commissariat à l'énergie atomique* in 1960. In the postwar decades, he became known worldwide as a television personality for bringing the undersea world to life. His American television series, *The Undersea World of Jacques Cousteau*, which ran from 1966 to 1976, enamored him to the American public: his thick French accent, epic adventures, and unmistakable red bonnet were uniquely appealing. Building on this fame, he created the Cousteau Society, a US-based international ENGO, in 1973 as part of a campaign to win funding to finance expeditions around the world. His society grew into a leading body for environmental protection. Cousteau's choice to operate out of the United States was driven by the weakness of environmentalism in France at the time. He created a sister organization in France in 1981, but even then he continued to focus the majority of his efforts stateside. The French public was much less receptive to his ideas than the American public, and he was continually frustrated by the red tape that stymied his French society. Still, as he campaigned hard against the minerals convention, painting mining as a grave risk to Antarctica's fragile environment, this vision gained enough ground in France to make a critical difference. When Cousteau's petition against the convention gained 180,000 signatures, the French government was forced to sit up and take notice.[94]

Cousteau, along with Victor, also directly lobbied the French government, and the two respected voices had the ear of President Mitterrand and Prime Minister Michel Rocard. Victor wrote to Mitterrand with an urgent plea: "The recent catastrophe on the Antarctic peninsula [the *Bahia Paraiso* spill], which may have worldwide consequences for certain fundamental ecosystems, demonstrates the extent to which it would be aberrant to not definitively protect the Antarctic continent from all aggressions including those that it would suffer as a consequence of [mineral] exploitation."[95] "With force and urgency," Victor continued, "I take the liberty to ask you to demonstrate to the world international civic spirit by refusing to sign the Wellington Convention of June 1988 [the minerals convention]." In the spring of 1989, Mitterrand declared publicly that he had consulted Cousteau on the minerals convention. "His proposition to make the Antarctic continent an international natural reserve has seduced me," said Mitterrand: "I am going to ask the French government to study this proposition and to see if whether, together with the countries who share our preoccupations, it would be possible to implement this idea without delay."[96]

Through early to mid-1989, Antarctic issues were discussed at high levels in the French government, and soon both Mitterrand and Rocard adopted the Antarctic as a personal crusade.[97] In the aftermath of the oil spills, Rocard argued, the mineral convention's provisions for environmental protection could no longer be considered adequate, and neither could its fundamental basis—that is, that mining in the Antarctic was in principle acceptable.[98] This represented a reversal of the position France had held since the 1970s. Protecting Antarctica's environment, Rocard announced in the autumn of 1989, is "my most fervent desire."[99] Rocard's personal rapport with the Australian prime minister Robert (Bob) Hawke, who likewise decided to reject the minerals convention, was also central to shaping the French government's position on the Antarctic. This rapport, nurtured by Rocard's personal charm, was critical to reviving the French-Australian bilateral relationship, which had been in tatters for a decade.[100] Gone were the days in which Australia treated France as a political rival in the Antarctic; on the minerals protocol, the two countries formed a united front. In France, the minerals convention was also opposed by the National Assembly, whose president, Laurent Fabius, was irritated that he had been shut out of the negotiations. Together, these voices called for France to fight for a complete ban on mineral exploitation and to protect the Antarctic "from any and all risks of pollution regardless of their origin."[101] Mitterrand's final decision echoed Cousteau's position: "I am preoccupied by the safeguarding of the Antarctic continent," he said, and with the "idea of transforming this continent into a vast natural and peaceful reserve."

This decision was part of a nascent but limited validation of environmental concerns in government. Elected in the spring of 1988, France's new Socialist government included committed environmentalists, most importantly Brice Lalonde. A political ecologist, founding member of *Les amis de la terre* (which campaigned against the French nuclear program through the 1970s), and ecological candidate in the 1981 presidential election, Lalonde was recruited to government from a European think tank. He was named secretary of state and then minister for the environment—the first ecologist to hold this position. He immediately launched an assertive environmental agenda at home and abroad, ratifying international treaties including the Montreal Protocol (CFCs/ozone), the Bonn Convention (protection of migratory species), and the Bern Convention (protection of natural habitats), as well as banning ivory imports into France. Domestically, his government's *plan vert* was adopted in October 1990. For Lalonde, opposition to mining in the Antarctic was a matter of identity. But even with his environmentalist credentials, he was in no position to change the government's stance on issues of significant national importance, such as nuclear testing. The Socialist government he served was, as Robert Gildea writes, "happy to steal individual policies from the ecologists, but not to let them interfere with the overall thrust of their strategy."[102] On the Antarctic minerals question, Lalonde's views carried weight as Mitterrand and Rocard formulated their position.

The French rejection of the minerals convention cannot, however, be attributed simply or solely to an environmental turn in government. Several analyses of this volte-face argue that it was steeped in environmental altruism, or, an explicit desire to improve the country's image on the world stage after having been lambasted for a trio of environmental mistakes in the 1980s: the *Rainbow Warrior* bombing, the Terre Adélie airstrip, and nuclear testing in the Pacific.[103] While this explanation makes logical sense, it is not supported by the archival material. It is important not to conflate environmental credentials and choices with conversion to the cause. This is not a story of simple altruism, or adoption of environmentalism. It is more complicated than that, entangled with two strongly political rationales: domestic politics and electoral strategy, and strategic considerations in the Antarctic.

Electoral pressure from the ecological movement and from pro-environmental voters made the environment matter on the French political agenda in late 1988 and into 1989.[104] Domestically, green candidates were making strong inroads. In the cantonal elections of autumn 1988, the Greens broke through the 5 percent barrier for the first time. And in municipal elections the following spring, Nantes, Toulouse, Lyon, and Bordeaux all saw victories for Green lists. In total, two thousand Green or Green-leaning candidates were elected to municipal councils in what Brendan Prendiville has called a "green wave" sweeping over France.[105] Mitterrand's refusal to ratify the minerals convention was meant to counter this momentum. On the European front, too, pollsters predicted dramatic breakthroughs for the surging Green parties in the mid-1989 parliamentary elections.[106] In the lead-up to those elections, Green interests in France came together for the first time and presented a single list, whose popularity soared. Mitterrand's volte-face on Antarctic minerals was part of his strategy for those elections, designed to attract potential Green voters and to demonstrate that the Socialists were responsive to environmental concerns. Still, Mitterrand was hugely tarnished by the *Rainbow Warrior* scandal and even with the minerals decision he found it hard to win the environmentalists back. In a major breakthrough the Greens won 10 percent of the vote and made their entrance on the European parliamentary scene, with a significant portion of those votes coming from former Socialist supporters.

The rise of green politics in France at the end of the 1980s is representative of the new life environmentalism enjoyed in the country at that time. After decades of stagnation, environmentalism was beginning to spread wings in French society: environmentalist ideas circulated more widely and in many aspects of social life, ecology and the environment became "in" topics. As business leaders, intellectuals, and politicians pronounced themselves "green," environmentalism edged toward the mainstream. Still, while it was chic to be concerned about environmental issues, real action still lagged. Even with major policy announcements such as the Antarctic minerals convention rejection, France continued to be seen internationally as among the worst offenders in the realm of environmental protection. And this environmental spirit did not persist for long: after the Rio de Janeiro Earth Summit in 1992, environmental issues again took on a leisurely pace in France.[107] Three years later, when newly elected president Jacques Chirac ordered a series of nuclear tests in the South Pacific coinciding with the negotiation of the Comprehensive Test Ban Treaty, France again became a pariah in the international environmental community. Still, there was relatively more acceptance of environmental ideas and the environment continued to matter in the Antarctic arena.

Mitterrand's rejection of the Antarctic minerals convention also spoke directly to strategic concerns about the French claim to Terre Adélie. In the late 1980s, as the environment came to matter in a way it had not earlier in the decade, the developing country group and ENGOs who had long been focused on Antarctica found their leverage. Malaysia spoke out at the United Nations, portraying the minerals convention and the Antarctic Treaty System as antienvironment. The ENGOs argued that the consultative parties would not be able to make good on the convention's environmental safeguards and portrayed the protocol as a slippery slope toward environmental degradation in the Antarctic.[108] For the ENGOs, the ongoing Terre Adélie airstrip saga was proof that the ATS would not reign in problematic projects, and was as such a red flag for minerals exploration and exploitation. The penalty for France if it was to ignore these voices, as Marie Françoise Labouz has written, was "discredit, or even disappearance" from Antarctic affairs.[109] In this context, senior figures in the French government considered the rejection of the minerals convention on environmental grounds and the proposal of the Madrid Protocol as the most effective way to protect the French claim to Terre Adélie: by championing a protocol for environmental protection within the existing ATS, they negated the environmental arguments for the creation of a supranational control authority.[110]

Indeed, while held up as an environmental victory, the Madrid Protocol was also designed to serve narrower French and Australian interests. For those two countries, the protocol was both a tool for environmental protection and a tool for restoring the Antarctic Treaty System's moral legitimacy. By trading autonomy in action for a more stable and robust ATS, it was, in Bruce Byers's terms, a "sovereignty bargain" that maintained Antarctica's power dynamics firmly in the ATS's court, exactly as France and Australia wanted it.[111] Foreign Minister Roland Dumas made this explicit: France's rejection of the minerals convention, he wrote, aimed at "the consolidation of the Antarctic Treaty System and its improvement to counter the doubts and criticisms levied against it."[112] This power play is generally regarded as having been successful both within France and by historians.[113] In this way, France retained authority on Antarctica's political scene and legitimacy in Terre Adélie. Further, France's leadership in this context built its reputation as a powerhouse in Antarctic environmental governance, important to French diplomats as it gave the country a means of exerting influence outside the Anglo-Saxon dominated SCAR.[114]

The French government also saw the rejection of the minerals convention as a way of preventing other countries from increasing their power in Antarctica, thereby preserving France's place as a major player in the Antarctic sphere. Countries such as Chile and China, Jean-Yves Le Deaut of the Parliamentary Office for Evaluating Scientific and Technological Choices noted, were acting aggressively in the Antarctic, by sending pregnant women to Antarctica to give birth (Chile) or by building large numbers of "supposedly scientific" bases in order to secure presence (China).[115] If Antarctic mining were to go ahead, Le Deaut emphasized, "we cannot completely exclude the opening by a claimant country of 'political' mining or petroleum installations which will serve only to affirm their rights to a territory. This could also be the case for countries which until now have not presented claims but which do not want the Antarctic to remain a domain reserved for a small club of developed countries." For France, limiting possibilities on the white continent was a means of self-preservation. And Le Deaut's assessment that significant mineral deposits in the Antarctic, should they exist, would be economically and technologically unexploitable for a long time into the future quelled any push for France to capitalize on the opening of the continent to minerals activity.

With these decisions, France found itself in a new position vis-à-vis other Antarctic actors: the many voices that had criticized France, often vociferously, through the 1980s, from Australia to the developing country group led by Malaysia to the ENGO group led by Greenpeace, now publicly supported France's new environmental stance.[116] Greenpeace even invited French diplomats in Wellington to a reception on board the *Gondwana*, declaring that "we have had our differences with France, but we support your policy in the Antarctic"—an impressive offer given that the French state had bombed a Greenpeace ship in New Zealand only five years previously.[117]

The volte-face on Antarctic minerals also represents another instance in which France broke with its normal policy of positive cooperation in the Antarctic Treaty System. After six years of negotiations, there was every reason to expect all countries to ratify the convention, especially given the informal rules governing common behavior at the ATS. A high degree of trust—the belief that governments are acting and negotiating in good faith—is critical to the effective functioning of the ATS.[118] For France to break these rules and reject a convention for which it had fought hard for years was remarkable. Here we see a similarity with France's decision on living marine resources: in both cases, France put sovereignty above adhering to the ATS's norms. While in the case of living marine resources, France's defense of its sovereignty priorities did not kill the convention as it did in the minerals case, both are representative of the limits of French adherence to the cooperative nature of the ATS.

The End of the Airstrip

As these events were swirling in Paris, the construction team in Terre Adélie dynamited and moved almost two million tons of rock, leveling Cuvier, Lion, Zeus, and Buffon Islands and lacing them together with the debris.[119] Gradually a long airstrip emerged, its straight sides and flat grayness an anomaly in its icy environment. By mid-1989, the blasting was all but complete: the causeway reached the last island and a zone had been prepared for a hangar and control tower (figure 20).

The Terre Adélie airstrip was finally completed in early 1993, over ten years after construction first began. The first plane to land on the airstrip, a French Air Force Hercules C-130, was scheduled for February 1994. In celebration, France released a stamp showing an airplane swooping above the rocky tip of Terre Adélie, the long airstrip gleaming in the background. But the stamp was premature: just two weeks before the plane was due to land, a storm hit Pointe Géologie. Winds whipped over two hundred kilometers per hour, causing ice to shelve from a nearby glacier and a tidal wave to slam into the causeway. The air-

FIGURE 20. High-altitude aerial view to the southeast, 1990: In the foreground is the airstrip under construction, with the razed islands clearly visible. The archipelago, the Dumont-d'Urville base, and the continent can also be seen (Antoine Guichard, Archipôles, IPEV).

strip was destroyed. Over two decades of planning, building, and strategizing was laid to waste by a single storm; what had taken years of political wrangling and on-the-ground earth moving to build was gone in a flash.

Why had such an event not been foreseen? The district chief in Terre Adélie blamed the storm's intense violence, calling it without precedent and utterly unpredictable.[120] But it is clear that Expéditions polaires françaises grossly underestimated the action of the sea and waves in its preparatory studies. This oversight is due to self-bias: the studies were strongly influenced by Expéditions polaires françaises' steadfast desire for the airstrip project to go ahead, by the belief that only an airstrip could resuscitate France's position in the Antarctic. It is also representative of the concentration of knowledge in Expéditions polaires françaises, its long history as a private organization, and its general disdain for external consultation. Government auditors lambasted the outcome, calling it a "poorly thought out [and] unhappy affair" that had "gravely underestimated" both the risks of natural disaster and the environmental damage wrought and led to the "pure loss" of more than 100 million francs.[121]

With the airstrip destroyed, the French government found itself in a delicate situation: on one hand, one basic premise underpinning the airstrip had always been to reinforce French sovereignty over Terre Adélie—something that could not simply be cast aside. On the other hand, it was not clear that rebuilding the airstrip would be successful, even if the necessary rock could be found, blasted, and moved. It was also unclear where the money to do so would come from. And, more importantly, given France's push for environmental governance in the Antarctic, the environmental consequences of rebuilding were hard to justify. In fact, the contradiction had been visible for some time and had been a quiet source of tension during the final years of construction.

The airstrip's fate was announced by Michel Barnier, the new minister of the environment in Mitterrand's government. With a long history of environmental interest, Barnier was a natural choice for the portfolio. He had been *chargé de mission* in Robert Poujade's cabinet in the early 1970s and had advocated environmental protection throughout his long tenure as the deputy for Savoie. After deliberation, Barnier declared the end of the airstrip project in the autumn of 1994. France's Antarctic airstrip had never been used and would never be used. Barnier gave two reasons for ending the project: "France's desire to better protect the Antarctic environment" and the cost and difficulty of rebuilding.[122] This decision went against the explicit wishes of Terre Adélie's district chief.

With French Antarctic diplomacy now guided by an environmental protocol that had given new wind to the Antarctic Treaty System's legitimacy, the political situation facing the French government was starkly different than it had been during the airstrip's construction. Through the 1980s, the airstrip had been a physical symbol of French commitment to its Antarctic claim and was seen as essential to maintaining that claim. But once French authority in Terre Adélie and legitimacy in Antarctic affairs had been bolstered by the minerals convention and Madrid Protocol decisions, the argument that the airstrip was primal to the territorial claim lost its driving force. Further, France's new, very public commitment to environmental protection in the Antarctic meant that rebuilding the airstrip was not defensible in light of the amount of further blasting, harm to birds, and damage to the landscape that would incur. By citing environmental protection as a key reason for terminating the airstrip project, Barnier reinforced France's strategic position within Antarctica's evolving political dynamics.

9

AN UNCERTAIN FUTURE

At the same time as President François Mitterrand's volte-face on the minerals convention reoriented his country's Antarctic stance, major changes were shaking up French polar research. In early autumn 1989, the overseas minister and the minister for research and technology demanded an evaluation of France's polar activities in order to get to the bottom of TAAF's persistent funding crises. The report, delivered just two months later by Claude Fréjacques (the president of the *Centre national de la recherche scientifique* and of TAAF's consultative council) and Frédéric Thiriez (a senior director at the Overseas Ministry), was damning. France was weak in both Arctic and Antarctic affairs, the men wrote, with a polar budget of half or less than that of comparable countries: while France's polar budget in 1989 was 110 million francs, those of Britain and West Germany were 250 million francs and 230 million francs, respectively. France used to be a strong player in Arctic research, they continued, but "has now been reduced to participation in a few operations here and there via international partnership."[1] The risk of an Arctic treaty between the bordering countries meant France would be entirely excluded from that region of the globe unless it augmented its presence. The outlook in Antarctica was better, but still French Antarctic science was clearly suffering, and unless France demonstrated more commitment and investment it would soon be without means and left out of international cooperation. Fréjacques and Thiriez then linked the two polar worlds, recommending that France establish a new polar organization to cover both Arctic and Antarctic research.

The idea of a new French polar organization had been floated for a while but had not been championed by anyone until this moment. Emboldened by high-level political interest in the Antarctic, the ministries saw a chance to act, to reform French polar research to their liking after years of frustration. As Mitterrand and Prime Minister Michel Rocard shone a spotlight on Antarctica's environment, the idea of France abandoning the Dumont-d'Urville base, long mooted, was definitively off the table. Environmentalism in the Antarctic was now official government policy and enjoyed support at the highest levels. Publicly, the ministries announced that the conditions had "come together for French polar research to have a new momentum and for our country to preserve its place in this peaceful competition between nations, that is to say among the first"—a clear harkening back to Jean-Baptiste Charcot's vision enunciated nearly a century earlier.[2] Still, they were not about to let go of their battle with TAAF. The ministries made it clear that they wanted a new structure for French polar research not only to revitalize it and create robust support mechanisms for it, but also to reduce TAAF's authority in wake of the auditors' criticisms. But there were competing interests and strong feelings.

With Mitterrand's and Rocard's push for an environmental protocol in the Antarctic, and especially with the environment acting as the public face behind their rejection of the minerals convention, France staked a claim: the Antarctic was a place where France was going to be active and decisive, a place where the environment was going to matter in decision-making. Armed with this high-level support, the ministries decided that France should aim to capture a big slice of the polar environmental research pie. The Antarctic and the Arctic, the ministries explained, held "the key to numerous questions about our universe and its future," from the ozone layer to the general circulation of the atmosphere to climate history and change.[3] Speaking in the summer of 1990, Louis Le Pensec, the overseas minister, made clear his aim: pointing to France's championing of a global convention for the protection of the Antarctic, he called for the "exceptional natural laboratory" of Antarctica to be preserved and for polar science to progress in the interests of humanity as a whole—and for France to lead these efforts.[4] But these steps toward shedding France's long-held international reputation as an environmental pariah were as motivated by internal French politics as they were by environmental concerns.

The plan to link the Arctic and Antarctic in a new polar organization was fueled by a trio of reasons: pride, pragmatism, and punishment. Given that all big countries possessed a polar organization covering both the Arctic and the Antarctic, the ministries felt that France should follow suit. France's pride and prestige in the polar spheres mandated it, the ministries insisted, and without joining the two poles, France would fall further behind and be unable to cooperate and compete on the international scene. Given the similarities of the themes, methods, and logistical problems of scientific research in the Arctic and the Antarctic, too, the ministries thought it pragmatic to link them. A new organization was also seen as a practical way of amalgamating the various disparate forces governing French polar science at the time. Lastly, linking the Arctic and Antarctic was a convenient way for the ministries to punish TAAF for decades of financial and administrative turmoil. Since France had no territorial possession in the Arctic region, the ministries argued, TAAF could not take on the role of an interlocutor with foreign partners in that region—and thus could not take a leading role in the new polar organization.[5] This was part of a broader argument which held that TAAF's legal structure and political connections meant that it was not the best vehicle for French research in the austral territories.

At the heart of the proposal for a new polar organization was a scientific station in the interior of Antarctica—something French scientists had long hoped for, but which was very expensive and logistically difficult. At the time, there were only two interior stations (Amundsen-Scott, run by the Americans, and Vostok, by the Soviets), but the interior offered unparalleled access to knowledge about the planet. By building an interior station, France would be able to both prove that it could keep up with the superpowers in the Antarctic and contribute to answering pressing environmental questions. While scientists and Expéditions polaires françaises saw Dome C (as the yet-unbuilt station was known) as crucial for boosting France's image in the international scientific community, for the government it represented a place where France could stake out its new environmental position in the Antarctic.

The site chosen for Dome C was located in Australia's Antarctic territory, taking advantage of the free access for scientific research allowed by the Antarctic Treaty. One of the coldest places on Earth, it is under the ozone hole and isolated from pollution and maritime influences, making it an ideal natural geophysical and astronomical observatory. In the mid-1970s, the French—with essential American help—drilled an impressive kilometer-long ice core there, extracting samples reaching back fifty thousand years. And during the austral summer of 1979, a joint French-American team undertook ice core drilling and seismological and meteorological studies at the site, work again only made possible by American logistics and funding. But still the site lacked a permanent station. In 1990, the two ministers leading the reorganization of French polar research, Hubert Curien (research and technology) and Louis Le Pensec (overseas), publicly announced their intention to move forward with a permanent Dome C station. The new French commitment to an environmental path in the Antarctic seemed to have legs. But despite multiple public announcements and much backroom maneuvering, through the end of 1990 and into 1991 no real progress was made. There was a fundamental discord between the ministries, who were eager to take authority away from TAAF, and TAAF itself, forced into a posture of self-defense. Power, authority, and control were at stake.

At TAAF, the government's sudden intense interest in the polar worlds was viewed with suspicion. Bernard Morlet and Bernard de Gouttes (TAAF's chief administrator from 1990 to 1991) correctly saw the new polar organization as a mechanism for sidelining TAAF, in effect punishing the territory for years of financial problems.[6] Concerned that TAAF's control over its scientific mission would be reduced, Morlet petitioned for TAAF to maintain its authority over French Antarctic and sub-Antarctic science, pointing to the science-sovereignty link that had underpinned Antarctic legitimacy for decades. Research, Morlet argued, was TAAF's raison d'être, the means by which TAAF assured French sovereignty over its districts—and thus research "cannot be dissociated from the Territory," as he repeated over and over in public and private.[7] Morlet's position, however, was weakened by the damning auditors' report, which made it difficult for him to defend TAAF in government circles.

Pushed to the wall, Morlet and de Gouttes dug in their heels, obstructing and obfuscating, refusing to assist with tasks to build the new polar organization. When asked for documents about TAAF's personnel, Morlet did not reply; for his part, de Gouttes deliberately muddled his responses to questions about TAAF's budget—all of which, complained officials at the Ministry of Research and Technology, made it impossible to figure out staffing and a provisional budget.[8] Thoroughly fed up with TAAF, the Overseas Ministry decided that funding for Antarctic research would not be increased until the new polar body was up and running.[9] New projects in the Antarctic, the ministry hoped, would be removed from TAAF's hands. Indeed, the ministry's contribution to TAAF had fallen by a quarter between 1980 and 1990—a decline significant enough to threaten the entire scientific program in Terre Adélie. The Overseas Ministry was so incensed that it even proposed dissolving Expéditions polaires françaises completely despite it being the chief repository of polar logistical knowledge in France.[10]

For his part, Paul-Emile Victor was furious. In the late autumn of 1990, he appealed publicly to Prime Minister Rocard to establish the new polar organization immediately. The delay, he said, was "a catastrophic lateness" due to "interpersonal quarrels, heavy and slow administrative structures, a general lack of dynamism, and no financing"—an accurate, if damning, assessment.[11] "At this rate, in two years France will lose the enviable place in the polar regions she has built up over the past 30 years," he continued: "She will be absent from European Arctic science; and she will have definitively lost her pioneer rank in Antarctica." Victor was soon granted a meeting with Rocard—confirmation of his continued influence in government even after retirement. At the meeting,

Rocard assured Victor that action would be taken within a fortnight. But when Rocard was forced to resign after clashing with Mitterrand, with whom he had a notoriously poor relationship, and Laurent Fabius, the matter was once again delayed.[12]

It was not until a year and a half later, in early 1992, that the new polar organization, called *Institut français pour la recherche et la technologie polaire* (French Institute for Polar Research and Technology), was created. Headquartered in Paris, it was responsible for selecting and financing scientific programs, organizing expeditions, participating in international scientific work, and managing laboratories in the polar and subpolar regions, as well as building a station at Dome C. It brought together representatives from the Overseas Ministry, the Ministry of Research and Technology, TAAF, Expéditions polaires françaises, and national scientific institutes—the key French structures, in short, whose work touched on the polar and subpolar regions. In 2002, its name was changed to *Institut polaire français Paul-Emile Victor* (often simply called the *Institut polaire français*, or IPEV) in honor of the dean of modern French polar work who had passed away seven years earlier.

While the new organization was instructed to assure the continuity of existing research, scientific activities, and operations, the animosity of the past two decades persisted, driven by long-standing mistrust and resentment. TAAF's chief administrator was prevented from taking a leading role in the new system—a serious blow to the territory, which continued to feel that it was treated as a second-class political citizen. Morlet himself was pushed aside because he would not come into line—something he saw as an immense deception and which he looked back on bitterly for the rest of his life.[13] And rather than ending the ongoing intragovernmental feuds, the creation of the new organization merely transformed their setting.

Following the Narrative to the Present Day

Since the early 1990s, the environmental approach that followed from France's rejection of the minerals convention and sponsorship of the Madrid Protocol has provided a clear narrative for the country's course in the Antarctic. It has not, however, put an end to the peaks and troughs of the preceding decades. This approach has also by no means been perfect; in particular, it took France far too long to pass legal and regulatory measures to enshrine the Madrid Protocol stipulations in law. Samuel Deliancourt rightly calls France's delays in this respect embarrassing in the context of the country's desire to be a leader in the protection of Antarctica's environment.[14]

The creation of the *Institut français pour la recherche et la technologie polaire* did boost French Antarctic science, and France remains a significant actor in that field. In cooperation with Italy, France finally built a scientific station at the Dome C site in the interior of the Antarctic Continent—something its scientists had long hoped for. The station, named Concordia, opened for the austral summers in 1996 and as a year-round facility in 2005. It represents a place where the French government can stake out its environmental position in Antarctic research. Due to the failure of the airstrip project, Concordia relies on overland convoys to cover the 1,100 kilometers of ice separating it from the coastal Dumont-d'Urville base.[15] The partnership with Italy, while not France's preferred option, was necessary for both countries: Italy provided money, which France lacked, and the French provided to the Italians a foothold into the Antarctic. France is also participating in the ambitious European "Beyond EPICA" ice core project, which aims to drill a 2.7-kilometer-long ice core and shed new light on Earth's climate history over the past 1.5 million years. Begun in 2019, Beyond EPICA's first results are expected in 2025. Ironically, the project is being led by Italian scientists, who had been shown the ropes in the Antarctic by the French. It is clear that the French government continues to see Antarctic research, and particularly ice core research, as a potent political symbol, a means of showing that France is "powerful and scientifically sophisticated," as Christian Gaudin of the Parliamentary Office for the Evaluation of Scientific and Technological Choices put it.[16] Indeed, this environmentally oriented scientific research is performing a political task toward legitimating the French claim. But still, even as France remains a world leader in terms of the number of scientific publications on the Antarctic and sub-Antarctic, investment in scientific resources, logistics, and human capital continues to falter.[17]

The political and institutional bickering that so colored France's polar efforts for decades has not abated. The two main players in French polar work, the Institut polaire français and TAAF, continue to disagree, especially in areas where their mandates overlap. Instead of cooperating, they often act as rivals. Government reports repeatedly stress that the lack of clarity surrounding their mandates is causing duplication, confusion, and waste, even going so far as to call on the prime minister's office to step in and regularize Terre Adélie's management.[18] TAAF's financial mismanagement, too, shows little improvement: problems with receipts, ordering, and accounts abound and there is a painful lack of transparency over simple matters such as the sale of stamps.[19]

The old funding problem also persists. French investment in the Antarctic remains significantly lower than that of other comparable countries, something regularly pointed out in the National Assembly, by scientists, in government reports, and in the media. Terre Adélie's budget is strained and the Dumont-d'Urville base suffers for it, with serious sanitation and maintenance problems. "The Dumont-d'Urville base is the major symbol of our presence," wrote Gaudin in 2007: "It is our duty to have a station in line with our rank and not a disorganized series of dilapidated buildings."[20] The base has not greatly improved since then. Chronically insufficient funding is continually complained about by those in charge of, and in charge of evaluating, France's role in the Antarctic: scientific research is not as robust as it could be, morale among personnel is low, and logistics are weak.[21] While the Institut polaire français and TAAF have made it clear that €70 million are necessary over the next twenty-five years to renovate the Dumont-d'Urville base, of which €40 million are needed immediately, no money appears to be forthcoming. Perhaps most embarrassing is that France is being outspent by countries with no territorial claim in the polar regions: while France spent about €18 million on polar research in 2019, Italy spent €20 million, and both were far eclipsed by other nonclaimant countries such as South Korea (€45 million) and Germany (€50 million).[22]

The link between investment in its myriad forms and sovereignty is clear. When the Institut polaire français' director, Jérôme Chappellaz, addressed the National Assembly in mid-2019, he asked the French government to consider carefully whether the country was still committed to playing a role in the Antarctic.[23] Without more investment, Chappellaz asserted, "not only will we lose our rank as a nation currently located at the forefront of scientific production in Antarctica, but France's weight in the Antarctic diplomatic context as well as its initial claim of sovereignty in Terre Adélie could be called into question." These issues were almost verbatim those that had defined the preceding several decades of France's relationship with the Antarctic. In particular, Chappellaz's appeal to the sovereignty question to push for additional funding recalls Morlet's earlier efforts to link sovereignty and science. As Olivier Poivre d'Arvor, France's ambassador for the polar regions, added in early 2022, France's legitimacy in the Antarctic sphere on all levels—politically, morally, scientifically, and potentially legally—will continue to fall if France is not seen to be invested, literally and figuratively, in the continent's future.[24] Once again, France risks being left out and left behind in the Antarctic arena.

The high cost of operating in the polar regions has of late been pushing France toward a European-based strategy, something it had been loath to pursue in earlier decades. In the 1980s, France chose to stay out of European projects in order to emphasize French-specific capacity in the Antarctic, something seen clearly when Morlet refused to join a European icebreaker project for reasons of sovereignty.[25] Now, the "colossal" costs of polar logistics are making cooperation more appealing.[26] France already cooperates with the Italians in the Antarctic (Concordia Station) and the Germans in the Arctic (the AWIPEV research base in Ny-Ålesund), among other projects. But cooperation is more appealing to France in the north than in the south given the lack of French capacity and territorial claims in the north. In the south, there is an underlying wariness since most European countries do not recognize France's claim to Terre Adélie, as Germany made very clear in its United Nations submission on continental shelf claims in 2005.[27] Still, France is embarking on a two-pronged European strategy in the Antarctic: First, eager to build the Institut polaire français into the leading European Antarctic projects body, France is increasingly coordinating, organizing, and participating in cooperative scientific projects. Here, there is a strong element of prestige; while France is open to scientific cooperation, it wants to be directing that work, not merely participating. Despite a persistent lack of money, the feeling of entitlement that has long colored France's polar affairs endures. Second, France is opening its bases to EU member countries with little Antarctic experience, at once enabling them to undertake Antarctic work and promoting French capacity on the continent. To France, a European strategy represents a means of competing with the great powers in the Antarctic, something which it is increasingly clear that isolated European nations cannot do on their own.[28] But even as this is understood in principle, practical commitment is lacking. While France and Italy agreed in early 2021 to renovate Concordia Station, for example, the Institut polaire français has no means of contributing France's €10 million share of the costs.[29]

Access weaknesses, too, continue to pose challenges to France's Antarctic future. The new French icebreaker, again called the *Astrolabe*, developed a major defect during its first trip to Terre Adélie in late 2019.[30] As a result, planned scientific work was canceled and the French were forced to rely on Australia to service Terre Adélie. As pointed out in the National Assembly, this meant that access to a French territory was once again entrusted to a foreign country, a "critical situation which puts research and French sovereignty in the TAAF in danger."[31] Between the lack of air access and the pack ice that can completely block maritime access, France cannot be said to have fully independent access to Terre Adélie—certainly not through the long austral winters nor to its vast interior. The icebreaker situation is particularly poignant since France's lack of a dedicated scientific icebreaker divides it from other major polar powers, a clear sign of not belonging with the "big players."[32] Even when it is running, the new *Astrolabe* is heavily used by the French Navy to patrol France's Exclusive Economic Zones, and the Institut polaire français only has access to it for four months each year for supply voyages. As such, French researchers have little capacity to conduct lengthy polar oceanographic campaigns.

France is also the only country highly active in the Antarctic with no air access to the continent.[33] To the Foreign Affairs Commission, which reported in

2019, the access problems speak to a quintuple weakness: inadequate servicing of a French territory, reliance on foreign nations, limitations on science and cooperation, danger to personnel on the ground, and a blow to France's legitimacy in Antarctic affairs.[34] The decision to end the airstrip project in 1994 still resonates, especially now that the Australians have an air link between Hobart and Casey Station, a four-hour flight that makes crystal clear what France still lacks: efficient access to a territory, a demonstration of commitment and control, and the ability to protect national interests via aerial surveillance.[35] France's inability to rapidly connect Hobart, Dumont-d'Urville, and Concordia Station, as well as not-infrequent appeals to other countries for supply and emergency help, Poivre d'Arvor emphasizes, weakens Terre Adélie's territorial continuity and integrity.[36] It will also make it more difficult in the future to argue for sovereign power if France cannot independently and securely access the territory—for example, to evacuate an ailing or injured scientist. These problems are not new. Gaudin's complaint that "among the great Antarctic nations, France suffers from the weakest logistics," written in 2007, could have been written at almost any time over the past seventy years.[37]

High-Level Engagement

Early in the twenty-first century, high-level concern over Antarctic geopolitics emerged in government, sending signs that France was eager to revitalize its stance in the Antarctic. This renewed interest can be traced to Michel Rocard's term as the first French ambassador for the polar regions, a position he held from 2009 until 2016. With his long-standing support for Antarctica's environment and his reputation as one of the "heroes" responsible for the moratorium on mineral exploitation, Rocard fought to make the Antarctic matter on France's political scene throughout his ambassadorship. His efforts bore fruit the year after his term finished when newly elected president Emmanuel Macron incorporated the Antarctic into his agenda. Macron's government has vocally engaged with the polar regions as a means of promoting broader geopolitical aims, a renewal of French diplomacy and revitalization of French influence across the globe.

Macron's frequent stressing of the Antarctic as a unique place for peace, science, and partnership, a place of extreme environmental fragility requiring cooperative protection, is a deliberate counterbalance to growing tensions in the region. Chinese and Russian assertiveness, in particular, have sparked high-level concern throughout Macron's presidency, something only reinforced by the re-emergence of Russia as the common Western enemy with the invasion of Ukraine in early 2022. In 2019, Prime Minister Édouard Philippe made clear France's mistrust of Chinese intentions in the Antarctic, pointing to the lack of transparency at Kunlun Station, located in Australia's Antarctic territory.[38] It does not help that China gives its Antarctic stations patriotic names and uses terms such as "conquest" to describe its activities on the continent, suggesting a latent nationalism.[39] Macron's new ambassador for the polar regions, Poivre d'Arvor, too, writes that China is working to destabilize the Antarctic Treaty System, dividing the consultative powers against each other and trying to destroy the governance consensus that has reigned for the past half century.[40] On the environmental front, French officials are concerned about Russian and Chinese agendas for Antarctic minerals, especially if one of these countries chooses to leave the Madrid Protocol and operate outside its constraints.[41] These threats have fed a growing French desire to reinforce its claim over Terre Adélie and to push the science and peace agenda of the ATS, a system in which France is highly invested.

In keeping with the environmental stance that has guided French involvement in the Antarctic for three decades, France has of late been pushing hard for the protection of eastern Antarctic waters. As China and Russia have stymied these efforts, explicitly opposing the creation of a protected marine reserve next to Terre Adélie, the French government has recognized the need to step up and protect its strategic interests. The Chinese and Russian opposition is entirely political, emphasized the Foreign Affairs Commission in 2019, demanding an equally strong political response from France.[42] For China and Russia, new marine protection areas are perceived as an implicit acknowledgment of Antarctic territorial claims as well as a threat to future fishing activities. Likewise, these countries are steadily undermining the existing living marine resources convention by deliberately stalling proceedings intended to impose consequences for rule breaking and blocking progress on other issues for political reasons.[43] In Japan, too, conservation and rational use are too often conflated. France must do more to ensure that conservation remains the primary focus in the region—especially as the biggest remaining underexploited fishery in the world, the Antarctic krill fishery, is poised to become a source of dispute between the fishing industry and environmentalist states and organizations. French efforts to engage with these issues in 2020 through the European Union were unsuccessful, and over the past few years little has been accomplished because of the COVID-19 pandemic.[44] This is representative of a larger battle: as more and more countries join the Antarctic Treaty System, the claimant states are finding themselves outnumbered, challenging their power on the continent.[45] For China especially, the Antarctic is a region that offers an important means for the expansion of soft power as well as a region in which China can challenge the hegemony of the original ATS powers, all of which is wrapped up in larger political strategies.

France has also actively been pushing for stringent restrictions on Antarctic tourism.[46] At least until interrupted by COVID-19, tourism numbers had been rising sharply for decades, representing both the physical presence of another interest group on the continent and the commercialization of the Antarctic. While the vast majority (upward of 98 percent) of this tourism takes place in the Antarctic Peninsula region, far from Terre Adélie, France is vocally speaking out against the environmental consequences of tourism, calling for strict limits on the number of passengers per ship and on the construction of land-based tourist infrastructure. French authorities are particularly concerned about the perturbation of fauna by tourists, especially given the coincidence of the high tourist season and wildlife reproduction periods. In Terre Adélie itself, France also wants to ensure that tourism does not detrimentally affect scientific work and is loath to have state logistical resources assist the growing industry.[47]

Hand in hand with these concerns is the potential for tourism to become a vector for legal challenges to the French claim. The arrest of a foreign national tourist for breaking French law, for example, would undoubtedly call into question jurisdiction and authority in Terre Adélie, highlighting the fragility of the claim. This raises a broader point: Terre Adélie's uncertain legal regime has long been of quiet concern to France.[48] While the state has on occasion tried to clarify the territory's legal situation (for example, by giving the district chief limited police functions and by stipulating that the French penal code applies with certain exceptions), the practicalities are tricky. By what means could a district chief detain a French suspect in Terre Adélie during the austral winter, for example, when removal by a French vessel might be up to nine months away? Moreover, any attempt to arrest a foreign national in Terre Adélie would almost certainly result in a jurisdictional dispute—one that, at its limit, could conceivably destabilize the Antarctic Treaty System and exacerbate tensions on the continent. This has long been on France's radar, dating back to the negotiation of the Antarctic Treaty, when French diplomats argued against establishing exclusive criminal jurisdiction on the basis of nationality. These uncertainties are by no means unique to France: as James Crawford and Donald R. Rothwell note using the fictional example of a foreign observer who kills an Australian scientist during a private brawl on an Australian base, the application of national law in the Antarctic is a Pandora's box best not opened.[49] This also applies in the regulatory arena. When France attempted to impose a mooring tax on foreign ships and a visitor tax on tourists to Terre Adélie in 2001, the United States argued that the move was not allowed under the ATS, and France was forced to retract the taxes—an unwelcome reminder of the limits on sovereignty imposed by the Antarctic Treaty. In contrast, France does impose taxes on ships and visitors to its sub-Antarctic islands, where sovereignty is not at play.[50]

These efforts to revitalize France's stance in the Antarctic have led to a number of practical results.[51] In mid-2019, the National Assembly set up an information mission to define a strategic vision for French presence in the polar regions. Later that year, France sent a minister to Terre Adélie for the first time. The visit was a calculated gesture intended to underline France's commitment to Antarctic research and marine protection at a time of increasing tension. And Macron instructed his ambassador for the polar regions, Poivre d'Arvor, to produce France's first polar strategy roadmap. More visibly, Macron's government used the French presidency of the 2021 Antarctic Treaty consultative meeting and Madrid Protocol meeting to publicly push environmental governance on the white continent. Speaking on the occasion of the sixtieth anniversary of the Antarctic Treaty in June 2021, Macron highlighted France's environmental credentials in the Antarctic.[52] The Antarctic Treaty System is still central to France's vision of the continent, and Macron's emphasis on France's responsibility for the perpetuation of that system was a not-so-subtle warning to China and other countries who have begun to test its strength.

With this high-level engagement, by early 2022 all elements were in place for significant French reinvestment in the Antarctic, and hope among polar officials and scientists was high. But promises and action—specifically, money—are different things. Despite the repeated promises made by Macron in 2021 and early 2022—promises that linked renewed polar commitment with broader geopolitical and environmental strategies—neither money nor other tangible investment have materialized. The road map for French polar strategy released by Poivre d'Arvor in the spring of 2022 reads not as a policy document but as a litany of complaints: chronic underinvestment in scientific research, embarrassingly weak logistics, crumbling infrastructure, no coherent strategic vision, burned-out personnel, and a falling reputation.[53] This was the end of the line for the Institut polaire français' director, Jérôme Chappellaz, who has for years been sounding alarm bells about France's Antarctic engagement. Tired of repeated promises but no follow-through, Chappellaz resigned his position and plans to now pursue polar research with another country—a serious blow to French polar interests.[54]

Epilogue

AN ANTARCTIC POWER *MALGRÉ SOI*

It is crystal clear that France cannot remain a major player in the Antarctic without significant new investment. That investment needs to come in the form of real money; promises, announcements, and reports are not enough. The goals enunciated by President Emmanuel Macron—championing the protection of Antarctica's environment, standing out as a scientific powerhouse, and playing a leading role in the management of the continent and its surrounding waters—are all critical to France's legitimacy in the Antarctic world. As the balance of influence in the Antarctic Treaty System shifts and other powerful countries make their weight felt, France finds itself in an uncomfortable position. Moreover, since claims to sovereignty over Antarctic territory are not constitutive principles of governance, the influence enjoyed by France in the decades immediately following the signing of the Antarctic Treaty is waning. This predicament is shared with other claimant states: as Anthony Bergin and his colleagues point out in their assessment of Australia's Antarctic interests, the politics of the white continent are in flux as the "old" Antarctic countries reduce or maintain their capabilities and activities while the "new" Antarctic countries (namely, China, India, and South Korea) continue to increase their investments.[1] Today, Antarctica's future looks less predictable than ever over the past sixty years.

That France once again finds itself at a crossroads in the Antarctic is not surprising from a historical perspective. As the long narrative of this book shows, France became and has remained an Antarctic power *malgré soi*. Indeed, France discovered a portion of the white continent, became an Antarctic claimant state, and grew into an Antarctic Treaty System leader all despite only intermittent political and cultural interest at home. With no sense of urgency and few immediate advantages to be gained from Terre Adélie, successive French governments had nothing to lose by ignoring the territory, often for long periods. Each critical stage in France's journey to Antarctic power was propelled not by internal desire or motivation but by a deep need to respond to an adversary, whether it be a rival state or a more nebulous threat such as alternative governance structures.[2] Terre Adélie has long been a site used by France to show itself superior to rivals, from Britain in the nineteenth century to the United States in the postwar period to China and Russia today. The story of France in the Antarctic is rooted in national pride and honor rather than strictly in territory.

Dumont d'Urville's *prise de possession* of 1840 was more a product of imperial rivalries than of eagerness to claim a tract of inhospitable land so far from home. His entire voyage, from the king's command to the navigator's decision to push south of Hobart, was motivated by the desire to best both France's old rival, Britain, and the new, impudent challenger, the United States. But for the rest of the nineteenth century and into the early twentieth century, when there was no threat to the claim, no outside pressure, Terre Adélie remained absent from French political and cultural interests. When France finally enacted legal decrees in the 1920s, it was only because Britain and its Dominions had begun to make claims on the continent and challenge France's hold over Terre Adélie. And the French state committed money for an expedition to Terre Adélie after World War II only when Victor made it clear that other countries were preparing a political solution to tensions on the Antarctic Continent and that France could not retain its territory without presence. As the International Geophysical Year and the Antarctic Treaty negotiations raised the white continent's profile, the potential of being left out of international projects and losing control of Terre Adélie again forced France to act. De Gaulle's commitment to permanent presence at the very end of the 1950s, too, was a response to the need to support France's status as a *puissance mondiale moyenne* after the collapse of empire, as well as a means of standing up to American hegemony. Similarly, Mitterrand's and Rocard's decision to merge questions of environment and sovereignty and stake out a new, spirited French position for the white continent at the very end of the 1980s was motivated by challenges to the Antarctic Treaty System and to French authority in the Antarctic world.

This pattern of French engagement with Terre Adélie in response to adversaries or threats is indicative of the territory's outlier status in broader French conceptions of colonialism, empire, and global power.[3] Whereas the primacy of French presence abroad has long been weighted in commercial potential and cultural influence, Terre Adélie has offered neither real economic promise nor populations conducive to *rayonnement* (or its past incarnations of evangelization and the imperial mission). Nor did the Antarctic territory serve France in the way faraway territories were supposed to: returning profits and raising revenues to cover (and indeed exceed) the expenses of keeping them, providing valuable raw materials, building a market for French goods and products, and—less concretely but no less importantly—helping to solve national problems. The strategic, economic, and political advantages Terre Adélie has offered to France have always been difficult to measure and hard to explain in quantitative terms. Unpopulated, frozen, and fiendishly difficult to access, Terre Adélie remained a land apart well into the twentieth century. As Alexandre Simon-Ekeland notes, too, with no Indigenous or permanent inhabitants, the Antarctic was detached from French cultural exploration.[4] But this also meant that Terre Adélie stood above the immense anger and shame associated with the fall of empire after World War II—"a discreet form of revenge on history" indeed, a territory immune from the complex emotions of decolonization—again emphasizing its separation from wider historical and cultural themes.[5]

It is this apartness from the imperial project, too, that has driven the gulf separating Terre Adélie and the Hexagon in both the political and cultural imaginations. Unlike in South America and Australia, with their geographic proximity and historical-emotional ties to the white continent, the Antarctic has never been strongly connected to French identity nor integrated into the broader French worldview. For the South American claimants, environmental and geographic connections—weather patterns, contiguous rocks, even fauna—play a role altogether absent from the French experience. And the Australian belief that geographic proximity confers territorial rights and responsibilities, too, reveals a nationalism toward the Antarctic entirely lacking in the French case. This is not simply a matter of physical distance: as Francis Spufford shows, Britain has long had a "hazy love affair" with the polar regions, a spirit of popular interest bordering on obsession.[6] While the French were certainly greatly interested in the world beyond the Hexagon through the nineteenth century and into the twentieth century, this was driven by the expansion of the French colonial empire, exotic populated territories ripe for the *mission civilisatrice* and blooming with economic promise. The polar regions were decidedly secondary, if not entirely absent, even at universities and in geographical societies, where again the utilitarian focus was on France's colonial possessions and their prospects. Unlike in Britain, where the Antarctic was seen in both scientific and public circles to be an integral part of empire, in France Terre Adélie did not fit into the imperial fabric. Never did France have to contend with the anti-imperial rhetoric with which Argentine president Juan Domingo Perón challenged Britain's Antarctic claim; never did France meet with any direct territorial challenge for Terre Adélie such as that which the British faced when, upon arrival at the Antarctic Peninsula in 1952, they were confronted by an armed Argentine naval party. Terre Adélie's much quieter history both furthered its distance from the imperial project and meant that the French state was able to ignore the territory for long periods with no repercussions.

But the idea of losing Terre Adélie to a rival has long been anathema. France had already lost Bouvet, Prince Edward, and Marion Islands for lack of pursuing claims—losses that paled in significance with the failure to claim and colonize land in Australia and New Zealand despite early landings, failures that enabled British hegemony in the South Pacific. And while French explorers made many discoveries in and around the Antarctic Peninsula, they never made any claims to territory there, shutting France out of that region as well. If Voltaire had underevaluated the strategic importance and economic value of territory in Canada, calling France's holdings there but "a few acres of ice," what future regrets might a similarly premature evaluation of Terre Adélie bring? The idea that this situation of loss, of regret, might replicate itself in Terre Adélie has long driven support for that territory, tying together prestige, honor, and international influence. More broadly, since World War II, Terre Adélie has become central to *grandeur*, faraway and yet essential to the redefinition of France as a global political entity following decolonization, resonating as strongly for geopolitical purposes as for environmental ones. With its arresting landscapes and striking visual imagery, Terre Adélie—land of ice and barrenness, home to those extraordinary birds that breed in the heart of the Antarctic winter, the Emperor penguins, emblems of Earth's climactic fragility—is now symbolic of French environmental diplomacy, part of a larger strategic foreign policy.

A Way Forward

As France finds itself in another crisis in the Antarctic arena, what can be learned from the past? If France is to continue to pursue Antarctic engagement, the best course of action lies in environmental governance. France has constructed an identity as a claimant country through environmental leadership since 1989, explicitly aiming to produce an Antarctic space in which environmental issues steer decision-making. By rejecting the minerals convention and championing the Madrid Protocol, Mitterrand and Rocard deliberately used environmental authority to support France's Antarctic claim and to justify political control in the Antarctic. This builds on France's earlier use of scientific research toward epistemological sovereignty, the creation of new knowledge to legitimate authority over territory. But while France can certainly point to environmental successes in the Antarctic over the past thirty years and still commands international respect in this arena, it now faces an evolving geopolitical situation that threatens once again to destabilize governance, and specifically environmental protections, on the continent. The need to increase those protections (including for the surrounding waters), prevent tourism and living resource activity from further harming the environment, and ensure the compliance of all states active in the Antarctic, is pressing. So too is the need to control the deployment of "dual use" technologies and creep in the security dimension. France's record of conducting inspections of other countries' Antarctic facilities under the Antarctic Treaty and the Madrid Protocol is embarrassingly poor; while expensive, inspections are a key means of promoting transparency and displaying interest in the Antarctic.[7] France would be well served to cooperate with like-minded states and undertake regular inspections at shared cost. As both a claimant state and a state vowing to champion Antarctica's environment, France has a particular responsibility in these regards.[8]

There is no time to waste. Record-breaking high temperatures are being regularly recorded across the continent. At the French-Italian Concordia Station, the mercury rose to minus 11.5°C in mid-March 2022, a reading that took even climate scientists by surprise.[9] Melting Antarctic ice will severely affect sea levels, ocean currents, and the atmospheric circulation around the world, while warming temperatures are already threatening Antarctica's iconic penguins as well as its less well-known species of flora and fauna. Not a week goes by that a major newspaper fails to publish an article about the dire consequences of global warming for the Antarctic, but real political commitment to change still lacks. Over the past half century our vision of the Antarctic has been transformed from one of a hostile, impenetrable place, the most implacable of foes, to a place of unparalleled environmental fragility in need of the strongest protections. With the Madrid Protocol, advanced by France and Australia, the Antarctic is now one of Earth's most protected environments. The past shows us that this transformation was propelled not only by environmental concern but equally by political motivations, from domestic electoral strategy to the protection of territorial claims to the relegitimization of authority and power through environmental policy. As French actions of the past suggest, the continued sculpting of environmental responsibility toward the white continent will necessarily be politicized on both domestic and international levels.

While France's claim to Terre Adélie benefits greatly from the "freezing" of sovereignty claims under the Antarctic Treaty, and while that framework still offers an advantageous governance structure vis-à-vis France's aims for the continent, the claimant states are now being forced to reconsider how to strengthen their position.[10] For the claimant states, continued displays of legitimacy and moral authority are essential, both individually and as part of the Antarctic Treaty System. As with the minerals volte-face of 1989, this will require flexibility and strategic thinking in order to meet present and future challenges such as the conservation of the surrounding waters, rapidly growing interest in bioprospecting, and the potential (if unlikely) reopening of the minerals question in 2048. In a manner parallel to what Andreas Østhagen points out for Norway's Arctic interests, Chinese and Russian actions are producing a new political landscape in the Antarctic, one increasingly at odds with French security and environmental policies.[11]

In the past, France has successfully translated environmental decisions and leadership into strong moral claims to Antarctic legitimacy. This transformation from a state long considered an environmental pariah has given France a scaffolding on which future action can be built. In the current climate, France's advocacy for increased protections in Antarctica and especially in its surrounding waters builds on this past and, if successful, will shape Antarctica's future legal geography in a way that benefits both France's strategic interests and the natural environment. France's continued push for strong limitations on Antarctic tourism, too, must be maintained; indeed, France is well positioned to take this one step further by pushing for internationally negotiated, legally binding regulations for tourism.[12] But success is by no means guaranteed. While continued tight ties between environmental governance and the construction of Antarctic space in political discourse show that France is committed to again trying to relegitimize the Antarctic Treaty System's voice through environmental policy, this will become more difficult in the coming years and decades. It is only by strengthening its position now that France will be able to withstand future challenges to its claim to Terre Adélie.

As control of waters adjacent to territorial possessions becomes more pressing, France has twice extended the external limits of the continental shelves around many of its overseas possessions, including its sub-Antarctic islands. This is a long-term project and the stakes are high: France is at once asserting its Pacific presence, preserving its rights for the future, and extending the jurisdiction over which it has sovereignty in order to increase resource potential.[13] But while this projection of power is relatively simple around Kerguelen, Crozet, Saint-Paul, and Nouvelle-Amsterdam, application of the United Nations Convention on the Law of the Sea (UNCLOS) to the Antarctic itself is a complex and unsettled matter. First, the freezing of sovereignty claims under the Antarctic Treaty precludes any new claims or any enlargement of existing claims. Second, the lack of broad international recognition of the existing claims suggests that claimant states will encounter opposition if they try to exert control over the maritime zones adjacent to their Antarctic territories, or to exert legal authority over nonnationals operating in those zones.[14] While all seven claimant countries belong to UNCLOS and maintain that their Antarctic claims give them the status of coastal states, many have been cautious in defining extended continental shelves. For its part, France deliberately excluded Terre Adélie from its 2009 submission, but noted that a submission for the Antarctic territory may later be made.[15] This prevents arguments that, if pursued, could backfire on French interests in the Antarctic sphere. Still, the waters near Terre Adélie are another area in which France will need to act decisively and strategically in the near future.

While France's claim to Terre Adélie is essentially protected so long as the Antarctic Treaty remains in force, this claim is still legally tenuous.[16] The claim is underpinned by discovery and *prise de possession*, as well as legal decrees, administrative and government activities, presence, infrastructure, and scientific research, but still the territory lacks more traditional (and widely accepted) ingredients of sovereign control. Moreover, the claim is not recognized by most other states. While there is no serious potential rival claimant, no country with a stronger claim under international law, France's hold over Terre Adélie could conceivably be threatened by the breakdown of the Antarctic Treaty System or by a challenge to the treaty from a multilateral forum.[17] This is precisely why French officials have been speaking out about the need to buttress the existing governance system. It is also why France has continued to perform sovereignty in Terre Adélie in public ways, from issuing stamps to minting commemorative coins to creating official websites.[18] Since 1993, TAAF has also been inventorying historical sites in Terre Adélie and adding them to the country's cultural heritage.[19] The sites include Rocher du Débarquement (where Dumont d'Urville's men set foot in 1840), what is left of the fire-damaged Port-Martin (used from 1950 to 1952), Mario Marret's wooden hut on Île des Pétrels (site of the postfire 1952 overwinter), and the iron cross on the northeast promontory of Île des Pétrels erected in memory of André Prud'homme, who disappeared during a blizzard in 1959.[20] With their emphasis on the earliest French encounters with Terre Adélie, these sites contribute to building and reinforcing a narrative of lengthy historical engagement in the territory. Such visible performances of sovereignty are all careful steps meant to improve France's chance of retaining Terre Adélie in case the sovereignty issue is forced in the future. They are an explicit recognition that much in the Antarctic, as Francis Auburn has noted, depends on the creation of facts.[21] But these performances of sovereignty alone are not enough: they will mean little without significant new scientific, logistical, and infrastructure investment.

Science remains an important currency of influence in the Antarctic Treaty System, a measure of political power on the continent, and it is at its own peril that France continues to underinvest in scientific research in the Antarctic. If

France wants to maintain a leading role in Antarctic governance and continue to support its claim to a slice of the Antarctic pie, it needs to finance a robust program of scientific inquiry at the coastal Dumont-d'Urville base, deep into Terre Adélie, and in the nearby waters; it also needs to build the logistical capacity necessary to lead large European and international projects. The creation of new geographic and scientific knowledge about Terre Adélie cannot be left to other states with superior logistics and higher budgets. At the same time, France needs to strengthen security in and around Terre Adélie and its sub-Antarctic possessions, and particularly to build maximal coverage capacity through Terre Adélie's vast expanse. Negotiating this balance—supporting both national and international interests, both France's territorial claim to Terre Adélie and the continent's multilateral governance system—will not become easier in the coming years.

The Many Costs of Territory

The story told in this book is neither one of domination nor of colonialism as traditionally understood, but one of imperial motivation and global ambition nonetheless. Since its discovery, Terre Adélie has offered to France a stage on which to play out broader rivalries, a means of showcasing national pride and prestige, and a way to support its status as a midsize world power. From besting the Brits and the Americans in 1840 to lending weight to *grandeur* at a time of empire collapse to the invocation of environmental authority toward political legitimacy, Terre Adélie has long been constructed as a geopolitical statement in one of Earth's most remote areas. Today more than ever, the vision of the French state as a territorial entity that reaches around the world is dependent on remote and even uninhabited possessions. From a geopolitical perspective, these possessions—including Terre Adélie—lend credence to the idea of a global France.[22]

In the twenty-first century, there remains a political conviction that the Antarctic offers to France a privileged space. But the money to back up that conviction has not been forthcoming and Terre Adélie's situation seems precarious. Since 1840, France's journey to Antarctic power has been propelled by a deep need to respond to and best adversaries. This is precisely the case France faces again today. With China, Russia, and other countries emerging as challengers, even opponents, in the Antarctic arena, France's interests are again threatened. France has the opportunity to respond by making the Antarctic a real political priority. Doing so would allow France to continue to play a key role in Antarctic governance, environmental protection, and scientific research going forward—but only if the political will to back words with euros emerges. As it stands, lack of money means dilapidated bases, logistical shortcomings, discouraged personnel, and faltering scientific research and partnerships. Without significant new investment, France will neither be able to respond to the evolving geopolitical situation that threatens to reconfigure the white continent's political landscape nor support its currently frozen claim to Terre Adélie in an uncertain future.

Notes

INTRODUCTION

1. Howitt 2019; Spufford 1996.
2. See Collis 2017.
3. Dodds 2011, 232; also see Dodds 2008.
4. Naylor et al. 2008; Elzinga and Bohlin 1989.
5. Howkins 2015.
6. Frioux and Lemire 2012.
7. P. Whitney Lackenbauer and Matthew Farish (2007) make a similar observation for the Canadian Arctic.
8. On this more broadly, see Roberts 2011.
9. Ingold 2011.
10. For environmental authority, see Howkins 2017; Dodds 2012; Turchetti et al. 2008.
11. Litfin 1997, 1998. On global environmental thinking, also see Schleper 2017; Poole 2008.
12. Kuehls 1996; Mairet 2015.
13. For an earlier view of the "greening of Antarctica," see Antonello 2019.
14. Howkins 2017, 7; Hall 2009, 140.
15. Hecht 2001, 254.
16. For a broader discussion of French identity in this context, see Hecht 1998.
17. See, for example, Jensen 2016; Østhagen 2020; Bergin et al. 2013.
18. Commission des affaires étrangères 2019b. See Berger 2019 for commentary.
19. See, for example, Wienecke, Klekociuk, and Welsford 2021; Chown et al. 2022.
20. For example, Adrian Howkins's (2017) work on Britain, Argentina, and Chile; Klaus Dodds (2002, 2008) as well as Dodds and Alan D. Hemmings (2013) on Britain; Malcolm Templeton (2017) on New Zealand; Leif Christian Jensen (2016) on Norway; Roger D. Launius (2018) and Evan Bloom (2022) on the United States; and Donald Rothwell and Shirley Scott (2007), as well as Dodds and Hemmings (2009) and Daniel Bray (2016), on Australia.

1. "ALL THAT IS REQUIRED IS TO DISCOVER IT"

1. The evolution of ideas about and the search for a great southern continent have been widely discussed in the literature. See the excellent Hiatt 2008, as well as Hiatt 2011; Scott et al. 2011; Romm 1992; and the ever-relevant Rainaud 1893. Here, the focus is on the role of France and of Frenchmen, and in particular the territories that now constitute French possessions in the Antarctic and sub-Antarctic. For French explorations of other parts of the Southern Hemisphere, including Australia, New Zealand, Polynesia, and Brazil, Blais 2005; Deckker and Toullelan 1989; La Roncière 1932; Tremewan 2013; and Sankey 2013 provide a good start.
2. Wehi et al. 2021; McFarlane 2008.
3. Zumthor 1993; Tattersall 1981. The term *Antipodes* was used more broadly at this time to refer to lands imagined or postulated to be "opposite" the known world.
4. Hiatt 2008; also see Broc 1986.

5. Understanding the physical separation between the continents we now call Oceania and Antarctica was a slow process. Indeed, the southernmost boundaries of Australia were only determined in the early nineteenth century, when Englishman Matthew Flinders and Frenchman Nicolas Baudin circumnavigated the island in opposite directions, meeting at Encounter Bay. As Christopher Wortham (2011) notes, the term *Terra Australis* continued to be used for both Australia and Antarctica through the eighteenth century.

6. Anthiaume 1911, 178; also see Toulouse 2012, 2007.
7. Le Testu 1555, fol. 34.
8. D'Albaigne 1570, 456.
9. Hamy 1896.
10. In 1555, Coligny sent the Chevalier de Villegagnon to set up a French colony in Brazil. Called "la France Antarctique," an appellation that underlines the fluidity of the term at the time, this colony only survived for four years before falling victim to internal conflict and Portuguese takeover (see Mariz and Provencal 2005).
11. La Popelinière 1582, 50, 78. Anne-Marie Beaulieu's (1997) edited edition of La Popelinière's work offers extensive commentary. She suggests that La Popelinière was inspired by the d'Albaigne brothers. On La Popelinière, also see Conley 1996; Lestringant 2007; Martinière 1997.
12. La Popelinière 1582, 78.
13. For de Courtonne, see Lestringant 2006.
14. De Courtonne 1663.
15. See, for example, Maneuvrier 2016; Perrone-Moisés 1995.
16. For more on this fascinating but convoluted story, see Scott et al. 2011; Sankey 2011; Sankey 2001. The latter two references offer an insightful treatment of the veracity of Gonneville's voyage. Other commentaries assume the man and his voyage to be real but provide no specific source evidence; see, for example, Marchant 1988.
17. Maupertuis 1756, 343–99.
18. While Bouvet's expedition is regarded as the first to have seen Cap de la Circoncision, it is today a Norwegian, not a French, possession. Following Bouvet, several expeditions attempted to refind Cap de la Circoncision, but owing to Bouvet's inaccurate plotting, these all failed. In 1825, British sealing ship captain George Norris landed on the island and claimed it for King George IV (Norris 1825). But, like France before, Britain didn't take any steps to assert sovereignty over the island. In 1927, a Norwegian expedition led by Harald Horntvedt hoisted the Norwegian flag and claimed the island following explicit instructions to claim any land found for Norway. This act was followed with a royal decree early the next year. While Britain initially protested this annexation, the ensuing diplomatic negotiations led Britain to renounce its claim in late 1929, "having regard to the friendly relations existing between the two countries" (C. H. Smith 1932). France's protest was both late and negligible (Fleuriau 1931). The island is now called Bouvetøya (Bouvet Island). This is not the only case in which French navigators failed to claim territory or French authorities failed to follow through on claims; similar examples exist in locations as varied as the Antarctic, Australia, New Zealand, South America, and the Indian Ocean. See Costa 1958 for discussion.
19. Buffon 1749, 212–17.
20. For de Brosses, see Leoni 2006; Racault 2006.
21. De Brosses 1756.
22. On this, see Chesneaux and Maclellan 1992, 55.
23. Saint-Aloüarn was the first European to make a claim on Australia's western coast, but this claim was never secured by France. That Saint-Aloüarn died before returning to France didn't help, as he was unable to report about the region to court.

24. For European traditions of territorial claim, see Seed 1995.
25. La Pérouse 1850.
26. Kerguelen de Trémarec 1782.
27. He was freed in 1778 and his naval rank restored to him.
28. On the Kerguelen cabbage, see Hatt 1949.
29. Cook 1821, 146–51.
30. On regret for the English names, see Hulot 1911.
31. For Marion Dufresne, see Duyker's (1994) biography.
32. In contrast, another set of islands seen by Marion Dufresne is not today French. Most likely originally discovered in 1663 by a Dutch East India Company ship, they were refound by Marion Dufresne and next sighted by James Cook in 1776. Cook named them Prince Edward and Marion for the fourth son of King George and the French navigator, respectively. When Britain claimed sovereignty over the islands, France accepted the annexation with no protest. After all, as the minister for colonies, Georges Trouillot, noted, no Frenchman had ever made a claim to the islands—not the first time, he complained, that such a mistake led to the loss of territory that might otherwise have been French. Some French sources, however, considered the islands to be French well into the twentieth century (e.g., Costa 1958, 73). In 1947–1948, they were transferred from Britain to South Africa.
33. Cook 1777.
34. Cited in Taillemite 1981, 5.
35. For La Pérouse's expedition, see Jacob 2004; Fauque 1985.
36. For this voyage, see Richard 1986.
37. For an interesting look at Baudin, see Fornasiero and West-Sooby 2011.
38. See Bloomfield 2017; Mandelblatt 2009; McClellan and Regourd 2000.
39. For the Falkland Islands, historical etymology is interesting given the dispute over the islands between Britain and Argentina: the Spanish name for these islands, *Islas Malvinas*, has its roots in the French *Îles Malouines*, the name given by Bougainville in 1764 when he founded the islands' first settlement. *Îles Malouines* is a reference to the French port of Saint-Malo, the departure point for Bougainville's ships.
40. For a particularly interesting look at nineteenth-century Antarctic sealing, see Basberg and Headland 2008. For nineteenth-century French whaling, see De Pasquier 1982.
41. These sightings and the controversies they caused have been written about extensively. See, for example, Riffenburgh 2007; Day 2013; Beck 1986.
42. See Gascoigne 2015; Jore 1958; J. Martin 1987. For an account from the time, see Carné 1843.
43. Bougainville 1837.
44. Jean-Paul Faivre (1953) sees this shift as happening around 1836, while Hélène Blais (2005) and John Dunmore (1969) date it to the 1820s.

2. AN UNEXPECTED TERRITORY

1. The most complete biographical treatment of Dumont d'Urville is Duyker (2014). Guillon (1986) and Bellec (2019) are also recommended. See Vergniol (1930) for an interwar treatment and I. Lebrun (1843) for an account written shortly after his death.
2. Kousser 2005; Tarral and Reinach 1906.
3. Dillon 1829.
4. *Revue des deux mondes* 1829; Dumont d'Urville 1829.
5. Dumont d'Urville 1834.
6. *Journal des débats politiques et littéraires* 1834.
7. For Dumont d'Urville's instructions, see Rosamel 1842.

8. Dumont d'Urville's voyage was part of a group of five expeditions dispatched by the king to the Pacific in 1836–1837. The others were those of Auguste-Nicholas Vaillant, who commanded a political and scientific circumnavigation; Abel Aubert du Petit-Thouars, whose three-year voyage brought him to the Aleutians, Easter Island, and Galapagos; and Cyrille Laplace and Jean-Baptiste Cécile, both of whom sailed to protect the interests of French missionaries and whalers far from Europe.

9. Dumont d'Urville 1842b, LXVIII.

10. Mawer 2006, 4–5; also see Larson 2011.

11. Roche 2005, 127, 477.

12. Dumont d'Urville 1837.

13. For this voyage, in addition to Duyker (2014) and Mawer (2006), Reybaud (1841) and D'Arcy Wood (2020) are recommended, as is the original day-to-day description reproduced in Ladrange (1990).

14. There is also a D'Urville Island in New Zealand.

15. Nordenskjöld 1905, 46.

16. Pépin 1837.

17. Dumont d'Urville 1842a, 83–84.

18. For example, *Hobart Town Courier* 1839.

19. See Howitt 2019, 17.

20. Dumont d'Urville 1845, 106.

21. Dumont d'Urville 1855, 180.

22. Dumont d'Urville 1845, 101–3. For accounts of the expedition's medical and health aspects, and particularly the devastating effects of scurvy and dysentery, see Chevanne 1994; Pendu 1993.

23. Dumont d'Urville 1845, 137–38.

24. For example, Hobbs 1932, 635; République française 2006, 5.

25. French geologists studied the rock samples brought back by Dumont d'Urville and his men, noting that they seemed to be similar to the rock found in Egyptian obelisks (e.g., Godard-Faultrier 1850, 9). The rocks were recently reanalyzed; see Godard et al. 2017.

26. Joseph-Fidèle-Eugene Dubouzet writing in Dumont d'Urville 1845, 149–51.

27. Dumont d'Urville 1845, 153–54.

28. Hombron and Jacquinot 1841, 320.

29. For Ringgold, see his account in Wilkes 1844, vol. 2, 344, 371; for Dumont d'Urville, see Dumont d'Urville 1845, 171–73.

30. Le Guillou and the two captains were already not on good terms owing to a long-running dispute over the medical situation aboard the ships. After the voyage, Dumont d'Urville accused Le Guillou of negligence while Le Guillou accused the captains of risking the mens' lives at sea (Dumont d'Urville 1842a; Le Guillou 1842, 198–99).

31. For example, *Hobart Town Courier* 1840; *Commercial Journal and Advertiser* 1840.

32. *The Hobart Town Courier and Van Diemen's Land Gazette* 1840.

33. Matterer 1842, 772–73.

34. I. Lebrun 1843, 47.

35. The best recent treatments of the three voyages are Mawer (2006) and D'Arcy Wood (2020). S. L. Millar (2017) is also recommended.

36. For the Exploring Expedition and Wilkes, in addition to the references given earlier, see Haskell 1942; Stanton 1975; Viola and Margolis 1985. For the expedition in broader context, see Bertrand 1971.

37. On the expedition's chief naturalist, Titian Ramsay Peale, see Porter 1985.

38. *New-York Daily Tribune* 1842.

39. *Sydney Herald* 1840b.
40. For example, *Australasian Chronicle* 1840; *Sydney Herald* 1840a.
41. Of the others, the *Sea Gull* disappeared with all hands in 1839 somewhere off Cape Horn; the *Relief* was sent back to the United States partway through the expedition; the *Flying Fish*, worn out, was sold in Singapore; and the *Peacock* was wrecked in Oregon's Columbia River in 1841.
42. *New-York Daily Tribune* 1842.
43. Still later, in his official expedition narrative, published in 1844, Wilkes claimed 16 January as the date of the first sighting (Wilkes 1844).
44. *New-York Daily Tribune* 1842; *Alexandria Gazette* 1842.
45. Vincendon-Dumoulin 1845, 256, emphasis in original.
46. For example, Lesson 1846, 128.
47. Officially, the US Navy recognized Wilkes's account at the time, asserting in its annual report for 1840 that the *Vincennes* discovered land on 19 January 1840 (Paulding 1840, 404).
48. For example, Costa 1958, 70; M. Emmanuel 1947, 137.
49. For example, Mill 1903; Plott 1969.
50. Hobbs 1932, 632.
51. Mawer 2006, 126. Mawer provides an excellent analysis of these questions.
52. For example, Department of State 1959.
53. Larson 2011, 35.
54. Cited in Mawer 2006, 173.
55. For example, *The Spectator* 1845.
56. Ross 1847, 116–17.

3. APATHY AND NEGLECT

1. For example, *Gazette du Bas-Languedoc* 1842; also see Guillemin 1842.
2. *Le moniteur universel* 1842.
3. *Les coulisses* 1842.
4. Pontécoulant 1844. De Pontécoulant's praise was, even in the circumstances, overdone, as the continental nature of the Antarctic had not yet been proven.
5. I. Lebrun 1843; Joubert 1871; Achille and Demoulin 1890; Meissas 1889; Postel 1887.
6. There are many such examples; Cortambert 1873, 115, and Pagès 1875 are representative.
7. "Wilkes Land" was widely used both inside and outside France at this time to refer to the Antarctic coast south of Van Diemen's Land along which the American captain had sailed. See, for example, Lassailly 1895, 46.
8. For discussion, see Simon-Ekeland 2021, 101.
9. Robert 1990, 92.
10. Verne 1871.
11. See Clode 2016. On fiction and Antarctica more broadly, see Leane 2012.
12. It is worth noting that the empire did have detractors, critics who argued that it was more important for France to focus on strengthening its position within Europe than to continue to expand outwardly, as well as those who thought that recapturing the provinces of Alsace and Lorraine (annexed by Germany at the end of the Franco-Prussian War in 1871) should take precedence over overseas activity. These critics were, however, consistently in the minority.
13. The Hexagon refers to the area of France geographically situated in Europe, excluding French islands in the Mediterranean Sea, the English Channel, and the Atlantic Ocean. The terms *mainland France* and *metropolitan France* are also used similarly.

14. Changes to the island's name over time reflect political realities: prior to 1793, the island now called Île de la Réunion was called Isle de Bourbon. It was renamed Réunion following the fall of the House of Bourbon during the French Revolution. The name was chosen to commemorate the union of revolutionaries from Marseille with the Parisian National Guard. In 1801, the island was renamed Île Bonaparte after Napoleon Bonaparte. But not long afterward, in 1810, Britain invaded and returned to the name Bourbon. When the island was restored to France five years later at the Congress of Vienna, the name Bourbon was retained. Finally, when the restored Bourbons fell during the French Revolution of 1848, the island was again renamed Réunion.

15. Vélain 1878.
16. Bertie 1905.
17. Ross 1847, 72–81.
18. Foreign Office 1887.
19. B. Smith and Drummond 1886.
20. Hertslet 1886; Foreign Office 1887.
21. There is an interesting parallel to be made here with Clipperton Island, an uninhabited island in the eastern Pacific claimed by France, where both British and American companies exploited guano with no French interference. Clipperton was the subject of a sovereignty dispute between France and Mexico; following binding international arbitration, in 1931 it was declared to be a French possession despite a lack of effective occupation. There is a significant amount of legal literature on this case and it has become a standard by which other disputes are measured. See V. Emmanuel 1932; Oraison 2007; Dickinson 1933; Inch 1965.
22. Hulot 1911; Semalle 1893.
23. Mercié 1897; *Politique coloniale* 1893.
24. Lieutard 1893.
25. Bossière 1894.
26. Copeland 1899, 4.
27. For Antarctica at this time, see Baughmann 1994; Basberg 2017.
28. Similar forces were at work in the Arctic at the same time; see Riffenburgh 1994.
29. For the Belgian expedition, see Decleir and Broyer 2001.
30. Griffiths 2007.
31. At the same time, whaling in the southern seas was on the rise and by the beginning of the twentieth century whaling was a leading factor in Antarctic and sub-Antarctic exploration. The development of new whaling weapons, together with growing demand for the whale species abundant in the Antarctic seas, fueled this exploration. By the opening of World War I, the southern seas supplied two-thirds of the world's whale oil, used in the production of lubricants, soap, and margarine. Its strategic value soared during the war, especially in Britain, where the by-product glycerin was essential to the manufacture of explosives. See Mawer 1999; Stackpole 1972.
32. For Charcot, see Simon-Ekeland 2021, pt. 3; Khan 2008; Zimmermann and Gallois 1936; Hoisington 1975.
33. Charcot 1908, 425–26.
34. Nordenskjöld was found in late 1903 by the Argentinian Navy; Charcot later met him in Buenos Aires.
35. Charcot 1908, 428–29.
36. Froidevaux 1903, 286.
37. Charcot 1905, 500.
38. Charcot, 426. For an excellent analysis of Charcot's position, see Simon-Ekeland 2021, 185ff.
39. Charcot 1905, 499; Charcot 1906.

40. Typical examples include *La vie moderne* 1905; *Le Matin* 1905; *Le Figaro* 1905.
41. *Le Matin* 1907.
42. Cited in Costa 1958, 71 n 9.
43. Charcot 1910; Rouch 1936.
44. Hobbs 1939, 68.
45. Charcot 1905, 498.
46. This decision was seen with regret by some later commentators, such as Marthe Emmanuel (1947), who felt that France should be entitled to lands in the Antarctic Peninsula region.
47. Foreign Office 1905.
48. Cambon 1905.
49. Ministère des colonies 1911.
50. British Letters Patent 1908.
51. Howkins 2017, 43.
52. Beck 1983b, 451.
53. Rabot 1901, 211.
54. Mallet 1911.
55. British Ambassador to France 1911; British Embassy, Paris 1911.
56. A. Lebrun 1912.
57. Ministère de la marine 1912.
58. Ministre des colonies 1912.
59. Poincaré 1912.
60. Bertie 1913.
61. For Mawson and the Australasian Antarctic Expedition, see Roberts 2004; Hains 2002; Corbett 1999.
62. *Sydney Morning Herald* 1910.
63. *Sydney Morning Herald* 1911; *The Daily Telegraph* 1911.
64. Mawson 1914, 257.
65. On the uncertainty surrounding Mertz's death, see Carrington-Smith 2005.
66. Renaud 1911, 398.
67. *Le Matin* 1912.
68. Mawson 1915, chap. 1; Mawson 1930, 47; also see Price 1962a, 176.
69. Mawson 1915, chap. 1; also see Mawson 1914.
70. Mawson 1920.
71. Mawson was also concerned that Britain was likely to allocate a sizable portion of the Antarctic to New Zealand, and argued that Australia's claim, geographic proximity, and strategic need were stronger.
72. *Le Petit Parisien* 1914.
73. For example, Jager-Schmidt 1914; *Navigazette* 1914; Zimmermann 1913.

4. FORMALIZING SOVEREIGNTY

1. First enunciated by Canada in the Arctic context, the sector principle dates to 1907. In that year, as Canada wrestled with formalizing possession of the lands and islands to the north of the Dominion, the idea of extending the territorial possessions of Arctic nations along meridian lines to the North Pole was raised in the Canadian Senate; see Cavell 2019. There is extensive discussion on the sector principle in the literature: Svarlien 1960; Auburn 1982, 17ff; G. W. Smith and Lackenbauer 2014; and Carlson et al. 2013 are recommended.

2. Cited in Beck 1983a, 475. On this, also see Beck 1983b; Howkins 2017; Dodds 2002; and Dudeney and Sheail 2019.

3. In the Antarctic context, Norway stands out as not making use of the sector principle, a geopolitical decision taken in order not to compromise the Svalbard Archipelago. It is in Norway's long-term strategic interests to not recognize the Russian sector principle claim to Arctic territories, since that claim includes Svalbard. Norway's claim to Antarctica's Dronning Maud Land, made in 1939, contained no explicit northern or southern limits (Norwegian Ministry of Foreign Affairs, 2014–2015, 16–18).

4. The French seem to have had second thoughts about the Antarctic Peninsula region in 1928, when the French ambassador in London was instructed to ask the British government if it had indeed annexed the parts of that region sighted by Dumont d'Urville and Charcot and, if so, on what date—a decidedly strange question, reflective of the state of ignorance over the Antarctic that had so long persisted in the French government (Ambassade de France à Londres 1928). The British were quick to reply that these territories were now part of the Falkland Islands Dependencies and under British control (Villiers 1928). France made no further moves in this direction.

5. *Annales coloniales* 1925.
6. Ministère des colonies 1924.
7. Ministère des colonies 1924.
8. Gerard 1925, 15.
9. Ministère des colonies 1924.
10. *Dépêche coloniale et maritime* 1925, 35.
11. Peau 1923–1924.
12. Bocher 2021.
13. Ministère des colonies 1924.
14. Berthier 1926, 870.
15. Floch 1982.
16. Regelsperger 1924, 137–38.
17. *The Register* 1925.
18. *The Daily Mail* (Brisbane) 1925a.
19. For example, *The Telegraph* (Brisbane) 1925.
20. *The Daily Mail* (Brisbane) 1925b.
21. Howitt 2019, 309–10.
22. Masson 1925; Charteris 1929.
23. Price 1962b.
24. At 432,000 square kilometers, Terre Adélie covers an area equivalent to just 7 percent of the six million square kilometers claimed by Australia.
25. Australian Antarctic Territory Acceptance Act 1933, emphasis added.
26. Bertie 1913.
27. Corbin 1933.
28. His Majesty's Governments 1937; also see Leigh-Smith 1934.
29. Ministère des affaires étrangères 1938.
30. Imperial Conference London 1937.
31. Garnier 1938; Journal officiel 1938, 4098–99.
32. His Majesty's Governments 1937.
33. Ministère des affaires étrangères 1938.
34. For Norway and the Antarctic, see Norwegian Ministry of Foreign Affairs 2014–2015; Jensen 2016; Apelgren and Brooks 2021.
35. Welles 1939b.
36. Bullitt 1939.
37. Bonnet 1939.
38. J-P C 1940.
39. Coppet 1940.

40. Kiesewetter 1942, 4.
41. For example, Stalinsky 1938; J-P C 1940.
42. Fawcett 1941.
43. Delépine 1964.
44. Admiralty Secretariat 1942.
45. For legal discussions of French sovereignty over Terre Adélie, see Costa 1958 and Guillaume 1987.
46. The literature on sovereignty and territorial claims is vast; in addition to the foundational Crawford 2019, pt. 3, and Shaw 2008, chap. 10, the following are suggested: Thomson 1995; Simsarian 1938; Smedal 1931. Today, environmental problems, which do not obey political boundaries, are increasingly challenging the ways in which states conceive of sovereignty; see Litfin 1997, 1998; Poole 2008.
47. For scientific activity and the Greenland case, see Martin-Nielsen 2013, 116–17.
48. Permanent Court of International Justice 1933, 63.
49. On effective occupation in the Antarctic, see Joyner 1998; Beck 1986; Crawford and Rothwell 1992, 57ff; Auburn 1982, chap. 1.
50. Shaw 2008, 511. On this, also see Thomson (1995), who stresses enforcement authority as critical to sovereignty and provides an overview of the issues in scholarship.
51. Huber 1928, 36.
52. Plott 1969, 29; US Navy General Board 1924. Plott's study offers a thorough analysis of the United States' position on Antarctic claims.
53. Hughes 1924a, 1924b.
54. This continued into the later interwar period with Richard E. Byrd and Lincoln Ellsworth's Antarctic expeditions. Already a national hero for his 1926 flight over the North Pole and his trans-Atlantic flight the following year, Byrd led an Antarctic expedition from 1928 to 1930, building a base called Little America on the Ross Ice Shelf and even flying to the South Pole. Soon thereafter, the polar explorer Ellsworth dropped a cylinder containing a claim from his plane while attempting to fly across the continent from Dundee Island to the Ross Sea in 1935. But Byrd's and Ellsworth's expeditions were without state endorsement and the United States chose to not pursue their claims beyond the usual reservation of rights. See Secretary of State (Hull) 1938.
55. Lüdecke and Summerhayes 2013.
56. Welles 1939a.
57. Roosevelt 1939, 17.

5. SCIENCE AND PRESENCE

1. For Mawson's comments, see *Northern Standard* (Darwin) 1946; for the *New York Times* story, see *The New York Times* 1946.
2. Aucouturier 1946; also see M. Emmanuel 1947.
3. *Combat: Hebdomadaire du Mouvement de libération française* 1946.
4. Goblet 1946.
5. US Navy 1946.
6. *The New York Times* 1947.
7. Cumming 1946.
8. For biographical treatments of Victor, see T. Fournier 2001 and Garde 2006. While the latter is both anecdotal and insightful, it needs to be approached cautiously as it contains factual errors.
9. For an excellent study of French anthropology and ethnology and their relations to empire and race at this time, see Conklin 2013. For Mauss, also see M. Fournier 1994.
10. Gessain 1989, 114.

NOTES TO PAGES 79–88

11. Victor 1938, 1939.
12. On the Arctic, Desert, and Tropic Information Center, see Farish 2005.
13. Victor 1947a.
14. Victor 1949, 135.
15. On Victor's vision of polar exploration, see Martin-Nielsen 2013, 39–59.
16. Victor 1987.
17. *Le Monde* 1946; J.-A. Martin, Vallette, and Pommier 1947.
18. Expéditions polaires françaises 1947.
19. Victor 1947b.
20. Victor 1947c, 5–6.
21. Beck 1986, 126, emphasis in original.
22. On Operation Tabarin and British Antarctic policy at this time, see Dudeney and Walton 2012.
23. Argentina had earlier established a permanently occupied weather station in the South Orkney Islands.
24. Victor 1947b.
25. For example, *Combat: Hebdomadaire du Mouvement de libération française* 1947, 2.
26. Auriol 1947; Ramadier 1947.
27. Le Président du Conseil, défense nationale 1947.
28. Ferrière 1949; Rougeron 1947, 1; Dollot 1949.
29. *Time* 1946.
30. Le Président du Conseil, défense nationale 1947.
31. For French attitudes toward the United States, see Roger 2006.
32. For the rebuilding of academic and industrial science in postwar France, see Pestre and Jacq 1996; Prost 1988. For the reconstruction of European science after World War II, see Krige 2006.
33. For reconstruction, see, among others, Vayssière 2009; Chapman 2018. And for France in the early postwar period more broadly, see Hitchcock 1998.
34. Hanessian 1960.
35. Hecht 2001, 254; Hecht 1998.
36. Had it not been for Victor's prior connections to Greenland from his prewar expeditions, his intense and long-standing fascination with that land, the French government would never have looked north in the postwar years. From a practical or territorial point of view, French investment in Greenland made little sense; indeed, it was a mission driven by one man, a singular personality, a connection that would persist for decades under Victor's careful nurturing. See Martin-Nielsen 2013, chap. 2.
37. Expéditions polaires françaises 1949.
38. Liotard 1948a, 1948b.
39. For Expéditions polaires françaises' early work in Greenland, see Expéditions polaires françaises 1956a.
40. For the *Commandant Charcot*, see Bayle and Dubard 1951.
41. Le Secrétaire d'état chargé de la marine et le Ministre de la France d'outre-mer 1948.
42. Victor 1948.
43. For US military thinking on the polar regions during the Cold War, see Doel 2009; Doel, Harper, and Heymann 2016; Farish 2013.
44. Commission des territoires d'outre-mer 1949, 258.
45. Capdeville 1949.
46. France—Madagascar 1949, 1831.
47. République française 1950.

48. For the seaplane, see Préfontaine 2001.
49. Liotard and Pommier 1952, 27.
50. Le Président du Conseil des ministres 1948.
51. Le Ministre de la France d'outre-mer 1948.
52. Liotard 1953; Ministère de la justice 1953; Journal officiel 1948; Gautier 1950.
53. Postage stamps and post offices have been used (and continue to be used) by many countries to demonstrate symbolic administration in the Antarctic; however, the ease of issuing stamps and establishing "post offices" in remote territories weakens their effectiveness. See Bagshawe and Goldup 1951; Auburn 1982, 39–41.
54. Le Ministre de la France d'outre-mer 1950. Since Terre Adélie was administratively attached to Madagascar at this time, the stamps used were Madagascan 100-franc airmail stamps. French Antarctic stamps have regularly been issued over the past seventy years and the rare ones are highly valued by collectors.
55. Ministère de la France d'outre-mer 1951, 7321.
56. Liotard and Pommier 1952, 23–24.
57. Mawson 1915.
58. Tabuteau 1952, 195.
59. Bayle and Dubard 1951.
60. For the co-opting of penguins in the production of French Antarctic space, see Martin-Nielsen forthcoming.
61. Liotard and Pommier 1952; Expéditions polaires françaises 1950, 1952b.
62. Liotard 1951b.
63. Expéditions polaires françaises 1956a.
64. Marret 1953b.
65. Expéditions polaires françaises 1951.
66. Marret 1954, 33.
67. For example, Bayle and Dubard 1951, 13.
68. Marret 1951.
69. Marret 1953a.
70. Expéditions polaires françaises 1954; Victor 1959, 7.
71. Victor and Pflimlin 1952; Victor 1952.
72. Liotard 1951a.
73. Ironically, at the same time French authorities were appealing to Expéditions polaires françaises for photographs of the Antarctic to display in Indochina as a means of showcasing French prestige (Chef du bureau de presse du Ministère des états associés 1951).
74. Victor 1950, 1951a; Cortadellas 1950.
75. Service hydrographique de la marine 1951; Vaugelade 1951; General Ghislain 1950.
76. Schmitt 1932; Fiekers 1958.
77. American Association of Jesuit Scientists 1933.
78. Les secrétaires perpétuels de l'Académie des sciences 1950; Victor 1951b.
79. Liotard 1951a.
80. *Le Monde* 1949; *Combat: Hebdomadaire du Mouvement de libération française* 1949, 2.
81. Marret 1955, audio 3:29.
82. Marret 1954, 240.
83. As Alexander Simon-Ekeland (2021, 320) notes, this was not unique to France.
84. Courtet 1950.

6. GROWING MATURITY

1. Bargues 1950.
2. Buriot 1954.
3. Gildea 2002, 21; Tronchon 1986; Fremigacci, Rabearimanana, and Razafimbelo 2008.
4. A. W. M. Smith 2014, 93.
5. Bargues 1950; Barjot 1952.
6. Assemblée nationale 1955, 7979. In 2007, the territory expanded to include the Îles Éparses (Scattered Islands). Situated around Madagascar, sovereignty over these islands is variously contested by Madagascar, Mauritius, and the Comoros. For these disputes, which are still at play today, see Foyer 1982; Oraison 2010; Verneau 2020.
7. As of 1996, it is headquartered in Réunion.
8. On the evolving legal status of *la France d'outre-mer* (overseas France), see Oraison 2004.
9. Garde 2002.
10. Chamberlain 1952; Jacka 1953.
11. Kerguelen is 3,900 kilometers from Durban and 4,100 kilometers from Perth.
12. Genty 1955, 169; Sicaud 1952.
13. In 1979, it was renamed Base Martin-de-Viviès after the death of meteorologist and explorer Paul de Martin de Viviès, the base's founder.
14. Contrary to the other territories mentioned here, Algeria was not administratively a French colony; it was annexed in 1848 and governed as an integral part of France until 1962. This did not, however, mean equal rights: Algerian Muslims did not enjoy the same rights as other French citizens. For the Algerian War, Courrière (2001) and Horne (1977) are particularly interesting.
15. For Operation Windmill, see Nutt 1948.
16. Bost 1957.
17. Richert 1957, 7.
18. Rolland and Victor 1959; Expéditions polaires françaises 1956b, 1956c.
19. Rolland 1965; Vinay 1979, 20.
20. LeSchack 1964, 7.
21. Expéditions polaires françaises 1968, 61–62.
22. For example, Faure 1955.
23. Here, the literature is vast. The following are recommended: Collis and Dodds 2008; Nicolet 1984; Korsmo 2007; Elzinga 1992.
24. See, for example, Dewart 1989.
25. See Beck 1986, 49. Beck (1986, chap. 3) provides a good discussion of the IGY's political aspects, while Elzinga (2011) offers an insightful retrospective. The Australians were particularly concerned about Soviet bases situated in the Australian Antarctic Territory (Goldie 1958).
26. Sudre 1955, 130.
27. Victor 1955.
28. Reppe 1957, 14ff.
29. Danjon 1958; Victor and Pflimlin 1952. Note that the franc was soon thereafter revalued at a rate of 100:1.
30. Sudre 1957; Couvreur 1955.
31. For example, Expéditions polaires françaises 1952a. Garde (2006, 91) provides a secondary account of this conflict.
32. Imbert 1956a.
33. Guillard 1955.
34. Cited in Lorius, Tahi, and Schlich 2008, 29.

35. For the ship, see Hansen 1996.
36. Reppe 1957, 71.
37. Imbert 1956b.
38. Novel 1958.
39. Lorius 1957–1958; Imbert 1959.
40. Morlet 1956; Lorius, Tahi, and Schlich 2008.
41. The Suez crisis showed clearly the reduced status of the old European powers, and especially France, in face of the two new superpowers.
42. See Jardel 1960; *Les cahiers français* 1957.
43. Rebeyrol 1958.
44. By locating their station at the geographic south pole, the converging point of most existing Antarctic territorial claims, the Americans implicitly challenged those claims.
45. Elzinga 2011, 66.
46. The first overwinter was accomplished by Claude Lorius, Jacques Dubois, and Roland Schlich, and the second by René Garcia, Henri Larzillière, and Guy Ricou.
47. Emery 1956.
48. Siple 1959.
49. Lorius, Tahi, and Schlich 2008, 100.
50. TAAF 1958.
51. It was originally, and briefly, called the Special Committee on Antarctic Research. SCAR was intended to provide a permanent body for international scientific cooperation in the Antarctic.
52. See, for example, Alduy 1956, 5940.
53. For example, Guillard 1958.
54. US Department of State 1958.
55. *Le Monde* 1958a.
56. For readable accounts of the Antarctic Treaty negotiations, see Peterson 1988; Beck 1986; Hall 1994; Howkins 2017, chap. 5; Berkman 2011.
57. Argentina's claim also rests on occupation in the South Orkneys, where it has had a meteorological station since 1904. These islands are also claimed by Britain. Further, while the Argentinian and Chilean claims overlap, in the 1940s the two South American countries agreed to mutually recognize their respective indisputable sovereignty rights over the claimed territories.
58. For discussion, see Gleason 1958; Chaturvedi 2009; Beck 1986, chap. 4.
59. Heap 1983, 105.
60. For the Soviet position, see Toma 1956; Gan 2010.
61. Merle 1961; Victor 1959; Expéditions polaires françaises 1961.
62. *Le Monde* 1958b.
63. Dupuy 1958, 210.
64. The literature on de Gaulle is vast. Two excellent books are Berstein (1989) and Julian Jackson's (2018) biography.
65. Conseil des ministres 1958; Victor 1961a.
66. Le Secrétaire d'état au Sahara 1961, 2997.
67. See Braun 2018 and Gildea 1994, chap. 3 for the concept of *grandeur* in French history.
68. French Polynesia also served as France's nuclear testing ground after Algerian independence, becoming an integral part of France's nuclear deterrent and thus of the Gaullist landscape.
69. Chesneaux 1991, 256.
70. Garde 2006, 112.

71. Reppe 1957, 11.
72. Gaulle 1959, 1962; Victor 1961a.
73. For example, Gaulle 1963. This was widely covered by the news media; *La Dordogne libre* 1959 is typical.
74. Charpentier 1959a.
75. Department of State 1958.
76. Phleger 1959a.
77. Phleger 1959d.
78. Phleger 1959c.
79. T. B. Millar 1972, 330.
80. Phleger 1959b.
81. Cited in Robert 1990, 98.
82. See Dodds and Hemmings 2009.
83. Antarctic Treaty 1959.
84. Charpentier 1959b.
85. Sudre 1963; TAAF 1960, 7; Charpentier 1971.
86. Government of France 1984.
87. See, for example, Vinay 1979.
88. For discussion, see Elzinga 1992; Turchetti et al. 2008.
89. See Sulikowski 2013.
90. Victor 1962.
91. Guillard 1968; TAAF 1964. See Salazar 2013 for the geopolitics of everyday life on Antarctic bases and settlements.
92. For example, during the IGY, Expéditions polaires françaises negotiated preferential telegram tariffs for Terre Adélie (Rouillon 1957).
93. *Le Monde* 1969; Boussin 1966. For food and emotion in British polar exploration, see McCorristine and Mocellin 2016.
94. For gender and the Antarctic, and particularly the integration of women into Antarctic programs, see Seag 2017 and McCahey 2021.
95. Chalumeau 1967.
96. Bauer 1965; Petit 2012.
97. Swithinbank 1966, 467.
98. Delépine 1973.
99. Rolland 1968.
100. Secretariat of the Antarctic Treaty 1968.
101. Victor 1969.
102. United States Observers 1964, 655–56.
103. Victor 1961b, 1961c, 1962.
104. Vaugelade 1962.
105. Thellier 1963.
106. Tahi, Gadioux, and Jacquin 2019, 170.

7. CRISIS AND CHOICES

1. Barberot 1979.
2. Vaugelade 1978.
3. Le Ministre d'état chargé de la défense nationale 1971.
4. Ten million francs: Chaussade 1979; previous year: Vinay 1979, 37ff.
5. Vinay 1979; Secrétariat d'état—DOM-TOM 1979.
6. Vaugelade 1978.
7. Vaugelade 1976.

8. Barberot 1979.
9. Président du conseil consultatif des TAAF 1979.
10. Vinay 1979; Secrétariat d'état—DOM-TOM 1979.
11. Heckel 1979.
12. Chaussade 1979.
13. Mosse 1979.
14. More generally, the more unproductive and unpromising an overseas territory, the harder it was to convince politicians and the public to contribute the (often high amounts of) money needed to support it. This was not only theoretical; France did abandon several African enclaves for these reasons.
15. Forrnet 1985.
16. Secrétariat d'état—DOM-TOM 1979; B. Pons 1986.
17. Vinay 1979, 44ff.
18. Président du conseil consultatif des TAAF 1979.
19. Morlet 1987, 54–55.
20. TAAF 1984a.
21. Dutac 1985.
22. Ministère de la recherche et de la technologie 1989b; also see Waldteufel 1990.
23. For the ship, see Buiron and Dugast 2017.
24. *Le Monde* 1988, 1990.
25. For a public evaluation of this funding decrease, see Coles 1991.
26. Pieri 1985b.
27. Ministère de la recherche et de la technologie 1989b, 1989c.
28. Expéditions polaires françaises 1990a; Maurin 1991; Rabourdin 1991.
29. Morlet 1989a.
30. TAAF 1985.
31. Sous-direction des affaires politiques, bureau Océan Indien 1991.
32. *Le Monde* 1991b; also see Pastre 1991.
33. *Libération* 1991.
34. *Le Monde* 1991a.
35. *Le Monde* 1954.
36. Labouz 1992, 42.
37. *Libération* 1991.
38. See Cornevin and Cornevin 1990; Aldrich 1996.
39. Cited in Chesneaux and Maclellan 1992, 99.
40. For the Arctic Ocean, France awkwardly points to Saint-Pierre et Miquelon.
41. Chesneaux 1991, 263–65.
42. For the Antarctic as a colonial space, see Collis and Stevens 2007.
43. Of the large literature available on this, the following are recommended: Joyner 1992; Oraison 2005b; Overholt 1990; Rothwell 1996, 127ff.
44. The Soviets, in particular, saw krill as a strategic resource; see Boczek 1984.
45. See Antonello 2019.
46. Heckel 1979; Guillaume 1985b; Robin 1979.
47. CAMLR Convention Text 1980.
48. Auburn 1982, 222; Beck 1986, 228.
49. Carraud 1979.
50. On UNCLOS, see Joyner 1992; Beurier 1989; Hemmings and Stephens 2010. On France in this context, see Journal officiel 1978.
51. Portail national des limites maritimes 2021; Bouron 2017.
52. Permanent Mission of France to the United Nations 2009.
53. See Haron 1986; Joyner 1998, chap. 8; Jayaseelan 2019; Østreng 1991.

54. United Nations Secretary General 1984.
55. Cited in Bermejo 1990, 58.
56. Henault 1979; Brochenin 1985; Guillaume 1987, 43.
57. Schricke 1984.
58. For a sociological discussion of this divide, see Jouvenet 2016.
59. It was in part these blows to self-confidence that led to France insisting on imposing particular organizational structures during negotiations for the failed European Antarctic Project of the early 1970s, ultimately offending potential partners such as West Germany. See Elzinga 2011; Martin-Nielsèn 2013.
60. Lemoine 1984.
61. Morlet 1987, 57.
62. Victor 1988.
63. For example, *Libération* 1991; Pange 1988.
64. Lemoine 1984.
65. Lorius 1989.
66. Praderie 1989.
67. Ministère de la recherche et de la technologie et Ministère des DOM-TOM 1990.
68. Centre national de la recherche scientifique 1989.
69. Ministère des affaires étrangères, affaires juridiques 1990; Praderie 1990c.
70. Lavezzari 1989. For analysis, see Joenniemi 1989.
71. Ministère des affaires étrangères, affaires juridiques 1989b.
72. Praderie 1990a.

8. ENVIRONMENTAL AUTHORITY

1. Expéditions polaires françaises 1982; Beaux 1981; Moulton 1982; Le Ministre de la défense 1981.
2. Rebeyrol 1982.
3. For example, Vinay 1979, 81ff.
4. Expéditions polaires françaises 1978; Secrétariat d'état—DOM-TOM 1979.
5. Morice 1976.
6. See Howkins 2017; Dodds 2012; Naylor et al. 2008.
7. Comité national français des recherches antarctiques 1962, 32; Expéditions polaires françaises 1974.
8. Martin-Nielsèn 2013, chap. 2.
9. P. M. Smith and Dana 1973.
10. Expéditions polaires françaises 1974.
11. Vinay 1984; also see Morlet 1984. French envy of foreign air capacity in the Antarctic was by no means diminished by the not-infrequent airplane accidents suffered by other countries. Even the three American planes that suffered a series of disasters (including takeoff failures, an exploding rocket, a motor fire, a cockpit fire, broken skis, and a pinned nose) while trying to rescue a French expedition from the ice sheet in the summer of 1975 put no noticeable dent in this desire.
12. Laking 1983, 18.
13. Roberts 2011, 157; Dodds and Hemmings 2009.
14. Brochenin 1985; Lemoine 1984; Secrétariat d'état—DOM-TOM 1985a.
15. For a look at the airstrip from the perspectives of infrastructure, science, and environment, see Christian Kehrt's contribution in Heine and Meiske 2022.
16. Engler 1985.
17. Ironically, in 1995 Greenpeace purchased the ship and renamed it the *Arctic Sunrise*.
18. Montgomery 1984; TAAF 1984b; Ministère des affaires étrangères 1985.

19. For example, *Canberra Times* 1983.
20. Académie des sciences 1983; Germain and Courrier 1983.
21. On this, see Overholt 1990, 249.
22. See Antonello and Howkins 2020 for discussion.
23. Turlin and Lilin 1991; Sanchez 1993; Szarka 2000.
24. Vaugelade 1983.
25. Thaler 1984.
26. Union internationale pour la conservation de la nature et des ressources 1984.
27. Pieri 1984.
28. Minahan 1983; Australie—aide-mémoire 1984; New Zealand Embassy 1984.
29. Can 1984.
30. Secrétariat d'état—DOM-TOM 1985b.
31. Vaugelade 1983; Brachet 1984; Chef de district de Terre Adélie 1988.
32. Aldrich 1987; X. Pons 1987.
33. For example, Meadmore 1984.
34. Secrétariat d'état—DOM-TOM 1984; TAAF 1983; Schweitzer 1983.
35. Comité scientifique 1984; Le Secrétaire d'état auprès du Ministre pour DOM-TOM 1984/1985; Lemoine 1983.
36. Brochenin 1985.
37. Secrétariat d'état—DOM-TOM 1985a.
38. Victor 1985; also see Pieri 1985a.
39. Brochenin 1985.
40. Victor 1986; Ministère des DOM-TOM 1987; Pieri 1986.
41. JO Sénat 1987, 923.
42. May 1988.
43. Pieri 1985d.
44. Greenpeace 1988; Ministère des affaires étrangères, affaires juridiques 1989a.
45. Thibau 1985a.
46. Greenpeace 1988; Greenpeace 1989a; Greenpeace 1989b.
47. Ministère des affaires étrangères 1987; Stefanini 1988.
48. Réunion interministérielle 1988; Waldteufel 1989.
49. Corbier 1987; Greenpeace 1984a, 1984b.
50. Beale 1986; Follin 1986.
51. *New Scientist* 1986.
52. Ambassade de France à Canberra 1985.
53. Australia, Parliamentary Debates 1986.
54. Thibau 1985b.
55. On environmentalism in France, see Cans 2006; Dobré 1995; Serne 2014; Lascoumes and Le Bourhis 1997; Charvolin 2003; Pronier and Jacques le Seigneur 1992.
56. Dorst 1965.
57. Poujade 1975.
58. Theys 1998, 19.
59. Pincetl 1993, 87.
60. Garraud 1979.
61. Rucht 1994; Topçu 2013; Duclos and Smadja 1985.
62. On this, see Sainteny 1998; Heijden, Koopmans, and Guigni 1992, 21; Rucht 1989, 86.
63. Secrétariat d'état—DOM-TOM 1985c.
64. Le Maho and Groscolas 1983; Le Maho 1984; Groscolas 1984.
65. Greenpeace 1988.
66. Pieri 1985c.

67. Victor 1985, emphasis in original.
68. Victor 1983.
69. Jouventin and Bretagnolle 1990; Jouventin and Weimerskirch 1990.
70. Expéditions polaires françaises 1990b.
71. Collis and Stevens 2007.
72. See Bornstein 1988; Roussel 2015, 440–42.
73. For discussion, see Chesneaux 1991, 263; Chesneaux and Maclellan 1992, chap. 6.
74. For Chernobyl and France, see Cans 2006, 223–24; Morin and Prieur 2006.
75. Nagtzaam 2009, 125.
76. Académie des sciences 1983; Greenpeace 1988.
77. Beck 1986, 109, 223; also see Overholt 1990, 234.
78. Lemoine 1984.
79. For example, Joyner 1988a, 74.
80. Piketty and Maitre 1974.
81. Courcel 1974.
82. Literature on the minerals negotiations is extensive; the following are recommended: Bermejo 1990; Andersen 1991; Beck 1989; Joyner 1991; Elliott 1994.
83. Beeby 1988, 9, emphasis in original.
84. Renouard 1984; Ministère des affaires étrangères 1984; Gouttes 1984.
85. Guillaume 1985a.
86. See, for example, Secrétariat d'état—DOM-TOM 1979; Henault 1979; Ministère des affaires étrangères 1984; Renouard 1985.
87. Puissochet 1988.
88. Senemaud 1988.
89. For example, in Peter Beck's thoughtful and knowledgeable paper from 1989 there isn't even a hint that the minerals convention might not be ratified (Beck 1989). Also see Labouz 1992, 52, and Beurier 1989, 14–16.
90. For Australia, see Bergin 1991; Crawford and Rothwell 1992.
91. Hawke and Rocard 1989; République française 1989.
92. For the Madrid Protocol, see A. Jackson 2021; Elliott 1994; Puissochet 1991; Oraison 2005a; Labouz 1992.
93. Secretariat of the Antarctic Treaty 1991.
94. See Rocard 1989b; Le Goff 1999; Shortis 2015; Nagtzaam 2009, 126. As Malcolm Templeton notes, Cousteau's efforts were poorly received in New Zealand, where Christopher Beeby tried to convince him to rethink his position (Templeton 2017, 228).
95. Victor 1989.
96. Le Deaut 1989.
97. Duquin 1990; Ministère des DOM-TOM 1989a, 1989b.
98. Rocard 1989a, 1932.
99. *Le Monde* 1989a, 1989b.
100. At the same time, Rocard also worked to improve France's relationship with New Zealand and to repair France's image in the South Pacific more broadly, including brokering a peace deal in New Caledonia in mid-1988. See McCallum 1991; Mohamed-Gaillard 2010; Aldrich 1993.
101. Le Deaut 1989, 85.
102. Gildea 2002, 237.
103. For example, Clark 2013; Sulikowski 2013, 116–17.
104. See Sainteny 1998; Szarka 2002.
105. Prendiville 1994, 45; Rüdig 2019.
106. Franklin and Rüdig 1992; Palmer 1989.
107. Cans 2006, 255.

108. Herber 1991; Barnes 1986.
109. Labouz 1992, 52; also see Beck 1991.
110. Ministère des DOM-TOM 1989a, 1989b.
111. Byers 1991; Crawford and Rothwell 1992. For the greening of Antarctica, also see Antonello 2019.
112. Dumas 1990, 7.
113. For example, Dodds 2011, 235; Howkins 2017, 193.
114. Boidevaix 1991.
115. Le Deaut 1989.
116. Puissochet 1990a, 1990b.
117. Bellescize (Ambassade de France à Wellington) 1990.
118. On this, see Joyner 1998, 94.
119. Meau and Faivre 1990.
120. Durieux 1994.
121. Cour des comptes 1996, 55.
122. Barnier 1994, 2720.

9. AN UNCERTAIN FUTURE

1. Fréjacques and Thiriez 1989.
2. Ministère de la recherche et de la technologie et Ministère des DOM-TOM 1990.
3. Ministère de la recherche et de la technologie 1989a; Ministère des DOM-TOM 1990.
4. Le Pensec 1990.
5. Ministère de la recherche et de la technologie et Ministère des DOM-TOM 1990.
6. TAAF 1989; Administrateur supérieur des Terres australes et antarctiques 1990.
7. Morlet 1987, 1989b, 1989c, 1990; Jouventin, Morlet, and Trehen 1990.
8. Praderie 1990b.
9. JO Sénat 1991.
10. Ulmann 1990.
11. Agence France-Presse 1990.
12. *Le Monde* 1991b.
13. Praderie 1991; Schlich 2010.
14. Deliancourt 2008.
15. Villemain and Godon 2015, 2020.
16. Gaudin 2007, 100.
17. As of 2021, France was first for production of scientific articles on the sub-Antarctic, fifth for the Antarctic, and second in terms of citation indices (Tiegna and Préville 2021, 21).
18. Cointat 2007; Poivre d'Arvor 2022, 69.
19. Cour des comptes 2005, 443–44.
20. Gaudin 2007, 125.
21. See, among others, Poivre d'Arvor 2022; Girardin and Habib 2019; Tiegna and Préville 2021. For discussion in the Senate, see, for example, Fernique 2021; Lopez 2021.
22. Girardin and Habib 2019, 95.
23. Commission des affaires étrangères 2019b; also see Berger 2019; Dessibourg 2020.
24. Poivre d'Arvor 2022, 92–93.
25. French scientists did earlier cooperate with Americans and Soviets, especially in glaciology and ice core drilling, forced by France's weak logistical capabilities.
26. Cointat 2007, 53.
27. Permanent Mission of Germany to the United Nations 2005.

28. This is part of a much broader balancing game played by France: given the country's relatively small population, its influence can be greatly multiplied by a cooperative European political interface—something that contradicts with the independence so sought through the Fifth Republic.

29. Tiegna and Préville 2021, 25.

30. The previous *Astrolabe* had been sold in 2017, when it was too old to be usefully modernized.

31. Lagleize 2020.

32. Tiegna and Préville 2021, 26; Poivre d'Arvor 2022, 30.

33. While New Zealand flies its own planes to the Antarctic, these planes land on an American-operated airstrip, something made possible by the proximity of New Zealand's Scott Base to McMurdo Station.

34. Commission des affaires étrangères 2019b, 104.

35. The Casey airstrip is not without its own problems; see Bergin et al. 2013, 17–18, and Fogarty 2011, 8–9.

36. Poivre d'Arvor 2022, 30, 68.

37. Gaudin 2007, 148.

38. Philippe 2019.

39. See Stone 2007.

40. Poivre d'Arvor 2022.

41. Gaymard and Mamère 2015; Girardin and Habib 2019. For the future of the Madrid Protocol, see Choquet 2018. Given the stipulations of the protocol, lifting the ban even after 2048 seems unlikely.

42. Commission des affaires étrangères 2019a, 106; Girardin and Habib 2019.

43. Bloom 2022, 13–14; Lukin 2014.

44. Pompili 2021.

45. See Rothwell and Scott 2007 for discussion.

46. Commission des affaires étrangères 2019a, 87ff; Gaymard and Mamère 2015; Le Drian 2021; Poivre d'Arvor 2022, 94–95.

47. Frenot 2007; Strobel and Tétart 2007.

48. Cour des comptes 2005, 442; Assemblée nationale 1971.

49. Crawford and Rothwell 1992, 78ff; also see Hemmings 2008.

50. Journal officiel, TAAF 2002; Journal officiel 2019.

51. This focus on the Antarctic has also given rise to a number of popular books on France's polar explorations and activities, some personal reminiscences, most celebratory: Dugast 2019; Buiron and Dugast 2017; Bellec 2019; Le Brun 2020; Tahi, Gadioux, and Jacquin 2019.

52. Macron 2021.

53. Poivre d'Arvor 2022.

54. Cherki 2022.

EPILOGUE

1. Bergin et al. 2013.

2. Similarly, Jean Chesneaux and Nic Maclellan argue that France has historically always done better in the Pacific arena with an adversary, whether it be England in the eighteenth and nineteenth centuries, German antagonism after 1870, Australia and the Soviets during the Fifth Republic, or ecological protesters in the 1980s (Chesneaux and Maclellan 1992, 90–91).

3. Certainly no single idea of empire can encapsulate the French experience; see Girardet 1972; Aldrich 1996, chap. 3.

4. Simon-Ekeland 2021.

5. Garde 2006, 112.

6. Spufford 1996, 8.

7. France last undertook inspections in 2006–2007, and prior to that in 1998–1999; in both cases, these were joint inspections conducted in cooperation with other countries (Secretariat of the Antarctic Treaty 2023).

8. On this "double status," see Oraison 2005a.

9. Météo France 2022.

10. Daniel Bray (2016) discusses this in the Australian context.

11. Østhagen 2020.

12. For example, forbidding tourists from approaching animals, especially during their reproduction season.

13. Choquet 2021; Roest 2017; Dobelle 2016.

14. The legal literature here is extensive and growing; the following are recommended: Kaye 2001; Oude Elferink 2002; Rothwell 1994; Joyner 1988b; Homan 2006.

15. Permanent Mission of France to the United Nations 2009.

16. Rothwell and Scott (2007) point out the same thing for Australia, and Bentley (2021) for Britain. It holds for all claimant countries. On Australia, also see Triggs 1986; for a broader view, see Mancilla 2018.

17. On tensions in the Antarctic Treaty System, see Hemmings 2014; Brady 2013.

18. For commemorative coins, see Journal officiel 1992, 2008.

19. On heritage preservation in Antarctica, see Hyde 2017, and on the strengthening of Antarctic sovereignty claims via public culture, see Dodds 2011.

20. Journal officiel 2009, 2020.

21. Auburn 1982, 5.

22. For France in the Indian Ocean in this context, see Bouchard and Crumplin (2011).

References

ABBREVIATIONS

ADD	Antarctic Documents Database, University of Tasmania
ANOM	Archives nationales d'outre-mer, Aix-en-Provence
CAD	Centre des archives diplomatiques de Nantes
CBA	Archives de la Cinémathèque de Bretagne, Brest
GPM	Greenpeace Media Archives
ICWA	Institute of Current World Affairs Archives
IPEV	Archives polaires françaises—Institut polaire français Paul-Emile Victor, Plouzané
JO	Journal officiel de la République française
NAA	National Archives of Australia
NAF	Archives nationales, France
NARA	National Archives and Records Administration, USA
SHD	Service historique de la défense, Brest/Vincennes
SPRIA	Scott Polar Research Institute Archives
UKNA	National Archives, UK

Académie des sciences. 1983. "Voeu relatif à la création d'une piste d'avions en Antarctique." 19940221/37, NAF.

Achille, Isidore Gilbert, and Anaïs Gillet Demoulin. 1890. *Jules-Sébastien-César Dumont d'Urville*. Paris: Hachette et Cie.

Administrateur supérieur des Terres australes et antarctiques. 1990. "Letter to Monsieur le Ministre de la recherche et de la technologie, 22 October 1990." 19990442/2, NAF.

Admiralty Secretariat. 1942. "Kerguelen Island: General Review of Mines Laid by HMAS Australia." ADM1/12148, UKNA.

Agence France-Presse. 1990. "Paul-Emile Victor réclame la mise en place immédiate de l'Institut français de recherches et technologies polaires." AFP/Papeete/Régions polaires/France, 22 November 1990.

Aldrich, Robert. 1987. "L'Australie et la France dans le Pacifique: Contentieux actuel et arrière-plan historique." *Journal de la Société des océanistes* 84:93–98.

———. 1993. *France and the South Pacific Since 1940*. Honolulu: University of Hawaii Press.

———. 1996. *Greater France: A History of French Overseas Expansion*. Houndmills: Palgrave Macmillan.

Alduy, Paul. 1956. "Séance no. 73–137." Assemblée nationale, débats parlementaires, 13 December 1956.

Alexandria Gazette. 1842. "Naval Court Martial." 10 September 1842.

Ambassade de France à Canberra. 1985. "Telegram to the Ministère des affaires étrangères, 3 April 1985." 19940221/35, NAF.

Ambassade de France à Londres. 1928. "Annexion de la Terre Louis-Philippe, de l'Île Joinville, des Terres Loubet, Fallières et Charcot, 9 June 1928." FO 371 W5540 /532/50, UKNA.
American Association of Jesuit Scientists. 1933. "Ziccawei Observatory; Shanghai, China." *Bulletin of the American Association of Jesuit Scientists, Eastern Section* 11:120.
Andersen, Rolf Trolle. 1991. "Negotiating a New Regime: How CRAMRA Came into Existence." In *The Antarctic Treaty System in World Politics*, edited by Arnfinn Jorgensen-Dahl and Willy Østreng, 94–109. London: Macmillan/The Fridtjof Nansen Institute.
Annales coloniales. 1925. "Le rattachement des terres australes." 6 March 1925, 2.
Antarctic Treaty. 1959. "The Antarctic Treaty, 1 December 1959." Conference on Antarctica, Washington, DC. https://www.ats.aq/e/antarctictreaty.html.
Anthiaume, Albert-Marie-Ferdinant. 1911. "Un pilot et cartographe havrais au XVIe siècle: Guillaume Le Testu." *Bulletin de géographie historique et descriptive* 26:135–202.
Antonello, Alessandro. 2019. *The Greening of Antarctica: Assembling an International Environment*. Oxford: Oxford University Press.
Antonello, Alessandro, and Adrian J. Howkins. 2020. "The Rise of Technocratic Environmentalism: The United States, Antarctica, and the Globalization of the Environmental Impact Statement." *Journal of Historical Geography* 68:55–64.
Apelgren, Nora, and Cassandra M. Brooks. 2021. "Norwegian Interests and Participation Towards the Creation of Marine Protected Areas in the Southern Ocean." *Polar Journal* 11:393–412.
Assemblée nationale. 1955. "Loi no. 55-1052 du 6 août 1955 conférant l'autonomie administrative et financière aux Terres australes et antarctiques françaises." JO Lois et décrets, no. 0187, 9 August 1955, 7979.
———. 1971. "Rapport fait par M. Fontaine sur le projet de loi (no. 1612) relatif au TAAF." Assemblée nationale, 4e législature.
Auburn, F. M. 1982. *Antarctic Law and Politics*. London: C. Hurst.
Aucouturier, Gustave. 1946. "La France rappelle qu'elle a des droits sur la Terre Adélie découverte en 1840 par Dumont d'Urville." *Paris-Dakar: Hebdomadaire d'informations illustré*, 15 December 1946, 1.
Auriol, Vincent. 1947. "Letter to Paul-Emile Victor, 2 July 1947." 20110210/212, NAF.
Australasian Chronicle. 1840. "Antarctic Discovery." 10 December 1840, 3.
Australia, Parliamentary Debates. 1986. "Questions with Notice, 1622–23, Senate." Hansard, Australia, 21 November 1986.
Australian Antarctic Territory Acceptance Act. 1933. "An Act to Provide for the Acceptance of Certain Territory in the Antarctic Seas as a Territory Under the Authority of the Commonwealth and for the Government Thereof [Australian Antarctic Territory Acceptance Act 1933]." A1559, 1933/8, Item ID 12244340, NAA.
Australie—aide-mémoire. 1984. "Construction d'une piste d'attérrissage en Terre Adélie, 29 November 1984." 19940221/35, NAF.
Bagshawe, Richard W., and John Goldup. 1951. "The Postal History of the Antarctic, 1904–49." *Polar Record* 6:45–79.
Barberot, Roger. 1979. "Le territoire des Terres australes et antarctiques françaises en septembre 1979." 19940218/70, NAF.
Bargues, Robert. 1950. "Discours." JO Madagascar et dépendances, no. 3424, 23 December 1950.
Barjot, Pierre. 1952. "Importance stratégique des TAAF." Madagascar et ses dépendances, 8H257, 1952/1958, ANOM.

Barnes, James N. 1986. "The Future of Antarctica—Environmental Issues and the Role of NGOs." In *Antarctic Challenge II: Conflicting Interest, Cooperation, Environmental Protection, Economic Development*, edited by Rüdiger Wolfrum, 413–45. Berlin: Duncker & Humblot.

———. 1991. "Protection of the Environment in Antarctica: Are Present Regimes Enough?" In *The Antarctic Treaty System in World Politics*, edited by Arnfinn Jorgensen-Dahl and Willy Østreng, 186–228. London: Macmillan/Fridtjof Nansen Institute.

Barnier, Michel. 1994. "Conséquences sur l'environnement de l'exploitation de l'aérodrome de la base Dumont-d'Urville en Terre-Adélie, réponse du ministère: Environnement." JO Sénat, 10e législature, 17 November 1994.

Basberg, Bjørn. 2017. "Commercial and Economic Aspects of Antarctic Exploration—from the Earliest Discoveries into the 'Heroic Age.'" *Polar Journal* 7:205–26.

Basberg, Bjørn, and Robert Headland. 2008. "The 19th Century Antarctic Sealing Industry—Sources, Data and Economic Significance." Norges Handelshøyskole SAM21, ISSN 0804-6824.

Bauer, Albert. 1965. "Travaux du groupe de glaciologie de la IXe expédition antarctique soviétique." *La houille blanche* 5:489–98.

Baughmann, T. H. 1994. *Before the Heroes Came: Antarctica in the 1890s*. Lincoln: University of Nebraska Press.

Bayle, Luc-Marie, and Pierre Dubard. 1951. "Penguin Island." *L'Atlantique*, 1 January 1951.

Beale, Bob. 1986. "France Accused of Breaking Eggs to Make Airstrip." 19940221/35, NAF.

Beaulieu, Anne-Marie, ed. 1997. *Les trois mondes de La Popelinière*. Geneva: Droz.

Beaux, Henri. 1981. "Letter to the Directeur des affaires politiques administratives et financières—DOM-TOM, 30 October 1981." 19940221/35, NAF.

Beck, Peter J. 1983a. "British Policy in Antarctica in the Early 20th Century." *Polar Record* 21:475–83.

———. 1983b. "Securing the Dominant 'Place in the Wan Antarctic Sun' for the British Empire: The Policy of Extending British Control over Antarctica." *Australian Journal of Politics and History* 29:448–61.

———. 1986. *The International Politics of Antarctica*. London: Croom Helm.

———. 1989. "Convention on the Regulation of Antarctic Mineral Resource Activities: A Major Addition to the Antarctic Treaty System." *Polar Record* 25:19–32.

———. 1991. "The Antarctic Resources Conventions Implemented: Consequences for the Sovereignty Issue." In *The Antarctic Treaty System in World Politics*, edited by Arnfinn Jorgensen-Dahl and Willy Østreng, 229–76. London: Macmillan/Fridtjof Nansen Institute.

Beeby, Christopher. 1988. "The Convention on the Regulation of Antarctic Mineral Resource Activities." Paper presented to the International Bar Association of Auckland, 13 October 1988, AU ATADD 4-BB-AQ-16, ADD.

Bellec, François. 2019. *Dumont d'Urville*. Paris: Tallandier.

Bellescize (Ambassade de France à Wellington). 1990. "Antarctique. Position Neo-Zélandaise, 24 August 1990." 19990442/3, NAF.

Bentley, Michael. 2021. "The Future of UK Antarctic Science: Strategic Priorities, Essential Needs and Opportunities for International Leadership." Grantham Institute Discussion Paper 9, Imperial College London.

Berger, Annick. 2019. "Antarctique, la fin du miracle français?" *Slate*, 13 October 2019.

Bergin, Anthony. 1991. "The Politics of Antarctic Minerals: The Greening of White Australia." *Australian Journal of Political Science* 26:216–39.

Bergin, Anthony, Marcus Haward, Andrew Jackson, Anthony Press, Sam Bateman, Peter Jennings, Julia Jabour, Stephen Nicol, Patrick Quilty, and Lyn Goldsworthy.

2013. "Cold Calculations: Australia's Antarctic Challenges." *Strategic Insights* 66, Australian Strategic Policy Institute.
Berkman, Paul Arthur. 2011. "President Eisenhower, the Antarctic Treaty, and the Origin of International Spaces." In *Science Diplomacy: Science, Antarctica, and the Governance of International Spaces*, edited by Paul Arthur Berkman, Michael A. Lang, D. W. H. Walton, and Oran R. Young, 17–27. Washington, DC: Smithsonian Institution.
Bermejo, Romualdo. 1990. *L'Antarctique et ses ressources minérales: Le nouveau cadre juridique*. Paris: P.U.F.
Berstein, Serge. 1989. *La France de l'expansion. I. La République gaullienne, 1958–1969*. Paris: Seuil.
Berthier, Hughes. 1926. "Actes du gouvernement général." JO Madagascar et dépendences, no. 2109, 18 September 1926.
Bertie, Francis. 1905. "Crozet Islands, 24 April 1905." FO83/2092, no. 149, UKNA.
———. 1913. "Note to the French Government, 29 March 1913." AU ATADD 1-BB-FR-13, ADD.
Bertrand, Kenneth. 1971. *Americans in Antarctica, 1775–1948*. New York: American Geographical Society and the National Science Foundation.
Beurier, Jean-Pierre. 1989. "Le droit de la mer dans l'Antarctique." *Revue juridique de l'environnement* 1:5–16.
Blais, Hélène. 2005. *Voyages au grand océan. Géographies du Pacifique et colonisation 1815–1845*. Paris: Comité des travaux historiques et scientifiques.
Bloom, Evan T. 2022. "Meeting Antarctica's Diplomatic Challenges: Joint Approaches for Australia and the United States." Australian Strategic Policy Institute, February 2022.
Bloomfield, Noelene. 2017. "Overview: France's Quest for Terra Australis: Strategies, Maladies and Triumphs." *Great Circle* 39:8–24.
Bocher, Elsa. 2021. "La carte, outil de pouvoir pour l'accès, le contrôle et la gestion des ressources naturelles des Îles Kerguelen, des années 1860 aux années 1920." Rencontres interdisciplinaires: Pouvoirs et ressources naturelles, Université Polytechnique des Hauts-de-France.
Boczek, Boleslaw A. 1984. "The Soviet Union and the Antarctic Regime." *American Journal of International Law* 78:834–58.
Boidevaix, Serge. 1991. "Telegram, XVIe réunion consultative du Traité sur l'Antarctique (Bonn, 7–18 octobre 1991), de la part de la délégation française, 16 October 1991." 19990442, NAF.
Bonnet, Georges. 1939. "Note to Ambassador Bullitt, Paris, 21 February 1939." DOS 741/5127/7, NARA.
Bornstein, Stephen E. 1988. "The Greenpeace Affair and the Peculiarities of French Politics." In *The Politics of Scandal: Power and Process in Liberal Democracies*, edited by Andrei S. Markovits and Mark Silverstein, 91–121. New York: Lynne Rienner.
Bossière, E. R. 1894. *Notice sur les Îles Kerguelen (possession française)*. Paris: Challamel.
Bost, R. 1957. "Organisation scientifique des Terres australes et antarctiques françaises." *TAAF Revue* 1:14–23.
Bouchard, Christian, and William Crumplin. 2011. "Two Faces of France: 'France of the Indian Ocean'/'France in the Indian Ocean.'" *Journal of the Indian Ocean Region* 7:161–82.
Bougainville, Hyacinthe de. 1837. *Journal de la navigation autour du globe de la frégate 'La Thétis' et de la corvette 'l'Espérance' pendant les années 1824, 1825 et 1826, tome 1*. Paris: Arthus Bertrand.

Bouron, Jean-Benoît. 2017. "Mesurer les zones économiques exclusives." *Géoconfluences* 23.
Boussin, Jean-Pierre. 1966. "A l'intérieur du bâtiment de séjour, la cuisine (base Dumont d'Urville)." Photo, Archipôles, DDU.66.61465, IPEV.
Brachet. 1984. "Rapport de mission d'étude en Terre Adélie de Madame Brachet, 19 février–10 mars 1984." 20010098/46, NAF.
Brady, Anne-Marie. 2013. "Diplomatic Chill: Politics Trumps Science in Antarctic Treaty System." *World Politics Review*, 19 March 2013.
Braun, Eric. 2018. *La grandeur de la France: Ses métamorphoses dans la Cinquième République*. Versailles: Carneade.
Bray, Daniel. 2016. "The Geopolitics of Antarctic Governance: Sovereignty and Strategic Denial in Australia's Antarctic Policy." *Australian Journal of International Affairs* 70:256–74.
British Ambassador to France. 1911. "Letter to Justin de Selves, 20 December 1911." Série BB4, no. 2453, Archives de la Marine, SHD.
British Embassy, Paris. 1911. "Note to French Government, 20 December 1911." AU ATADD 1-BB-FR-11, ADD.
British Letters Patent. 1908. "Great Britain: Falkland Islands Dependencies, Letters Patent, 21 July 1908." British and Foreign State Papers, 1907–1908, Vol. 101, London, 76–77.
Broc, Numa. 1986. *La géographie de la Renaissance 1420–1620*. Paris: Bibliothèque nationale.
Brochenin, M. 1985. "Letter to the Secrétaire général, 24 January 1985." 19940221/35, NAF.
Brosses, Charles de. 1756. *Histoire des navigations aux Terres Australes contenant ce que l'on sait des mœurs & productions des contrées découvertes jusqu'à ce jour: & ou il est traité de l'utilité d'y faire de plus amples découvertes, & des moyens d'y former un établissement*. Paris: Durand.
Buffon, Georges Louis Leclerc de. 1749. *Premier discours—de la manière d'étudier et de traiter l'histoire naturelle; Second discours—histoire et théorie de la Terre, preuves de la théorie de la Terre*. Paris: Imprimerie royale.
Buiron, Daphné, and Stéphane Dugast. 2017. *L'Astrolabe. Le passeur de l'Antarctique*. Vanves: E/P/A.
Bullitt, William. 1939. "Diplomatic Note to the French Ministry of Foreign Affairs, 17(?) May 1939." DOS file 741.5127/7, NARA.
Buriot. 1954. "Rapport fait au nom de la Commission des territoires d'outre-mer sur le projet de loi (no. 1203) tendant a ériger en territoire distinct de Madagascar les Terres australes et antarctiques françaises." JO Documents parliamentaires, annexe no. 8249, 1 April 1954, 672.
Byers, Bruce. 1991. "Ecoregions, State Sovereignty, and Conflict." *Bulletin of Peace Proposals* 22:68–72.
Cambon, Paul. 1905. "French Memorandum to the United Kingdom Offering to Renounce Any French Claims to the Crozet Islands in Return for the Neutrality of the Minquiers Islands, 28 November 1905." FO83/2092, 95, UKNA.
CAMLR Convention Text. 1980. "Statement by the Chairman of the Conference on the Conservation of Antarctic Marine Living Resources." https://www.ccamlr.org/en/organisation/camlr-convention-text.
Can, Bronwyn. 1984. "MP Calls for Ban on French Antarctic Ship." *The Age*, 1 December 1984, 4.
Canberra Times. 1983. "Airstrip Plans Called Threat to Wildlife." 17 January 1983.

Cans, Roger. 2006. *Petite histoire du mouvement écolo en France*. Paris: Delachaux et Niestlé.
Capdeville, Jean. 1949. "Débats." Assemblée nationale, 4 November 1949, 5980–83.
Carlson, Jon D., Christopher Hubach, Joseph Long, Kellen Minteer, and Shane Young. 2013. "Scramble for the Arctic: Layered Sovereignty, UNCLOS, and Competing Maritime Territorial Claims." *SAIS Review of International Affairs* 33:21–43.
Carné, Louis de. 1843. "Des intérêts français dans l'Océanie." *Revue des deux mondes* 2:288–301.
Carraud. 1979. "Note diplomatique: Antarctique, 30 March 1979." 20010098/77, NAF.
Carrington-Smith, Denise. 2005. "Mawson and Mertz: A Re-Evaluation of Their Ill-Fated Mapping Journey During the 1911–1914 Australasian Antarctic Expedition." *Medical Journal of Australia* 183:638–41.
Cavell, Janice. 2019. "The Sector Theory and the Canadian Arctic, 1897–1970." *International History Review* 41:1168–93.
Centre national de la recherche scientifique. 1989. "Note sur une politique française dans l'Arctique, 27 February 1989." 19990442/2, NAF.
Chalumeau, Pierre. 1967. "Terre Adélie: Campagne d'été 1966–67." Film, 16 mm, 16:06, 25533, CBA.
Chamberlain, N. G. 1952. "Observations of Terrestrial Magnetism at Heard, Kerguelen and Macquarie Islands (Carried out in Cooperation with the Australian National Antarctic Research Expedition, 1947–1948)." Report no. 5, Ministry of National Development, Bureau of Mineral Resources, Geology, and Geophysics, Australia.
Chapman, Herrick. 2018. *France's Long Reconstruction: In Search of the Modern Republic*. Cambridge, MA: Harvard University Press.
Charcot, Jean-Baptiste. 1905. "The French Antarctic Expedition." *Geographical Journal* 26:497–516.
———. 1906. *Le 'Français' au pôle Sud: Journal de l'expédition antarctique française 1903–1905*. Paris: Flammarion.
———. 1908. "Pourquoi faut-il aller dans l'Antarctique?" *Bulletin de la Société astronomique de France* 10:425–39.
———. 1910. *Le 'Pourquoi-Pas?' dans l'Antarctique: Journal de la deuxième expédition au pôle Sud, 1908–1910*. Paris: Flammarion.
Charpentier, Pierre. 1959a. "Statement by Mr. Charpentier (France), Conference Doc. 12, October 15, 1959." In *The Conference on Antarctica, Washington, October 15 to December 1, 1959: Conference Documents—the Antarctic Treaty and Related Papers*.
———. 1959b. "Statement by Mr. Charpentier (France), Conference Doc. 25, Annex E, December 1, 1959." In *The Conference on Antarctica, Washington, October 15 to December 1, 1959: Conference Documents—the Antarctic Treaty and Related Papers*.
———. 1971. "Notes de voyage en Antarctique et au pôle Sud." *Revue de défense nationale* 303:1267–89.
Charteris, A. H. 1929. "Australasian Claims in Antarctica." *Journal of Comparative Legislation and International Law* 11:226–32.
Charvolin, Florian. 2003. *L'invention de l'environnement en France: Chroniques anthropologiques d'une institutionnalisaion*. Paris: La Découverte.
Chaturvedi, Sanjay. 2009. "IGY (1957–58) and the Discursive Transformation of the Antarctic." In *International Encyclopedia of Human Geography*, edited by Rob Kitchin and Nigel Thrift, 133–39. Amsterdam: Elsevier.
Chaussade, Jean. 1979. "Note à l'attention de M. Diefanbacher—Situation du territoire des Terres australes et antarctiques françaises, June 1979." 19940218/70, NAF.

Chef de district de Terre Adélie. 1988. "Confidential Telegram to Bernard Morlet, 6 January 1988." 20010098/46, NAF.
Chef du bureau de presse du Ministère des états associés. 1951. "Letter to Expéditions polaires françaises, 31 January 1951." 20110210/213/4, NAF.
Cherki, Marc. 2022. "Antarctique: La recherche polaire française souffre." *Le Figaro*, 22 March 2022.
Chesneaux, Jean. 1991. "The Function of the Pacific in the French Fifth Republic's 'Grand Design': Theory and Practice of the 'Puissance Mondiale Moyenne.'" *Journal of Pacific History* 26:256–72.
Chesneaux, Jean, and Nic Maclellan. 1992. *La France dans le Pacifique: De Bougainville à Moruroa*. Paris: La Découverte.
Chevanne, Isabelle. 1994. "Les journaux sanitaires de l'expédition en Terre Adélie: 1837–1840." PhD thesis, Université de Nantes.
Choquet, Anne. 2018. "Interdiction de l'exploitation minière en Antarctique, une réalité menacée?" *Natures sciences sociétés* 26:49–59.
———. 2021. "L'extension du plateau continental au large de l'Antarctique: Entre volonté de ménager les susceptibilités et défendre ses intérêts." *VertigO—la revue électronique en sciences de l'environnement* 33. https://doi.org/10.4000/vertigo.29658.
Chown, S. L., R. I. Leihy, T. R. Naish, C. M. Brooks, P. Convey, B. J. Henley, A. N. Mackintosh, L. M. Phillips, M. C. Kennicutt II, and S. M. Grant, eds. 2022. "Antarctic Climate Change and the Environment: A Decadal Synopsis and Recommendations for Action." Scientific Committee on Antarctic Research, Cambridge, UK. https://scar.org/library/scar-publications/occasional-publications/.
Clark, M. L. 2013. "The Antarctic Environmental Protocol: NGOs in the Protection of Antarctica." In *Environmental NGOs in World Politics: Linking the Local and the Global*, edited by Matthias Finger and Thomas Princen, 160–85. London: Routledge.
Clode, Danielle. 2016. "Terres Australes: Rewriting Australia's French History (with the Help of Jules Verne)." *Writing the Ghost Train: Rewriting, Remaking, Rediscovery (Refereed Proceedings of the 20th Conference of the Australasian Association of Writing Programs, Melbourne)*, 1–11.
Cointat, Christian. 2007. "Rapport d'information no. 132: Arctique, Antarctique, terres australes: Un enjeu pour la planète, une responsabilité pour la France." Sénat, session ordinaire de 2007–2008, 12 December 2007.
Coles, Peter. 1991. "French Research Threatened." *Nature* 349:553.
Collis, Christy. 2017. "Territories Beyond Possession? Antarctica and Outer Space." *Polar Journal* 7:287–302.
Collis, Christy, and Klaus Dodds. 2008. "Assault on the Unknown: The Historical and Political Geographies of the International Geophysical Year (1957–8)." *Journal of Historical Geography* 34:555–73.
Collis, Christy, and Quentin Stevens. 2007. "Cold Colonies: Antarctic Spatialities at Mawson and McMurdo Stations." *Cultural Geographies* 14:234–54.
Combat: Hebdomadaire du Mouvement de libération française. 1946. "L'uranium remet en vedette la 'Terre Adélie.'" 14 December 1946, 6A.
———. 1947. "Expédition antarctique française." 8 July 1947.
———. 1949. "On découvre les carnets de Dumont d'Urville." 6 January 1949.
Comité national français des recherches antarctiques. 1962. "Bulletin d'informations no. 14." *TAAF Revue* 21:31–33.
Comité scientifique. 1984. "Procès-verbal de la réunion du 2 mars 1984." 20010098/56, NAF.

Commercial Journal and Advertiser. 1840. "Expedition of the French Corvettes 'l'Astrolabe' and 'La Zelee,' Under the Command of Commodore d'Urville, and Captain Jacquinot." 18 April 1840.

Commission des affaires étrangères. 2019a. "Rapport d'information no. 2042. Mers et océans: Quelle stratégie pour la France?" Assemblée nationale, 15e législature, 19 June 2019. https://www.assemblee-nationale.fr/dyn/15/rapports/cion_afetr/l15b 2042_rapport-information.pdf.

———. 2019b. "Table ronde sur les pôles: Enjeux stratégiques et environnementaux." Assemblée nationale, 15e législature, 18 September 2019.

Commission des territoires d'outre-mer. 1949. "Rapport fait au nom de la Commission des territoires d'outre-mer sur la proposition de résolution de M. Louis Rollin et plusieurs de ses collègues tendant à inviter le gouvernement à affirmer et matérialiser les droits de la souveraineté de la France sur les îles australes françaises." JO Assemblée nationale, 12 April 1949, 258.

Conklin, Alice L. 2013. *In the Museum of Man: Race, Anthropology, and Empire in France, 1850–1950*. Ithaca, NY: Cornell University Press.

Conley, Tom. 1996. *The Self-Map Map: Cartographic Writing in Early Modern France*. Minneapolis: University of Minnesota Press.

Conseil des ministres. 1958. "Décision de présence permanente." Comptes rendus du Conseil des ministres, 4 July 1958.

Cook, James. 1777. *A Voyage Towards the South Pole and Round the World. Performed in His Majesty's Ships the Resolution and Adventure, in the Years, 1772, 1773, and 1775*. London: W. Strahan & T. Cadell.

———. 1821. *The Three Voyages of Captain James Cook Round the World, Vol. 5.* London: Longman, Hurst, Rees, Orme, and Brown.

Copeland, Henry. 1899. *Kerguelen Island and Australian Commerce*. Sydney: John Sands.

Coppet, Jules Marcel de. 1940. "Mines." JO Madagascar et dépendances, no. 2840, 27 April 1940, 520.

Corbett, David. 1999. "Douglas Mawson: The Geologist as Explorer." *Records of the South Australian Museum* 30:107–36.

Corbier, Claude. 1987. "Letter to Monsieur le Commissaire de police, 5 November 1987." 20110210/2, NAF.

Corbin, Charles. 1933. "Note to the Under Secretary of State for Foreign Affairs, 24 October 1933." Imperial Conference 1937, Committee on Polar Questions, Annex I, 16, FO 371/1231, UKNA.

Cornevin, Robert, and Marianne Cornevin. 1990. *La France et les Français outre-mer*. Paris: Tallandier.

Cortadellas, Jacques. 1950. "Letter to M. le Ministre des postes, télégraphes et téléphones, 18 September 1950." 20110210/76, NAF.

Cortambert, Eugène. 1873. *Géographie générale de l'Asie, de l'Afrique, de l'Amérique et de l'Océanie pour la classe de sixième a l'usage des lycées et des collèges*. Paris: Hachette et Cie.

Costa, J.-F. da. 1958. *Souveraineté sur l'Antarctique*. Paris: Librarie générale de droit et de jurisprudence.

Cour des comptes. 1996. "La piste aéroportuaire de Terre Adélie." Rapport au président de la République, octobre 1996, suivi des réponses des administrations, collectivités, organismes, et entreprises.

———. 2005. "L'administration des Terres australes et antarctiques françaises." Rapport au président de la République suivi des réponses des administrations, collectivités, organismes, et entreprises, 439–59. https://www.ccomptes.fr/fr/documents/1330.

Courcel, Geoffroy Chodron de. 1974. "Note confidentielle, Ministère des affaires étrangères, 8 October 1974." 19810057/24, NAF.
Courrière, Yves. 2001. *La guerre d'Algérie, tomes 1 et 2*. Paris: Fayard.
Courtet, François. 1950. "S'étendre au pôle Sud?" *La croix du nord*, 18–19 June 1950, 1.
Couvreur, Jean. 1955. "Le R. P. Lejay nous parle de la plus vaste opération scientifique qui ait jamais été tentée." *Le Monde*.
Crawford, James. 2019. *Brownlie's Principles of Public International Law (9th Edition)*. Oxford: Oxford University Press.
Crawford, James, and Donald R. Rothwell. 1992. "Legal Issues Confronting Australia's Antarctica." *Australian Year Book of International Law* 13:53–88.
Cumming, Hugh S. 1946. "Memorandum of Conversation, Chief of the Division of Northern European Affairs." *Foreign Relations*, 30 December 1946.
d'Albaigne, André. 1570. "Remontrance d'André d'Albaigne." Reproduced in *Études historiques et géographiques*, edited by Ernest-Théodore Hamy, 1890, 456–59. Paris: Ernest Leroux.
Danjon, André. 1958. "L'Année géophysique internationale touche à sa fin: La coopération géophysique internationale la prolongera en 1959." *Le Monde*, 26 December 1958.
D'Arcy Wood, Gillen. 2020. *Land of Wondrous Cold: The Race to Discover Antarctica and Unlock the Secrets of Its Ice*. Princeton, NJ: Princeton University Press.
Day, David. 2013. *Antarctica: A Biography*. New York: Oxford University Press.
de Courtonne, Jean Paulmier. 1663. *Mémoires pour l'établissement d'une mission chréstienne dans le troisième monde, autrement appellé, la terre australe, meridonale, antarctique, & inconnue*. Paris: Claude Cramoisy.
de Gaulle, Charles. 1959. "Letter to Paul-Emile Victor, 31 July 1959." 20110210/212, NAF.
———. 1962. "Transcript of a Note Read over the Telephone to the Ministre des finances, 6 June 1962." 20110210/212, NAF.
———. 1963. "Letter to Paul-Emile Victor, 8 January 1963." 20110210/212, NAF.
De Pasquier, J. Thierry. 1982. *Les baleiniers français au XIXe siècle*. Grenoble: Terre et mer.
Deckker, Paul de, and Pierre-Yves Toullelan. 1989. "La France et le Pacifique." *Revue française d'histoire d'outre-mer* 76.
Decleir, Hugo, and Claude de Broyer, eds. 2001. *The Belgica Expedition Centennial: Perspectives on Antarctic Science and History*. Brussels: VUB.
Delépine, Gracie. 1964. "Les Allemands aux Kerguelen durant la Deuxième Guerre mondiale." *Revue TAAF* 26:8–29.
———. 1973. *Toponymie des terres australes*. Paris: Commission territoriale de toponymie.
Department of State. 1958. "Memorandum of Conversation: Daniels, Luboeansky (RPA), Landy, Lucet (French Embassy), Washington, 28 April 1958." DOS Central Files 702.022/4-2858, NARA.
———. 1959. "Statement Issued by the Department of State on the Occasion of the Signing of the Antarctic Treaty, Department of State Press Release 827, December 1." In *The Conference on Antarctica, Washington, October 15 to December 1, 1959: Conference Documents—the Antarctic Treaty and Related Papers*.
Dépêche coloniale et maritime. 1925. "Les dépendances de Madagascar: Les Comores, les Glorieuses, Saint-Paul et Amsterdam, Kerguelen et Terre Adélie."
Dessibourg, Olivier. 2020. "Jérôme Chappellaz: 'Pour l'instant, la France n'a pas d'ambition importante pour l'Antarctique.'" *Le Monde*, 24 February 2020.
Dewart, Gilbert. 1989. *Antarctic Comrades: An American with the Russians in Antarctica*. Columbus: Ohio State University Press.

Dickinson, Edwin D. 1933. "The Clipperton Island Case." *American Journal of International Law* 27:130–33.
Dillon, Peter. 1829. *Narrative and Successful Result of a Voyage in the South Seas Performed by Order of the Government of British India, to Ascertain the Actual Fate of La Pérouse's Expedition Interspersed with Accounts of the Religion, Manners, Customs and Cannibal Practices of the South Sea Islanders*. London: Hurst, Chance.
Dobelle, Jean-François. 2016. "La délimitation des frontières maritimes de la France." *Annuaire français de droit international* 62:519–40.
Dobré, Michelle. 1995. *L'opinion publique et l'environnement*. Orléans: Institut français de l'environnement.
Dodds, Klaus. 2002. *Pink Ice: Britain and the South Atlantic Empire*. London: I. B. Tauris.
———. 2008. "The Great Game: Britain and the 1959 Antarctic Treaty." *Contemporary British History* 22:43–66.
———. 2011. "Sovereignty Watch: Claimant States, Resources, and Territory in Contemporary Antarctica." *Polar Record* 1:1–13.
———. 2012. *The Antarctic: A Very Short Introduction*. Oxford: Oxford University Press.
Dodds, Klaus, and Alan D. Hemmings. 2009. "Frontier Vigilantism? Australia and Contemporary Representations of Australian Antarctic Territory." *Australian Journal of Politics and History* 55:513–29.
———. 2013. "Britain and the British Antarctic Territory in the Wider Geopolitics of the Antarctic and the Southern Ocean." *International Affairs* 89:1429–44.
Doel, Ronald E. 2009. "Quelle place pour les sciences de l'environnement physique dans l'histoire environmentale?" *Revue d'histoire moderne et contemporaine* 56:137–64.
Doel, Ronald E., Kristine C. Harper, and Matthias Heymann, eds. 2016. *Exploring Greenland: Cold War Science and Technology on Ice*. New York: Palgrave Macmillan.
Dollot, René. 1949. "Le droit international des espaces polaires." *Hague recueil* 75:115–200.
Dorst, Jean. 1965. *Avant que nature meure*. Neuchatel: Delachaux et Niestlé.
Dubard, Pierre, and Luc-Marie Bayle. 1951. *Le 'Charcot' et la Terre Adélie*. Paris: France Empire.
Duclos, Denis H., and Jocelyne J. Smadja. 1985. "Culture and the Environment in France." *Environmental Management* 9:135–40.
Dudeney, John R., and John Sheail. 2019. *Claiming the Ice: Britain and the Antarctic 1900–1950*. Newcastle upon Tyne: Cambridge Scholars.
Dudeney, John R., and David W. H. Walton. 2012. "From Scotia to 'Operation Tabarin': Developing British Policy for Antarctica." *Polar Record* 48:342–60.
Dugast, Stéphane. 2019. *Polar circus: Les expéditions polaires à la française*. Paris: Trésor.
Dumas, Roland. 1990. "The Antarctic in World Politics." *International Challenges: Fridtjof Nansen Institute Newsletter* 10.
Dumont d'Urville, Jules Sébastien César. 1829. "Polynésie. 'L'Astrolabe' à Vanikoro." *Revue des deux mondes* 2:242–56.
———. 1834. *Voyage pittoresque autour du monde; résumé général des voyages de découvertes*. Paris: L. Tenré et Henri Dupuy.
———. 1837. "Décompte de M. Dumont d'Urville pendant son séjour à Londres, 11 May 1837." Dumont d'Urville Papers, CC7/A/772.34, Vincennes, SHD.
———. 1842a. *Voyage au pôle Sud et dans l'Océanie sur les corvettes 'l'Astrolabe' et la 'Zélée' exécuté par ordre du roi pendant les années 1837-1838-1839-1840 sous le commandement de J. Dumont d'Urville, tome III*. Paris: Gide et Cie.

———. 1842b. *Voyage au pôle Sud et dans l'Océanie sur les corvettes 'l'Astrolabe' et la 'Zélée' exécuté par ordre du roi pendant les années 1837-1838-1839-1840, histoire du voyage, tome I.* Paris: Gide et Cie.

———. 1845. *Voyage au pôle Sud et dans l'Océanie sur les corvettes 'l'Astrolabe' et la 'Zélée' exécuté par ordre du roi pendant les années 1837-1838-1839-1840 sous le commandement de J. Dumont d'Urville, tome VIII.* Paris: Gide et Cie.

———. 1855. *Voyage au pôle Sud et dans l'Océanie sur les corvettes 'l'Astrolabe' et la 'Zélée' exécuté par ordre du roi pendant les années 1837-1838-1839-1840 sous le commandement de J. Dumont d'Urville, tome X.* Paris: Gide et Cie.

Dunmore, John. 1969. *French Explorers in the Pacific, Vol. 2: The Nineteenth Century.* Oxford: Clarendon.

Dupuy, René-Jean. 1958. "Le statut de l'Antarctique." *Annuaire français de droit international* 4:196-229.

Duquin, G. 1990. "Consultation des scientifiques au sujet du document franco-australien révisé sur les éléments constitutifs d'une convention globale de protection de l'Antarctique, 11 May 1990." 19990442/3, NAF.

Durieux, Jacques. 1994. "Note to Monsieur l'Administrateur supérieur des TAAF, 31 January 1994." 20010098/46, NAF.

Dutac, P. 1985. "Budget 1985: Présentation, 15 March 1985." 19940389/35, NAF.

Duyker, Edward. 1994. *An Officer of the Blue: Marc-Joseph Marion Dufresne 1724-1772, South Sea Explorer.* Melbourne: Miegunyah/Melbourne University Press.

———. 2014. *Dumont d'Urville: Explorer and Polymath.* Dunedin: Otago.

Elliott, Lorraine M. 1994. *International Environmental Politics: Protecting the Antarctic.* Houndmills: St. Martin's.

Elzinga, Aant. 1992. "Antarctica: The Construction of a Continent by and for Science." In *Denationalizing Science: The Contexts of International Scientific Practice*, edited by Elisabeth Crawford, Terry Shinn, and Sverker Sörlin, 73-106. Dordrecht: Kluwer Academic Publications.

———. 2011. "Origin and Limitations of the Antarctic Treaty." In *Science Diplomacy: Antarctica, Science, and the Governance of International Spaces*, edited by Paul Arthur Berkman, Michael A. Lang, David W. H. Walton, and Oran R. Young, 59-67. Washington, DC: Smithsonian Institution.

Elzinga, Aant, and Ingemar Bohlin. 1989. "The Politics of Science in Polar Regions." *Ambio* 18:71-76.

Emery, Sydney. 1956. "Letter to Monsieur le Chef de bataillon, commandant de l'École de haute montagne, 3 July 1956." 20110210, NAF.

Emmanuel, Marthe. 1947. "A propos des rivalités antarctiques: La conquête du pôle Sud." *L'information géographique* 11:135-38.

Emmanuel, Victor. 1932. "Arbitral Award on the Subject of the Difference Relative to the Sovereignty over Clipperton Island." *American Journal of International Law* 26:390-94.

Engler, Michel. 1985. "Aérodrome Terre Adélie: Définition du projet, 24 September 1985." 20140342/179, NAF.

Expéditions polaires françaises. 1947. "Les Expéditions polaires françaises au Groenland, 1947." 20110210/113, NAF.

———. 1949. "Publicités." 20110210/113, NAF.

———. 1950. "Compte-rendu d'un raid avec chiens, 1949-1950." 20110210/181, NAF.

———. 1951. "Note 0193, 6 July 1951." 20110210/76, NAF.

———. 1952a. "Note, 25 April 1952." 20110210/1, NAF.

———. 1952b. "Récits des premières expéditions en Terre Adélie, 1948-1952." 20110210/181, NAF.

———. 1954. "Subventions, 23 January 1954." 20110210/218, NAF.
———. 1956a. "Terre Adélie-Groenland, 1947–1955: Rapport d'activités." Paris: Arthaud.
———. 1956b. "Fonctionnement." 20110210/3, NAF.
———. 1956c. "Protocole concernant les Expéditions polaires françaises (Missions Paul-Emile Victor)." 20110210/1, NAF.
———. 1961. "10e campagne en Terre Adélie." 20110210/183, NAF.
———. 1968. "Twentieth anniversary of Expéditions polaires françaises (Missions Paul-Emile Victor)." *Arctic* 21:59–66.
———. 1974. "Note sur la participation française au projet américain de transport aérien international dans l'Antarctique et sur le possibilité de desserte aérienne de la Terre Adélie, 25 June 1974." 20110210/147, NAF.
———. 1978. "Desserte de la Terre Adélie par voie aérienne: Comparison avec la voie maritime." 20110210/147, NAF.
———. 1982. "Le transport aérien en Terre Adélie pour la réalisation de programmes de recherche sur la calotte glaciaire antarctique." 19940221/36, NAF.
———. 1990a. "Analyse comptable des comptes définitifs, 2 July 1990." 20060368/7, NAF.
———. 1990b. "Terre Adélie: La France innove la technologie polaire et s'efforce de protéger l'environnement." 20060368/7, NAF.
Faivre, Jean-Paul. 1953. "L'expansion française dans le Pacifique de 1800 à 1842." PhD thesis, Université de Paris.
Farish, Matthew. 2005. "Archiving Areas: The Ethnogeographic Board and the Second World War." *Annals of the Association of American Geographers* 95:663–79.
———. 2013. "The Lab and the Land: Overcoming the Arctic in Cold War Alaska." *Isis* 104:1–29.
Fauque, Danielle. 1985. "Il y a deux cents ans: L'expédition Lapérouse." *Revue d'histoire des sciences* 38:149–60.
Faure, Edgar. 1955. "Letter to Paul-Emile Victor, 8 April 1955." 20110210/212, NAF.
Fawcett, Nigel. 1941. "Midshipman's Journal (*Neptune*), January 1940 to February 1941." Neptune Association. http://www.hmsneptune.com/nigel-fawcett-journal.htm.
Fernique, Jacques. 2021. "Position de la France et de la recherche scientifique en Antarctique." Sénat, débats parlementaires, 11 March 2021, 1536.
Ferrière, M. 1949. "'La Zélée' à la Terre Adélie." *Le Monde*, 26 February 1949.
Fiekers, B. A. 1958. "Rev. Pierre Lejay, S.J." *Woodstock Letters* 87:334.
Fisher, Denise. 2013. "French Motivations in the Pacific." In *France in the South Pacific: Power and Politics*, edited by Denise Fisher, 239–70. Canberra: ANU.
Fleuriau, Aimé-Joseph de. 1931. "Enclosure 1 in No. 207 (Memorandum to the United Kingdom Requesting Information Concerning the British Position as Regards Bouvet Island), 1 December 1931." PRO DO114/34, 224, UKNA.
Floch, Daniel. 1982. *Les oubliés de l'Île Saint-Paul*. Rennes: Ouest France.
Fogarty, Ellie. 2011. "Assessing and Protecting Australia's National Interests." Lowy Institute for International Policy.
Follin, Bernard. 1986. "Letter to Roland Dumas, 19 March 1986." 19940221/35, NAF.
Foreign Office. 1887. "Memorandum by Mr. Alfred S. Green Relative to the Claim of France to the Island of Desolation, or Kerguelen's Land, June 25, 1867." FO 83/1781/5372, UKNA.
———. 1905. "British Memorandum to France Explaining the British Wish to Clarify French Intentions with Regard to the Crozet Islands, 6 December 1905." FO 83/2092/221-222, UKNA.
Fornasiero, Jean, and John West-Sooby. 2011. "Naming and Shaming: The Baudin Expedition and the Politics of Nomenclature in the Terres Australes." In *European*

Perceptions of Terra Australis, edited by Anne M. Scott, Alfred Hiatt, Claire McIlroy, and Christopher Wortham, 165–84. London: Routledge.
Forrnet, Jacques. 1985. "Letter to the Administrateur supérieur des Terres australes et antarctiques, 18 July 1985." 19940389/36, NAF.
Fournier, Marcel. 1994. *Marcel Mauss*. Paris: Fayard.
Fournier, Thierry. 2001. "Paul-Émile Victor, biographie d'un explorateur polaire (1907–1995)." PhD thesis, École des chartes.
Foyer, Jean. 1982. "Les Îles Éparses resteront-elles françaises?" *La nouvelle revue des deux mondes*, January, 54–61.
France—Madagascar. 1949. "Arrêté créant un district austral." JO Madagascar, 31 July 1949.
Franklin, Mark N., and Wolfgang Rüdig. 1992. "The Green Voter in the 1989 European Elections." *Environmental Politics* 1:129–59.
Fréjacques, Claude, and Frédéric Thiriez. 1989. "Pour un nouvel élan de la recherche polaire (DGRT)." 19990442/2, NAF.
Fremigacci, Jean, Lucile Rabearimanana, and Célestin Razafimbelo, eds. 2008. *L'insurrection de 1947 et la décolonisation à Madagascar, tome 1*. Tananarive: Tsipika.
Frenot, Yves. 2007. "L'émergence d'un tourisme de masse en Antarctique." *Le cercle polaire* [online]. http://counterdimension.free.fr/Robin/pole/art_y_frenot_emergence_tourisme.htm.
Frioux, Stéphane, and Vincent Lemire. 2012. "Pour une histoire politique de l'environnement au 20e siècle." *Vingtième siècle. Revue d'histoire* 113:3–12.
Froidevaux, Henri. 1903. "M. Froidevaux's Paris Letter." *Bulletin of the American Geographical Society* 35:283–88.
Gan, Irina. 2010. "Soviet Antarctic Plans After the International Geophysical Year: Changes in Policy." *Polar Record* 46:244–56.
Garde, François. 2002. "L'administration des îles désertes." *Revue française d'administration publique* 101:59–67.
———. 2006. *Paul-Emile Victor et la France de l'Antarctique*. Paris: Audibert.
Garnier, Jacqueline. 1938. "Limite des territoires français de la Terre Adélie." *L'information géographique* 3:66.
Garraud, Philippe. 1979. "Politique électro-nucléaire et mobilisation: La tentative de constitution d'un enjeu." *Revue française de science politique* 29:448–74.
Gascoigne, John. 2015. "From Science to Religion: Justifying French Pacific Voyaging and Expansion in the Period of the Restoration and the July Monarchy." *Journal of Pacific History* 50:109–27.
Gaudin, Christian. 2007. "La place de la France dans les enjeux internationaux de la recherche en milieu polaire: Le cas de l'Antarctique." Rapport no. 230, Office parlementaire d'évaluation des choix scientifiques et technologiques. https://www.assemblee-nationale.fr/12/pdf/rap-off/i3702.pdf.
Gautier, Georges. 1950. "Arrêté portant ouverture du bureau postal de Terre Adélie au service de la télégraphie officielle et privée." JO Madagascar et dépendences, no. 3393, 20 May 1950, 899.
Gaymard, Hervé, and Noël Mamère. 2015. "Rapport no. 2704: Les enjeux écologiques, économiques et géopolitiques du changement climatique en Arctique et en Antarctique." Assemblée nationale, 14e législature, 8 April 2015.
Gazette du Bas-Languedoc. 1842. "Catastrophe du chemin de fer: Suite des détails." 22 May 1842, 2.
General Ghislain. 1950. "Letter to Paul-Emile Victor, 15 December 1950." 20110210/217, NAF.

Genty, Robert. 1955. "Le rôle stratégique de l'île Kerguelen." *Revue de défense nationale* 128:166–75.

Gerard, F. 1925. "La pêche dans les îles australes." *La pêche à Madagascar* (supplément illustré du *Courrier colonial*), 15 September 1925.

Germain, P., and R. Courrier. 1983. "Letter to Admiral Pieri (with Annexes), 25 March 1983." 19940221/37, NAF.

Gessain, Robert. 1989. *Un homme marche devant: La dernière traversée du Groenland en traîneaux à chiens*. Paris: Arthaud.

Gildea, Robert. 1994. *The Past in French History*. New Haven, CT: Yale University Press.

———. 2002. *France since 1945*. 2nd ed. Oxford: Oxford University Press.

Girardet, Raoul. 1972. *L'idée coloniale en France de 1871 à 1962*. Paris: La table ronde.

Girardin, Éric, and Meyer Habib. 2019. "Rapport d'information no. 4082 déposé en application de l'article 145 du règlement par la Commission des affaires étrangères en conclusion des travaux d'une mission d'information constituée le 23 juillet 2019 sur la problématique des pôles: Arctique et Antarctique." Assemblée nationale, 15e législature. https://www.assemblee-nationale.fr/dyn/15/rapports/cion_afetr/l15b4082_rapport-information.pdf.

Gleason, S. Everett. 1958. "Memorandum: Discussion at the 357th Meeting of the National Security Council, 6 March 1958, Washington." Whitman File, Eisenhower Library.

Goblet, Yves-Marie. 1946. "L'Antarctique française et la Terre Adélie." *Le Monde*, 23 December 1946.

Godard, Gaston, Julien Reynes, Jérome Bascou, René-Pierre Ménot, and Rosaria Palmeri. 2017. "First Rocks Sampled in Antarctica (1840): Insights into the Landing Area and the Terre Adélie Craton." *Comptes rendus Géoscience* 349:12–21.

Godard-Faultrier, Victor. 1850. "Nouvelles archéologiques et diverses." *Procès-verbaux: Société nationale d'agriculture, sciences et arts d'Angers* 24:1–10.

Goldie, L. F. E. 1958. "International Relations in Antarctica." *Australian Quarterly* 30:7–29.

Gouttes, Bernard de. 1984. "Note sur les activités liées aux ressources minérales de l'Antarctique, 24 February 1984." 19940389/36, NAF.

Government of France. 1984. "French Contribution to the United Nations Study on the Question of Antarctica, 1984-06-18." UN Document 8/39/583 (pt. 2), vol. 2, 2 November 1984, 5267.

Greenpeace. 1984a. "Greenpeace Activists Dressed as Penguins Protest on the *Polarbjørn* Ship Against the Construction of a French Airstrip in Antarctica, 22 October 1984." Photo, Solara, GP0VH8, GMA.

———. 1984b. "Greenpeace Activists Dressed as Penguins in Front of the TAAF Headquarters (Terres australes et antarctique françaises) to Deliver Postcards Against the Construction of a French Airstrip in Antarctica, 29 July 1984." Photo, Solara, GP0S0N, GMA.

———. 1988. "Les faits sur la piste d'attérrissage de Dumont d'Urville." 19990442/3, NAF.

———. 1989a. "Adelie Penguins Threatened by Airstrip Construction at French Dumont D'Urville Base, 1 January 1989." Photo, Steve Morgan, GP02BB, GMA.

———. 1989b. "Adelie Penguins on the Run from a Caterpillar Digger at the French Dumont D'Urville Base. Greenpeace Protested Non-Violently Against the Construction of the Airstrip, 1 January 1989." Photo, Steve Morgan, GP033KM, GMA.

Griffiths, Tom. 2007. *Slicing the Silence: Voyaging to Antarctica*. Cambridge, MA: Harvard University Press.

Groscolas, René. 1984. "Letter to the Secrétariat d'état—DOM-TOM, 26 October 1984." 19940221/36, NAF.

Guillard, Robert. 1955. "Au port de Rouen." Photo, reproduced in Lorius, Tahi, and Schlich 2008, 28.
———. 1958. "Letter to Commandant Jean Schmitt, 20 March 1958." 20110210/212, NAF.
———. 1968. "Dans le très confortable bâtiment séjour (bt n°31), partie de cartes dans le coin salon-bibliothèque-discothèque (base Dumont d'Urville)." Photo, Archipôles, DDU.68.00582, IPEV.
Guillaume, Gilbert. 1985a. "Instructions pour la délégation française à la 6e réunion des parties consultatives sur les ressources minérales de l'Antarctique, 19 February 1985." 19940389/36, NAF.
———. 1985b. "Note diplomatique: Régime juridique applicable à la zone économique des Kerguelen, 20 December 1985." 2010098/77, NAF.
———. 1987. "La France et le droit de l'Antarctique." *Espaces et ressources maritimes* 2:33–44.
Guillemin, Alexandre. 1842. *Lamentation sur la catastrophe du 8 mai 1842, au chemin de fer de Versailles*. Paris: Chez Gaume Frères.
Guillon, Jacques-Gibert. 1986. *Dumont d'Urville, 1790–1842. La Vénus de Milo, les épaves de La Pérouse, l'Antarctique et la Terre Adélie*. Paris: France Empire.
Hains, Brigid. 2002. *The Ice and the Inland: Mawson, Flynn, and the Myth of the Frontier*. Melbourne: University of Melbourne Press.
Hall, H. Robert. 1994. "International Regime Formation and Leadership: The Origins of the Antarctic Treaty." PhD thesis, University of Tasmania.
———. 2009. "The 'Open Door' into Antarctica: An Explanation of the Hughes Doctrine." *Polar Record* 25:137–40.
Hamy, Ernest-Théodore. 1896. "Francisque et André d'Albaigne, cosmographes lucquois au service de la France." *Études historiques et géographiques*, 241–60.
Hanessian, John. 1960. "Letter to Richard Nolte, 12 April 1960." 4/12/1960, JH-14, ICWA.
Hansen, Odd Magnus Heide. 1996. *Ishavsskutenes historie, vol. 1*. Tromsø: Nordlys.
Haron, Mohamed. 1986. "Antarctica and the United Nations—the Next Step?" In *Antarctic Challenge II: Conflicting Interest, Cooperation, Environmental Protection, Economic Development (Proceedings of an Interdisciplinary Symposium, 17–21 September 1985)*, edited by Rüdiger Wolfrum, 321–32. Berlin: Duncker & Humblot.
Haskell, Daniel C. 1942. *The United States Exploring Expedition, 1838–1842, and Its Publications, 1844–1874*. New York: New York Public Library.
Hatt, H. H. 1949. "Vitamin C Content of an Old Antiscorbutic: The Kerguelen Cabbage." *Nature* 164:1081–82.
Hawke, Robert J. L., and Michel Rocard. 1989. "Joint Statement on International Environment Issues Agreed by Prime Ministers Hawke and Rocard, Canberra, 18 August 1989." AU ATADD 1-BB-AU-203, ADD.
Heap, John A. 1983. "Cooperation in the Antarctic: A Quarter of a Century's Experience." In *Antarctic Resources Policy: Scientific, Legal and Political Issues*, edited by F. Orrego Vicuna, 103–8. Cambridge: Cambridge University Press.
Hecht, Gabrielle. 1998. *The Radiance of France: Nuclear Power and National Identity after World War II*. Cambridge, MA: MIT Press.
———. 2001. "Technology, Politics, and National Identity in France." In *Technologies of Power: Essays in Honor of Thomas Parke Hughes and Agatha Chipley Hughes*, edited by Michael T. Allen and Gabrielle Hecht, 253–93. Cambridge, MA: MIT Press.
Heckel, B. 1979. "Instructions pour la délégation française." 19940218/70, NAF.
Heijden, H.-A. van der, R. Koopmans, and M. Guigni. 1992. "The West European Environmental Movement." In *Research in Social Movements, Conflicts and Change: The Green Movement Worldwide*, edited by Matthias Finger, 1–41. Greenwich, CO: JAI.

Heine, Eike-Christian, and Martin Meiske. 2022. *Beyond the Lab and the Field: Infrastructures as Places of Knowledge Production since the Late Nineteenth Century.* Pittsburgh, PA: University of Pittsburgh Press.
Hemmings, Alan D. 2008. "Problems Posed by Attempts to Apply a Claimant's Domestic Legislation Beyond Its Own Nationals in Antarctica." *Asia Pacific Journal of Environmental Law* 11:207–20.
———. 2014. "Rights, Expectations and Global Equity: Re-Justifying the Antarctic Treaty System for the 21st Century." In *Polar Geopolitics: Knowledges, Resources and Legal Regimes*, edited by Richard C. Powell and Klaus Dodds, 55–73. Cheltenham: Edward Elgar.
Hemmings, Alan D., and Tim Stephens. 2010. "The Extended Continental Shelves of Sub-Antarctic Islands: Implications for Antarctic Governance." *Polar Record* 46:312–27.
Henault, P. 1979. "Instructions pour la délégation française à la Xe réunion consultative du Traité sur l'Antarctique, 19 September 1979." 19940218/70, NAF.
Herber, Bernard P. 1991. "The Common Heritage Principle: Antarctica and the Developing Nations." *American Journal of Economics and Sociology* 50:391–406.
Hertslet, E. 1886. "Memoranda on the Chesterfield Islands, the Lacepede Islands, Desolation Island, and St. Paul and Amsterdam Islands." PRO FO83/1781, 22 December 1886, UKNA.
Hiatt, Alfred. 2008. *Terra Incognita: Mapping the Antipodes before 1600.* London: British Library.
———. 2011. "Terra Australis and the Idea of the Antipodes." In *European Perceptions of Terra Australis*, edited by Anne M. Scott, Alfred Hiatt, Claire McIlroy, and Christopher Wortham, 9–43. London: Routledge.
His Majesty's Governments. 1937. "Draft Note to the French Government Elaborating Reasons for Insisting Upon Confining Adélie Land to Narrow Limits." FO 371 W17129/1365/50/1937, UKNA.
Hitchcock, William I. 1998. *France Restored: Cold War Diplomacy and the Quest for Leadership in Europe, 1944–1954.* Chapel Hill: University of North Carolina Press.
Hobart Town Courier. 1839. "Discovery of a New Continent." 25 January 1839, 3.
———. 1840. "Expedition of the French Corvettes 'l'Astrolabe' and 'La Zelée,' Under the Command of Commodore d'Urville, and Captain Jacquinot." 28 February 1840, 3.
Hobbs, William H. 1932. "Wilkes Land Rediscovered." *Geographical Review* 22:632–55.
———. 1939. "The Discoveries of Antarctica Within the American Sector, as Revealed by Maps and Documents." *Transactions of the American Philosophical Society* 31:1–71.
Hoisington, William A. 1975. "In the Service of the Third French Republic: Jean-Baptiste Charcot (1867–1936) and the Antarctic." *Proceedings of the American Philosophical Society* 119:315–24.
Homan, Anna. 2006. "Maritime Zones in Antarctica." *Australian and New Zealand Maritime Law Journal* 20:69–77.
Hombron, Jacques Bernard, and Honoré Jacquinot. 1841. "Description de plusieurs oiseaux nouveaux ou peu connus provenant de l'expédition autour du monde faite sur les corvettes 'l'Astrolabe' et la 'Zélée'." *Annales des sciences naturelles, 2e série* 16:312–20.
Horne, Alistair. 1977. *A Savage War of Peace: Algeria 1954–1962.* London: Macmillan.
Howitt, Rohan. 2019. "Ideological Origins of the Australian Antarctic, 1839–1933." PhD thesis, University of Sydney.
Howkins, Adrian. 2015. *The Polar Regions: An Environmental History.* New York: Wiley.

———. 2017. *Frozen Empires: An Environmental History of the Antarctic Peninsula.* New York: Oxford University Press.
Huber, Max. 1928. "The Island of Palmas Case (or Miangas)—the United States of America vs. The Netherlands, Case No. 1925-01." Permanent Court of Arbitration, The Hague, 4 April 1928.
Hughes, Charles E. 1924a. "Letter to Mr. A. W. Prescott, 13 May 1924." DOS file 811.014/101, NARA.
———. 1924b. "Note to the Norwegian Minister, 2 April 1924." DOS, Correspondence Between Norwegian Minister and United States Secretary of State Regarding Polar Claims, Foreign Relations of the United States, vol. 2, 519–20.
Hulot, Étienne. 1911. "Les Kerguelen." *Revue des deux mondes* 1:187–217.
Hyde, Timothy. 2017. "Architecture at the End of the World: The Pasts and Futures of Heritage Preservation in Antarctica." *Future Anterior: Journal of Historic Preservation, History, Theory, and Criticism* 14:73–86.
Imbert, Bertrand. 1956a. "Letter to Monsieur le Ministre de la défence nationale, 2 March 1956." 20110210/217, NAF.
———. 1956b. "Metal Buildings at the French Antarctic Base on Île des Pétrels." *Polar Record* 8:246–53.
———. 1959. "La France antarctique." *L'astronomie* 73:241–53.
Imperial Conference London. 1937. "Committee on Polar Questions: New Hebrides, Western Samoa, the Antarctic." CAB 32/129, UKNA.
Inch, Donald R. 1965. "An Examination of Canada's Claim to Sovereignty in the Arctic." *Manitoba Law School Journal* 1:31–53.
Ingold, Alice. 2011. "Écrire la nature: De l'histoire sociale à la question environnementale?" *Annales. Histoire, sciences sociales* 1:11–29.
Jacka, Fred. 1953. "Magnetic Observations at Heard, Kerguelen and Macquarie Islands, 1947–1951." *ANARE Reports* 17.
Jackson, Andrew. 2021. *Who Saved Antarctica? The Heroic Era of Antarctic Diplomacy.* Cham: Palgrave Macmillan.
Jackson, Julian. 2018. *A Certain Idea of France: The Life of Charles de Gaulle.* Milton Keynes: Allen Lane.
Jacob, Yves. 2004. *L'énigme Lapérouse.* Paris: Tallandier.
Jager-Schmidt, André. 1914. "Le docteur Mawson faillit mourir sur la banquise." *Excelsior*, 2 May 1914, 3.
Jardel, F. H. 1960. "Une expédition scientifique en Terre Adélie." *Revue des deux mondes*, January, 118–30.
Jayaseelan, Sumitra. 2019. "Development of Malaysia's Position in Antarctica: 1983 to 2017." *Polar Journal* 9:214–35.
Jensen, Leif Christian. 2016. "From the High North to the Low South: Bipolar Norway's Antarctic Strategy." *Polar Journal* 6:273–90.
JO Sénat. 1987. "Construction d'une piste d'avions en Terre Adélie, réponse du ministère: Départements et territoires d'outre-mer." 8e législature, 11 June 1987, 923.
———. 1991. "Situation de la station polaire de Terre Adélie, réponse du ministère: Départements et territoires d'outre-mer." 9e législature, 1 August 1991, 1618.
Joenniemi, Pertti. 1989. "Competing Images of the Arctic: A Policy Perspective." *Current Research on Peace and Violence* 3:111–22.
Jore, Léonce. 1958. *L'océan Pacifique au temps de la Restauration et de la monarchie de Juillet (1815–1848).* Paris: Besson et Chantemerle.
Joubert, Fr. 1871. *Dumont-d'Urville.* Tours: Alfred Mame et fils.
Journal des débats politiques et littéraires. 1834. "Le 'Voyage pittoresque autour du monde.'" 27 February 1834, 3.

Journal officiel. 1938. "Décret fixant les limites des territoires français de la région antarctique dite Terre Adélie." JO Madagascar et dépendences, no. 2723, 30 April 1938.
———. 1948. "Réponses des ministres aux questions écrites, 3e séance." Assemblée nationale, débats parlementaires, 25 August 1948, 6263.
———. 1978. "Décret no. 78-963 fixant les conditions dans lesquelles certains navires étrangers pourront obtenir des droits de pêche dans les zones économiques." JORF, 19 September 1978, 3342.
———. 1992. "Arrêté du 15 décembre 1992 relatif à la frappe et à la mise en circulation d'une pièce commémorative de 5F et de deux pièces commémoratives de 100F." JORF no. 299, 24 December 1992.
———. 2008. "Arrêté du 27 août 2008 relatif à la frappe et à l'émission de pièces de collection de 100 €, de 50 €, de 20 €, de 15 €, de 10 €, de 5 €, de 1 1/2 € et de 1/4 €." JORF no. 0202, 30 August 2008.
———. 2009. "Décret no. 2009-1060 du 26 août 2009 portant publication de la mesure 3 (2006)—Sites et monuments historiques de l'Antarctique—Rocher du Débarquement, adoptée à Edimbourg le 23 juin 2006." JORF no. 0200, 30 August 2009.
———. 2019. "Arrêté du 7 février 2019, no. 2019-19, fixant les taxes de séjour et de mouillage dans les TAAF." JORF no. 83, 7 February 2019.
———. 2020. "Décret no. 2020-51 du 27 janvier 2020 portant publication de la mesure 9 (2016) relative à la liste révisée des sites et monuments historiques de l'Antarctique, adoptée à Santiago le 1er juin 2016, lors de la XXXIXe réunion consultative du Traité sur l'Antarctique." JORF no. 0024, 29 January 2020.
Journal officiel, TAAF. 2002. "Arrêté no. 2002-17 du 1 juillet 2002 relatif à l'application de la taxe de mouillage et de la taxe territoriale de séjour pour la Terre Adélie." JO TAAF, no. 15, 1 July 2002, 4.
Jouvenet, Morgan. 2016. "Des pôles aux laboratoires: Les échelles de la coopération internationale en paléoclimatologie (1955-2015)." *Revue française de sociologie* 57:563-90.
Jouventin, Pierre, and Vincent Bretagnolle. 1990. "French Biologists Reply to Greenpeace Report." *Polar Record* 26:54.
Jouventin, Pierre, Bernard Morlet, and Paul Trehen. 1990. "La recherche en matière d'environnment dans les T.A.A.F." *Aménagement et nature* 98:22-24.
Jouventin, Pierre, and Henri Weimerskirch. 1990. "Long-Term Changes in Seabird and Seal Populations in the Southern Ocean." In *Antarctic Ecosystems, Ecological Change and Conservation*, edited by K. R. Kerry and G. Hempel, 208-13. Berlin: Springer-Verlag.
Joyner, Christopher C. 1988a. "The Evolving Antarctic Minerals Regime." *Ocean Development & International Law* 19:73-95.
———. 1988b. "The Exclusive Economic Zone and Antarctica: The Dilemmas of Non-Sovereign Jurisdiction." *Ocean Development & International Law* 19:469-91.
———. 1991. "CRAMRA: The Ugly Duckling of the Antarctic Treaty System?" In *The Antarctic Treaty System in World Politics*, edited by Arnfinn Jorgensen-Dahl and Willy Østreng, 161-85. London: Macmillan/Fridtjof Nansen Institute.
———. 1992. *Antarctica and the Law of the Sea*. Dordrecht: Martinus Nijhoff.
———. 1998. *Governing the Frozen Commons: The Antarctic Regime and Environmental Protection*. Columbia: University of South Carolina Press.
J-P C. 1940. "La Terre Adélie." *Paris-Midi*, 2 February 1940, 5.
Kaye, Stuart B. 2001. "The Outer Continental Shelf in the Antarctic." In *The Law of the Sea and Polar Maritime Delimitation and Jurisdiction*, edited by Alex G. Oude Elferink and Donald R. Rothwell, 125-37. The Hague: Kluwer Law International.

Kerguelen de Trémarec, Yves Joseph de. 1782. *Relation de deux voyages dans les mers australes et des Indes, faits en 1771, 1772, 1773, et 1774. Extrait du journal de sa navigation pour la découverte des Terres Australes.* Paris: Knapen & fils.
Khan, Serge. 2008. *Jean-Baptiste Charcot: Pionnier des mers polaires.* Grenoble: La bibliothèque des explorateurs.
Kiesewetter, Ernest. 1942. "Un grand problème colonial d'après-demain: Terre Adélie." *L'union française*, 31 January 1942.
Korsmo, Fae L. 2007. "The Genesis of the International Geophysical Year." *Physics Today* 60:38–43.
Kousser, Rachel. 2005. "Creating the Past: The Vénus de Milo and the Hellenistic Reception of Classical Greece." *American Journal of Archaeology* 109:227–50.
Krige, John. 2006. *American Hegemony and Postwar Reconstruction of Science in Europe.* Cambridge, MA: MIT Press.
Kuehls, Thom. 1996. *Beyond Sovereign Territory: The Space of Ecopolitics.* Minneapolis: University of Minnesota Press.
La Dordogne libre. 1959. "Le Président de Gaulle a reçu à l'Élysée les membres de l'expédition française en Terre Adélie." 22 April 1959.
La Pérouse, Jean-Francois de Galaup. 1850. *Nouvelle bibliothèque des voyages anciens et modernes, tome VI.* Paris: Didot.
La Popelinière, Henri Lancelot Voisin de. 1582. *Les trois mondes.* Paris: P. L'Huillier.
La Roncière, Charles de. 1932. *Histoire de la marine française.* Paris: E. Plon.
La vie moderne. 1905. "L'expédition antarctique du docteur Charcot." 27 August 1905.
Labouz, Marie Françoise. 1992. "Les politiques juridiques de l'environnement antarctique, de la Convention de Wellington au Protocole de Madrid." *Revue belge de droit international* 25:44–66.
Lackenbauer, P. Whitney, and Matthew Farish. 2007. "The Cold War on Canadian Soil: Militarizing a Northern Environment." *Environmental History* 12:920–50.
Ladrange, Paul. 1990. "Il y a 150 ans Dumont d'Urville decouvrait la Terre Adélie." *Cols bleus: Hebdomadaire de la Marine française* 2063:10–15.
Lagleize, Jean-Luc. 2020. "Avarie du navire polaire 'l'Astrolabe' et moyens octroyés à l'IPEV." Assemblée nationale, 15e législature, débats parlementaires, 11 February 2020, 981.
Laking, George. 1983. "Antarctic Perspectives." *New Zealand International Review* 8:13–19.
Larson, Edward J. 2011. "Public Science for a Global Empire: The British Quest for the South Magnetic Pole." *Isis* 102:34–59.
Lascoumes, Pierre, and Jean-Pierre Le Bourhis. 1997. *L'environnment ou l'administration des possibles. La création des directions régionales de l'environnement.* Paris: Harmattan.
Lassailly, Charles. 1895. *Cours moyen et supérieur de géographie à l'usage des élèves des lycées (classes de 8e et de 7e) et des candidats au certificat d'études primaires: Livre-atlas.* Paris: Larousse.
Launius, Roger D. 2018. "Creating Open Territorial Rights in Cold and Icy Places: Cold War Rivalries and the Antarctic and Outer Space Treaties." In *Ice and Snow in the Cold War: Histories of Extreme Climatic Environments*, edited by Julia Herzberg, Christian Kehrt, and Franziska Torma, 139–62. New York: Berghahn.
Lavezzari, Bertrand. 1989. "Projet de conférence à Helsinki sur la protection de l'environnement Arctique, 6 February 1989." 19990442/2, NAF.
Le Brun, Dominique. 2020. *Les pôles: Une aventure française.* Paris: Tallandier.

Le Deaut, Jean-Yves. 1989. "Rapport sur les problèmes posés par le développement des activités liées à l'extraction des ressources minérales de l'Antarctique (Office parlementaire des choix scientifiques et technologiques)." 19990442/3, NAF.
Le Drian, Jean-Yves. 2021. "Déclaration de M. Jean-Yves Le Drian, Ministre de l'Europe et des affaires étrangères, sur le Traité de Washington sur l'Antarctique et la protection de ce continent à Paris le 15 juin 2021." République française, Collection des discours publics. https://www.vie-publique.fr/discours/.
Le Figaro. 1905. "Le Docteur Charcot conférencier." 18 June 1905, 2.
Le Goff, Gaëlle. 1999. "L'influence des organisations non gouvernementales sur la négociation de quelques instruments internationaux." Master's thesis, McGill University.
Le Guillou, Élie. 1842. *Voyage autour du monde de 'l'Astrolabe' et de la 'Zélée' sous les ordres du contre-amiral Dumont d'Urville pendant les années 1837 38 39 et 40. Tome 2*. Paris: Berquet et Pétion.
Le Maho, Yvon. 1984. "Letter to the Administrateur supérieur des TAAF, 24 October 1984." 19940221/36, NAF.
Le Maho, Yvon, and René Groscolas. 1983. "La construction d'une piste d'aviation en Terre Adélie." *Le Monde*, 15 June 1983.
Le Matin. 1905. "Le retour de Charcot." 31 May 1905.
———. 1907. "Au pôle Sud. Pour la science, pour la France, Charcot va repartir." 19 August 1907.
———. 1912. "L'entente cordiale dans l'Antarctique." 7 May 1912, 1.
Le Ministre d'état chargé de la défense nationale. 1971. "Letter to Paul-Emile Victor, 28 January 1971." 20110210/217, NAF.
Le Ministre de la défense. 1981. "Letter to Monsieur le Secrétaire d'état auprès du Ministre d'état, Ministre de l'intérieur et de la décentralisation, chargé des départements et territoires d'outre-mer, 2 October 1981." 20110210/147, NAF.
Le Ministre de la France d'outre-mer. 1948. "Letter to André F. Liotard, secret, 29 Novembre 1948." 20110210/213/4, NAF.
———. 1950. "Letter to M. le Haut commissaire de la République à Madagascar, 13 September 1950." 20110210/213/4, NAF.
Le Monde. 1946. "Trois explorateurs français reviennent du Spitzberg." 14 December 1946.
———. 1949. "Les carnets de route de Dumont d'Urville auraient été retrouvés." 6 January 1949.
———. 1954. "Les sénateurs ajournent l'examen du statut des Îles Kerguélen et de la Terre Adélie." 10 July 1954.
———. 1958a. "Les États-Unis proposent pour l'Antarctique le maintien du 'statu quo' établi pour l'Année géophysique internationale." 6 May 1958.
———. 1958b. "Seule la base Dumont-d'Urville sera maintenue en Terre Adélie." 7 July 1958.
———. 1969. "La routine ou l'aventure." 26 February 1969.
———. 1988. "'L'Astrolabe'—navire de plein Sud." 26 October 1988.
———. 1989a. "La conférence sur l'Antarctique: M. Michel Rocard suggère la création d'une réserve naturelle." 11 October 1989.
———. 1989b. "M. Fabius et l'exploitation minière en Antarctique." 11 April 1989.
———. 1990. "'L'Astrolabe' bloqué par les glaces en Antarctique." 14 December 1990.
———. 1991a. "Annoncée le 14 février 1990 la création de l'institut polaire se heurte à de nouvelles difficultés." 3 December 1991.
———. 1991b. "Faute de crédits suffisants: La recherche polaire au frigo." 27 April 1991.
Le moniteur universel. 1842. "Obsèques de M. le contre-amiral Dumont d'Urville." 16/17 May 1842.

Le Pensec, Louis. 1990. "Discours, Ministre des départements et territoires d'outre-mer." 19990442/2, NAF.
Le Petit Parisien. 1914. "L'explorateur Douglas Mawson est arrivé, hier soir, à Paris." 3 May 1914, 3.
Le Président du Conseil, défense nationale. 1947. "Letter to M. le Ministre des forces armées, 12 November 1947." 20110210/217/337, NAF.
Le Président du Conseil des ministres. 1948. "Letter to André F. Liotard, 22 November 1948." 20110210/212, NAF.
Le Secrétaire d'état auprès du Ministre pour DOM-TOM. 1984/1985. "Letter to Monsieur le Premier ministre, late 1984 or early 1985." 20010098/46, NAF.
Le Secrétaire d'état au Sahara. 1961. "Débats parlementaires, 1e session." JORF, Assemblée nationale, 25 October 1961.
Le Secrétaire d'état chargé de la Marine et le Ministre de la France d'outre-mer. 1948. "Protocole, 25 May 1948." 20110210/218, NAF.
Le Testu, Guillaume. 1555. *Cosmographie universelle, selon les navigateurs tant anciens que modernes.* D.1.Z14, Archives de la Marine, SHD.
Leane, Elizabeth. 2012. *Antarctica in Fiction: Imaginative Narratives of the Far South.* Cambridge: Cambridge University Press.
Lebrun, Albert. 1912. "Letter to Delcassé: Demande de renseignements Terre Adélie ou Wilkes, 22 January 1912." Serie BB4, no. 2453, Archives de la Marine, SHD.
Lebrun, Isidore. 1843. *Biographie du contre-amiral Dumont d'Urville.* Caen: H. Le Roy.
Leigh-Smith, P. 1934. "Letter to His Excellency M. André Charles Corbin, 13 April 1934." FO W3227/23/50, 317, UKNA.
Lemoine, Georges. 1983. "Letter to Monsieur le Ministre de l'industrie et de la recherche, 12 September 1983." 20010098/46, NAF.
———. 1984. "Actes du colloque sur la recherche française dans l'Antarctique, Grenoble, 19–21 September 1984." 19940389/36, NAF.
Leoni, Sylviane. 2006. "Un coup de force intellectuel ou la naissance d'un mythe." In *Mythes et géographies des mers du Sud: Études suivies de l'histoire des navigations aux Terres Australes de Charles Brosses,* edited by Sylviane Leoni and Réal Ouellet, 7–15. Dijon: Éditions universitaires de Dijon.
Les cahiers français. 1957. "L'année géophysique: Les français dans l'Antarctique." 13, 44–45.
Les coulisses. 1842. "Nécrologie: Mort du contre-amiral Dumont-d'Urville." 12 May 1842, 2.
Les secrétaires perpétuels de l'Académie des sciences. 1950. "Letter to Monsieur le Ministre de la défense nationale, 12 June 1950." 20110210/217, NAF.
LeSchack, Leonard A. 1964. "The French Polar Effort and the Expéditions polaires françaises." *Arctic* 17:2–14.
Lesson, René-Primevère. 1846. *Notice historique sur l'amiral Dumont d'Urville.* Rochefort: Henry Loustau et Cie.
Lestringant, Frank. 2006. "L'abbé Paulmier et l'évangélisation de la Terre australe." In *Mythes et géographies des mers du Sud: Études suivies de l'histoire des navigations aux Terres Australes de Charles Brosses,* edited by Sylviane Leoni and Réal Ouellet, 17–25. Dijon: Éditions universitaires de Dijon.
Lestringant, Frank, and Monique Pelletier. 2007. "Maps and Descriptions of the World in Sixteenth-Century France." In *The History of Cartography, Vol. 3: Cartography in the European Renaissance,* edited by David Woodward, 1463–79. Chicago: University of Chicago Press.
Libération. 1991. "La débâcle de l'Antarctique français: Et si la base française de Terre Adélie devait être fermée?" 13 March 1991.

Lieutard, Louis Édouard Paul. 1893. "Îles Saint-Paul, Amsterdam et Kerguelen." *Revue française de l'étranger et des colonies* 17:266–69.
Liotard, André-Frank. 1948a. "Letter to Leon Blum, 26 August 1948, written on behalf of Paul-Emile Victor." 20110210/212, NAF.
———. 1948b. "Letter to Monsieur le Gouverneur de la Vignette [Delavignette], 20 September 1948." 20110210/213/5, NAF.
———. 1951a. "Letter to Monsieur le Président de la République, 21 June 1951." 20110210/212, NAF.
———. 1951b. "L'expédition en Terre Adélie, 1949–1951." *Le Figaro*, July 1951.
———. 1953. "Procès-verbal d'André-Frank Liotard." JO no. 266, 10 November 953, 10112.
Liotard, André-Frank, and Robert Pommier. 1952. *Terre Adélie: 1949–1952*. Paris: Arthaud.
Litfin, Karen T. 1997. "Sovereignty in World Ecopolitics." *Mershon International Studies Review* 41:167–204.
———. 1998. "The Greening of Sovereignty: An Introduction." In *The Greening of Sovereignty in World Politics*, edited by Karen T. Litfin, 1–27. Cambridge, MA: MIT Press.
Lopez, Vivette. 2021. "Maintien de la compétitivité scientifique française en Antarctique." Sénat, débats parlementaires, 25 February 2021, 1267.
Lorius, Claude. 1957–1958. "Carnet d'hivernage: Terre Adélie—Station Charcot, AGI 1957–1958." Reproduced in *365 jours sous les glaces de l'Antarctique*, edited by Claude Lorius, Djamel Tahi, and Roland Schlich, 2008, 158–59. Grenoble: Glénat.
———. 1989. "Arctique et Antarctique: Note sur les recherches françaises dans les régions polaires, 27 January 1989. Recherche—DGRT." 19990442/2, NAF.
Lorius, Claude, Djamel Tahi, and Roland Schlich. 2008. *365 jours sous les glaces de l'Antarctique*. Grenoble: Glénat.
Lüdecke, Cornelia, and Colin Summerhayes. 2013. *The Third Reich in Antarctica: The German Antarctic Expedition, 1938–39*. Norwich: Bluntisham.
Lukin, V. V. 2014. "Russia's Current Antarctic Policy." *Polar Journal* 4:199–222.
Macron, Emmanuel. 2021. "Message de M. Emmanuel Macron, président de la République, à l'occasion du 60e anniversaire du Traité sur l'Antarctique le 24 juin 2021." République française, Collection des discours publics. https://www.vie-publique.fr/discours/.
Mairet, Gérard. 2015. "Nature et souveraineté. Philosophie politique en temps de crise écologique." In *L'enjeu mondial. L'environnement*, edited by François Gemenne, 37–44. Paris: Sciences Po.
Mallet, Louis. 1911. "Foreign Office Despatch to His Majesty's Ambassador at Paris, written on behalf of Edward Grey, 18 December 1911." PRO file CAB32/47, British Policy in the Antarctic, Memorandum E101, Appendix IV, Annex A, UKNA.
Mancilla, Alejandra. 2018. "The Moral Limits of Territorial Claims in Antarctica." *Ethics & International Affairs* 32:339–60.
Mandelblatt, Bertie. 2009. "'On the Excellence of the Vegetable Diet': Scurvy, Antoine Poissonnier-Desperrières's New Naval Diet and French Colonial Science in the Atlantic World." Working Paper 0914, International Seminar on the History of the Atlantic World, 1500–1825, Harvard University.
Maneuvrier, Christophe. 2016. "Paulmier de Gonneville et le Portugal: Un navigateur normand dans la première mondialisation." *Revista de História Da Sociedade e Da Cultura* 95:95–109.
Marchant, Leslie R. 1988. *France australe*. Paris: France Empire.
Mariz, Vasco, and Lucien Provencal. 2005. *Villegagnon e a França Antártica: Uma reavaliação*. Rio de Janeiro: Nova Fronteira.

Marret, Mario. 1951. "Terre Adélie." Film, 35mm, 22:40, 4027, CBA.
——. 1953a. "Aptenodytes Forsteri." Film, 16mm, 15:00, 26610, CBA.
——. 1953b. "Réflexions techniques." 20110210/1, NAF.
——. 1954. *Sept hommes chez les pingouins*. Paris: Julliard.
——. 1955. "Björn et Yfaut, chiens polaires." Armor Films, 35mm, 18:00.
Martin, Jacques-André, Yves Vallette, and Robert Pommier. 1947. "L'expédition française de 1946 au Spitzberg." *Acta geographica* 2:9–11.
Martin, Jean. 1987. *L'empire renaissant, 1789–1871*. Paris: Denoël.
Martinière, Guy, and Martine Acerra. 1997. *Coligny, les protestants et la mer*. Paris: Université Paris-Sorbonne.
Martin-Nielsen, Janet. 2013. *Eismitte in the Scientific Imagination: Knowledge and Politics at the Center of Greenland*. New York: Palgrave Macmillan.
Masson, David Orme. 1925. "Memorandum on Australian Sector of the Antarctic and Recent French Claim to Administer Adelie Land." A981, ANT 4 PART 3, NAA.
Matterer, Aimable. 1842. *Notes nécrologiques et historiques sur M. le contre-amiral Dumont d'Urville*. Paris: Imprimerie royale.
Maupertuis, Pierre Louis Moreau de. 1756. *Oeuvres de M. de Maupertuis, tome 1*. Lyon: Jean-Marie Bruyset.
Maurin, Alain. 1991. "Letter to J. P. Schwaab, 4 April 1991." 20060368/7, NAF.
Mawer, Granville Allen. 1999. *Ahab's Trade: The Saga of South Seas Whaling*. New York: St. Martin's.
——. 2006. *South by Northwest: The Magnetic Crusade and the Contest for Antarctica*. Kent Town: Wakefield.
Mawson, Douglas. 1914. "Australasian Antarctic Expedition, 1911–1914." *Geographical Journal* 44:257–84.
——. 1915. *The Home of the Blizzard: Being the Story of the Australasian Antarctic Expedition 1911–1914*. London: W. Heinemann.
——. 1920. "Letter on Future Policy in Antarctic Regions." Navy Office, 1920–1937, MP1185/9, 453/204/938, NAA.
——. 1930. *The Home of the Blizzard*. London: Hodder & Stoughton.
May, John. 1988. *The Greenpeace Book of Antarctica: A New View of the Seventh Continent*. London: Dorling Kindersley.
McCahey, Daniella. 2021. "'The Last Refuge of Male Chauvinism': Print Culture, Masculinity, and the British Antarctic Survey (1960–1996)." *Gender, Place & Culture* 29:751–71.
McCallum, Wayne. 1991. "The Rocard Visit: Symbol of Rapprochement." *New Zealand International Review* 1992:7–10.
McClellan, James E., and François Regourd. 2000. "The Colonial Machine: French Science and Colonization in the Ancien Régime." *Osiris* 15:31–50.
McCorristine, Shane, and Jane S. P. Mocellin. 2016. "Christmas at the Poles: Emotions, Food, and Festivities on Polar Expeditions, 1818–1912." *Polar Record* 52:562–77.
McFarlane, Turi. 2008. "Maori Associations with the Antarctic—Tiro o Te Moana Ki Te Tonga." PhD thesis, Canterbury University.
Meadmore, Jean. 1984. "Letter to the Ministère de l'intérieur (DOM-TOM), 29 June 1984." 19940221/37, NAF.
Meau, Y., and J. Faivre. 1990. "Rapport de mission sur la construction d'un aérodrome en Terre Adélie." 20140342/179, NAF.
Meissas, Gaston. 1889. *Les grands voyageurs de notre siècle*. Paris: Hachette et Cie.
Mercié, M. E. 1897. "Aux terres de Kerguelen, Îles de Saint-Paul et d'Amsterdam." *Le tour du monde* 3:397–408.

Merle, René. 1961. *Terre Adélie 1958–1960: Rapport d'activités.* Paris: Expéditions polaires françaises.
Météo France. 2022. "Antarctique: Des températures plus de 35°C au-dessus de la normale." 25 March 2022. https://meteofrance.com/actualites-et-dossiers/actualites/planete/antarctique-des-temperatures-de-30-degc-au-dessus-des-normales.
Mill, Hugh Robert. 1903. "Review of 'Antarctica' by Edwin Swift Balch." *Geographical Journal* 21:525–29.
Millar, Sarah Louise. 2017. "Science at Sea: Voyages of Exploration and the Making of Marine Knowledge, 1837–1843." PhD thesis, University of Edinburgh.
Millar, T. B., ed. 1972. *Australian Foreign Minister: The Diaries of R. G. Casey, 1951–60.* London: Collins.
Minahan, Sharyn. 1983. "Letter to Bernard Morlet, 17 June 1983." 19940221/37, NAF.
Ministère de la France d'outre-mer. 1951. "Fixation de l'heure légale dans le territoire français de la Terre Adélie." JO Lois et décrets, no. 161, 10 July 1951.
Ministère de la justice. 1953. "Décret no. 53-1095: Portant publication du procès-verbal d'installation d'une cellule administrative en Terre Adélie." JO no. 266, 10 November 1953, 10112.
Ministère de la marine. 1912. "Note pour l'E.M.G.: Renseignements sur les expéditions antarctiques françaises, 7 February 1912." Service hydrographique, Archives de la Marine, SHD.
Ministère de la recherche et de la technologie. 1989a. "Enjeux: Antarctique, 8 December 1989." 19990442/2, NAF.
———. 1989b. "Recherche des TAAF et JADE, 12 June 1989." 19990442/2, NAF.
———. 1989c. "Rapport no. 5313, June 1989." 19990442/2, NAF.
Ministère de la recherche et de la technologie et Ministère des DOM-TOM. 1990. "Un nouvel élan pour la recherche polaire, 13 February 1990." 19990442/3, NAF.
Ministère des affaires étrangères. 1938. "Décret fixant les limites des territoires français de la région antarctique dite 'Terre Adélie'." JO Lois et décrets, no. 82, 6 April 1938.
———. 1984. "Rapport sur la 4e réunion consultative spéciale pour l'élaboration d'un régime des ressources minérales, tenue à Washington du 18 au 27 janvier 1984." 19940389/36, NAF.
———. 1985. "Réunion préparatoire à la XIIIe réunion des parties consultatives, 23 April 1985." 19940389/36, NAF.
———. 1987. "Participation d'ASOC à la prochaine réunion de la CCAMLR, 28 August 1987." 20010098/77, NAF.
Ministère des affaires étrangères, affaires juridiques. 1989a. "Piste aérienne Terre Adélie, 11 January 1989." 19990442/2, NAF.
———. 1989b. "Note aux missions diplomatiques: Comité international des sciences de l'Arctique, 15 February 1989." 19990442/2, NAF.
———. 1990. "Note de convocation: Réunion sur l'Arctique, 22 January 1990." 19990442/2, NAF.
Ministère des colonies. 1911. "No. 2453, 20 July 1911 and 5 August 1911." Série Marine BB4, Vincennes, SHD.
———. 1924. "Décret du 21 novembre 1924 rattachant les Îles Saint-Paul, Amsterdam, les archipels Crozet et Kerguelen, et la Terre Adélie au gouvernement général de Madagascar." JO Lois et décrets, no. 304, 27 November 1924, 10452.
Ministère des DOM-TOM. 1987. "Relève de décisions, 4 November 1987." 20010098/46, NAF.
———. 1989a. "Note pour le Directeur des affaires politiques, administratives et financières de l'outre-mer: Protection de l'environnement en Antarctique, 14 July 1989." 19980006/3, NAF.

———. 1989b. "Note pour Monsieur le Ministre, 6 July 1989." 19980006/3, NAF.
———. 1990. "La recherche polaire, 14 February 1990." 19990442/2, NAF.
Ministre des colonies. 1912. "Letter to le Ministre de la marine: Îles et terres australes, 9 April 1912." Série Marine BB4, Vincennes, SHD.
Mohamed-Gaillard, Sarah. 2010. *L'archipel de la puissance? La politique de la France dans le Pacifique Sud de 1946 à 1998*. Bruxelles: Peter Lang.
Montgomery, Bruce. 1984. "Hobart Braces for Protest to Save Antarctic Birdlife." *The Australian*, 4 December 1984, 17.
Morice, R. 1976. "Note pour Monsieur le Ministre: Désenclavement de la Terre Adélie, 25 February 1976." 20110210/147, NAF.
Morin, H., and C. Prieur. 2006. "Pierre Pellerin serein sur son nuage." *Le Monde*.
Morlet, Bernard. 1956. "Station Charcot." Film, 16 mm, 16:55, 26702, CBA.
———. 1984. "Note sur les pistes aériennes de l'Antarctique, 8 November 1984." 19940221/35, NAF.
———. 1987. "Scientific Research on the Antarctic in France." In *Proceedings of the Belgian National Colloquium on Antarctic Research (Brussels, 20 October 1987)*. Brussels: Prime Minister's Services—Science Policy Office.
———. 1989a. "Bilan des besoins et procédure d'optimisation, 20 September 1989." 19990442, NAF.
———. 1989b. "Contribution à l'étude d'une structure nouvelle pour la recherche et la technologie polaires et subantarctiques, 5 November 1989." 19990442/2, NAF.
———. 1989c. "La recherche scientifique et technique dans les Terres australes et antarctiques françaises (Recherche—DGRT), 1 May 1989." 19990442/2, NAF.
———. 1990. "'L'Astrolabe': Budget nécessaire à son emploi en océanographie, 12 July 1990." 19990442, NAF.
Mosse, Yves. 1979. "Relevé de décisions: Réunion sur le TAAF présidée par Monsieur le Ministre, 12 December 1979." 19940218/70, NAF.
Moulton, Kendall M. 1982. "Letter to Colonel Guy Archer, 29 July 1982." 19940221/35, NAF.
Nagtzaam, Gerry. 2009. *The Making of International Environmental Treaties: Neoliberal and Constructivist Analyses of Normative Evolution*. Cheltenham: Edward Elgar.
Navigazette. 1914. "L'expédition antarctique du Docteur Mawson." 5 March 1914, 6.
Naylor, Simon, Martin Siegert, Katrina Dean, and Simone Turchetti. 2008. "Science, Geopolitics and the Governance of Antarctica." *Nature Geoscience* 1:143–45.
New Scientist. 1986. "France Dynamites Antarctic Penguins." 24 January 1986, 4.
New Zealand Embassy. 1984. "Antarctic: French Airstrip, 31 July 1984." 19940221/35, NAF.
New-York Daily Tribune. 1842. "Trial of Lieut. Charles Wilkes, U.S.N. Naval Court Martial on Board the U.S. Ship North Carolina, Lying in the New York Harbor, Tenth Day, Saturday, August 27." 29 August 1842.
Nicolet, Marcel. 1984. "The International Geophysical Year (1957–1958): Great Achievements and Minor Obstacles." *GeoJournal* 8:303–20.
Nordenskjöld, Otto. 1905. *Antarctica, or, Two Years Amongst the Ice of the South Pole*. London: Hurst and Blackett.
Norris, George. 1825. "MS 101/7—Log Notes, 10 December to 15 December 1825 [Regarding Discovery of Bouvetøa]." GB 15, George Norris Collection, British Sealing Voyage, SPRIA.
Northern Standard (Darwin). 1946. "Uranium Deposits in Antarctic." 20 September 1946, 7.
Norwegian Ministry of Foreign Affairs. 2014–2015. "Norwegian Interests and Policy in the Antarctic." Report to the Storting, Meld. St. 32 (2014–2015). https://www.regjeringen.no/en/find-document/white-papers-/id1754/.

Novel, Roland. 1958. "Raid: Dumont d'Urville à Charcot, 1958." 20110210/76, NAF.
Nutt, David C. 1948. "Second (1948) U.S. Navy Antarctic Development Project." *Arctic* 1:73–144.
Oraison, André. 2004. "Quelques réflexions sur l'article 72–3 de la loi fondamentale de la Ve République, introduit par la loi constitutionnelle du 28 mars 2003 concernant les DOM-TOM." *Les cahiers d'outre-mer* 225:101–8.
———. 2005a. "La position et le rôle particulier de certains états dans le processus de protection du continent Antarctique. Le cas spécifique de la France en sa double qualité d'état possessionné et d'état conservationniste." *Revue juridique de l'environnement* 2:147–62.
———. 2005b. "Nouvelles réflexions sur le statut protecteur du continent Antarctique et des eaux avoisinantes: Le bilan de 1959 à 2005 et les nouveaux défis à relever." *Revue de droit international, de sciences diplomatiques et politiques* 83:37–77.
———. 2007. "Le différend franco-mexicain sur le récif corallien de Clipperton revisité." *Revue de la recherche juridique—droit prospectif* 1:431–41.
———. 2010. "Radioscopie critique de la querelle franco-malgache sur des Îles Éparses du canal de Mozambique." *Revue juridique de l'Océan Indien* 11:147–233.
Østhagen, Andreas. 2020. "What Is the Point of Norway's New Arctic Policy?" Arctic Institute. https://www.thearcticinstitute.org/point-norway-new-arctic-policy/.
Østreng, Willy. 1991. "The Conflict and Alignment Pattern of Antarctic Politics: Is a New Order Needed?" In *The Antarctic Treaty System in World Politics*, edited by Arnfinn Jorgensen-Dahl and Willy Østreng, 433–50. London: Macmillan/Fridtjof Nansen Institute.
Oude Elferink, Alex G. 2002. "The Continental Shelf of Antarctica: Implications of the Requirement to Make a Submission to the CLCS Under Article 76 of the LOS Convention." *International Journal of Marine and Coastal Law* 17:485–518.
Overholt, Deborah H. 1990. "Environmental Protection in the Antarctic: Past, Present, and Future." *Canadian Yearbook of International Law*, 227–60.
Pagès, A. 1875. *Atlas universel comprenant 75 cartes coloriées, avec un texte en regard*. Paris: Société de géographes/Librarie de l'écho de la Sorbonne.
Palmer, J. 1989. "Progress by Greens Expected as Europe Heads for Polls." *Guardian Weekly*, 23 April 1989, 7.
Pange, Marie-Françoise de. 1988. "La France va-t-elle abandonner l'Antarctique?" *Quotidien*, 4 February 1988.
Pastre, Claude. 1991. "Letter to Louis Le Pensec, 16 January 1991." 19990442/2, NAF.
Paulding, James Kirke. 1840. "Annual Report of the Secretary of the Navy, 5 December 1840." Navy Department Library.
Peau, Étienne. 1923–1924. "Mission aux Îles Kerguelen d'Étienne Peau, conservateur adjoint au Muséum d'histoire naturelle du Havre." MIS 99, 1923–1924, ANOM.
Pendu, Thierry. 1993. "La pharmacopée de Dumont d'Urville lors de son voyage en Terre-Adélie, 1837–1840." PhD thesis, Université de Nantes.
Pépin, Adelie. 1837. "Letter to J. S. C. Dumont d'Urville, 10 November 1837." Marine 5JJ 158 Bis, Dumont d'Urville Papers, 1838–1841, Vincennes, SHD.
Permanent Court of International Justice. 1933. "Legal Status of Eastern Greenland (Den. v. Nor.)." Publications of the Permanent Court of International Justice, Series A/B, No. 53, 5 April 1933, Collection of Judgments, Orders and Advisory Opinions. Leyden: A. W. Sijthoff.
Permanent Mission of France to the United Nations. 2009. "France: UNCLOS Submission. The French Continental Shelf: Partial Submission to the Commission on the Limits of the Continental Shelf in Respect of the Areas of the French Antilles and

the Kerguelen Islands." https://www.un.org/Depts/los/clcs_new/submissions_files/submission_fra1.htm.
Permanent Mission of Germany to the United Nations. 2005. "Note to the Secretariat of the United Nations, Note No. 88, 5 April 2005." https://www.un.org/depts/los/clcs_new/submissions_files/aus04/clcs_03_2004_los_deu.pdf.
Perrone-Moisés, Leyla. 1995. *Le voyage de Gonneville (1503–1505): Et la découverte de la Normandie par les indiens du Brésil*. Trans. Ariane Witkowski. Paris: Chandeigne.
Pestre, Dominique, and François Jacq. 1996. "Une recomposition de la recherche académique et industrielle en France dans l'après-guerre, 1945–1970: Nouvelles pratiques, formes d'organisation et conceptions politiques." *Sociologie du travail* 38:263–77.
Peterson, M. J. 1988. *Managing the Frozen South: The Creation and Evolution of the Antarctic Treaty System*. Berkeley: University of California Press.
Petit, Jean-Robert. 2012. *Vostok: Le dernier secret de l'Antarctique*. Paris: Paulsen.
Philippe, Édouard. 2019. "Stratégie nationale de sûreté des espaces maritimes." Bureau du Premier ministre, 10 December 2019. https://www.gouvernement.fr/sites/default/files/contenu/piece-jointe/2019/12/snsem_2019_finale.pdf.
Phleger, Herman. 1959a. "Memorandum from Phleger, 12 October 1959." DOS Central Files, 702.022/10-1259, NARA.
———. 1959b. "Memorandum from the Head of the U.S. Delegation to the Conference on Antarctica (Phleger) to the Secretary of State, Washington, 19 October 1959." Foreign Relations of the United States, 1958–1960, United Nations and General International Matters, Vol. II.
———. 1959c. "Memorandum from the Head of the U.S. Delegation to the Conference on Antarctica (Phleger) to the Secretary of State, Washington, 20 October 1959." Foreign Relations of the United States, 1958–1960, United Nations and General International Matters, Vol. II.
———. 1959d. "Memorandum from the Head of the U.S. Delegation to the Conference on Antarctica (Phleger) to the Secretary of State, Washington, 21 October 1959." Foreign Relations of the United States, 1958–1960, United Nations and General International Matters, Vol. II.
Pieri, Claude. 1984. "Letter to the Secrétariat d'état, 13 July 1984." 19940221/37, NAF.
———. 1985a. "Letter to Monsieur le Secrétaire d'état—DOM-TOM, 31 December 1985." 20010098/46, NAF.
———. 1985b. "Letter to the Secrétariat d'état, 17 April 1985." 19940389/35, NAF.
———. 1985c. "Letter to the Secrétariat d'état, 22 March 1985." 19940389/35, NAF.
———. 1985d. "Mesure de police administrative en Terre-Adélie." Arreté territoriale no. 034, TAAF, 30 October 1985.
———. 1986. "Letter to Monsieur le Ministre des DOM-TOM, 26 May 1986." 20010098/46, NAF.
Piketty, G., and M. Maitre. 1974. "Avis sur l'exploration minière en Antarctique, 1 October 1974." 19810057/24, NAF.
Pincetl, Stephanie. 1993. "Some Origins of French Environmentalism: An Exploration." *Forest & Conservation History* 37:80–89.
Plott, Barry Merrill. 1969. "The Development of United States Antarctic Policy." PhD thesis, Fletcher School of Law and Diplomacy.
Poincaré, Raymond. 1912. "Letter to the British Ambassador in Paris, 16 April 1912." AU ATADD 1-BB-FR-12, ADD.
Poivre d'Arvor, Olivier. 2022. "Équilibrer les extrêmes: Stratégie polaire de la France à horizon 2030." Ministère de l'Europe et des affaires étrangères, R2070-QI3. https://

www.gouvernement.fr/upload/media/default/0001/01/2022_04_strategie_polaire_de_la_france_a_horizon_2030.pdf.
Politique coloniale. 1893. "Prise de possession des Îles Kerguelen." 21 March 1893, 56.
Pompili, Barbara. 2021. "Lutte contre le dérèglement climatique." Assemblée nationale, XVe législature, 30 March 2021.
Pons, Bernard. 1986. "Politique du gouvernement a l'égard des TAAF." Sénat, compte rendu integral, 20 June 1986, 1867.
Pons, Xavier. 1987. "L'Australie, le nucléaire et la présence française en Nouvelle-Calédonie." *Politique étrangère* 52:47–60.
Pontécoulant, Gustave de. 1844. *Discours à l'occasion de l'inauguration de la statue de Dumont d'Urville à Condé-sur-Noireau en 1844, le 20 octobre 1844*. Condé-sur-Noireau: J.-P. Auger.
Poole, Robert. 2008. *Earthrise: How Man First Saw the Earth*. New Haven, CT: Yale University Press.
Portail national des limites maritimes. 2021. "Superficies des espaces maritimes de souveraineté et de juridiction de la France." https://limitesmaritimes.gouv.fr/ressources/tableau-des-superficies.
Porter, Charlotte M. 1985. "The Lifework of Titian Ramsay Peale." *Proceedings of the American Philosophical Society* 129:300–312.
Postel, Raoul. 1887. *La marine et les grands marins français*. Paris: Librarie général de vulgarisation (A. Degorge).
Poujade, Robert. 1975. *Le ministère de l'impossible*. France: Calmann-Lévy.
Praderie, Françoise. 1989. "Letter to Philippe Waldteufel, 23 March 1989." 19990442/2, NAF.
———. 1990a. "Letter to Claude Lorius, 2 August 1990." 19990442/2, NAF.
———. 1990b. "Letter to M. C. Becle, 5 December 1990." 19990442/2, NAF.
———. 1990c. "Mission recherche polaire, Ministère de la recherche et de la technologie, 24 January 1990." 19990442/2, NAF.
———. 1991. "Letter to P. Hermelin, 5 April 1991." 19990442/2, NAF.
Préfontaine, Patrick Vinot. 2001. "Stinson en Antarctique." *Le trait d'union: Journal de la branche française d'Air Britain* 195:1–8.
Prendiville, Brendan. 1994. *Environmental Politics in France*. Boulder, CO: Westview.
Président du conseil consultatif des TAAF. 1979. "Letter to Raymond Barre, 12 June 1979." 19940218/70, NAF.
Price, A. Grenfell. 1962a. "Appendix A: Mawson's Part in the Wilkes Controversy." In *The Winning of Australian Antarctica: Mawson's B.A.N.Z.A.R.E. Voyages 1929–31, Based on the Mawson Papers*, edited by A. Grenfell Price, 174–81. Sydney: Angus and Robertson.
———. 1962b. *The Winning of Australian Antarctica: Mawson's B.A.N.Z.A.R.E. Voyages 1929–31, Based on the Mawson Papers*. Sydney: Angus and Robertson.
Pronier, Raymond, and Vincent Jacques le Seigneur. 1992. *Génération verte: Les écologistes en politique*. Paris: Presses de la Renaissance.
Prost, Antoine. 1988. *Les origines de la politique de la recherche en France, 1939–1958*. Paris: CNRS.
Puissochet, Jean-Pierre. 1988. "Telegram, Ambassade de France à Wellington, 2 June 1988." 19980006/3, NAF.
———. 1990a. "Affaires juridiques: Antarctique—le point de la situation à la suite du colloque d'Oslo, 25 May 1990." 19990442, NAF.
———. 1990b. "Antarctique—suite du colloque d'Oslo." 19990442/3, NAF.
———. 1991. "Le protocole au Traité sur l'Antarctique relatif à la protection de l'environnement—Madrid." *Annuaire français de droit international* 37:755–73.

Rabot, Charles. 1901. "Le manuel antarctique anglais." *Bulletin de la Société de géographie* 4.
Rabourdin, Henri. 1991. "Letter to Expéditions polaires françaises, 19 March 1991." 20060368/7, NAF.
Racault, Jean-Michel. 2006. "Résonances utopiques de l'histoire des navigations aux terres australes du président de Brosses." In *Mythes et géographies des mers du Sud: Études suivies de l'histoire des navigations aux Terres Australes de Charles Brosses*, edited by Sylviane Leoni and Réal Ouellet, 43–61. Dijon: Éditions universitaires de Dijon.
Rainaud, Armand. 1893. *Le continent austral. Hypothèses et découvertes*. Paris: Armand Colin.
Ramadier, Paul. 1947. "Letter to Paul-Emile Victor, 6 October 1947." 20110210/212, NAF.
Rebeyrol, Yvonne. 1958. "Premier bilan de travaux français en Terre Adélie." *Le Monde*, 2 April 1958.
———. 1982. "Convoitises sur le continent blanc." *Le Monde*.
Regelsperger, Gustave. 1924. "Les Îles Crozet et la Terre Adélie." *L'Océanie française* 78:137–38.
Renaud, J. 1911. "Régions polaires." *La géographie: Bulletin de la Société de géographie* 24:398–402.
Renouard, François. 1984. "Rapport sur la réunion pour l'élaboration d'un régime de ressources minérales tenue à Tokyo du 22 au 31 Mai 1984, Ministère des affaires étrangères." 19940389/36, NAF.
———. 1985. "Note, Ministère des affaires étrangères, 8 March 1985." 19940389/36, NAF.
Reppe, Xavier. 1957. *Aurore sur l'Antarctique*. Paris: Nouvelles éditions latines.
République française. 1950. "Loi no. 50-248 du 1er mars 1950 relative à la création d'un établissement administratif permanent à l'Île Amsterdam." JORF, 2 March 1950, 2391.
———. 1989. "Final Report of the Fifteenth Antarctic Treaty Consultative Meeting, Paris, 9–20 October." Antarctic Treaty System. https://documents.ats.aq/ATCM15/fr/ATCM15_fr001_e.pdf.
———. 2006. "Proposition de classement du Rocher du Débarquement dans le cadre des sites et monuments historiques." Antarctic Treaty Consultative Meeting 2006, WP 19, CPE 7.
Réunion interministérielle. 1988. "Compte-rendu de la réunion interministérielle tenue le lundi 24 octobre 1988." 19990442/2, NAF.
Revue des deux mondes. 1829. "Dernières nouvelles du naufrage de La Peyrouse." *Journal des voyages, découvertes et navigations modernes* 41:112–14.
Reybaud, Louis. 1841. "Expédition de 'l'Astrolabe.'" *Revue des deux mondes* 25:621–56.
Richard, Hélène. 1986. *Le voyage de d'Entrecasteaux à la recherche de Lapérouse*. Paris: Comité des travaux historiques et scientifiques.
Richert, Xavier. 1957. "Terres australes et antarctiques françaises." *TAAF Revue* 1:3–13.
Riffenburgh, Beau. 1994. *The Myth of the Explorer: The Press, Sensationalism, and Geographical Discovery*. Oxford: Oxford University Press.
———. 2007. *Encyclopedia of the Antarctic*. New York: Routledge.
Robert, Jean. 1990. *L'Antarctique et la Terre Adélie*. Aix-en-Provence: Edisud.
Roberts, Peder. 2004. "Specimens, Skins, and Souvenirs: Rethinking the Australasian Antarctic Expedition." Master's thesis, University of New South Wales.
———. 2011. *The European Antarctic: Science and Strategy in Scandinavia and the British Empire*. New York: Palgrave.
Robin, C. A. 1979. "Note à l'attention de M. le Ministre: Project de convention sur la conservation des ressources marines vivantes de l'Antarctique, 8 June 1979." 20010098/77, NAF.

Rocard, Michel. 1989a. "Préservation de l'Antarctique, réponse du Premier ministre." JO Sénat, 9e législature, 23 November 1989.
———. 1989b. "Transcript of Interview with Prime Minister Rocard, July 1989." AU ATADD 1-BB-FR-85, ADD.
Roche, Jean-Michel. 2005. *Dictionnaire des bâtiments de la flotte de guerre française de Colbert à nos jours, tome 1: 1671–1870*. Toulon: J.-M. Roche.
Roest, Walter. 2017. "EXTRAPLAC: Les enjeux, pour la France, de son plateau continental." *Annales des mines* 85:62–66.
Roger, Philippe. 2006. *The American Enemy: The History of French Anti-Americanism*. Chicago: University of Chicago Press.
Rolland, Pierre. 1965. "Arrêté no. 8 portant création d'un conseil scientifique au sein des TAAF, 28 May 1965." 19940218/70, NAF.
———. 1968. "Letter to M. le directeur des Expéditions polaires françaises, 22 May 1968." 20110210/76, NAF.
Rolland, Pierre, and Paul-Emile Victor. 1959. "Convention entre les Terres australes et antarctiques françaises et les Expéditions polaires françaises." 20110210/2, NAF.
Romm, James S. 1992. *The Edges of the Earth in Ancient Thought*. Princeton, NJ: Princeton University Press.
Roosevelt, Franklin D. 1939. "President Roosevelt's Order of November 25, 1939, to Admiral Byrd." RG 126, no. 56–8, Appendix I, 15–18, NARA.
Rosamel, Claude du Campe de. 1842. "Lettre." In *Voyage au pôle Sud et dans l'Océanie sur les corvettes 'l'Astrolabe' et la 'Zélée' exécuté par ordre du roi pendant les années 1837–1838–1839–1840. Histoire du voyage, tome 1* (Paris: Gide), V–XIII.
Ross, James Clark. 1847. *A Voyage of Discovery & Research in the Southern and Antarctic Regions During the Years 1839–1843: Vol. 1*. London: John Murray.
Rothwell, Donald R. 1994. "A Maritime Analysis of Conflicting International Law Regimes in Antarctica and the Southern Ocean." *Australian Year Book of International Law* 15:155–81.
———. 1996. *The Polar Regions and the Development of International Law*. Cambridge: Cambridge University Press.
Rothwell, Donald R., and Shirley V. Scott. 2007. "Flexing Australian Sovereignty in Antarctica: Pushing Antarctic Treaty Limits in the National Interest?" In *Looking South: Australia's Antarctic Agenda*, edited by Lorne K. Kriwoken, Julia Jabour, and Alan D. Hemmings, 7–20. Annandale: Federation.
Rouch, J. 1936. "Avec Charcot dans l'Antarctique." *Revue des deux mondes* 36:180–99.
Rougeron, René. 1947. "20 français vont explorer les solitudes glacées de la Terre Adélie." *Ce soir: Grand quotidien d'information indépendant*, 6–7 July 1947.
Rouillon, Gaston. 1957. "Letter to M. l'Ingénieur général, directeur des services radioélectriques, 12 April 1957." 20110210/76, NAF.
Roussel, Eric. 2015. *François Mitterrand: De l'intime au politique*. Paris: Perrin.
Rucht, Dieter. 1989. "Environmental Movement Organisations in West Germany and France: Structure and Interorganisational Relations." In *Organising for Change: Social Movement Organisations in Europe and the United States*, edited by Bert Klandermans, 61–94. Greenwich, CO: JAI.
———. 1994. "The Anti-Nuclear Movement and the State in France." In *States and Anti-Nuclear Movements*, edited by Helena Flam, 129–62. Edinburgh: Edinburgh University Press.
Rüdig, Wolfgang. 2019. "Green Parties and Elections to the European Parliament, 1979–2019." In *Greens for a Better Europe*, edited by Wolfgang Rüdig and Liam Ward, 3–48. London: London Publishing Partnership.

Sainteny, Guillaume. 1998. "L'émergence d'un nouvel enjeu de politique publique: Le pouvoir face à l'environnement." *Politiques et management public* 16:129–58.

Salazar, Juan. 2013. "Geographies of Place-Making in Antarctica: An Ethnographic Approach." *Polar Journal* 3:1–19.

Sanchez, Luis Enrique. 1993. "Environmental Impact Assessment in France." *Environmental Impact Assessment Review* 13:255–65.

Sankey, Margaret. 2001. "L'abbé Paulmier méconnu: Le mythe et l'histoire des terres australes en France au dix-septième et dix-huitième siècles." *Australian Journal of French Studies* 38:54–68.

———. 2011. "Mapping Terra Australis in the French Seventeenth Century: The Mémoires of the Abbé Jean Paulmier." In *European Perceptions of Terra Australis*, edited by Anne M. Scott, Alfred Hiatt, Claire McIlroy, and Christopher Wortham, 111–34. London: Routledge.

———. 2013. "The Abbé Paulmier's Mémoires and Early French Voyages in Search of Terra Australis." In *Discovery and Empire: The French in the South Seas*, edited by John West-Sooby, 41–68. Adelaide: University of Adelaide Press.

Schleper, Simone. 2017. "Life on Earth: Controversies on the Science and Politics of Global Nature Conservation, 1960–1980." PhD thesis, Maastricht University.

Schlich, Roland. 2010. "Notice nécrologique: Bernard Morlet." Notices nécrologiques, 22 December 2010, Archives des Amicale des missions australes et polaires françaises.

Schmitt, Richard B. 1932. "Zikawei Observatory, Shanghai, China." *Bulletin of the American Association of Jesuit Scientists, Eastern Section* 9:175–78.

Schricke, C. 1984. "France." United Nations General Assembly, 52nd meeting, 1st Committee, 29 November 1984, A/C.1/39/PV.52, A/39/251 66, Question of Antarctica.

Schweitzer, L. 1983. "Letter to the Secrétariat d'état." 19940389/35, NAF.

Scott, Anne M., Alfred Hiatt, Claire McIlroy, and Christopher Wortham, eds. 2011. *European Perceptions of Terra Australis*. London: Routledge.

Seag, Morgan. 2017. "Women Need Not Apply: Gendered Institutional Change in Antarctica and Outer Space." *Polar Journal* 2:319–35.

Secretariat of the Antarctic Treaty. 1968. "Rapport de la cinquième réunion consultative, Paris, 18–29 Novembre 1968." https://www.ats.aq/devAS/Meetings/Past/6.

———. 1991. "The Protocol on Environmental Protection to the Antarctic Treaty." https://www.ats.aq/e/protocol.html.

———. 2023. "List of Inspections." Inspections Database [online]. https://www.ats.aq/devAS/Ats/InspectionsDatabase.

Secrétariat d'état—DOM-TOM. 1979. "Note pour Monsieur le Ministre: Principaux problèmes posés par la situation actuelle du territoire des TAAF." 19940218/70, NAF.

———. 1984. "Piste d'aviation en Terre Adélie, 4 September 1984." 19940221/37, NAF.

———. 1985a. "Note à l'attention de Monsieur le Président de la République." 19940221/35, NAF.

———. 1985b. "Note de présentation du projet." 20010098/46, NAF.

———. 1985c. "Note de présentation du projet: Annexe III—questions d'environnement." 20010098/46, NAF.

Secretary of State (Hull). 1938. "Telegram to the Consul at Capetown (Denby), 22 October 1938." Foreign Relations of the United States Diplomatic Papers, 1938, General, Vol. 1, Ellsworth Antarctic Expedition/93.

Seed, Patricia. 1995. *Ceremonies of Possession: Europe's Conquest of the New World, 1492–1640*. Cambridge: Cambridge University Press.

Semalle, Réne de. 1893. *De l'établissement d'une colonie pénale à Kerguelen*. Versailles: Veuve E. Aubert.
Senemaud, François. 1988. "Rapport de mission: Session finale de la 4e réunion consultative spéciale du Traité de l'Antarctique relative aux ressources minérales de l'Antarctique, 6 June 1988." 19980006/3, NAF.
Serne, Pierre. 2014. *Des verts à EELV: 30 ans d'histoire de l'écologie politique*. Paris: Les petits matins.
Service hydrographique de la Marine. 1951. "Note, 9 August 1951." Box 9.JJ.40, SH2/EMG1/SH5411/SHO, SHD.
Shaw, Malcolm N. 2008. *International Law (6th ed.)*. Cambridge: Cambridge University Press.
Shortis, Emma. 2015. "Who Can Resist This Guy? Jacques Cousteau, Celebrity Diplomacy, and the Environmental Protection of the Antarctic." *Australian Journal of Politics and History* 61:366–80.
Sicaud, Pierre. 1952. "Importance stratégique des Îles Kerguelen." Madagascar et ses dépendances, 8H257, 1952/1958, ANOM.
Simon-Ekeland, Alexandre. 2021. "Making French Polar Exploration, 1860s–1930s." PhD thesis, University of Oslo.
Simsarian, James. 1938. "The Acquisition of Legal Title to Terra Nullius." *Political Science Quarterly* 53:111–28.
Siple, Paul. 1959. *90° South: The Story of the American South Pole Conquest*. New York: Putnam.
Smedal, Gustav. 1931. "Acquisition of Sovereignty over Polar Areas." *Skrifter om Svalbard og Ishavet* 36:5–135.
Smith, Andrew W. M. 2014. "Of Colonial Futures and an Administrative Alamo: Investment Reform and the Loi Cadre (1956) in French West Africa." *French History* 28:92–113.
Smith, Bruce, and J. Brougham Drummond. 1886. "Letter to Earl Granville, 8 September 1886." FO 83/1781, 209–13, UKNA.
Smith, C. Howard. 1932. "Letter to His Excellency A. de Fleuriau, 14 January 1932." PRO file DO114/34, 224, UKNA.
Smith, Gordon W., and P. Whitney Lackenbauer. 2014. "The Sector Principle and the Background of Canada's Sector Claim." In *A Historical and Legal Study of Sovereignty in the Canadian North: Terrestrial Sovereignty, 1870–1939*, edited by Gordon W. Smith and P. Whitney Lackenbauer, 181–98. Calgary: University of Calgary Press.
Smith, Philip M., and John B. Dana. 1973. "Airbus: An International Air Transportation System for Antarctica." *Antarctic Journal* 8:16–19.
Sous-direction des affaires politiques, bureau Océan Indien. 1991. "Note à l'attention de M. le Préfet, directeur du cabinet. Objet: Difficultés financières des TAAF pour 1991." 19990442/2, NAF.
Spufford, Francis. 1996. *I May Be Some Time: Ice and the English Imagination*. London: Faber and Faber.
Stackpole, Edouard. 1972. *Whales & Destiny: The Rivalry between America, France, and Britain for Control of the Southern Whale Fishery, 1785–1825*. Amherst: University of Massachusetts Press.
Stalinsky, E. 1938. "La Terre d'Adélie: Aujourd'hui perdue dans les déserts antarctiques, deviendra-t-elle un jour un centre de grande activité humaine?" *Paris-Midi*, 31 July 1938.
Stanton, William. 1975. *The Great United States Exploring Expedition of 1838–1842*. Berkeley: University of California Press.

Stefanini, Laurent. 1988. "Note: Ministère des affaires étrangères, direction affaires juridiques, 25 July 1988." 20010098/77, NAF.
Stone, Richard. 2007. "Long (and Perilous) March Heralds China's Rise as a Polar Research Power." *Science* 315:1516.
Strobel, Mathias, and Frank Tétart. 2007. "Le tourisme en Antarctique: Un enjeu géopolitique?" *Hérodote* 127:167–77.
Sudre, René. 1955. "À l'assaut du pôle Sud." *Revue des deux mondes* 1–XII:128–34.
———. 1957. "L'année géophysique." *Revue des deux mondes* 1–IX:141–46.
———. 1963. "Le froid et les âges glaciaires." *Revue des deux mondes* 1–III:115–20.
Sulikowski, Chavelli. 2013. "France and the Antarctic Treaty System." PhD thesis, University of Tasmania.
Svarlien, Oscar. 1960. "The Sector Principle in Law and Practice." *Polar Record* 10:248–63.
Swithinbank, Charles. 1966. "A Year with the Russians in Antarctica." *Geographical Journal* 132:463–74.
Sydney Herald. 1840a. "Highly Important Discovery." 8 December 1840, 2.
———. 1840b. "The Antarctic Continent: Official Report of Lieutenant Wilkes." 19 December 1840, 2.
Sydney Morning Herald. 1910. "To the Antarctic." 14 June 1910.
———. 1911. "Antarctic Exploration." 9 January 1911.
Szarka, Joseph. 2000. "Environmental Policy and Neo-Corporatism in France." *Environmental Politics* 9:89–108.
———. 2002. *The Shaping of Environmental Policy in France*. New York: Berghahn.
TAAF. 1958. "L'expédition antarctique française 1956–1957, reçue par le Président de la République." *TAAF Revue* 3:15.
———. 1960. "Le Traité sur l'Antarctique." *TAAF Revue* 10:5–7.
———. 1964. "Relève 1964–1965 dans les TAAF." *TAAF Revue* 29:54–59.
———. 1983. "Réunion sur les TAAF, procès-verbal, 17 October 1983." 19940389/35, NAF.
———. 1984a. "Budget." 19940389/35, NAF.
———. 1984b. "Compte rendu des incidents survenus le 29 juin 1984 au siège du territoire des TAAF." 19940221/37, NAF.
———. 1985. "Note à l'attention de Madame Haye-Guillaud, 22 February 1985." 19940389/36, NAF.
———. 1989. "Compte rendu de la réunion du 16 décembre 1989." 19990442/2, NAF.
Tabuteau, François. 1952. "Deux ans en Terre Adélie." *Études: Revue fondée en 1856 par des pères de la Compagnie de Jésus* 275:191–204.
Tahi, Djamel, Georges Gadioux, and Jean-Pierre Jacquin. 2019. *La grande odyssée: Une histoire des Expéditions polaires françaises*. Paris: Paulsen.
Taillemite, Étienne. 1981. "Les français dans le Pacifique." *Cols bleus: Hebdomadaire de la Marine et des arsenaux* 7–XI:4–9.
Tarral, Claudius, and Salomon Reinach. 1906. "La découverte de la Vénus de Milo. Mémoire inédit de Tarral." *Revue archéologique* 7:193–202.
Tattersall, Jill. 1981. "Terra incognita: Allusions aux extrêmes limites du monde dans les anciens textes français jusqu'en 1300." *Cahiers de civilisation médiévale* 24:247–55.
Templeton, Malcolm. 2017. *A Wise Adventure II: New Zealand and Antarctica after 1960*. Wellington: Victoria University Press.
Thaler, Louis. 1984. "Commission des sages sur le projet de piste d'aviation en Terre Adélie: Principales conclusions du rapport." 19940221/36, NAF.
The Daily Mail (Brisbane). 1925a. "Adelie Land." 13 July 1925, 6.
———. 1925b. "Adelie Land: French Annexation." 6 March 1925, 6.

The Daily Telegraph. 1911. "Dr. Mawson's Antarctic Expedition." 9 January 1911.
The Hobart Town Courier and Van Diemen's Land Gazette. 1840. "Local." 21 February 1840.
The New York Times. 1946. "Antarctic is Held Uranium Source." 6 November 1946.
———. 1947. "U.S. Maps Formal Claims." 6 January 1947.
The Register. 1925. "Adelie Land." 1 July 1925, 8.
The Spectator. 1845. "The United States Exploring Expedition." 15 February 1845.
The Telegraph (Brisbane). 1925. "Adelie Land: French Claim Ridiculed." 27 July 1925, 16.
Thellier, M. 1963. "Note sur un différend qui s'aggrave entre M. Victor et les scientifiques (universitaires et CNRS) à propos des recherches scientifiques à la station Dumont d'Urville, en Terre Adélie." 20110210/13, NAF.
Theys, Jacques. 1998. "Vingt ans de politique française de l'environnement: Les années 70–90. Un essai d'évaluation." In *Les politiques d'environnement. Évaluation de la première génération: 1971–1995*, edited by Bernard Barraqué and Jacques Theys, 17–40. Paris: Recherches.
Thibau. 1985a. "French Diplomatic Telegram, Greenpeace et l'Antarctique, 11 October 1985." 20010098/46, NAF.
———. 1985b. "French Diplomatic Telegram, XIIIe réunion Antarctique: Piste d'attérrissage en Terre Adélie, 15 October 1985." 20010098/46, NAF.
Thomson, Janice E. 1995. "State Sovereignty in International Relations: Bridging the Gap Between Theory and Empirical Research." *International Studies Quarterly* 39:213–33.
Tiegna, Huguette, and Angèle Préville. 2021. "La recherche française en milieu polaire: Revenir dans la cour des grands." Office parlementaire d'évaluation des choix scientifiques et technologiques, Report no. 643 (2020–2021), 27 May 2021. https://www.vie-publique.fr/rapport/281289-rapport-opecst-sur-la-recherche-francaise-en-milieu-polaire.
Time. 1946. "Science: Bombs on Ice?" 11 February 1946.
Toma, Peter A. 1956. "Soviet Attitude Towards the Acquisition of Territorial Sovereignty in the Antarctic." *American Journal of International Law* 50:611–26.
Topçu, Sezin. 2013. *La France nucléaire: L'art de gouverner une technologie contestée*. Paris: Seuil.
Toulouse, Sarah. 2007. "Marine Cartography and Navigation in Renaissance France." In *The History of Cartography, Volume 3: Cartography in the European Renaissance*, edited by David Woodward, 1550–68. Chicago: University of Chicago Press.
———. 2012. "Les hydrographes normands, XVIe et XVIIe siècles." In *L'âge d'or des cartes marines: Quand l'Europe découvrait le monde*, edited by Catherine Hofmann, Hélène Richard, and Emmanuelle Vagnon, 136–59. Paris: Seuil.
Tremewan, Peter. 2013. "La France Australe: From Dream Through Failure to Compromise." *Australian Journal of French Studies* 50:100–114.
Triggs, Gillian D. 1986. *International Law and Australian Sovereignty in Antarctica*. Sydney: Legal Books.
Tronchon, Jacques. 1986. *L'insurrection malgache de 1947*. Paris: Karthala.
Turchetti, Simone, Simon Naylor, Katrina Dean, and Martin Siegert. 2008. "On Thick Ice: Scientific Internationalism and Antarctic Affairs 1957–1980." *History and Technology* 24:351–76.
Turlin, Monique, and Charles Lilin. 1991. "Les études d'impact sur l'environnement: L'expérience française." *Aménagement et nature* 102:4–7.
Ulmann, Martine. 1990. "Letter to Paul Hermelin, 21 August 1990." 19990442/PH, NAF.

Union internationale pour la conservation de la nature et des ressources. 1984. "Résolution 16/38: Piste d'attérrissage de Pointe Géologie, 16e session de l'Assemblée générale, Madrid, 14 November 1984." 20010098/77, NAF.

United Nations Secretary General. 1984. "Study Requested Under General Assembly Resolution 38/77: Report of the Secretary-General." A/39/583 (Part I), A/39/251 66, Question of Antarctica.

United States Observers. 1964. "Report of United States Observers on Inspection of Antarctic Stations, 1963–64 Austral Summer Season." *International Legal Materials* 3:650–61.

US Department of State. 1958. "United States Invitation to Twelve-Nation Antarctic Conference, 2 May 1958." DOS file 399.829/6–2058, Foreign Relations of the United States 1958–1960, CA-11231, NARA.

US Navy. 1946. "Operation Order, Operation Highjump, 26 August 1946." Library of the US Naval Support Force (Antarctica), Washington, DC.

US Navy General Board. 1924. "Sovereignty of Crozet Island and Wilkes Land." Study no. 414–5, Serial no. 1225, 9 December 1924, Archives of the US Naval History Division, Department of the Navy.

Vaugelade, Jean. 1951. "Letter to Monsieur le Secrétaire général du gouvernement, 24 July 1951." 20110210/212, NAF.

———. 1962. "Letter to Gilbert Weill, 11 January 1962." 20110210/13, NAF.

———. 1976. "Letter to Monsieur le Premier ministre, 28 February 1976." 20110210/212, NAF.

———. 1978. "Letter to Paul-Emile Victor, 1 February 1978." 20110210/13, NAF.

———. 1983. "Projet de piste pour avion Cuvier-Lion-Buffon: Étude générale d'impact sur l'environnement." 19940221/36, NAF.

Vayssière, Bertrand. 2009. "Relever la France dans les après-guerres: Reconstruction ou réaménagement?" *Guerres mondiales et conflits contemporains* 236:45–60.

Vélain, Charles. 1878. *Description géologique de la presqu'île d'Aden, de l'île de la Réunion, des îles Saint-Paul et Amsterdam.* Paris: Hennuyer.

Vergniol, Camille. 1930. *Dumont d'Urville: La grande légende de la mer.* Paris: La renaissance du livre.

Verne, Jules. 1871. *Vingt mille lieues sous les mers.* Paris: J. Hetzel et Cie.

Verneau, Laure, and Laurence Caramel. 2020. "Madagascar: La France augmente son aide mais ne cède rien sur les Îles Éparses." *Le Monde*, 21 February 2020.

Victor, Paul-Emile. 1938. *Boréal.* Paris: Bernard Grasset.

———. 1939. *Banquise.* Paris: Bernard Grasset.

———. 1947a. "Curriculum vitae." 20110210/1, NAF.

———. 1947b. "Letter to Ministère de l'économie nationale, 19 May 1947." 20110210/255, NAF.

———. 1947c. "Projet préliminaire des Explorations polaires françaises dans l'Arctique et dans l'Antarctique, 1947–1950, B—développement." 20110210/1, NAF.

———. 1948. "Letter to Major Sadlers, 14 December 1948." 20110210/76, NAF.

———. 1949. "The French Expedition to Greenland, 1948." *Arctic* 2:135–48.

———. 1950. "Letter to Monsieur le Ministre, 8 September 1950, Annexe I." 20110210/213, NAF.

———. 1951a. "Letter to General Delaye, 14 September 1951." 20110210/217, NAF.

———. 1951b. "Letter to Monsieur le Ministre de la marine, 4 May 1951." 20110210/218, NAF.

———. 1952. "Letter to Monsieur le Président de la République, 25 November 1952." 20110210/212, NAF.

———. 1955. "Coopération et rivalité autour du pôle Sud." *Le Monde*, 2 March 1955.
———. 1959. "Les expéditions françaises en Terre Adélie." *TAAF Revue* 7:3–14.
———. 1961a. "Letter to Jacques Foccart, 10 March 1961." 20110210/212, NAF.
———. 1961b. "Letter to M. le Président du conseil consultatif des TAAF, 1 December 1961." 20110210/1, NAF.
———. 1961c. "Note sur le projet de création d'un 'centre de recherches polaires,' 3 March 1961." 20110210/1, NAF.
———. 1962. "La base Dumont d'Urville en Terre Adélie: Perspectives d'avenir immédiat." *TAAF Revue* 21:4–11.
———. 1969. "Letter to Monsieur le Ministre des armées, 20 April 1969." 20110210/217, NAF.
———. 1983. "Faut-il abandonner la Terre-Adélie?" *Le Monde*, 9 December 1983.
———. 1985. "Réflexions concernant la construction de la piste d'attérrissage pour avions gros porteurs en Terre Adélie." 19940221/35, NAF.
———. 1986. "Letter to Monsieur le Président de la République, 20 February 1986." 20110210/212, NAF.
———. 1987. *L'iglou*. Paris: Stock.
———. 1988. "Note concernant le futur des Expéditions polaires françaises." 19990442/2, NAF.
———. 1989. "Letter to Bernard de Gouttes, 3 February 1989." 19980006/3, NAF.
Victor, Paul-Emile, and Pierre Pflimlin. 1952. "Compte rendu de l'entretien entre Paul-Emile Victor et Pierre Pflimlin, Ministre de la France d'outre-mer, 15 September 1952." 20110210/213, NAF.
Villemain, Aude, and Patrice Godon. 2015. "Construction de la fiabilité organisationnelle en environnement extrême à partir de la sécurité réglée et gérée: Étude de cas du raid Concordia." *Perspectives interdisciplinaires sur le travail et la santé* 17:1–24.
———. 2020. "Logistic Transport in Extreme Environments: The Evolution of Risk and Safety Management over 27 Years of the Polar Traverse." *Ergonomics* 63:1257–70.
Villiers. 1928. "Letter to His Excellency M. A. de Fleurier, 11 July 1928." FO file W6428/532/50, UKNA.
Vinay, Bernard. 1979. "Rapport no. 7, January 1979." 19940218/70, NAF.
———. 1984. "Letter to the Secrétaire d'état, 16 March 1984." 19940389/35, NAF.
Vincendon-Dumoulin, Clément Adrien. 1845. "Quelques réflexions sur les voyages au pôle Sud, des Captaines Wilkes, James Ross et Dumont-d'Urville." In *Voyage au pôle Sud et dans l'Océanie sur les corvettes 'l'Astrolabe' et la 'Zélée' exécuté par ordre du roi pendant les années 1837-1838-1839-1840, sous le commandement de J. Dumont d'Urville*, tome VIII (Paris: Gide et Cie), 187–256.
Viola, Herman J., and Carolyn Margolis, eds. 1985. *Magnificent Voyagers: The U.S. Exploring Expedition, 1838–1842*. Washington, DC: Smithsonian Institution.
Waldteufel, Philippe. 1989. "Letter to L. A. Leclerc, 20 January 1989." 19990442/2, NAF.
———. 1990. "La communication sur la recherche polaire, 17 February 1990." 19990442/2, NAF.
Wehi, Priscilla M., Nigel J. Scott, Jacinta Beckwith, Rata Pryor Rodgers, Tasman Gillies, Vincent Van Uitregt, and Krushil Watene. 2021. "A Short Scan of Māori Journeys to Antarctica." *Journal of the Royal Society of New Zealand*. DOI: 10.1080/03036758.2021.1917633.
Welles, Sumner. 1939a. "Letter to the President, 6 January 1939." DOS file 800.014, Antarctic 129A, NARA.
———. 1939b. "Reservation of Rights of the United States with Respect to Claims of Other Nations to Sovereignty in the Antarctic, 6 January 1939." DOS file 741.5127/3, Foreign Relations of the United States, Polar Correspondence, NARA.

Wienecke, Barbara, Andrew Klekociuk, and Dirk Welsford. 2021. "Antarctica." State of the Environment Report, Commonwealth of Australia. https://soe.dcceew.gov.au/antarctica/introduction.

Wilkes, Charles. 1844. *Narrative of the United States Exploring Expedition During the Years 1838, 1839, 1840, 1841, 1842.* Philadelphia: C. Sherman.

Wortham, Christopher. 2011. "Meanings of the South: From the Mappaemundi to Shakespeare's Othello." In *European Perceptions of Terra Australis*, edited by Anne M. Scott, Alfred Hiatt, Claire McIlroy, and Christopher Wortham, 61–82. London: Routledge.

Zimmermann, Maurice. 1913. "L'expédition antarctique australienne Douglas Mawson." *Annales de géographie* 123:287–88.

Zimmermann, Maurice, and L. Gallois. 1936. "Nécrologie: Le Dr. J.-B. Charcot." *Annales de géographie* 45:659–67.

Zumthor, Paul. 1993. *La mesure du monde: Représentation de l'espace au Moyen Âge.* Paris: Seuil.

Index

Academy of Sciences (*Académie des sciences*), 28, 98, 108–9, 113, 130, 153, 160, 162
Adélie penguins, 35, 91–92, 152, 154–55, 160
Agreed Measures for the Conservation of Antarctic Fauna and Flora, 158, 162–63
airstrip: construction, 152, 155–56, 172; destruction, 172–73; early planning, 148–49; environmental consequences, 152–55, 157–58, 160–61, 173–74; environmental impact studies, 153–54; motivation, 4, 145, 148–51; opposition to, 152–58, 160–63, 168, 170; political context, 149, 151, 155–56, 160–63, 173–74; repercussions, long-term, 180; termination, 173–74, 183
Algeria, 6, 104, 108, 116, 121–22, 139
Amundsen-Scott base, 113–14, 177
ancient Greece. *See* antiquity
Antarctica: and climate change, 7–8, 92, 166, 176, 191; continental nature, knowledge of, 1, 24, 32, 41, 50–51, 53; discovery of, 24; early ideas of, 9–17, 22; environment, shifting perceptions of, 5, 11–12, 15–16, 22, 81, 92, 117, 166–68, 173–74; environmental protection, 116, 163, 170, 191, 195; environmental protection, French interest in, 2, 5, 165–70, 173–74, 176, 179, 183–84, 187, 191–92; search for, 13–17, 19–24; strategic value, 59, 77, 81–82, 87, 133, 190, 192–94; strategic value, early, 13–14, 16–17, 20, 29–30; surrounding waters, 140–41, 184, 187, 191–94; "third part of the world," 13–14; tourism, 7, 185, 191–92; "treasure island" visions, 12, 16, 22, 56, 81–82, 164. *See also* Antarctic Treaty (System) (ATS)
Antarctic and Southern Ocean Coalition (ASOC), 153, 158
Antarctic Peninsula, 29–31, 39, 52–57, 63, 81, 95, 108, 185, 190; British-Argentine dispute, 97, 119, 190
Antarctic Treaty (System) (ATS): challenges to, 141–43, 151, 154, 164, 170, 184–85, 187–88, 191–93; and environmental infractions, 153, 158, 170; free access for scientific research, 118–19, 122–23, 177; "freezing" of claims, 3, 117, 123–25, 191–92; French engagement with, 5–7, 126, 129, 133, 138, 143, 157, 163, 171, 185–86, 192; French position during negotiations, 122–25; French reaction to proposal, 119–22, 188; inspections and observations under, 129–30, 156, 158, 191; negotiations, 122–25, 185; official languages, 124; origins, 116–19; relegitimization through environmental policy, 6, 170–71, 173, 191–92; and resources, 140–42, 164; science as currency, 3, 115, 123–26, 129, 133, 142, 147, 149, 193–94
Antipodes, 9–10
antiquity, 9–10, 12
Arctic: French research and activity in, 144–47, 175–78; and the sector principle, 69; and Victor, 79, 84. *See also* International Arctic Science Committee (IASC)
Argentina, 46, 54, 56, 81, 105, 107, 117; Antarctic claim, 55, 76, 78, 118–19; dispute with Britain, 46, 67, 97, 118–19, 189–90
Astrolabe (1826–1829 expedition), 28
Astrolabe (1837–1840 expedition), 30, 32, 37–38, 45, 137
Astrolabe (entered into operational service 2017), 182, 216n30
Astrolabe (purchased 1988), 136–37
Auriol, Vincent, 82, 98
Australasian Antarctic Expedition (1911–1914), 58–61, 66, 69, 92–93
Australia: Antarctic interests, political, 58–61, 63, 66–70, 73, 81, 105, 117–18, 123–24, 158; Antarctic interests, public, 2, 32, 40, 46, 65–66, 189; and Antarctic minerals, 165, 167; colonization of, French regrets, 25, 190; and exploration, 16, 23, 27–28, 48; interest in French possessions, 50, 58–61, 63, 65–69, 71–74, 87–88, 103–4; and the Madrid Protocol, 6, 165, 170, 191; relationship with France, 129, 154–55, 158, 168, 171, 182
Australian Antarctic Territory, 67–70, 74, 76
Australian National Antarctic Research Expedition, 85
aviation, 72, 82, 112, 128–29, 149, 151
aviation agreement, French-Commonwealth, 70–71

257

Barberot, Roger, 133
Bargues, Robert, 101–102
Barnier, Michel, 173–74
Barre, Raymond, 133, 135, 140
bases. See *individual bases and stations*
Baudin, Nicolas, 19, 23, 198n5
Bauer, Albert, 128
Bertie, Francis, 57
Bonnet, Georges, 70–71
Bossière brothers (René and Henry), 50, 56, 106
Bougainville, Hyacinthe de, 25
Bougainville, Louis Antoine de, 19, 21–22, 28
Bouvet (island), 108, 190, 198n18. See also Cap de la Circoncision
Bouvet de Lozier, Jean-Baptiste Charles, 16–17, 19, 21–22, 53
Brazil, 15, 156, 165, 197n1, 198n10
Bretagnolle, Vincent, 161
Britain: Antarctic claims, 55–58, 62–63, 67, 117–19; Antarctic interests, political, 1, 56–57, 62–63, 66–70, 81, 110, 123, 175; Antarctic interests, public, 2, 189; challenges to French territory, 48–50, 55–58, 65, 68–70, 87; concern about French possessions, World War II, 72; de Gaulle's dependence on, 120; dispute with Argentina, 46, 67, 97, 118–19, 189–90; and empire, 1, 46, 74, 189; and the International Geophysical Year, 107; recognition of French claim, 58, 66–67, 70, 74; rivalry with France, 1, 16–17, 22, 24–25, 29, 77, 188, 190
British Antarctic Expedition (1839–1843), 32, 42–43, 50. See also Ross, James Clark
Buffon, Georges Louis Leclerc de, 17
Byrd, Richard E., 71, 76–78, 205n54

Canada, 16, 69, 77, 81, 146–48, 190, 203n1
Cap de la Circoncision, 17, 21
Cape Denison, 59, 92
cartography, 9–13, 17, 51–54, 64, 91, 105, 108; Dieppe maps, 12–13
Casey, Richard, 123–24
Casey Station, 158, 183
Centre national de la recherche scientifique (CNRS), 82, 146–47, 175
Chappellaz, Jérôme, 7, 181, 186
Charcot, Jean-Baptiste, 51–57, 60, 63, 143, 146, 176
Charpentier, Pierre, 122–25
Chernobyl, 160, 162
Chevrette expedition (1819–1820), 27
Chile, 24, 31; Antarctic interests, 46, 55, 57, 78, 81, 105, 117–19, 171

China: Antarctic interests, 156, 171, 183–84, 187, 192, 194; relationship with France, 3, 7–8, 186, 188
Chirac, Jacques, 132–33, 169
climate change, 7–8, 166, 176, 191
Clipperton Island, 202n21
Cold War, 2–3, 83, 87, 107, 116–18, 120, 140
Coligny, Gaspard de, 13
Columbus, Christopher, 10, 13, 20, 51
Commandant Charcot, 85–88, 90, 97–99, 109, 148
Concordia Station, 180–83, 191
continental shelves. See Exclusive Economic Zones
Convention for the Conservation of Antarctic Marine Living Resources (CCAMLR), 140–42, 157, 164, 171, 184
Convention on the Regulation of Antarctic Mineral Resource Activities (CRAMRA), 134, 138, 142, 156; French volte-face, 165–71, 174–76, 179, 190, 192; negotiation of, 163–65
Cook, James, 12, 15–16, 20–22, 24, 199n32
Copeland, Henry, 50
Côte Clarie, 37
Cousteau, Jacques, 83, 166–68
Couve de Murville, Maurice, 124
Crozet (archipelago): administrative attachment to the Hexagon, 102; decrees (1924), 63; discovery, 21, 47; German wartime activity, suspected, 72; neglect and shipwreck (1887), 48; permanent base, 105; possible ceding in face of lack of money (1979), 133; and resources, 24, 141, 192; ship visits, prewar, 65; territorial challenges to, 55–57
Crozet, Julien Marie, 21
cultural heritage, 193

d'Albaigne brothers (André and Francisque), 13, 198n11
de Brosses, Charles, 17
de Coppet, Jules Marcel, 71
de Courtonne, Abbé Jean Paulmier, 14–16, 21
de Gaulle, Charles, 2, 6, 77, 104, 120–23, 129, 140, 188
Denmark, 73–74, 81, 146
d'Entrecasteaux, Antoine Reymond Joseph Bruny, 19, 23
de Selves, Justin, 57–58
Desolation Islands. See Kerguelen (archipelago)
Dillon, Peter, 28
dog (sledding), 59, 79, 80, 85, 90–93, 95, 99
Dome C, 177, 179–80. See also Concordia Station
Douguet, Max, 86–89

Dumont d'Urville, Jules Sébastien César, 46, 57–63, 67–69, 73–75, 81, 123, 143; Antarctic expedition, 1, 25, 29–43, 50, 91, 188; death, 43–46, 99; early expeditions, 27–28; early life, 26; family, 26, 30–31, 35–36, 38, 44–45; health, 31–32, 38; influence on Charcot, 53–55; and La Pérouse's fate, 27–28, 31, 45

Dumont-d'Urville base: and the airstrip, 145, 149, 152; construction and early use, 110–14, 116, 126–30; continual presence, 121, 125, 132, 150; problems with, 129–30, 132, 144, 149, 180–81, 183; and sovereignty, 120, 125, 129, 132–33, 149, 194; threatened closure, 116–17, 132–33, 135, 138, 145, 155–56, 176

Duperrey, Louis Isidore, 25, 27

Eisenhower, Dwight, 117, 120
Ellsworth, Lincoln, 82, 205n54
Emperor penguins, 92, 96, 110, 152, 158, 161, 190
environmental authority, 3–6, 74, 93, 107, 170, 173–74, 190–91, 194
environmental diplomacy, 2, 4–6, 8, 167–70, 173–74, 183–86, 190–92
environmental governance. *See* environmental diplomacy
environmental impact studies, 153–55, 160
environmental NGOs (ENGOs), 6, 151–54, 157–58, 160–61, 166, 170–71. See also *individual ENGOs*
European cooperation in the Antarctic, 180–82, 184, 194, 212n59
Exclusive Economic Zones, 141–42, 182, 192–93
Expéditions polaires Françaises: and the airstrip, 148, 151–53, 156–57, 173; creation, 80, 82, 84; and Dome C, 177; expeditions to Terre Adélie (1948–1953), 6, 84, 84–99, 101; and the French Navy, 85–87, 95–98, 109, 123; funding, 80, 82, 84, 97–98, 106, 119, 132, 136–39; and Greenland, 80, 82, 84, 110, 146; and the International Geophysical Year, 108–110, 116; problems at, 130–32, 136–39, 145, 178; and the reorganization of polar research, 135, 178–79; and science, role of, 87, 93, 97, 123; status and role, 84–85, 87, 106, 109, 121, 129–30, 145, 173, 179. See also Victor, Paul-Emile

exploration: changing conceptions of, 80, 90; dangers, 23–24; French views of, 13, 15–16, 19, 25, 46, 189; heroic age, 51–52, 59; impact on ideas of the Antarctic, 12, 15–16, 22; and the Pacific, 12, 19, 24–25; and the "third part of the world", 13–14. See also Antarctica, search for; *individual expeditions, explorers, and ships*

Fabius, Laurent, 168, 179
Falkland Islands, 24–25, 46, 50, 56, 67, 106, 119
Falkland Islands Dependencies, 56, 62, 67, 69
Falkland Islands Dependencies Survey, 81, 85, 105, 109
Fine, Oronce, 10–12
food, 93–94, 111, 114, 127
France: decolonization, 3, 6, 101–102, 104, 121–22, 140, 189–90; empire collapse, 2, 6, 87, 121, 188–89; empire, conceptions of, 3, 6, 45–46, 65, 103, 140, 188–89; empire expansion, 1, 13–17, 19–20, 25, 46, 48, 121, 189; environmental movement, domestic, 158–62, 166–67, 169–70; environmental politics and policy, 2–5, 8, 159–71, 173–77, 179–80, 183–88, 190–92, 194–95; environmental reputation, international, 141, 162–63, 165, 168–71, 176, 190–92; Fifth Republic, 6, 121, 216n28; Fourth Republic, 78, 98, 102–4, 121; identity, 3–7, 52, 71, 82–83, 104, 121, 125, 140, 189–90; overseas possessions, 6, 103–4, 116, 121, 123, 135, 139–42, 192, 194; polar budget, 7–8, 108, 137, 139, 175, 194–95; prestige and place in the world, 4, 6, 55, 83, 104, 120–21, 133, 140, 176, 190, 194; prestige and place in the world, 19th century, 19, 25; reconstruction, 78, 82–83, 120; Third Republic, 46, 61

France, sub-Antarctic possessions: administrative attachment to the Hexagon, 101–5; administrative attachment to Madagascar, 63–64, 88; Antarctic Treaty norms, 163, 165, 171; contribution to France's global dimension, 48, 104, 121, 133, 140, 194; cost of servicing, 131; discovery and claim, 19, 22, 47–48; effective occupation, diluted, 74; lack of Indigenous inhabitants, 6, 102–3, 121, 140; marine resources and sovereignty, 141; political (dis)interest, 49, 55–58, 64–65, 71, 87–88; and resources, 63, 134–35, 140–42; strategic importance, 61, 72, 87, 142, 192; taxes on ships and visitors, 185; weaknesses to title, 48–49, 61, 88. See also *individual possessions*

Franklin, John, 32, 37
French East India Company, 16–17, 21
French Navy: announcement of Terre Adélie's discovery, 38; and British blockades, 26, 30; disinterest in Terre Adélie, postwar, 87, 96–98, 123; and exploration, early, 15, 19, 24–25, 27; patrolling France's oceanic interests, 63, 182; relationship with Expéditions polaires françaises, 85–87, 95, 97–98, 109; role in establishing presence in Terre Adélie, 85, 89; support for Terre Adélie, early 20th century, 57

French Polynesia, 121, 132, 139, 155, 197n1
French Revolution, 19, 22–24
Freycinet, Louis Claude de, 25–26

gender, 127
Germany, 72, 76, 83, 103, 147, 151, 175, 181–82
Gillet, Christiane, 127
Giscard d'Estaing, Valéry, 132, 159
Glomar Challenger, 164
Gonneville, Binot Paulmier de, 14–16, 21
grandeur, 3, 6, 29, 120–21, 140, 162, 190, 194
Greenland: aviation and technology, 94, 146, 150; East Greenland case (1933), 73–74; French expeditions, postwar, 80, 82–84; Victor's connection with, 79, 110, 145
Greenpeace, 152–57, 160, 162, 171
Guillard, Robert, 109–12

Hobart, 28, 32, 37–38, 66, 137, 153–54, 157–58, 183
Hobbs, William Herbert, 41, 54
Hughes, Charles Evans, 75–76
Hughes Doctrine, 75–76
Hui Te Rangiora, 9

ice cores, 144, 177, 180, 215n25
Île des Pétrels, 96, 110, 193
Îles Éparses, 47, 208n6
Imbert, Bertrand, 108–10, 112–15
Indochina, 46, 97–99, 102, 104, 121–22, 134
Institut français pour la recherche et la technologie polaire (French Institute for Polar Research and Technology), 179–80. See also polar research, organization of
Institut polaire français Paul-Emile Victor (IPEV, French Polar Institute Paul-Emile Victor), 7, 179–82, 186. See also polar research, organization of
International Arctic Science Committee (IASC), 146–47, 175
International Geophysical Year (IGY), 98, 105, 107–17, 119, 123, 126, 136, 151, 188
Island of Palmas, 74
Italy, 180–82, 191

Jacquinot, Charles Hector, 30, 32, 37
Japan, 51, 106, 117, 184

Kerguelen (archipelago): administrative attachment to the Hexagon, 102; and communication with Terre Adélie, 89; continental shelf, 192; decrees (1924), 63–64; discovery and claim, 20–21, 47; German wartime incursions, 72, 103; permanent base, 87–88, 104–5; refuge park, 64; and resources, 24, 50, 56, 64, 141, 192; Ross's landing, 42; ship visits and presence, prewar, discussed and actual, 49, 56, 58, 65; strategic importance, 72, 103–4; territorial challenges to, 48–50, 87–88, 103–4
Kerguelen de Trémarec, Yves Joseph de, 19–21, 53
Kermadec, Jean-Michel Huon de, 23
krill, 135, 141, 184

La Coquille expedition (1822–1825), 27
Lalonde, Brice, 168
La Pérouse, Jean François de Galaup, comte de, 19–20, 22–23, 27–28, 31, 45, 137
La Popelinière, Henri Lancelot Voisin de, 13–14
Lebrun, Albert, 57
Le Deaut, Jean-Yves, 171
Le Français, 53–54
Lejay, R. Pierre, 98, 108–9, 116
Le Maho, Yvon, 160
Le Pensec, Louis, 176–77
Le Testu, Guillaume, 13
Liotard, André Frank, 83–85, 89–93, 99
living marine resources. *See* marine resources
logistics, French weaknesses, 7–8, 101, 129, 144, 151, 177, 180–83, 185–86, 194–95
Louis-Philippe, 1, 25, 29, 31
Louis XV, 19–20
Louis XVI, 19, 22

Macron, Emmanuel, 7, 183–84, 186–87
Madagascar, 63–66, 70–71, 73, 88–89, 101–3
Madrid Protocol, 2, 6, 165–66, 170, 174, 176, 179, 184, 186, 190–91
Magellan, Ferdinand, 10, 13, 47
magnetic poles, 29–30, 33, 36, 42, 58, 111, 113
Mahathir bin Mohamad, 142
Malaysia, 142–43, 170–71
Māori, 9, 21
mapping. *See* cartography
marine resources, 106, 135, 139–42, 164, 171, 184, 191–92. *See also* Convention for the Conservation of Antarctic Marine Living Resources; United Nations Convention on the Law of the Sea (UNCLOS)
Marion Dufresne, 131, 136
Marion Dufresne, Marc Joseph, 19, 21, 23, 199n32
Marret, Mario, 93, 96–97, 99, 110, 193
Martin, Jacques-André, 80, 90, 96
Mawson, Douglas, 58–61, 66–67, 69, 74, 77, 81, 85, 88, 91–93. *See also* Australasian Antarctic Expedition (1911–1914)

McMurdo, 113–14, 216n33
minerals, 20, 56, 59, 63, 71–72, 75, 117, 142, 184, 192. *See also* Convention on the Regulation of Antarctic Mineral Resource Activities (CRAMRA); Madrid Protocol
Ministry for Colonies, 56–57, 63–65
Ministry of Foreign Affairs: and France's Arctic interests, 146; position on the "freezing" of sovereignty claims, 124; response to Britain's challenge to Terre Adélie, 57–58; response to condominium proposal, 84; strategic interests in the Antarctic, 70, 129, 133–34, 149, 156, 165, 170
Ministry of Research (under various names), 135–36, 146, 153, 155–56, 175–79
Ministry of the Environment (and Protection of Nature), 159–61, 168, 173
Ministry of the Navy (Marine), 20, 32, 38, 49, 54, 56
Mirny, 113–14, 128
mission civilisatrice (civilizing mission), 6, 46, 104, 189
Mitterrand, François, 155, 162, 173, 179; on minerals and environment, 2, 165, 167–70, 175–76, 188, 190
Morlet, Bernard, 135–36, 138, 144–45, 178–79, 181

Napoleon, 24, 38
Napoleonic Wars, 24–25, 29
New Caledonia, 38, 89, 121, 139, 155, 214n100
New World, 10, 12, 13, 15, 72
New Zealand: air access, 151, 216n33; Antarctic claim and activity, 63, 105, 117–18; colonization, French regrets, 25, 190; overflight rights, 70; recognition of French claim, 70, 74; relationship with France, 25, 154–55. See also *Rainbow Warrior*
Nordenskjöld, Otto, 31, 52–53
Norsel, 109–10, 112, 115, 129
Norway: Antarctic claim and activity, 51, 76, 78, 105, 117–18, 123–24; and the Arctic, 146, 192; and Bouvetøya, 198n18; and Greenland, 73; recognition of French claim, 70, 80; ships leased to France, 95–96, 109–10, 132, 148, 153; whaling, 56, 80
Nouvelle-Amsterdam. *See* Saint-Paul and Nouvelle-Amsterdam
nuclear testing, 139, 155, 162, 168–70, 209n68

oceanographic research, 132, 136, 182
Operation Highjump, 77–78, 81–82, 91, 104–5, 122

Operation Tabarin, 81
Overseas Ministry: and the airstrip, 149, 153, 155–56, 163; and attachment of the austral possessions to the Hexagon, 102; conflict with TAAF, 133–35, 137–41, 175–78; disgruntlement with Terre Adélie, 134–35, 141; focus on economic potential, 134–35, 141; and minerals convention negotiations, 165; and the reorganization of polar research, 176–79; view of the role of overseas possessions, 135, 139–40

Peau, Étienne, 64
penguins, 7, 33–35, 40, 89, 110, 139, 153, 157–58, 191. See also *individual species*
Pépin, Adèle Dorothée, 26, 30–31, 35, 38, 44–45
Phleger, Herman, 123
Pieri, Claude, 137, 154, 161
Poincaré, Raymond, 57–58
Pointe Géologie, 35, 96, 154, 172
Poivre d'Arvor, Olivier, 181, 183–84, 186
Polarbjørn, 153–54, 157
polar legitimacy: and the airstrip, 145, 151, 156, 163; Australia's competing legitimacy, 59, 74; concerns about, 181, 183, 187; and the environment, 5–6, 170, 173–74, 191–92, 194; moral legitimacy, 3, 5–6, 15, 120, 149, 170, 181, 192; and performances of sovereignty, 3; and science, 59, 125, 178, 180, 190; and Terre Adélie, 96, 100, 133, 170
polar research, organization of, 138, 146, 175–79. See also *individual organizations*
Pommier, Robert, 80
Port-Martin, 90–97, 99, 107, 110–11, 116, 193
postal stamps, 3, 81, 89, 93, 115, 172, 193
post offices. *See* postal stamps
Poujade, Robert, 159, 173
Prince Edward and Marion Islands, 108, 190, 199n32
prise de possession: and France's sub-Antarctic possessions, 20–21, 48, 50; role in territorial acquisition, 72, 75; and Terre Adélie, 34, 38, 57–58, 73, 188, 193
Prud'homme, André, 115–16, 193
puissance mondiale moyenne (midsized world power), 2, 7, 121, 140, 188, 194

Rainbow Warrior, 155, 160, 162, 168–69, 171
resources: and Australian interest in the Antarctic, 59; and British interest in Kerguelen, 48–49; and discovery of the Antarctic, 24; French desire to secure (1920s), 63–64; private exploitation in Kerguelen, 50, 56, 63;

resources (*continued*)
and Terre Adélie's potential, 81–82, 103, 105–6; "treasure island" visions of the Antarctic, 12, 16, 22, 56, 81–82, 164; and value of overseas possessions, 63, 134–35, 139, 141–42. *See also* Convention for the Conservation of Antarctic Marine Living Resources; Convention on the Regulation of Antarctic Mineral Resource Activities (CRAMRA); marine resources; minerals
Ringgold, Cadwalader, 37, 40
Rocard, Michel, 2, 167–68, 176, 178–79, 183, 188, 190
Rocher du Débarquement, 33, 35, 89, 193
Roosevelt, Franklin D., 76, 120
Ross, James Clark, 29, 32, 38–39, 42–43, 48, 50, 63
Ross Dependency, 62–63, 69
Rouillon, Gaston, 112, 129
Russia, 3, 7–8, 24, 183–84, 188, 192, 194. *See also* USSR

Saint-Aloüarn, Louis François Marie Aleno de, 20, 23
Saint-Paul and Nouvelle-Amsterdam: administrative attachment to the Hexagon, 102; decrees (1924), 63; discovery and claim, 23, 47–50; neglect turns tragic, 65; permanent base, 87–88, 104–5; and resources, 56, 65, 192; ship visits and presence, prewar, discussed and actual, 48, 56, 65; territorial challenges to, 87–88
Scattered Islands. *See* Îles Éparses
Scientific Committee on Antarctic Research (SCAR), 115
scientific knowledge and research: and the Antarctic Treaty (System), 7, 118–19, 122–26, 129, 142, 149, 184, 193; French commitment to, 7, 123, 131–34, 144–47, 175–77, 180–82, 193–95; French funding for, 3, 137–39, 144, 149, 178, 186, 193–94; as political tool, 3, 74, 83, 108, 149, 162, 171, 180; and sovereignty, 80–81, 87, 93, 105, 107, 133–35, 138, 178, 180–81, 190; in Terre Adélie, 5, 85, 90–93, 109, 112–15, 119, 126–27, 145; and territorial legitimacy, 3, 59, 125–26
scurvy, 21, 23–24, 31, 54, 65
sealing, 21, 24, 48, 50, 63, 109
sector principle, 62–63, 68–69
South American Antarctic, 119, 189. *See also* Argentina; Chile
South Pole, 10, 17, 29, 51, 55–56, 62–63, 68–69, 113–14

sovereignty: differing interpretations, France-Australia, 66; and environment, 2–4, 5, 170, 188; legal basis, 49, 55, 57, 72–76, 120, 193; limits imposed by the Antarctic Treaty, 124–26, 185; and logistics, 151; and science, 2–3, 133, 135, 138, 149, 178, 181, 190; *terres de souveraineté*, 121; tripartite division of views, Antarctic Treaty, 117. *See also prise de possession*; scientific knowledge and research; Terre Adélie, sovereignty
Soviet Union. *See* USSR
stamps. *See* postal stamps
Station Charcot, 111–14, 116
Suez Canal, 49, 110, 112, 120

TAAF (*Terres australes et antarctiques françaises*, French Southern and Antarctic Lands): and the airstrip, 153; creation, 102–6; crisis (1970s–1980s), 131–38, 140–41, 144, 149, 175–79; and cultural heritage, 193; mapping and toponymy commission (*Commission de toponymie*), 129; missions, 105–6, 135, 138; presence-sovereignty link, 105, 107, 119, 121, 133; and the reorganization of polar research, 179; science-sovereignty link, 105, 133, 138, 178
Tasmania, 21, 32, 37, 149. *See also* Van Diemen's Land
Terra Australis (Incognita), 10–16, 20, 22, 198n5
Terre Adélie: access, 85–88, 98, 101, 110, 117, 129–33, 148, 182–83; access, air, 129–30, 144–45, 148–51, 153, 161, 182–83; access and sovereignty, 96, 136, 148, 182–83; administration and management, 63–64, 70, 73–74, 88–89, 101–104, 106, 130, 180; annexation threats, 63, 65–67, 73, 75, 99; appointment of official representatives, 89, 93; boundaries, 58, 67–70; controversy over first sighting, 38–42, 60, 96; and decolonization, 102–4, 121–22; decrees (1924), 63–65; discovery and claim (1840), 33–35, 37–38, 41; and empire, 45–46, 65, 140, 188–89; and foreign nationals, 126, 157, 185, 192–93; and French prestige, 4, 6, 83, 104, 120–21, 133, 140, 188, 190, 194; international recognition of, 66–67, 70–71, 74–77, 89, 182; legal status, 73–75, 81, 156–57, 185, 193; public interest, 45–46, 82, 99–100, 139; strategic value, 71–72, 77, 81–82, 104, 122, 139–40, 147, 189–90, 194; time zone, 89
Terre Adélie, funding: government commitment (1960s), 127–28; government commitment, postwar, 82–84; government commitment,

International Geophysical Year, 108; lack of, 20th century, 97–99, 116, 119, 131–32, 138–39, 144, 178; lack of, 21st century, 8, 180–81, 186, 195; private funding, 84, 119
Terre Adélie, sovereignty: and the airstrip, 151, 162–63, 173–74; and the Antarctic Treaty, 123–25, 191; and assertion of presence, postwar, 82, 85, 89, 93, 100; challenges to, 57–61, 63, 65–67, 73–75, 81, 99; and closure of the Dumont-d'Urville base, 116–17, 119–20, 132–33, 135, 138, 145, 155–56, 176; and continual presence, 119–22, 125, 132; dependence on foreign nations, 85, 89, 96, 114, 129, 131, 137, 148, 182; effective occupation, 74, 81, 88–89, 101, 126, 132; legality, 49, 72–75, 81, 157, 185, 193; and the Madrid Protocol, 170, 174; and minerals, 164, 170, 173–74; Navy's view of, 97; performances of, 2–3, 80, 89, 105, 107, 115, 129, 151, 193; science-sovereignty link, 93, 100; weaknesses, 57, 64, 74–76, 80–81, 105, 107–8, 181–83
Terre de Gonneville, 14–16, 21
Terre(s) Australe(s), 14, 17, 19, 23
Terre Wilkes. *See* Wilkes Land
Thala Dan, 129, 131
Thaler, Louis, 153–54
Tottan, 95–97

United Nations, 118, 120, 125, 141–43, 156, 170, 182
United Nations Convention on the Law of the Sea (UNCLOS), 142, 192–93. *See also* Exclusive Economic Zones
United States: Antarctic capacity vis-à-vis France, 104–5, 110, 121, 129–30, 144, 149, 151, 177; Antarctic claims policy, 39, 41–42, 70–71, 75–78, 81, 118–19; and the Antarctic Treaty, 117–19, 123; condominium proposal, 84; Hughes Doctrine, 75–76; interest in France's sub-Antarctic possessions, 65, 87, 104; and the International Arctic Science Committee (IASC), 146–47; and the International Geophysical Year, 107–8, 113–14, 116, 123; refusal to recognize Antarctic claims, 70–71, 74–78, 81–82, 89, 118; relationship with de Gaulle, 6, 120–21; relationship with France, 1, 3, 29, 76–78, 81–82, 123, 151, 185, 188. *See also individual explorers, expeditions, bases, and operations*
United States Exploring Expedition (1838–1842), 32, 37–42. *See also* Wilkes, Charles
uranium, 77
USSR: Antarctic interests, 81, 105, 117–18, 121, 123–24, 177; Antarctic logistical capacity, 110, 128–29, 148; and the International Arctic Science Committee, 146–47; and the International Geophysical Year, 107, 113–14

Vallette, Yves, 80, 85
Van Diemen's Land, 21, 38–39, 42
Vaugelade, Jean, 131–33, 149
Vénus de Milo, 27, 45
Verne, Jules, 46, 51, 54, 78
Victor, Paul-Emile: and the airstrip, 149–50, 156, 161; early life, 78–79; and Expéditions polaires françaises, 80, 82, 84, 98–99, 106, 130, 145; and Greenland, 79–80, 84, 110, 145; and the International Geophysical Year, 108–10; and the minerals convention, 167; polar vision, 79–80, 83, 90, 93–94, 97, 107, 144–45, 150; and the reorganization of polar research, 178–79; and Terre Adélie, 2, 80–87, 89, 96–97, 116–17, 119, 122, 126–27, 130, 188; and World War II, 79–80
Vietnam, 97. *See also* Indochina
Vinay, Bernard, 133–35, 151
Vincendon-Dumoulin, Clément Adrien, 36, 41, 99
Vostok, 113, 128, 177

Weasels, 79, 90, 92–93, 111
Weddell, James, 29–30
West Germany. *See* Germany
whaling, 24, 48, 50, 56–57, 63–64, 76, 80, 103
Wilkes, Charles, 29, 32, 37–43, 50, 60, 75–76, 96
Wilkes Land, 41, 43, 45, 64
World War II, 70–72, 76, 79–84, 103, 120–21

Zélée, 30, 32, 37–38

www.ingramcontent.com/pod-product-compliance
Lightning Source LLC
Chambersburg PA
CBHW050927240426
43670CB00023B/2957